MARYLAND

The Seventh State

A History

John T. Marck

Fourth Edition

For my wife Margo & our Goddaughter, Julia Noel Thompson

Creative Impressions, Ltd.
P.O. Box 188, Glen Arm, Maryland 21057

Printed and Bound in the United States of America

First Edition Printing October, 1993 (Softbound)
First Edition Printed By:
Creative Impressions, Ltd.
Second Edition Printing, June 1994 (Softbound)
Third Edition Printing, July 1995 (Hardbound)
Third Edition, Second Printing, July 1996 (Hardbound)
Fourth Edition, February, 1998 (Hardbound)
Second, Third & Fourth Editions Printed By:
JOSTENS Commercial Printing

All Rights Reserved
ISBN 1-884604-78-1

Cover Design:

Front Cover: State of Maryland Flag and Gold Cross Bottony.
Back Cover: The Great Seal of Maryland, Obverse & Reverse

Creative Impressions, Ltd., is a member of the
"Maryland With Pride" program, sponsored by
Maryland Department of Agriculture &
Maryland Department of Economic & Employment Development

I would like to convey a special thank you to my father
William John (Jack) Marck, Jr.,
For his help and wisdom in the making of this book.

A Splendid Time is Guaranteed For All.

Preface

When <u>Maryland The Seventh State A History</u> was first published it became increasingly obvious that it filled a long-standing gap. Until this time there was no comprehensive history of the State of Maryland and its twenty-four major subdivisions. One could go to each county's chamber of commerce and find a few pamphlets and learn about some tourist attractions. The success of the first edition led to an expansion of information in the second edition.

In this third edition, we find the basic information of the previous editions enhanced by more in-depth history of the counties and their subdivisions (cities, towns, metropolitan areas). All tourist attractions in each county and Baltimore City are profiled and detailed information is given. Additionally, the third edition contains interesting photographs and line art, and United States postage stamps, commemorating Maryland. Also featured are obsolete bank notes from Maryland banks, stock certificates, and miscellaneous documents from Maryland's past.

This is the definitive work for learning about all of Maryland, its history, geography, character and interrelationships.

Read and learn why Maryland is accurately called, "America in Miniature."

Jack Marck

MARYLAND

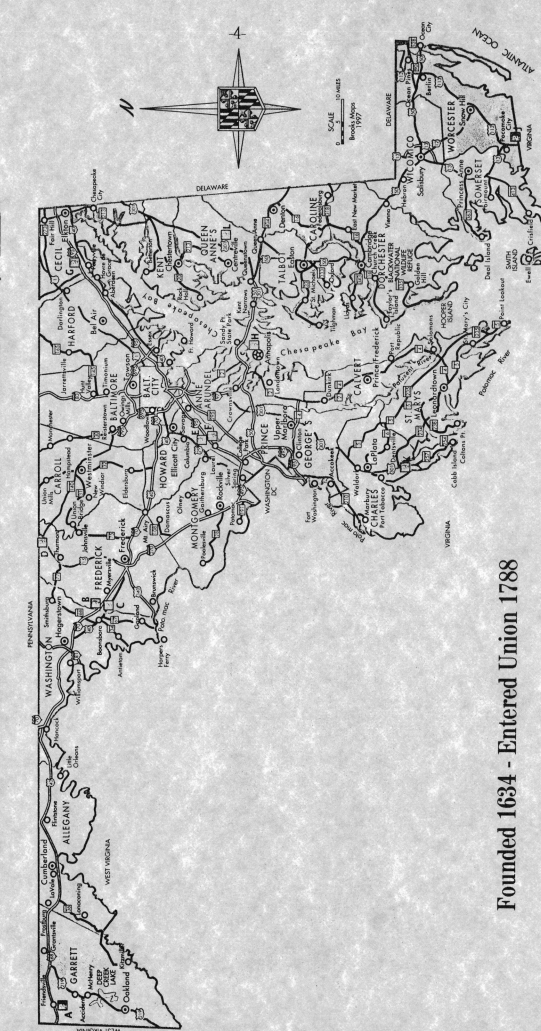

Founded 1634 - Entered Union 1788

We, the People of the State of Maryland, grateful to Almighty God for our civil and religious liberty, and taking into our serious consideration the best means of establishing a good Constitution in this State for the sure foundation and more permanent security therefore, declare:...

-Declaration of Rights, Constitution of Maryland, 1867

TABLE OF CONTENTS

MARYLAND CHRONOLOGY

c.10,000 B.C. to 1998

c.10,000 B.C.
First humans arrived by this date in what would become Maryland.

c.1500 B.C.
Oysters became an important food resource.

c.1000 B.C.
Introduction of pottery by Native-Americans.

c.800 A.D.
Introduction of domesticated plants by Native-Americans.

c.1200
Permanent villages established by Native-Americans.

1498
John Cabot, sailed along the Eastern Shore, in what is now Worcester County.

1524
Giovanni da Verrazano sailed the mouth of the Chesapeake Bay.

1572
Pedro Menendez de Aviles, the Spanish Governor of Florida, explored the Chesapeake Bay.

1608
Captain John Smith explored the Chesapeake Bay.

1629
George Calvert, 1st Lord Baltimore, left Avalon in Newfoundland, and visited Virginia.

1631
Kent Island settled by Virginians under William Claiborne.

1632
On June 20, the Maryland Charter was granted to Cecilius Calvert, 2nd Lord Baltimore, by Charles I, King of England.

1633
On November 22, The *Ark* and the *Dove* set sail from Cowes, England for Maryland.

1634
Leonard Calvert, Maryland's first governor and other settlers landed on St. Clement's Island.

1635
The First General Assembly met at St. Mary's City.

1645
Ingle's Rebellion.

1648
On January 21, Margaret Brent was denied the right to vote in the General Assembly.

1649
Religious Toleration law enacted on April 21.

1650
On April 6, the General Assembly was divided into an upper and lower house.

1652
Parliamentary commissioners hold jurisdiction over the colony, curtailing proprietary authority, on March 29.

1657
Lord Baltimore's claim to Maryland is reaffirmed, November 30.

1664
Slavery sanctioned by law; slaves to serve for life.

1685
The first printing press was used by William Nuthead in St. Mary's City by August 31.

1689
The Maryland Revolution (July 1689 - May 1690)

1690
Interim Government of Protestant Associators
(May 1690 - April 1692)

1692 - 1715
Maryland under Crown rule; governed as a royal colony rather
then as a proprietary province.

1692
The Church of England was made the established church.

1694
The Capital of Maryland moved from St. Mary's City to Annapolis
in February.

1696
King William School (later renamed St. John's College)
was founded in Annapolis.

1715
Restoration of proprietary rights given to Charles Calvert,
5th Lord Baltimore

1727
The *Maryland Gazette* was first published in Annapolis.

1729
Baltimore Town was established.

1732
The boundary lines were established with three lower counties of
Pennsylvania, which later became Delaware.

1744
On June 30, Native-American chiefs of Six Nations relinquished
by treaty all claims to land within the colony.

1747
Tobacco inspection law established, which enabled Maryland to
control the quality of exports.

1763 - 1767
Charles Mason and Jeremiah Dixon surveyed the boundary line
with Pennsylvania, now referred to as the Mason-Dixon Line.

1765
On November 23, the Stamp Act met with resistance at Frederick.

1772
On March 28, the cornerstone was laid for the State House
in Annapolis.

1774
On April 19, the last colonial General Assembly prorogued.

1774
On June 22, the First Provincial Convention met in Annapolis.

On October 19, the ship, *Peggy Stewart* was burned in
Annapolis harbor.

1775
The "Bush Declaration," was signed at Harford County
on March 22.

The Association of Freemen was formed on July 26.

1776
On July 4, the Declaration of Independence was adopted and was
signed by Marylanders William Paca, Charles Carroll of
Carrollton, Thomas Stone and Samuel Chase.

1776
On July 6, The Maryland Convention declared independence from
Great Britain.

1776
On November 3, the Declaration of Rights was adopted by the
Ninth Convention, and the Church of England was disestablished.

On December 20, through March 4, 1777, the Continental Congress
met in Baltimore.

1777
On February 5, the First General Assembly, elected under the
State Constitution of 1776, met in Annapolis.

1781
On March 1, Maryland ratified, and by doing so, made effective,
the Articles of Confederation,

John Hanson of Port Tobacco, Maryland was elected President of
the United States in Congress Assembled on November 5.

1782
Washington College was established in Chestertown.

1783 -1784
The Continental Congress met in Annapolis from
November 26 to June 3.

1783
On December 23, George Washington resigned his commission as
commander-in-chief of the Continental Army in the Old Senate
Chamber at the State House in Annapolis.

1784
St. John's College established in Annapolis.

On January 14, the Treaty of Paris, which ended the Revolutionary War, was ratified by Congress at Annapolis.

1785
On March 28, the Mt. Vernon Compact, which was an agreement on navigation and fishing in the Potomac River and Chesapeake Bay, was signed by Maryland and Virginia Commissioners.

Canton cargo arrived in Baltimore in August, beginning trade with China.

1785
Mt. Vernon Compact ratified by Maryland on November 22.

1787
On September 17, the U.S. Constitution was signed by Marylanders Daniel Carroll, James McHenry, and Daniel of St. Thomas Jenifer, at Philadelphia.

1788
Maryland ratified by U.S. Constitution as the seventh state on April 28.

1789
Maryland ratified the Bill of Rights to U.S. Constitution on December 19.

1797
Baltimore City incorporated.

1807
The University of Maryland chartered as College of Medicine in Maryland on December 18.

1810
Free blacks were disenfranchised.

1814
On August 24, the Battle of Bladensburg was fought.

The British were driven back at the Battle of North Point, also known as The Battle of Baltimore. On September 13, the British Bombardment of Fort McHenry took place, inspiring Francis Scott Key to write *Star-Spangled Banner.*

1815
The Cornerstone was laid for America's first war memorial, the Battle Monument, dedicated to those who fought at the Battle of North Point.

1818
The National Road was completed from Cumberland to Wheeling, West Virginia.

1824 -1829
The Chesapeake & Delaware Canal was constructed.

1827
The Baltimore & Ohio Railroad was chartered.

1828 -1848
The Chesapeake & Ohio Canal construction started, and extended to Cumberland by 1848.

1837
On May 17, the *Baltimore Sun* newspaper began publication.

1838
On October 3, the Governor and the State Senators were first elected by voters, rather than by the legislature.

1844
On May 24, Samuel F.B. Morse demonstrated the telegraph line from Washington, D.C. to Baltimore, using the "Morse Code," by transmitting the message, "What hath God Wrought."

1845
On October 10, the U.S. Naval Academy was founded in Annapolis.

1851
The Second State Constitution was adopted on June 14.

1854 -1859
The rise of the Know-Nothing Party. The Know-Nothing-Party was an American Political movement that was antagonistic toward immigrants and Roman Catholics. Baltimore Rioters named the city "Mobtown."

1859
On October 16, John Brown launched his raid from Maryland on federal arsenal at Harper's Ferry.

1861
On April 19, the Sixth Massachusetts Union Regiment was attacked by a Baltimore mob.

On May 13, General Benjamin F. Butler's Union forces occupied Baltimore.

1862
The Battle of South Mountain was fought on September 14.

On September 17, the Battle of Antietam, also known as the Battle of Sharpsburg, the bloodiest single battle in the Civil War was fought in Sharpsburg.

1863
The Army of Northern Virginia (Confederates) invaded Maryland en route to Gettysburg.

1864
On July 6, Hagerstown was held for ransom by the Confederates.

On July 9, the Battle of Monocacy was fought, and Frederick was held for ransom by the Confederates.

1864
Maryland slaves emancipated by State Constitution of 1864, November 1.

1867
The Fourth State Constitution was adopted on September 18.

1876
On October 3, the Johns Hopkins University opened in Baltimore.

1886
The Enoch Pratt Free Library opened in Baltimore on January 5.

1902
The Workmen's Compensation law was enacted, the first such law in the United States.

1904
The Baltimore Fire, on February 7, destroyed seventy blocks of the business district.

1909
On April 6, Matthew Henson, of Charles County, reached the North Pole with Robert Peary.

1920
The Merit System Law was established for State employees.

Women voted for the first time in Maryland on November 2.

1931
Francis Scott Key's *Star-Spangled Banner,* adopted as national anthem on March 3.

1937
Maryland State income tax first instituted.

1941
On December 7, the *U.S.S. Maryland*, was among the ships attacked at Pearl Harbor.

1947
The first State sales tax was instituted on July 1.

1950
On June 24, Friendship International Airport, later re-named Baltimore-Washington International Airport, began operation.

1952
On July 31, the Chesapeake Bay Bridge opened.

1954
The first baseball game ever played at Memorial Stadium by the Baltimore Orioles, was April 15. They defeated the Chicago White Sox, 3-1.

1955
Desegregation of public schools began in September.

1956
Voting machines were first used in Maryland.

1957
On November 30, the Baltimore Harbor Tunnel opened. It was completed at a cost of $130 million.

1958
First 49-star flag unfurled at Fort McHenry as Alaska is admitted to the Union.

1958
The Baltimore Colts win the World Championship by defeating the New York Giants, 23-17 in sudden death overtime with a touchdown scored by Alan Ameche.

1959
First 50-star flag is unfurled at Fort McHenry as Hawaii is admitted to the Union.

The Baltimore Colts again win the World Championship by defeating the New York Giants.

1962
The Baltimore Beltway (I-695) opened through Baltimore County in July, encircling Baltimore City.

1963
The Cambridge riots began on June 11, and as a result the National Guard was used and remained there until May,

Interstate 95 is dedicated by President John F. Kennedy in his last public appearance before his assassination in Dallas, Texas twelve days later. I-95 from Baltimore to the Delaware line is designated John F. Kennedy Highway.

1964
On August 16, the Capital Beltway (I-495) opened, encircling Washington, D.C., passing through Maryland's Prince George's and Montgomery Counties, and Virginia.

1966
The Baltimore Orioles win the World Series by defeating the Los Angeles Dodgers in four straight games.

1967
On July 25, riots again started in Cambridge.

1967
The town of Columbia opened, a planned community in Howard County.

1969
Maryland Public Television in Owings Mills, aired its first broadcast.

1970
The Baltimore Orioles win the World Series by defeating the Cincinnati Reds.

1971
The ship *Constellation* is moved to Pier I becoming the first Inner Harbor attraction.

1973
The second parallel of the Chesapeake Bay Bridge opened.

1975
In May, the Calvert Cliffs Nuclear Power Plant began operation in Calvert County.

1977
The *Pride of Baltimore*, a Baltimore Clipper ship was commissioned in May.

The Key Bridge was completed.

1980
On July 2, Harborplace, a three-acre center of restaurants and shops, opened in Baltimore City.

1981
The National Aquarium opened in Baltimore City.

1982
The Meyerhoff Symphony Hall, home to the Baltimore Symphony Orchestra, was built through the efforts of Maestro Sergiu Comissiona, Joseph Leavitt, and Joseph Meyerhoff, who contributed 10.5 million dollars.

1983
The Baltimore Orioles win the World Series by defeating the Philadelphia Phillies in five games.

1984
The Baltimore Colts Professional Football Club, betraying two generations of loyal fans, sneak out of town under the cover of darkness.

1985
The Fort McHenry Tunnel opened on November 24.

1986
The *Pride of Baltimore* capsized and sank near Puerto Rico on May 14. Its Captain and three of its eleven crew members were lost.

1986
The *News American* newspaper printed its final edition on May 27.

Halethorpe brewery, formerly the National Brewing Company closed its doors. With it ended an era of National Bohemian Beer (Natty Boh), National Premium, and Colt 45 and Mickey's malt liquor.

1987
Kurt Schmoke became Baltimore's first elected black mayor.

1988
The *Pride of Baltimore* II, was commissioned in October.

1991
On October 6, thirty-eight years of major league baseball ended at Memorial Stadium, with the Orioles season ending game against the Detroit Tigers.

1992
Oriole Park at Camden Yards, the new home of the Baltimore Orioles Professional Baseball Club opened on April 6.

1993
The Maryland Department of Transportation Light Rail System opened in Baltimore City.

1994
Kathleen Kennedy Townsend became Maryland's first lieutenant governor.

1995
Baltimore Metro extension opened from Charles Center to Johns Hopkins Hospital.

On September 5, Baltimore Orioles Cal Ripken, Jr., tied Lou Gerhig's long standing record of 2,130 consecutive games, reached by Gerhig on May 1, 1939. Cal's streak began on May 20, 1982.

On September 6, Cal Ripken, Jr., broke Gerhig's record, playing in his 2,131 consecutive baseball game.

Pope John Paul II visits Baltimore

1996
On June 13, Cal Ripken Jr., tied Hiroshima Carp star Sachio Kinugasa's international record by playing in his 2,215th consecutive game. On June 14, Cal broke this record, playing in his 2,216th consecutive game.

On December 6, the Cal Ripken, Jr. Museum opened in Aberdeen, Maryland, Cal's hometown.

Maryland once again received a professional football team in the NFL, The Baltimore Ravens, since losing the Baltimore Colts in the 1983 season to Indianapolis. The Ravens played their 1996 and 1997 seasons at Memorial Stadium.

1996
The Baltimore Colts Marching Band, who have continued to perform in spite of the Colts having left Baltimore, will become the Baltimore Ravens Marching Band with the 1998 season.

Maryland's two telephone area codes, 301 & 410 are required for all local calls.

1997
Cal Ripken, Jr., is moved to third base from shortstop .

The Hard Rock Cafe opened at Baltimore's Inner Harbor.

The Baltimore Orioles, who remained in first place the entire 1997 season, won the American League East Division.

1997
For about ten days in March, the *Pride of Baltimore* II was used to portray the ship *Amistad*, for the motion picture of the same name. The *Pride* sailed to Mystic Seaport, Conn., and Newport, Rhode Island, where it was used in various water and dock scenes. *Amistad*, which was directed by Stephen Spielberg, premiered at the Senator Theatre in Baltimore on December 12, as well as in other parts of the country.

On October 23, the Ecumenical Patriarch Bartholomew I, Archbishop of Constantinople and New Rome, and the spiritual leader of the world's 300 million Orthodox Christians, arrived in Baltimore. At 10:30 a.m., he conducted a Patriarchal Doxology, a formal prayer service at the Greek Orthodox Cathedral of the Annunciation with Rev. Constantine Monios, dean of the Cathedral. At 5:30 p.m., Bartholomew participated in a Service of Prayer and Praise at the Basilica of the National Shrine of the Assumption of the Blessed Virgin Mary, with Cardinal William H. Keeler. This was the first time an ecumenical patriarch would preach at a Roman Catholic church in the United States. He sat in the chair used by Pope John Paul II during his 1995 Camden Yards Mass. This chair was made for John Carroll, who was the first bishop of Baltimore when it was established as the nation's first Roman Catholic diocese in 1789.

On December 14, the last ever professional football game was played at Memorial Stadium. This was the last home game for the Baltimore Ravens before moving to their new stadium. In this game, the Ravens defeated the Tennessee Oilers, 21-19. Interestingly, the last game played by the Colts at Memorial Stadium was also against the then Houston Oilers.

1998
A new football stadium, future home of the Baltimore Ravens, is scheduled to open for the 1998 season, and is located directly across from Oriole Park at Camden Yards.

THE FOUNDING

OF

MARYLAND

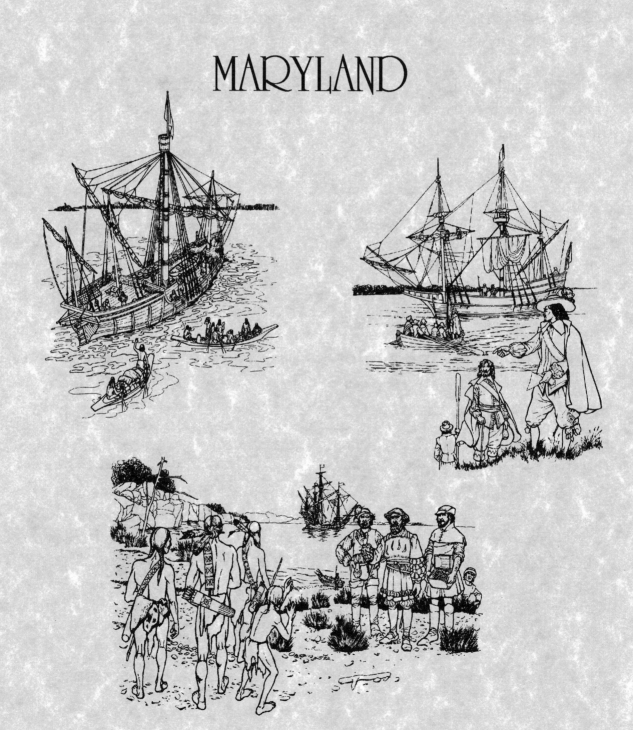

Millions of years ago, dinosaurs as well as other pre-historic animals roamed the land we now know as Maryland. We know this from the many fossils that have been discovered in Beltsville and Bladensburg, as well as in other parts of the state. Calvert Cliffs is another area in which many fossils have been discovered.

The first people in Maryland were "Indians." Christopher Columbus gave the people he met this name when he discovered America, because he believed he had found a shorter route to India, thus he named these people Indians. Scientists have determined through studying pottery, weapons and tools, that Indians lived in Maryland thousands of years ago.

After Columbus made his voyage in 1492, further exploration of this New World began. John Cabot, in 1498 sailed down the east coast to Maryland, and in 1524, Giovanni da Verrazano landed on the coast of the Delmarva Peninsula. During this time, explorers who sailed to the New World, upon finding land would claim this land for their king. Cabot claimed the land he found for King Henry VII of England, and Verrazano for the King of France. England claimed Maryland; however, this was disputed, as Spain claimed that the explorer Pedro Menendez Marques, first saw the Chesapeake Bay and as a result Maryland was Spanish territory.

In attempts to colonize the New World, Spain was quite active; however, England moved slowly. In 1580, the English settled in Roanoke, Virginia, but getting supplies was difficult due to the war with Spain. After years of trying to get supplies, in 1607 the first successful English colony was established at Jamestown, Virginia. Colony life in these early days was very hard. Killings by Indians and death by disease took a heavy toll. Soon, a leader by the name of Captain John Smith, arrived at Jamestown. He had learned to deal with the Indians and organize the colonists, and brought them through the first cold, very difficult winter. John Smith believed that the Chesapeake Bay extended to the Pacific Ocean. Being curious, he explored the Bay, mapping it as he went. These maps were in use for years to come.

Upon returning to England, John Smith spoke with a young man by the name of

William Claiborne, and told him of the land area that later would become Maryland. Claiborne first went to Virginia and mapped the entire state, becoming wealthy as a result. In 1628, Claiborne explored and found Palmer's Island and Kent Island. Liking these islands, he bought them from the Indians and set up trading posts. Having great success, Claiborne was granted a license from King Charles I, to trade in all areas of America not previously given to others. This gave Claiborne great power and status, making him similar in authority to a king.

George Calvert

George Calvert was born in 1580, to a wealthy family, and was educated at Oxford University, England. By 1624, Calvert had gained power and influence in England, and was granted the Island of Avalon in Newfoundland. In 1624, Calvert decided to leave the Church of England and become Catholic. Although he changed religions, he still maintained his friendship with King James I, and was thus retained by the King as a member of the Privy Council. In 1625, the King gave Calvert the title of Baron of Baltimore, First Lord Baltimore. During this time, it was not safe for Calvert in England because he was Catholic. Because of his unpopularity in England, and his desire to create a refuge for fellow catholics, he set out for his Colony on Avalon. Before his arrival on Avalon, he had sent other Catholics and non-Catholics to help colonize the island. Upon his arrival in 1627, he found that a house had been built for him as well as a church, a fort and other homes. In addition to being the leader of this new colony, Calvert also found himself fighting French warships at sea. Not only was fighting the French bad enough, but there were many other hardships to endure; cold weather, disease, and a shortage of food. Calvert had originally believed that the weather on Avalon would not be so cold, thinking that it would be similar to England. After learning he was wrong he decided to set out for Virginia, where warmer weather would make for better colonizing.

He arrived in Virginia in 1629. Because of his friendship with the King of England, he remained quite a powerful man. People in power in Virginia were worried that because of his relationship with the king, the king might grant Calvert land that the people wanted. These persons in power decided that Calvert should swear an oath of loyalty to the Crown and the Church of England. Calvert had no problem swearing an oath to the Crown, but could not swear loyalty to the Church of England, as he had left the

church to become Catholic. Since he refused to swear his
loyalty to the Church of England he was not permitted to stay.
On his original voyage to Virginia, Calvert had heard of the
many good lands both North and South of Virginia. After leaving
Virginia, he explored and witnessed the beautiful areas of the
Potomac River and Chesapeake Bay. He also liked and believed
the climate to be more suitable for colonization. He then
returned to England, but left his wife, the Lady Baltimore,
along with some of his children, in Virginia.

In 1629, Calvert sent for his wife and children to return to England. While waiting for
their return he asked the king to grant him the land he had explored south of Virginia.
However, the people of Virginia objected to him receiving these lands, so the King
granted him the lands north of the Potomac River. As the Charter of Maryland was being
prepared on April 15, 1632, George Calvert, First Lord Baltimore, died. His son, Cecil,
the principal but not the only heir, then inherited lands, wealth and title from his father,
making him the Second Lord Baltimore. Cecil Calvert had married Anne Arundell, the
daughter of Thomas Arundell in 1628. On June 20, 1632, King Charles I, met with Cecil
Calvert to sign the Maryland Charter. King Charles I, had made naming the colony after his
wife, Queen Henrietta Marie, a condition of the grant, and thus placed the name in the
body of the charter prior to the signing. The King used the name "Terra Mariae," which
means Mary Land. Cecil Calvert agreed. This is how Maryland received its name.

Cecil, the Second Lord Baltimore decided to send colonists to set up the
English colony of Maryland. However, he decided to stay in England and handle the family
estates, as well as maintain a good relationship with the King of England. In his place, Cecil
sent his brother, Leonard Calvert, as well as another brother, George, to lead the
expedition. On November 22, 1633, Leonard Calvert set out with two ships from Cowes
Isle, England, on a voyage to Maryland to set up a colony. The two ships were named
the "Ark" and the "Dove." The Ark, a large ship had a capacity of roughly 300 tons, while
the Dove, being a much smaller ship, had a capacity of only about 50 tons. Historians
say that approximately 140 people founded the first Maryland colony. Many people
chosen for this voyage on the Ark and the Dove, such as farmers, carpenters and brick
makers, were picked for their particular skills. Equally important to skillful people was
having the proper equipment, which had to be transported with them. Both winter and
summer clothes had to be taken, also cannons, knives and rifles for protection. Food
aboard the ships had to be stored very carefully so as not to spoil. Drinking water and

THE ARK AND THE DOVE

-by Moll

The Dove (left) and the Ark

beer were stored in large casks. Great care was taken to also store away plants and seeds needed to grow food in their farms and gardens. Planning this voyage was well-thought-out. They left on the journey in winter, so they would arrive in spring, in time to plant and grow the necessary foods for the forthcoming winter.

As the Ark and Dove started their voyage, they encountered many problems. After leaving Cowes, England, they came upon large masses of rocks at the Isle of Wight and rough breaking waves, making maneuvering difficult. Other problems faced the crews of the two ships. On the voyage, beside bad weather and rough seas, they also had to deal with pirates and raiders who were in the waters in which they had to sail. One ship they encountered at a distance was an Algerian vessel, which they assumed was hostile, but fortunately were not approached by it. In planning the voyage, they set their course not directly west to Maryland, due to the Atlantic current, but to the southwest, because the winds were more favorable (see map). Once they reached Barbados they would then have only a northern route.

In comparing the two ships', size was the major difference, but as a result the ships capabilities differed greatly. The Ark, being a much larger ship traveled better through the rough seas, was better armed and equipped, and had more crew members, with which to fend off pirates and raiders. The Dove in comparison, being so much smaller, did not handle well in rough seas, and was not capable of defending itself well. It seemed that the Dove was destined for problems.

Early in the voyage, the Ark and Dove came across another ship, the "Dragon." This ship was a large, well armed merchant vessel which was traveling their way. The Dragon therefore acted as a leader, a guide of sorts to follow, which pleased crews of both the Ark and Dove. Four days into the voyage, on November 25, a terrible storm began. The winds were so strong, and the waves so rough that the Dragon turned back toward England. The Captains of the Ark and Dove decided to go on. The Captain of the Dove advised the Ark that they would hang a lantern on the ship's mast so that they (the Ark) could keep them in view. The Captain of the Dove also advised that if they hung two lanterns this meant they were in trouble and needed help. As the night went on, the storm grew worse. Through the storm and strong winds, the crew of the Ark observed two lights coming from the Dove. The Ark, however could not reach the Dove

MAP SHOWING THE ROUTE OF THE ARK AND THE DOVE 1633-1634

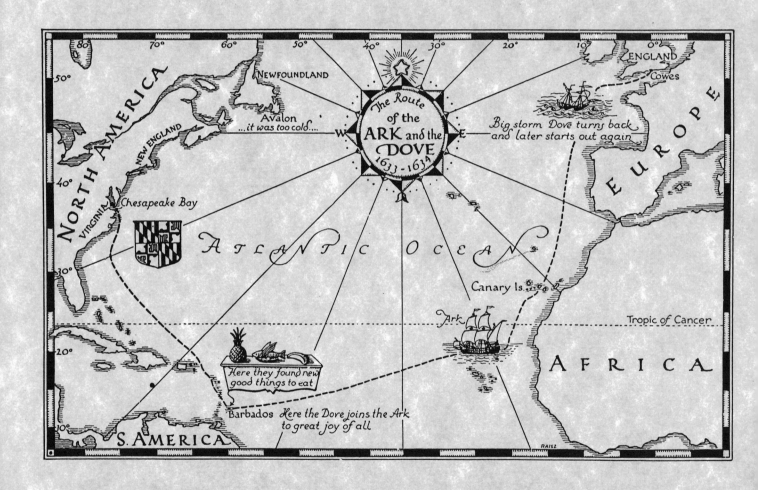

ENGLAND
Cowes

NEWFOUNDLAND

Avalon
...it was too cold...

The Route
of the
ARK and the
DOVE
1633-1634

Big storm Dove turns back
and later starts out again

NORTH AMERICA

NEW ENGLAND

VIRGINIA Chesapeake Bay

A T L A N T I C   O C E A N

EUROPE

Canary Is.

Ark

Tropic of Cancer

AFRICA

Here they found new
good things to eat

Barbados Here the Dove joins the Ark
to great joy of all

S. AMERICA

RAISZ

to help her, as it was all they could do to keep themselves afloat. During the storm the Ark lost sight of the Dove. Throughout the night they tried in vain to sight the Dove. Finally, as the storm subsided and morning came, they hoped to find her, but there was no trace of the Dove. The Ark, after passing the Canary Islands finally arrived in Barbados on January 5, 1634. There the crew rested and repaired their ship, damaged in the storm. One day as they were working in the harbor they looked out and saw something they could not believe. Sailing into the harbor was the Dove. Upon speaking with the crew of the Dove it seemed that because the storm was so great, they turned around and sought shelter of an English port. After the storm they set sail again, crossed the ocean and by providence, in time to meet the Ark.

As time passed, the Ark and Dove reached the Chesapeake Bay, bound for the Potomac River to Maryland. The Ark and Dove arrived at Maryland in early March, 1634. On March 25, they came ashore to celebrate the Feast of the Annunciation. Today we celebrate March 25 as Maryland Day.

Landing of Maryland colonists at St. Clements, March 1634.
Original painting by Leutze at the Maryland Historical Society

For several days the crews lived on the ships, while exploring parties looked for a suitable place to start their town. Searching the areas and rivers off the Potomac, they traveled a river called St. George's, which later became St. Mary's. They found an area inside St. Mary's River for the first settlement. This land was owned by the Yaocamicoe Indians. In this search for a suitable place to live, Governor Calvert used Captain Henry Fleet as a guide, because he knew the language of the Indians and was an experienced trader and interpreter. On March 27, 1634, Governor Calvert bought the land from the Yaocamicoes. Once the land was purchased, they sent word back to the crews of the Ark and Dove for them to move to this new town. As the settlers moved into the new town a celebration began. Dressed in their finest clothes, the new settlers fired cannons and flags were flown. The new village name changed from Yaocamico to St. Mary's City. This name was given in honor of the Virgin Mary.

The first black Marylander was Mathias de Sousa. Of African and Portuguese descent, he was one of nine indentured servants brought to Maryland by Jesuit missionaries and was on the Ark when Lord Baltimore's expedition arrived in the St. Mary's River in 1634. His indenture was finished by 1638 and he became a mariner and fur trader. In 1641, he commanded a trading voyage north to the Susquehannock Indians and, in 1642, sailed as master of a ketch belonging to the Provincial Secretary John Lewger. De Sousa departed and returned to the St. Mary's River many times. He anchored here (the location of the Maryland Dove today) and walked to Lewger's Manor House at St. John's. While living there he served in the 1642 legislative assembly of freemen. No record remains of de Sousa's activities after 1642, but his legacy of courage and success is regarded with great pride by all the citizens of St. Mary's County and Maryland. (a plaque dedicated in his honor is located today near the waters edge in the location of the Maryland Dove).

During this time, the Yaocamico and Susquehannock Indians were enemies. The Yaocamicoes, needing help defending themselves, found the settlers a welcome sight and learned many things from them. They received guns, steel knives and axes, which were used not only for protection but also enabled them to cut trees, farm and build homes. Some of the first homes the settlers built were cut wood with shingled roofs, and not log cabins as most believe. Soon thereafter many homes were made of brick. By the late 1670s, St. Mary's City, Maryland's first capital, had some houses and buildings of fine quality.

Margaret Brent

Margaret Brent (1601-1671) was a Catholic gentlewoman. She lived in Maryland from 1638 to 1650. In June 1647, the dying Governor, Leonard Calvert, made her executrix of his estate with power to pay the soldiers he had hired to put down a protestant rebellion. Margaret Brent's skill in carrying out this mission preserved Lord Baltimore's authority and his policy of religious toleration. During this crisis she unsuccessfully requested two votes in the assembly; one for herself and one as Lord Baltimore's agent. This was the first known effort of a woman in America to vote in a legislative assembly.

Written in the records of the Assembly proceeding of Friday, January 21, 1648 is the following: "Came Mrs. Margaret Brent and requested to have vote in the House for herself and voice also...as His Lordship's attorney. The Governor denied that the said Mrs. Brent should have any vote in the House. And the said Mrs. Brent protested against all proceedings in this present Assembly, unless she may be present and have vote as aforesaid." Additionally, in the Assembly to Lord Baltimore on April 21, 1649 was written: "Your Lordship's estate...was better for the Colony's safety at that time in her hands than in any mans else in the whole province after your brother's death. For the soldiers would never have treated any other with...civility and respect."

IN 1648 MARGARET BRENT ASKS FOR "VOTE...AND VOYCE"

The Mason-Dixon Line

During the 1660s, many land disputes arose because of settlers farming lands which were close to other states' borders. Consequently, disputes came about as to border lines. These disputes involved the states of Maryland and Virginia and Maryland and Pennsylvania. Over the next approximately one hundred years, Maryland lost many thousands of acres of land in these disputes, to Virginia and Pennsylvania.

Finally, in 1763, two men, Charles Mason and Jeremiah Dixon, who were employed by the Penns and Lord Baltimore were sent to survey the boundary line between Maryland and Pennsylvania. Once completed in 1767, Maryland lost almost three million acres of land to Pennsylvania. Because of this survey, the famous Mason-Dixon line was established; it is regarded as the popular dividing line between the northern and southern states. Today, one can still see the stone markers put in place by Mason and Dixon along the boundary line. The stone markers have the Calvert coat of arms on the Maryland side, and the Pennsylvania coat of arms on the Pennsylvania side (see picture).

Additionally, Mason and Dixon also surveyed and established the boundary line between Maryland and the Colony of Delaware. These various surveys by Mason and Dixon, along with the Chesapeake Bay and Potomac River, explain why Maryland today has such an unusual shape.

The French and Indian War

The French and Indian War was fought between 1754 and 1763. France and England began fighting because each believed they owned the land in the Ohio River Valley. During this time, French explorers had made friends with the Indians, and in doing so turned the Indians against the British. Once war began, the Indians helped the French fight the British. During the war many settlers in Western Maryland were killed. Several forts were built to help provide protection. Fort Cumberland was built around what is now the City of Cumberland, and Fort Frederick, near Hancock. Many Western Maryland

STONE MARKERS ALONG MASON-DIXON LINE

Stone Markers along the Maryland-Pennsylvania line. Marker on left represents Maryland side with coat of arms; the right Pennsylvania coat of arms.

settlers were frightened by all the killings, and fled their homes and farms, seeking safer areas. Most went to Frederick, Annapolis or Baltimore. Finally, after England won the war, most of the settlers who had left their homes in Western Maryland did not return. They stayed in Frederick, Annapolis or Baltimore, and by doing so increased the growth of these cities.

The main effect that the French and Indian War had on Maryland was merely that it slowed the growth of Western Maryland. This simultaneously increased the growth of Frederick, Annapolis, and Baltimore.

Maryland and the American Revolutionary War

Taxes in Maryland were already high. The Maryland Assembly had taxed the citizens, not only to meet the normal expenses, but to help repay the cost of the French and Indian War, including the cost to build Forts Frederick and Cumberland.

England wanted more money from Maryland, and other American colonies to pay off their war debts. In March 1765, the English Parliament passed the Stamp Act, which required that tax stamps be on all legal papers, as well as a variety of other things such as newspapers and playing cards. Although grateful to England for their assistance in the French and Indian War, the citizens felt that any further tax was excessive. On behalf of the citizens of Maryland, the Maryland Assembly sent a protest to the King of England.

England ignored the protest, and appointed a Marylander, Zachariah Hood, to be the stamp distributor and tax collector. Upon his arrival in Annapolis, he was met by angry citizens, who refused to let him off his ship. Hours later, Hood was able to get ashore. The angry citizens, in protest, tore down Hood's house. Fearing for his safety, he fled to New York.

In Frederick, Maryland, the county court refused to use the tax stamps on its legal papers. Situations began to intensify. Throughout Maryland angry groups tarred and feathered, burned or hanged mock effigies of Hood, in protest of the Stamp Act. In light of all the disruption caused by the Stamp Act, England repealed the law. But England was not finished.

In 1767, the English Parliament passed the Townshend Act, which taxed glass, lead, paint, tea, and paper. America again protested, and formed non-importation clubs, refusing to buy any of the taxed goods set forth in the Townshend Act. In Annapolis, an English ship named the Good Intent came into the harbor. Members of Maryland's non-importation club boarded the ship and found taxed items. Refusing to let the taxed cargo ashore, they sent the ship back to England, profitless. America again won as England repealed the Townshend Act, except the tax on tea. England believed that if Americans got used to the idea of the tea tax, they could gradually include all the previous items once set forth in Townshend. Americans were not fooled. They refused to buy any tea.

On November 28, 1773, a shipload of tea arrived in Boston, Massachusetts from England. On December 16, 1773, American colonists, dressed in Indian disguises boarded the ship and dumped the tea into the harbor. This is known as the "Boston Tea Party." In revenge, the King of England along with Parliament closed Boston's harbor until the tea was paid for. To help the people of Boston, many colonies, including Maryland sent food and supplies. Unable to use its port, they would ship the supplies to nearby towns, then using horses and wagons, transported the supplies to Boston. To combat this, England sent four regiments of British soldiers there.

Maryland, angry over the way all colonies were being treated by England, proposed that a representative from each colony meet in Philadelphia. Some thought that any fight between Boston and England would surely be lost. But what if all the colonies united? Thus far the American colonists had just about had enough of the various British laws. Included in these was the "Intolerable Acts of 1774." These were four Acts or laws imposed by England. They were: (1) Boston Port Act which closed the port of Boston to all shipping; (2) Massachusetts Government Act which gave power to the royal Governor. This meant that all Council Members who were previously elected by the General Assembly were now appointed by the royal Governor. Permission was required for town meetings and the sheriff as well as all juries fell under the authority of the royal Governor; (3) Administration of Justice Act allowed British officials and soldiers to be tried in a colony other than the one in which they were accused, or sent to England for trial; (4) Quartering Act which dictated the quartering of British troops inside the town of Boston.

In September 1774, the First Continental Congress met. Angry over the Intolerable Acts they prepared a petition for the repealing of these acts. Meanwhile, they decided not to import any goods from England. One law that England imposed actually helped the people from Maryland. The law stated that only English-owned ships may be used for trade between the colonies and England. As many of these ships were made along the shores of the Chesapeake Bay and considered English owned, the regulation helped the Maryland shipbuilders. When the First Continental Congress concluded, the Maryland delegates returned, and the Maryland Convention approved their work. Three matters which were important were: (1) The people of Maryland would be encouraged to produce more wool in order to clothe themselves, and not be dependant on England; (2) that a militia was to be organized in case of any fights or battles; (3) that Maryland was to, at all times, lend support to any other colony against England.

The Peggy Stewart

An Annapolis resident, Anthony Stewart owned a ship known as the Peggy Stewart, named for his daughter. Loaded with 2,000 pounds of tea the ship arrived at Annapolis harbor. Anthony Stewart decided that he would pay the tax on the tea, and have it quietly moved ashore; but soon the word of his intentions got out. Citizens became angry, and gathered at the harbor. As tempers grew hotter, the group of angry citizens went to Stewart's house and confronted him. They reminded him that he should be loyal to the non-importation agreement, although he had refused to sign it. The angry crowd gave him a choice; burn the ship "or be hanged right here at your front door."

Stewart agreed to burn the tea and offer a public apology, but pleaded to let him unload the rest of his valuable cargo. Although some people agreed, the mob continued to shout louder. Fearing for the safety of his family, he agreed to burn his ship. On October 19, 1774, Stewart ran his ship aground and applied the torch himself. The crowd cheered as the ship burned to the water. Not only did Stewart lose his valuable cargo, but also his ship worth thousands of dollars. Some people believe that the punishment was too harsh, that he should have been permitted to burn only the tea. But many experts do agree that this action clearly demonstrated the determination Marylanders felt against England and the taxes imposed. During the early hours of April 19, 1775, the four regiments of British troops sent to enforce the laws of England had arrived in Boston's harbor. Observing their arrival, Paul Revere and William Dawes galloped on their horses through the streets shouting "The British are coming!" All this day, the Americans and British fought in a bloody battle at Lexington and Concord. "The shot heard round the world" was fired, and the American Revolutionary War had begun.

At this time, the Governor of Maryland, Sir Robert Eden, who represented Henry Harford, the son of the last Lord Baltimore, found himself with little power. Although well-liked in Maryland, he was considerately placed on a ship in Annapolis harbor and returned to England. Meanwhile, Maryland had held several sessions of the Provincial Convention, in which each county sent a representative to Annapolis. A Council of Safety was formed which basically was the Executive branch of the government of Maryland. By July 1775, most of the powers of the state had been taken over by the Convention and the Council of Safety. During this month the Convention declared that if England attempted to enforce the laws of Parliament, the citizens of Maryland would fight.

Americans believed that the military training and experience they received by virtue of the French and Indian War would assist them in this fight. For England to fight a war, they would first have to cross three thousand miles of ocean to get here. But not all colonists felt the war was necessary. Many were still loyal to England, and England was quite a powerful country. Many wondered if the risk was worth the price. England, being the power that it was, was now quite aware that the colonists had no intention of obeying the English laws, and was amazed by this refusal. The English could not believe that America wanted to make its own laws and elect its own leaders. To stop this rebellion, England had sent additional troops, now on their way across the ocean. One attempt to halt the colonists' rebellion was by Lord Dunmore in Virginia. His orders were to gain control of the Potomac River, split the colonies, and stop the flow of supplies to the colonists. His plan was also to send his ships to meet the land troops loyal to England. As he sailed up the river, he had also planned to raid several plantations owned by two of America's leaders, known to be loyal to the American cause, George Washington and George Mason.

But Lord Dunmore's plan was not to be, thanks to an alert Marylander named John Hanson. He and his men captured the land troops sent to meet Lord Dunmore, and met Dunmore's ships with such resistance that he fled the Potomac. One of the first early English plans to split the colonies had failed. But much fighting was to come. This attempt by Dunmore was the only serious fighting to have taken place on the Potomac in the war. But Maryland played a major role. It sent thousands of troops to fight with George Washington and helped with large amounts of supplies. Maryland gave food, clothing and other supplies to the army without which the troops could not have endured the war.

By the time of the Second Continental Congress, which met on May 10, 1775, the rebelling colonists were already at war with England. America's struggle for independence had begun. John Hancock of Massachusetts, was elected president of the Congress, of which Maryland had seven delegates. They were: Thomas Johnson, Jr., Matthew Tilghman, Samuel Chase, William Paca, John Hall, Thomas Stone, and Robert Goldsborough. Thomas Johnson, the most active of the group, was the one who nominated George Washington as commander-in-chief of the Continental Army. In June 1775, the Battle of Bunker Hill was fought, with no real leadership. Washington then took over the command of the Continental Army and soon forced the British out of Boston.

The Second Continental Congress agreed that the colonies should be independent states. To accomplish this, America needed a document which expressed these feelings. Thomas Jefferson of Virginia was given the task of putting these feelings into words. He drafted a copy, and took it to Congress. Minor changes were made by John Adams of Massachusetts and Benjamin Franklin of Pennsylvania. Following this, Congress amended some articles, and adopted the document on July 4, 1776. This document was The Declaration of Independence, which was approved and passed in Philadelphia on July 4, but not signed. Later on August 2, 1776, fifty-three members signed a parchment copy, while others waited to sign. But the agreement was approved, and the American colonial times were over. All colonies were now states, no longer subjects under the King of England, and its people were now citizens of a new nation.

The Maryland Men Who Signed

Of the seven members of the Maryland delegation, four signed the Declaration of Independence. These men by signing risked their lives, lands and fortunes. They were: Charles Carroll of Carrollton, Samuel Chase, William Paca and Thomas Stone.

Charles Carroll

Samuel Chase

William Paca

Thomas Stone

Charles Carroll of Carrollton was born in Annapolis, Maryland in 1737, and was the only Roman Catholic to sign the Declaration of Independence.

He had added the "of Carrollton," to his signature to separate himself from the others named Charles in the large Carroll family. Although diminutive in physical structure, everything else about him was colossal; his brilliant mind, his determination, and his wealth. At this time he was the richest man in America.

Charles was educated by Jesuits until he was eleven years old, then completed his studies in France and England. He returned to America in the year of the Stamp Act (1765) and was given Carrollton Manor, a ten-thousand acre plantation in Frederick County, Maryland by his father. It was here that he married a cousin and raised his family.

During the Revolution in 1774, Charles became actively involved with his election to the provincial convention. Some months before the start of the war, he had predicted a victory should the war come to America. He had told a friend in England, "your armies will evacuate our soil, and your country retire, an enormous loser from this contest...though much blood may be spilt, we have no doubt of our ultimate success."

On July 4, 1776, Carroll was selected by the Maryland convention to join the delegates in Congress. Taking his seat on July 18, he was elected to the Board of War and Ordinance. Two weeks later, Charles Carroll of Carrollton, at the age of thirty-nine, signed the Declaration. Charles died in 1832, at the age of ninety-four, outliving all other signers. In 1828, four years before his death, he officially opened the Baltimore & Ohio Railroad. Consequently, he was the only Signer who ever saw a steam locomotive.

Samuel Chase, was born in Somerset County, Maryland on April 17, 1741, the son of an Episcopal Minister. Chase was a heavy set man, with a temper, who would pound the table when raging against the King of England, or when maddened by adversaries. When angered, his face would become flushed, thus his nickname, "Bacon Face."

Samuel studied law in Annapolis, and was admitted to the bar in 1761. At the age of twenty-three, he was elected to the Maryland legislature and immediately fought royal tyranny. It was Chase who led the charge on the Stamp Act and taxation. He was one of the few delegated at the First Continental Congress to violently criticize the Crown.

Chase continued to fight aggressively for independence at the Second Continental Congress, although his own Maryland delegation had been told to vote against freedom from Britain's control. In consideration of this, his determination never weakened. Along with his colleague, Charles Carroll of Carrollton, he took to the road on horseback, and made fervent speeches for independence at towns and farms throughout the colony. This campaign was successful, and the Maryland delegation reversed its position and urged an all-out vote in favor of independence. When Chase signed the Declaration he was thirty-five. Following the signing, Chase became very active as a congressman, serving on approximately thirty committees.

Chase was appointed chief judge of the Maryland criminal court in 1788. In 1791, he was named chief judge of the general court. In 1796, President Washington appointed him to the Supreme Court. Soon thereafter he made political attacks on the Jeffersonians and was tried under the Solution Act, which led to impeachment proceedings. Samuel Chase was acquitted and remained on the court until his death in Baltimore on June 19, 1811 at the age of seventy.

William Paca, was born in 1740 and held a distinction among the other signers of the Declaration of Independence. While most of the signers had been born in the colonies of English ancestry, Paca's family was of Italian ancestry and had been in Maryland for generations.

William was a sophisticated man who graduated from the College of Philadelphia, in 1759. Following graduation, he worked in an Annapolis law firm, then went on to London for two years at the Inner Temple. Upon his return home, he married a girl of considerable wealth, and settled in a luxurious home in Maryland. At this time Paca, was considered the finest lawyer in Maryland noted for his "incredible insight and logical power."

Although Paca was very well-liked and respected by all who knew him, the delegates did not relish his close ties with Samuel Chase, his school-days friend and fellow delegate from Maryland. Chase had a violent temper in his cause for independence, while Paca was good tempered, but allowed himself to be manipulated politically and socially by Chase. Consequently, Paca's reputation in public life was far less then his considerable talents. At the First and Second Congresses, Paca never took a side opposite from that supported by Chase. Although less vocal than Chase,

Paca was just as enthusiastic and determined to see independence. William Paca died in 1799, at the age of fifty-nine.

Thomas Stone was born in 1743, and called his residence near Port Tobacco, Maryland, "Habre-de-Venture." Stone was one of the most successful lawyers in Maryland. He was also one colonist who did not support the cause for independence as enthusiastically as his fellow delegates, William Paca and Samuel Chase. He once said, "I wish to conduct affairs so that a just and honorable reconciliation should take place."

Married at the age of twenty-five, he built his bride one of the finest homes in Maryland as a display of his love and affection for her. Additionally, at his young age, he had built a profitable law practice in Frederick, Maryland. Stone was a man who always thought for himself, and was not easily swayed by popular opinions or recommendations from others. In 1774, he defended a poll tax to support the clergy, much to the disappointment of his good friend and mentor, Thomas Johnson, as well as Samuel Chase and William Paca.

During the Second Continental Congress, Stone continued to oppose Samuel Chase. He was also very much against slavery. He once said, " I have never known a single instance of a Negro being contented in slavery." In reply a fellow congressional member said, " Stone was sometimes mistaken upon plain subjects."

In the cause for independence, Stone was patient in presenting his ideas. He is on record as announcing that, "We should pretty unanimous in a resolution to fight it out for independence. The proper way to effect this is not to move too quick. But then we must take care to do everything which is necessary for our security and defense, not suffer ourselves to be lulled or wheedled by any deceptions, declarations, or givings out. You know my heart wishes for peace upon terms of security and justice to America. But war, anything, is preferable to surrender of our rights."

By July 2, 1776, no word had arrived from England concerning peaceful negotiations. This was the final prompting Stone needed to cast his vote for complete independence. Thomas Stone died in 1787, at the age of forty-four.

Maryland's Government

After July 26, 1775, the Maryland Convention had complete control over the government of Maryland. As mentioned earlier, Governor Robert Eden was placed on a ship and sent back to England on June 23, 1776. Charles Carroll, during the Maryland Convention on June 28, 1776, recommended that Maryland join with other colonies agreeing with the Declaration of Independence. One day prior to the Declaration of Independence being adopted, the Maryland Convention decided that they needed a permanent form of government in Maryland. So, on August 1, 1776, each county in Maryland sent a representative to the Constitutional Convention, for the purpose of writing the first Maryland constitution. Meeting on August 14, 1776, they elected Matthew Tilghman as president of the convention. They then selected a committee whose function was to write and prepare the constitution for submission. The committee members were: Matthew Tilghman, Charles Carroll of Annapolis, William Paca, Charles Carroll of Carrollton, George Plater, Samuel Chase, and Robert Goldsborough.

Following the writing of the constitution, these same writers wrote Maryland's Bill of Rights, very similar to those outlined in the first ten amendments of the United States Constitution. Maryland's Constitution, outlined that there should be a governor, who at this time was to be chosen each year, serving no more than three terms consecutively. Also, the legislature was now to be called the General Assembly. This assembly shall consist of the House of Delegates and the Senate. The Governor's Council, made up of five men, was then formed. One of its function was to approve those men the governor selected for various State offices.

In October 1776, the Convention again met and went over the proposed document line by line. After long debates and some changes the Declaration of Rights was agreed upon on November 3, 1776. Five days later on November 8, the Form of Government was agreed upon, and two days later on November 10, the entire Constitution was adopted. This Constitution of Maryland endured for many years, although with various amendments over the years. Under Maryland's new Constitution, a legislature was formed and a governor was chosen. Thomas Johnson was the first, taking office on March 21, 1777.

Maryland in the Revolutionary War

Now that George Washington was Commander-in-Chief of the American forces, what he needed most was men. The first troops to come from the southern colonies to Washington's aid were from Maryland. Under the command of Captain Michael Cresap and Thomas Price, one hundred and thirty troops marched over five hundred miles to reach General Washington near Boston. These troops, armed with muskets were all excellent shots, from their experience in hunting game.

Another group of Maryland soldiers also provided important assistance during the war. At the Battle of Long Island in August 1776, as the British began to overrun the Americans, four hundred men from Maryland under the command of Major Mordecai Gist and Captain Samuel Smith took a position and held the British back, while the main body of the army escaped over the water to Manhattan Island, providing their further escape up the Hudson River Valley. Upon Washington getting the main body to safety, the Maryland troops retreated over the river they had held, an also returned to safety. Of the four hundred who fought this day, two hundred were killed. Out of the remaining two hundred who survived, only about twenty were not injured. Because of their bravery, these men were referred to as "Maryland Old Line." Through other battles which followed, Maryland troops displayed the same types of courage. This eventually led to Maryland being called the "Old Line State."

Many men from Maryland gave their lives during the war. George Washington wrote in a letter during the winter of 1777 "of the fifteen hundred brave young men who joined me from Maryland, only a scarce handful remained." Washington also praised another Maryland man, Tench Tilghman, who provided outstanding help to him as his secretary and aide-de-camp.

Maryland Doctors During the War

During the days of the Revolution, doctors had little knowledge of how to treat wounds, prevent infection, or how diseases spread. There was also no means of anesthesia. Surgeons of this day knew only two types of operations. One was amputation, and the other was trepanation, an operation in which the bones of the skull were bored or sawed relieving the brain of pressures caused by injuries, blood clots or fluids. There were no sterile medical instruments or bandages, nor did doctors realize that cleanliness helped wounds and that dressings must be changed.

Diseases such as typhoid and typhus spread quickly, due in large part to the small, cramped, crowded makeshift hospitals. In February 1777, Congress ordered that all soldiers be inoculated for smallpox, but doctors did not have a safe vaccination for the disease. They gave each soldier a mild strain of the disease, thinking that they would soon become immune. Instead of providing protection, many died of the disease. Smallpox, brought back to Maryland by returning soldiers spread through the civilian population having devastating results.

Several doctors from Maryland served in the war. One of the most important was Dr. James Craik of Charles County. As a surgeon he first served in the British Army, and then came to America during the French and Indian War, where he met George Washington. Washington soon made Craik Chief Medical Officer in the Virginia Militia. Following the French and Indian War, he settled at Port Tobacco, Maryland, and built a house known as "LaGrange" which stands today. Because of his friendship with George Washington, he soon became Washington's family doctor. At the outbreak of the Revolution, Dr. Craik joined the Continental Army and was made Assistant Director-General of the Army's Medical Department, and rose to Chief Physician and Surgeon of the Army. Following the war, during George Washington's final illness, Dr. Craik was one of the attending physicians. Upon Washington's death, Craik moved to Alexandria, Virginia where he practiced until his death in 1814. Other doctors from Maryland include Dr. James Wilkinson and Dr. James McHenry, after whom Fort McHenry in Baltimore was named. During the war McHenry served as a medical officer, and finally as a personal secretary to Washington. Following the war, he became a United States Senator, and Secretary of War in President Washington's cabinet.

Maryland Women During the Revolution

Women played a very important role during the war. While their men were off fighting, they assumed the work of running the plantations and farms. One notable lady was Mrs. Mary Lee, wife of the second Governor of Maryland, Thomas Lee. Mrs. Lee, along with others organized supplies, such as blankets, clothing, food and medical items, and sent them to Washington at Valley Forge. So grateful was Washington, he personally wrote a thank you letter to Mrs. Lee. When France made the Treaty of Alliance and joined the United States in the fight with the British, the women of Maryland also sent blankets, clothing and food to Lafayette for his troops. Maryland also supplied guns, cannons, powder, and shoes for the hundreds of soldiers.

The Articles of Confederation are Ratified

Continuing failure to put together the confederation could have undermined the Revolution. Quarreling among the states was hindering the war effort and threatened to break the already fragile nation. Additionally, France, Spain, and Holland were reluctant to grant loans to a nation that did not officially exist. In spite of this, Maryland continued to hold out. New York's cession of its western lands in 1780 was not enough. Unless Connecticut, which had minimal claims, and Virginia, which had a lot to lose, followed New York's lead, the Maryland Assembly would not support the Articles.

James Madison and Joseph Jones, Virginia delegates, led the Congressional attempt to break the deadlock. On September 6, 1780, Congress adopted a resolution urging the states to agree to "a liberal surrender of a portion of their territorial claims, since they cannot be preserved entire without endangering the stability of a general confederacy..." In further strength of the argument, Congress announced on October 10, that all ceded lands would be disposed of for the common benefit of the United States. In the future, they would become separate states, but for now it was up to the disputing parties to act.

At the same time that Jones returned to Virginia to personally promote adoption of the Congressional measure, Connecticut agreed to give up its controversial claims. Additionally, on November 22, the Maryland Assembly, meeting in Annapolis, agreed to consider ratification. A joint committee of the Maryland Assembly's two houses was appointed to consider the question and draft instructions to the state's Congressional delegates. Originally, opinions were divided and debate continued for over two months, but two events finally broke the stalemate.

On January 2, Virginia passed an act ceding to the United States the territory northwest of the Ohio River. At this same time, France's minister to the colonies, Chevalier de La Luzerne, refused to grant a loan request by Maryland, on the grounds of non-ratification. This information tipped the scales. As January closed, and during the first days of February, the Maryland Assembly came to its decision. It authorized the state's delegation in Congress to subscribe to the Articles of Confederation. On February 12, Daniel Carroll, a newly elected Congressional delegate, became the first

Maryland signer. The second required signature was affixed by John Hanson. Congress set March 1, at twelve midnight, as the time for the public announcement that the Confederation of the United States was officially born.

Upon the announcement, an enormous celebration ensued. A cannon on land in Philadelphia fired thirteen volleys, one for each of the thirteen states. A similar "fire of joy," began from John Paul Jones' frigate, the Ariel. Celebrations were held all over the United States, as fireworks lit up the nighttime sky. Local newspapers paid tribute to "A Union, begun by necessity, cemented by opposition and common danger, and now finally consolidated into a perpetual confederacy of these new and rising states."

On March 1, 1781, the Articles of Confederation were ratified at Annapolis, with Maryland being the last to sign, under which the thirteen original colonies establish a government of states.

The Treaty of Paris

Following the surrender of Cornwallis at Yorktown in 1781, most of the fighting ended. But the war was not formally over until the signing of the Treaty of Paris in 1783. In the Treaty of Paris, Great Britain formally recognized the independence of the United States. On January 14, 1784, the Congress of the Confederation met at the State House in Annapolis, Maryland, and ratified the Treaty.

BE IT REMEMBERED!

THAT on the 17th of October, 1781, Lieutenant-General Earl CORNWALLIS, with above Five thousand Britiſh Troops, ſurrendered themſelves Priſoners of War to his Excellency Gen. GEORGE WASHINGTON, Commander in Chief of the allied Forces of France and America.

LAUS DEO!

Washington Resigns at Old Senate Chamber

Eight years earlier, George Washington, dressed in his blue uniform of a colonel in the Virginia militia, stood before Congress and accepted their commission as Commander-in-Chief of the Continental Army. At the time, Washington said, "I do not think myself equal to the command I am honored with."

Now, on a cold December morning, two days before Christmas, he was before Congress again. Any doubts of that earlier day had all been laid to rest. As he stood to address Congress, his eyes were dimmed, his hands shaking, and his voice choked with emotion. At the age of forty-four, George Washington wanted now only to return to his beloved Mount Vernon to spend the remainder of his years. Several weeks earlier, On December 4, General Washington had bade farewell to his officers at Frances' Tavern in New York. It was a very emotional time for Washington, embracing some of the men, and shaking hands with others. Von Steuben was there, along with his trusted friends Henry Knox and Benjamin Tallmadge. As the day ended, Washington turned to take one last salute from the assemblage. He then set out for his journey to Annapolis, where Congress was in session.

His journey to Annapolis had been a pleasurable one, taking a barge across New Jersey, stopping briefly in Trenton, then on to Philadelphia and finally Annapolis. Along his route, he had received an outpouring of gratitude and affection from his fellow countrymen. On December 22, an elaborate dinner and reception was held in his honor. Among the two hundred guests were the aristocracy of Annapolis as well as members of Congress. Thirteen toasts were given, followed by the firing of thirteen cannons and a ball at the State House.

On December 23, 1783, General Washington entered the Senate Chamber of the State House in Annapolis. Crowded in the chamber were Congressmen, Maryland dignitaries, and a few army officers, all wishing to hear Washington speak. In a voice that was barely audible, despite the hushed silence, General Washington began by praising

his officers and congratulating Congress. Then after a short pause, he hurried to the business at hand: "Having now finished the work assigned me, I retire from the great theater of action; and bidding an affectionate farewell to this august body under whose orders I have so long acted, I here offer my commission, and take leave of all the employments of public life."

The speech lasted three minutes. When it was over, Washington took his commission from his pocket and handed it to Thomas Mufflin, the President of Congress, and quickly left the chamber. After bidding farewell to close friends, Washington rode to Mount Vernon in time to celebrate Christmas at home for the first time in many, many years. On April 30, 1789, George Washington was elected President of the United States. He served two terms, ending on March 4, 1797. Following the Presidency, he retired to Mount Vernon, where on December 14, 1799, he died of pneumonia at the age of 67. George Washington is buried at his beloved Mount Vernon, in Virginia.

Today, visitors may visit the Old Senate Chamber at the State House in Annapolis. On the floor in the chamber is a plaque marking the spot where George Washington resigned his commission, as well as a statue figure likeness of the general. Admission to the State House and the Old Senate Chamber is free.

Washington Resigning His Commission, by Edwin White. The original painting hangs in the State House.

The War of 1812

After the American Revolution, Maryland was involved in yet another war. America, was divided concerning the issue of war, and many argued against entering the War of 1812. But the causes need to be considered. English ships were stopping American ships quite frequently. The English used the excuse that they were looking for British military deserters. This practice made America quite angry. This idea of stopping American ships was also being done by the French. They would stop American merchant ships and search them. The United States came very close to entering a war with France in 1798. So close that George Washington came out of retirement to command. Washington appointed John Eager Howard brigadier general as war seemed certain. Remember that at this time, the United States felt grateful to France for their help in the American Revolutionary War, and felt bitter toward the British. Finally, ill feelings subsided without the necessity of war. George Washington, who died in 1799, did not live to see the next conflict.

In 1807, a British ship, the <u>Leopard</u>, attempted to stop and search an American ship by the name of the <u>Chesapeake</u>. The Captain of <u>Chesapeake</u>, refused to allow this search to occur. The British then fired on <u>Chesapeake</u>, killing crew members and wrecking the ship which was forced to surrender. President Thomas Jefferson, upon learning of this, issued a warning to the British to stay out of American ports and waters. In 1811, an American political group, the "War Hawks," urged war with England. The War Hawks members made up the majority in Congress and although public opinion was against war, the War Hawks view remained dominant.

Meanwhile, the British had been giving aid to the Indians, under Chief Tecumseh, who was making war on Americans who were taking the Indians' land when moving west. The American Congress then declared war on England on June 8, 1812. This move almost divided the nation as many New England states talked of seceding from the Union. The United States felt confident that this war would be easily won as England was busy fighting the French.

In 1813, the British blockade of U.S. ports increased. Generally the British controlled the Atlantic Ocean, and raided many areas of the Chesapeake Bay. To help with the war effort, the United States Government asked Maryland for a three million-dollar loan, which Maryland raised and paid. In May 1813, the British raided the town of Havre de Grace, Maryland. The British set fire to the town, looted the stores, stealing money, silver, food and clothing. In an attempt to fight back, a townsmember, John O'Neill returned cannon fire and held the British, requiring a very large force of British soldiers to capture him. O'Neill was wounded by his own cannon recoil, thus making his capture easy. The British planned to hang O'Neill, but two British soldiers had also been captured, and the United States told the British that if O'Neill died, they would in turn hang the British prisoners. This action saved the life of O'Neill. The United States, to thank O'Neill, gave him a job for life working the lighthouse at Havre de Grace. This position could also be retained by his family on his death, if they wanted. This lighthouse in Havre de Grace, which today is operated automatically, is the oldest working lighthouse in the United States.

The Battle of Baltimore

If the British had won the War of 1812, thus conquering Baltimore, one can only imagine the impact this would have had on the nation. The Battle of Baltimore, also known as the Battle of Northpoint, was most decisive toward the war's outcome. The British, who had defeated the Americans at Bladensburg and Washington, were quite confident in their ability to defeat the Americans again. The Americans, however, prepared well. They fortified the Baltimore Harbor with great care and planning. Fort McHenry was ready. Over Fort McHenry flew a huge American Flag. This flag was forty two feet long and thirty feet wide. America wanted the flag to be seen.

Other defensive measures were taken by the United States. They closed the mouth of the Patapsco River with wooden floats and chains. They sank ships in the channel to prevent the British from sailing up to the city. Baltimore and America were ready. On September 12, 1814, four thousand British soldiers landed at North Point.

The fighting began. At the beginning of the fighting, American sharpshooters Daniel Wells and Henry McComas, shot and killed the British commanding officer, Major Ross, leaving the British at a leadership disadvantage. At first the British drove the Americans back, in spite of the loss of Ross. What appeared to be a retreat by the United States was really a clever plan. American sharpshooters continued to shoot the advancing British. Finally the British approached close enough to see the City of Baltimore. The United States had twelve thousand troops waiting for the British at Hampstead Hill. The British, stopping just before Hampstead Hill, called back to their fleet for reinforcements.

Meanwhile, near the Bay, the British positioned sixteen ships in Baltimore's inner harbor. Positioned just out of range of United States guns, they heavily shelled Fort McHenry. The British then moved closer, and the guns at Fort McHenry opened fire, driving the British back. The British had also planned to use ladders to climb the walls of Fort McHenry. What they did not realize was that the United States had set up defenses at Fort Covington, Fort Babcock and Lazaretto Point, to counter such an attack. When the British attack again started, the United States returned heavy fire. For over two hours, the rockets and bombs lit up the sky.

The incident which led to Key's celebrated poem began with this battle in Baltimore's harbor. A pacifist at heart, Key had no desire for war. Following the passage by Congress of the War Act in 1812, Key became a lieutenant and quarter-master in a field company. In September, 1814, Dr. William Beanes, a physician from Upper Marlboro who had caused the arrest of a disorderly band of British soldiers, was unjustly captured. In retaliation against Dr. Beanes, Admiral Sir George Cockburn sent a detachment of troops who broke into Dr. Beanes' house, and dragged him from his bed. Transporting him to their ship, he was thrown in irons. The event was a disgrace; however his release could not be secured. Cockburn threatened to hang him from a yardarm. Friends of Key insisted that he intervene. Under a flag of truce, Key boarded an American sloop with Colonel John S. Skinner, and approached the British fleet in the Chesapeake Bay. Although Key was indifferently received, he possessed documents which described the care with which the captured doctor had treated wounded British soldiers. These documents, and pleas from Key swayed the argument and Cockburn released Beanes. By this time, the battle had begun, and the three Americans were detained on the British ship, being forced to watch the bombardment of Fort McHenry from within enemy lines. Over Fort McHenry flew a tremendous flag. Observing the battle on the 13th, Key watched the flashes of light from the rockets and bombs. In the morning on September 14, 1814, Key wondered if the flag was still there. As dawn approached he saw the U.S. flag. Additionally, the British had decided not to attack Hampstead Hill. The British invasion had failed. British troops pulled back and by the 15th, departed.

Francis Scott Key, during the battle, jotted notes aboard the ship on an envelope which described his feelings and emotions as he watched the bombardment at Fort McHenry, and his concern for the flag. This poem was originally titled "The Defense of Fort McHenry." That night at the Indian Queen Inn, a Baltimore hotel, Key wrote out the remainder of his poem. Key, upon finishing his poem, gave his copy to his brother-in-law, Judge J.H. Nicholson. Nicholson suggested the tune "Anacreon in Heaven" and had the poem printed, copies of which two survive today. First published in the Baltimore Patriot on September 20, 1814, it became known across the country as "Star-Spangled Banner." Eventually, Congress on March 3, 1931, made "Star-Spangled Banner" the official National Anthem of the United States. The copy that key wrote in the Indian Queen Inn on September 14, 1814, remained in the Nicholson family for 93 years. In 1907 it was sold to Henry Walters of Baltimore. In 1934 it was bought at auction in New York from the Walters estate by the Walters Art Gallery, Baltimore, for $26,000. The Walters Gallery in 1953 sold it to the Maryland Historical Society for the same price. It is displayed there today.

Indian Queen Inn Logo

The flag that Francis Scott Key saw during the bombardment is preserved in the Smithsonian Institute in Washington, D.C. The 30 X 42-foot flag has fifteen alternate red and white stripes and fifteen stars for the original 13 states, and Kentucky and Vermont. The flag was made by Mary Young Pickersgill from Baltimore. Her original house, c.1793, a National Historic Landmark originally known as the Baltimore Flag House, and known today as the Star-Spangled Banner Flag House and Museum, was restored in 1953 and is now a museum. It is located at 844 East Pratt Street, Baltimore, Maryland.

Francis Scott Key was born in 1779 at a manor house, "Terra Rubra" in Frederick County, Maryland, attended St. John's College in Annapolis, and practiced law there. After he married Mary Taylor Lloyd, the couple moved to Georgetown, where he practiced law with his uncle, Philip Barton Key. Francis Scott Key died in 1843, and is buried in Frederick, Maryland. Above his grave a flag is flown twenty four hours a day, three hundred sixty five days a year.

The War of 1812 closed with an honorable peace in 1814. The Treaty of Ghent, an agreement between the United States and England, was signed in Ghent, Belgium. The Treaty was ratified by the United States Congress in February 1815.

The Star-Spangled Banner Flag House and Museum

THE STAR-SPANGLED BANNER

O say, can you see by the dawn's early light
What so proudly we hailed at the twilight's last gleaming ?
Whose broad stripes and bright stars through the perilous fight,
O'er the ramparts we watched were so gallantly streaming !
And the rockets' red glare, the bombs bursting in air,
Gave proof through the night that our flag was still there.

O say, does that Star-spangled Banner yet wave
O'er the land of the free and the home of the brave ?

On the shore, dimly seen through the mist of the deep
Where the foe's haughty host in dread silence reposes,
What is that which the breeze, o'er the towering steep,
As it fitfully blows, half conceals, half discloses ?
Now it catches the gleam of the morning's first beam--
In full glory reflected, now shines on the stream;

'Tis the Star-spangled Banner, O long may it wave
O'er the land of the free and the home of the brave !

O thus be it ever when freemen shall stand
Between their loved homes and the foe's desolation !
Bless with victory and peace, may our heav'n-rescued land
Praise the Power that hath made and preserved us a nation.
Then conquer we must, for our cause it is just--
And this be our motto: "In God is our trust !"

And the Star-spangled Banner in triumph shall wave
O'er the land of the free and the home of the brave.

Francis Scott Key

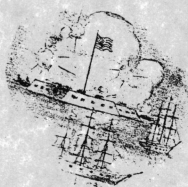

O say can you see by the dawn's early light
While so proudly we hail'd at the twilight's last gleaming,
Whose broad stripes & bright stars through the perilous fight
O'er the ramparts we watch'd, were so gallantly streaming?
And the rocket's red glare, the bomb bursting in air,
Gave proof through the night that our flag was still there,
O say does that star spangled banner yet wave
O'er the land of the free & the home of the brave?

On the shore dimly seen through the mists of the deep,
Where the foe's haughty host in dread silence reposes,
What is that which the breeze, o'er the towering steep,
As it fitfully blows, half conceals, half discloses?
Now it catches the gleam of the morning's first beam,
In full glory reflected now shines in the stream,
'Tis the star-spangled banner — O long may it wave
O'er the land of the free & the home of the brave!

And where is that band who so vauntingly swore,
That the havoc of war & the battle's confusion
A home & a Country should leave us no more?
Their blood has wash'd out their foul footstep's pollution.
No refuge could save the hireling & slave
From the terror of flight or the gloom of the grave,
And the star-spangled banner in triumph doth wave
O'er the land of the free & the home of the brave.

O thus be it ever when freemen shall stand
Between their lov'd home & the war's desolation!
Blest with vict'ry & peace may the heav'n rescued land
Praise the power that hath made & preserv'd us a nation!
Then conquer we must, when our cause it is just,
And this be our motto — "In God is our trust,"
And the star-spangled banner in triumph shall wave
O'er the land of the free & the home of the brave. —

Original copy of "Star-Spangled Banner" penned by Francis Scott Key. The original is on display at the
Maryland Historical Society.
Original Post Card depicting the Francis Scott Key Monument, Frederick, Maryland.

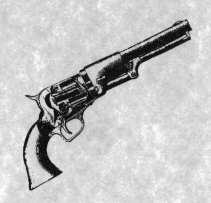

The Civil War in Maryland

Maryland before the Civil War was divided on the issue of slavery. There were three basic opinions concerning this issue. Some believed that owning slaves was wrong. Others believed that it was wrong to make a slave of any man, and still others believed that although they owned slaves, they should be freed when it was affordable to do so. These opinions came mostly from those Maryland plantation owners who did in fact own slaves.

As Maryland is located midway between the north and the south, most people could understand both sides of the slavery issue. As early as 1746, a Quaker named John Woolman traveled through Maryland and preached against slavery. Because of him, many Quaker families freed their slaves. In 1783, Maryland passed a law forbidding the importation of slaves to the state for the purpose of selling them. This law provided that people who already owned slaves could keep them, but any slave imported to be sold became a free man.

As time passed, more northern states were opposed to slavery. When the Republican party was formed, it prohibited slavery in the great western territories that had not yet been formed into states. The southern states, believing that the Republican party would try to do away with slavery in all states and territories threatened to secede. When Abraham Lincoln was elected President in 1860, many southern states seceded from the Union, and formed the new Confederate States of America. In 1860, there were as many free Negroes in Maryland as there were slaves. People wondered if Maryland would remain in the Union or join the Confederacy.

Maryland did not secede from the Union. When the war began with the bombing of Fort Sumter in 1861, Maryland was a divided state. Many families were split in their loyalty. Fathers and sons, brothers and cousins had different beliefs, and would now be fighting against each other. On April 19, 1861, the Sixth Massachusetts Regiment passed

through Baltimore on its way to Washington. People gathered to cheer the troops, others gathered and threw stones. As they marched along Pratt Street, the soldiers returned fire to the angry mob. Before the mob retreated, eleven citizens were killed and many more injured. Four soldiers were killed and thirty-six were wounded. Known as the Baltimore Riot, these killings were the first of the Civil War. A young Marylander who was living in Louisiana heard of the Baltimore Riot, and felt that the rights of Maryland's citizens had been interfered with. His name was James Ryder Randall. So incensed by the events of the riot, he wrote a poem titled, "My Maryland." It was set to music and became one of the most popular songs in the South, and became Maryland's State Song, later titled, "Maryland, My Maryland."

Many of Maryland's citizens were determined that no other Northern troops would pass through the city. Alarmed by the riots, the Mayor of Baltimore and the Governor of Maryland asked President Lincoln not to send any further troops. Lincoln agreed and in the future sent them by a different route. Although Maryland was still in the Union, many people in the state believed that the Confederate States were right in their beliefs. To ward off any further problems and watch over the city, General Butler and his Union army entered Baltimore on May 13, 1861, and without incident took possession of Federal Hill. From this time, until several months after the war, troops were kept there. The Union built other forts in and around the city. For a short time, the United States Government thought that supplies and ammunition were being sent to the Confederacy, so no shipments were permitted to or from Baltimore, by either ship or train.

Throughout the Civil War, approximately fifty thousand men from Maryland fought for the Union, and twenty thousand for the Confederacy. Colonel John R. Kenly commanded Maryland's first regiment of Union soldiers and Colonel Bradley T. Johnson commanded the Maryland Confederates. When the war began, the Maryland Confederates met at Point of Rocks, Virginia. These first troops had no guns, ammunition or uniforms. Because Maryland was part of the Union, the government refused to supply these men. Finally, Colonel Johnson's wife persuaded the State of North Carolina to supply her husband's regiment. Often during the war, Maryland soldiers, fathers, sons, and brothers, fought on opposite sides. One of the first battles took place at Front Royal, Virginia, in May 1862. It was here that the First Maryland Union Infantry met the First Maryland Confederate

Infantry. Following the Confederate victory, many Union soldiers were captured. Many Rebel soldiers knew the Union prisoners, and gave them food and tobacco, and talked about their mutual friends and relatives at home. These men who fought on opposite sides did not hate one another, as they were fighting for principles in which they believed, rather than just each other.

Other battles in which Marylanders exclusively fought other Marylanders were in June 1863, when the Union Baltimore Battery of Light Artillery exchanged cannon fire with the Second Maryland Confederate Artillery at Winchester, Virginia and again in June 1864, at New Bridge, on the Chickahominy River in Virginia.

Maryland had two famous men who fought in the Confederate Navy. Franklin Buchanan commanded the famous ironclad <u>Merrimac</u>, but because he was wounded he did not command during the famous battle with the Union ironclad <u>Monitor</u>. In later years, Buchanan would become the chief admiral of the Confederate Navy. The second Marylander was Captain Raphael Semmes who commanded the Confederate ship, <u>Alabama</u>. Because of Maryland's location just across the Potomac River, many battles took place on Maryland's soil. No important fighting took place in 1861, but many famous battles were to come.

Bloody Lane - Antietam National Battlefield

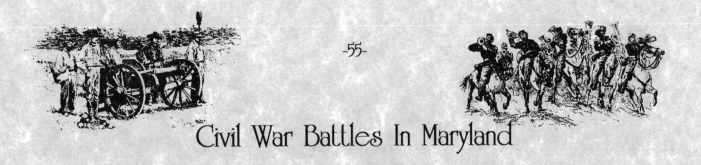

Civil War Battles In Maryland

In September 1862, General Robert E. Lee and the Army of Northern Virginia invaded Maryland. These were courageous men, being thin and tired from lack of food and long marches. Many soldiers had no shoes. Still as they marched, their band played and the men sang "Maryland, My Maryland."

On September 6, 1862, Lee's army marched into Frederick looking for volunteers. Because most of western Maryland favored the north, Lee received little assistance. On September 14, 1862, Lee's army met General George McClellan's Army of the Potomac at the Battle of South Mountain. Several days later the armies would meet again, in the most important battle on Maryland soil. This was at the Battle of Antietam, or the Battle of Sharpsburg as it is also known. For two days, September 16, and 17, the two armies clashed. The worst day in Civil War history came on September 17, when more lives were lost in a single day then in any other battle in history. Although neither side actually won, Lee's army was so weakened by the battle he was forced to retreat to Virginia. In this Maryland Campaign, Lee suffered 13,388 casualities, of which 10,941 fell at Antietam. McClellan's Army of the Potomac suffered 26,025 killed, wounded or captured, of which 12,440 were at Antietam.

In July 1864, General Jubal Early led another Confederate army into Maryland. During this occupation, he went to Frederick and Hagerstown. It was in these towns that he forced the residents to pay him large sums of money to prevent their towns from being destroyed. On July 9, 1864, Early's troops defeated Union General Lew Wallace at the Battle of the Monocacy River, outside Frederick. Other smaller battles took place in Maryland, mostly along the Potomac River, near Harper's Ferry. Rebels often destroyed parts of the rail lines of the Baltimore & Ohio Railroad outside Baltimore. Another famous Marylander, Lieutenant Colonel Harry Gilmor brought his famous Confederate cavalrymen to Cockeysville and Towson, only to be pushed back toward Virginia by Union troops. During this time Union troops continued to occupy Baltimore. They would arrest any person who was suspected of siding with the Confederates. The Union soldiers would search homes of those believed to be helping the Confederates.

The mayor of Baltimore as well as the chief of police was arrested. The telegraph offices were seized by Union soldiers and any singing or whistling of Confederate songs, or the wearing of Confederate colors was criticized.

Maryland was the only state which was so truly divided in the war. Many who lived in the northern and western sections sided with the Union. Others in southern sections, the Eastern Shore and many in Baltimore favored the Confederacy. When the war ended, bitterness Marylanders felt for each other who fought on opposite sides quickly diminished. Together they worked to rebuild and make the state again prosperous.

Antietam National Battlefield looking toward Dunker Church

Burnside Bridge, Antietam National Battlefield

Dunker Church, Antietam National Battlefield

Antietam National Battlefield Cannon

Clara Barton Monument, Antietam National Battlefield

MARYLAND'S 23 COUNTIES

&

BALTIMORE CITY

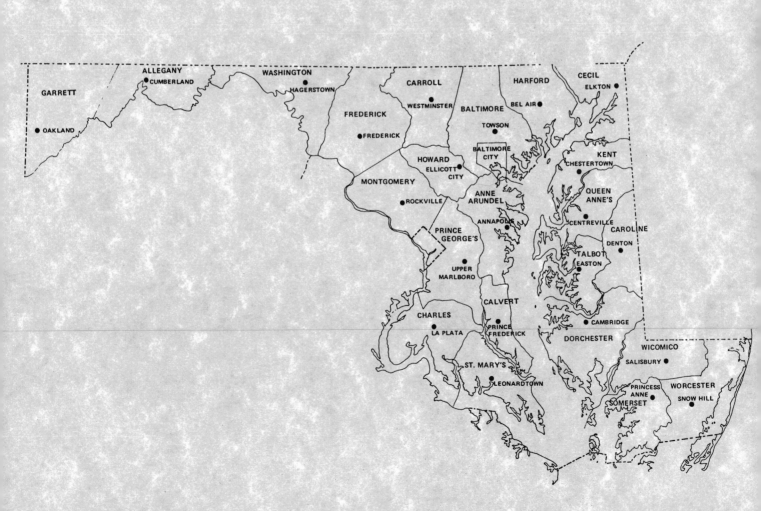

ALLEGANY COUNTY

The County was created in 1789 from Washington County (Acts of 1789). Allegany comes from the Indian word "Allegiwi" meaning "beautiful stream."

The sheaf of wheat that appears in the design is taken from the Allegany County Commissioners' seal that was adopted in 1829. Four lines radiate as compass points from the sheaf of wheat. Emphasis is placed on the west compass line to signify the location of the county in Maryland and to emphasize the historical importance of Allegany County in the westward movement. The lower section on the right side contains a pick and shovel and is symbolic of the coal mining industry that has been a vital part of the county history. The upper section of the seal is symbolic of the Appalachian location of Allegany County with its beautiful hills and streams. The largest section of the seal contains design elements representing the role that roads and various forms of transportation have played in the history of the county. The toll house and the wheel for the first national road, and the canal barge and railroad cars for the western movement. Also included in this segment of the seal is the symbol for industry and a cluster of building forms symbolizing the cultural and religious heritage of Allegany County.

Allegany County, the smallest of the four Maryland mountain counties, lies between Garrett to the west and Washington to the east. Its northern border is the State of Pennsylvania, and to the south the Potomac River separates it from West Virginia. The elevation of Allegany County is approximately six hundred to three thousand feet above sea level, with most of the ridges averaging two thousand five hundred feet. Some of the largest are Dan's Mountain, Will's Mountain, Warrior Mountain, Polish Mountain and Town Hill. Two smaller elevations are Fort Hill and Shriver Mountain. During the mid-eighteenth century, early English settlers moved into the area. One early pioneer was Thomas Cresap, who founded Oldtown, also known as Skipton in early days, about 1760. At Will's Creek, named for the last Shawnee Indian to inhabit this area, a fort was built, first known as Fort Mount Pleasant but later renamed Fort Cumberland. It was at the intersection of Washington and Green Streets, in the city of Cumberland, where the Emmanuel Episcopal Church stands today.

The early history of the fort is interwoven with the story of the early explorations of George Washington, the beginning of the French and Indian or Seven Years War, and Braddock's defeat in 1755. Washington first planned the fort as an outpost against the French who had built Fort Duquesne, now Pittsburgh, and were determined to check the western progress of the English-speaking people of the Colonies. When Braddock's army retreated in confusion, Fort Cumberland was the rallying point. Washington remained as commander for at least three years and the log cabin he occupied can now be seen in Riverside Park in Cumberland. It originally stood on the site of the Allegany County courthouse.

The city of Cumberland was laid out in 1785, and officially established in 1787, becoming the county seat in 1789. President Washington visited the area again during the Whiskey Rebellion of 1794. The first child born in Cumberland was Frederick Dent, the father-in-law of Ulysses S. Grant. Frederick died in the White House during his son-in-law's presidential term of office.

Because most westbound settlers passed through Allegany County, it became the focal point on the westward trail, and the main reason the Chesapeake and Ohio Canal was built from Georgetown to Cumberland. Because of the canal project, railroad builders were influenced to extend the Baltimore & Ohio Railroad in the same direction, from Baltimore City to insure the continued movement of supplies and products. In doing so the railroad builders worked faster than the canal diggers and arrived first at Cumberland.

The wagon road had been extended to Wheeling, Virginia (now West Virginia) in 1812, with the aid of the first federal funds appropriated for road building. The toll road was known as the "Cumberland Road" and the "National Road." The improved transportation facilities brought prosperity to the area for many years. The Western Maryland and Pennsylvania Railroads followed the Baltimore & Ohio, and Cumberland became a great rail center. Extensive coal production, an important industry at the time, provided fuel to the railroads, and kept both the trains and the canal boats busy hauling coal for many years. Today the mines and canal are no longer used.

Agriculture is an important resource in Allegany County. Corn, grains and hay are the chief products, raised mostly for local consumption. Additionally, some fruit growing has been commercially profitable, including apples, peaches and cherries.

Allegany County's population in 1990 was 74,946. By 1994, the population was 73,866, a slight decrease of 1.4% since 1990. In 1998, the population rose to 76,140, and by the year 2000, it is projected to rise to 77,500.

Allegany County has many historical and interesting places to visit. These include: 1742 Log Cabin: Located at the corner of Williams and Messick Road, Cumberland, this log cabin was originally located on "The Brothers" land tract that was sold to Mary McCleary by Thomas Beall of Samuel in 1810. It's original location was on Michigan Avenue. Visitors may view the cabin from the outside only. C & O Canal Boat Replica and Canal Park: Located on Rt. 51, North Branch, Cumberland, this canal boat replica features a captain's cabin with furnishings of the C & O Canal period (1828-1924). Nearby is a lock house and two restored canal locks. Other points of interest related to the C & O Canal are the C & O Canal National Historical Park Visitor's Center, located at Western Maryland Station Center, Canal Street, Cumberland. Located here are artifacts relating to the canal and Cumberland. Also located here are the Transportation and Industrial Museum, containing displays pertaining to the railroads, the canal and industries of the 1800s and the Western Maryland Scenic Railroad, where historic train rides are featured. These train rides travel from Cumberland on sixteen miles of track, winding through the Narrows, along scenic valleys, around Helmstetter's Curve, through Brush Tunnel to Frostburg, where the locomotive is rotated on a turntable for the return trip. The C & O Canal Paw Paw Tunnel is located on Rt. 51, 28 miles south of Cumberland. Described as a major engineering feat in the 1800s, the Paw Paw tunnel cut 3,118 feet through the mountain. Located on the C & O Canal towpath, the tunnel is open year round. The Tunnel Hill Trail is approximately two miles in length and crosses over the top of the tunnel. Flashlights are suggested, and wheelchairs are not recommended. Each year, generally in July, is the C & O Canal Boat Festival, located on Rt. 51 South, in Cumberland. Featured are reenactments of Civil War life in the 1800s, stage coach rides and canal boat tours, as well as music, arts and crafts.

Also located in Cumberland is George Washington's Headquarters, c.1755, located on Green Street. This structure can be viewed with a self-operated tape located on the porch. On Washington Street is the Emmanuel Episcopal Church/Fort Cumberland Earthworks. This church, was built in 1849 on the site of Fort Cumberland, over a series of tunnels. Portions of Fort Cumberland's earthworks still exist beneath the church. Tours of the church are available by appointment. The Washington Street Historic District, also in Cumberland, begins at Baltimore Street and extends to the 600 block.

The houses along this route are most interesting, maintaining a standard of architectural quality and uniformity of the 1800 period. Self-guided tour brochure is available.

In Mt. Savage is an interesting place known as The Castle. This 1880s stone structure is surrounded by a twenty foot stone wall. It has been restored to its original elegance, and is presently a bed & breakfast, available for tours, teas, and parties. Also in Mt. Savage is the Mt. Savage Historical Park, located on Old Row. Within the park a cabin has been constructed to honor the first settlers who lived west of Fort Cumberland. The Mt. Savage Museum is located within the park, and is the birthplace of Cardinal Edward Mooney. Mt. Savage is an interesting example of a surviving nineteenth century railroad town, and a fascinating place to visit.

The city of Frostburg is another interesting place to visit. As Frostburg owes its beginnings to the National Road, Main Street is lined with houses built before 1900, all unembellished in their original distinction. Other places of interest include:

The Depot Center, located at 19 Depot Street, Frostburg. Within the center is featured the renovated c.1891 Cumberland & Pennsylvania Railroad Depot, and the Thrasher Carriage Museum. The Old Depot houses a restaurant, lounge, bakery, ice cream parlor and gift shop. The Thrasher Carriage Museum contains one of the most comprehensive collections of carriages in the country. The museum houses over fifty pieces from the extensive private collection of the late James R. Thrasher. Included also is the presidential inaugural coach used by Teddy Roosevelt. Across the street is the Tunnel Hotel containing various arts, crafts, and souvenir shops. The Frostburg Museum at the corner of Hill and Oak Streets, Frostburg, is an 1890s school building with displays of local history and the Frostburg State University Planetarium, offers special monthly programs each year from September to May.

The only remaining toll house in the State of Maryland is located in Allegany County, at LaVale. This 1836, four room structure housed the gatekeeper who collected the tolls along the road until the 1900s. The LaVale Toll Gate House is open May through October and by appointment.

The <u>National Road and Narrows</u> can be viewed from North Centre Street to Route 40 in West Cumberland. This road was the first federally funded highway in the United States. It was authorized by the United States Government in 1806, in response to a need to connect East and West via a national transportation system. As a result of costly repairs, control of the road was turned over to the states and toll houses were built. In 1832, the road was re-routed through the Narrows, a natural gap in the mountains with sheer rock cliffs on one side, boasting the Lover's Leap Legend.

Form of Government: Code Home Rule (1974)

Map of Allegany County

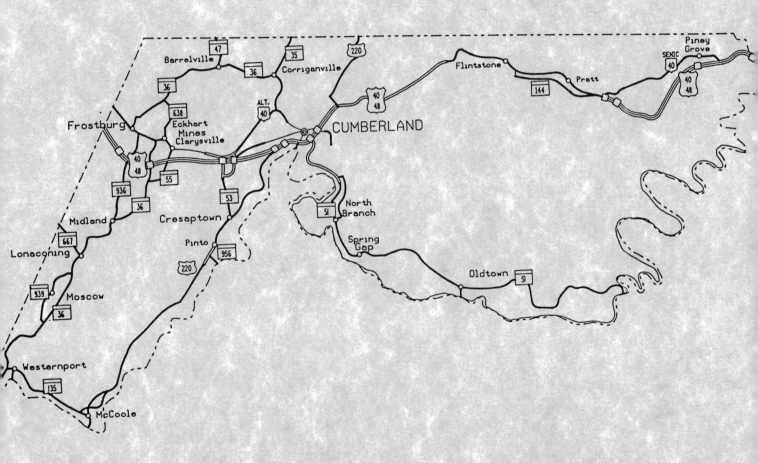

ANNE ARUNDEL COUNTY

Anne Arundel County was established in 1650 (Chapter 8, Acts of 1650). The County was named for England's Lady Anne Arundell, wife of Cecil Calvert, Second Lord Baltimore and founder of the colony of Maryland. Lady Anne Arundell married at the age of thirteen, and was the mother of many. She was known for her strong intellect, and her love of the arts. Anne Arundell died in 1649 at the age of thirty-four. On her tombstone her husband had engraved, "Farewell, you most lovely of earthly beauties."

Anne Arundel County is located on the Western Shore, south of Baltimore City, and extends along the Chesapeake Bay to Calvert County on the south. It has an area of four hundred seventeen square miles of land and seven of water. Its elevation rises to about three hundred feet northeast of Laurel, near the Anne Arundel, Howard and Prince George's counties junction.

The Anne Arundel County Seal varies only slightly from the flag of Maryland, which is the Coat of Arms of the Lords Baltimore representing the Calvert and Crossland families. Crossland is the family name of George Calvert's mother. George Calvert was the first Baron Baltimore. The county's official colors are gold, from the Calvert Arms, and red from the Crossland Arms.

The first settlement in Anne Arundel County was made in 1648 by the Puritans who had been living in Virginia, but found the climate of the religious toleration in Maryland more agreeable than conditions in the older colony. During this time, the English Civil War between the Cavaliers and the Puritan "Roundheads" of Oliver Cromwell was raging, and Virginia was loyal to the King and the Established Church. In 1649, Charles I was executed and the Puritans of Anne Arundel County attempted to seize control of Maryland. As a result, the county was established in 1650. In the following ten years, the new colonies' political life was confused, but by 1660, with the restoration of the Stuart kings, the proprietary authority was restored to the Calvert family.

Due to objections made concerning the remote location of St. Mary's as the capital of Maryland, and as the population began moving north, a decision was made to move the capital. Located on the Severn River was a tiny community, first known as Providence, then changed to Anne Arundel Town, and eventually Annapolis. In 1695, Annapolis became the capital of Maryland. It took its name, "Annapolis" from Princess Anne, later Queen Anne, the last of the Stuart line to rule England.

The first State House was built in 1697, the second in 1706, and the present structure began in 1772, and was completed in 1779. In the Old Senate Chamber of the existing State House, the Congress of the United States met from November 16, 1783 to June 3, 1784. In this chamber room George Washington resigned as commander-in-chief of the Army, and Congress ratified the Treaty of Paris, ending the Revolutionary War. This State House is the oldest in continuous use in the United States. The State House and the Old Senate Chamber are open to the public and admission is free. Inside the Old Senate Chamber is period furniture as well as a statue likeness of George Washington.

The State House dome is the largest wooden structure of its kind in North America. It was designed and constructed by Annapolis architect Joseph Clark between 1785 and 1797. Atop the dome is a carved Easter Shore cypress in the shape of an acorn which steadies a lightning rod. For over two-hundred years, this "Franklin" lightning rod, which was constructed and grounded to Benjamin Franklin's specifications, has served as the State House spire and in recent times as its flagpole. This innovation of Franklin's lightning rod, which pierces the acorn, continues to protect the dome.

Another interesting site in the State capital is the United States Naval Academy, which originally opened in 1845. Located on the academy grounds is the Naval Museum, Preble Hall, which features a collection of arms, artifacts, ship models and marine art; Tecumseh Stone, a bronze replica of the USS Delaware's wooden figurehead, which is frequently decorated by midshipmen; and the Chapel & Crypt of John Paul Jones, this chapel's cornerstone was laid in 1904 by Admiral Dewey. Beneath the chapel is the Crypt of John Paul Jones, noted naval hero of the American Revolution. Other places of interest include: St. John's College, which was chartered in 1784 as a successor to King William's School, established in 1696. The college was also the site of Revolutionary and Civil War encampments.

Many interesting buildings of colonial architecture, and historic points of interest can also be found in Annapolis. These include: Anne Arundel County Court House, built in 1824; the Public Library (1737); City Hall (1764); St. Mary's Church, Duke of Gloucester Street, (1735), a Victorian-Gothic structure. The interior displays the rib-vaulting and hand-carved altar screen characteristic of the Gothic Revival style; St. John's Parish, Duke of Gloucester Street, (1858) was the third church to be built on this site. In the church is a silver communion service presented by King William III in 1695 which is still in use; William Paca House and Garden, 186 Prince George Street, (1763), this Georgian mansion was built between 1763 and 1765 by William Paca, signer of the Declaration of Independence and Governor of Maryland. The William Paca Garden is a two-acre, neo-classical landscape, featuring four parterres, herb and vegetable, and wilderness gardens; Ogle House (1742); Chase-Lloyd House, 22 Maryland Avenue, (1769), built by Samuel Chase, signer of the

Declaration of Independence. This Georgian house is noted for its fine interior detail.

Hammond-Harwood House, 19 Maryland Avenue, (1774), considered one of the most beautiful examples of late Colonial architecture; Shiplap House Museum, was formerly a tavern which catered to colonial waterfront clientele, and is one of the oldest houses in Annapolis, built in 1715; Bordley-Randall House (1726); Dorsey House (1685); Jennings House (1737); Brice House, 42 East Street, (1766), is the stately residence of James Brice, featuring exceptional craftsmanship with beautifully carved moldings and detailed woodwork; Sands House (1680); Tobacco Prise House, 4 Pinkney Street, is an early nineteenth century warehouse. On display are exhibits of Maryland's colonial tobacco trade, including a tobacco press used to fill hogsheads for shipment to England; Ridout House (1750); Scott House (1784); and Jonas Green House (1680).

Charles Carroll House, 107 Duke of Gloucester Street, is the birthplace and dwelling of Charles Carroll of Carrollton (1737-1832). Charles Carroll was the only Catholic to sign the Declaration of Independence, and was one of the wealthiest men in colonial America; Banneker-Douglass Museum, 84 Franklin Street, includes African-American arts and culture; Old Treasury, State House Grounds, was built between 1735 and 1737. This is the oldest public building in Maryland; Maritime Museum, 77 Main Street, is a restored eighteenth century warehouse. Used by Revolutionary War victualling (food supplies) officer to store supplies for the Continental Army and Navy. Exhibits include "Maritime Annapolis 1751-1791"; Maryland Inn, built in 1772 on "Drummer's Lot" where the town drummer cried the daily news. This impressive structure has been operating as an inn since the 1770s.

Middletown Tavern, Market Space & Randall Street, operated as a tavern and ferry landing between 1745 and 1790, and was a popular dining and lodging place of American Patriots, and today is a popular restaurant; Kunta Kinte Plaque, this plaque in the sidewalk at the head of City Dock commemorates the arrival in 1767 of the African slave immortalized in Alex Haley's Roots; Liberty Tree, St. John's Campus in front of McDowell Hall, this four hundred year old tulip tree was a rallying point for meetings of Sons of Liberty prior to the Revolutionary War. The McDowell Hall of St. John's College was originally intended as the governor's mansion which was reconstructed in 1909 along with its original eighteenth century look.

For nearly forty years after the removal of Maryland's State capital from St. Mary's to Annapolis, little if nothing was done to find a suitable place for the governor to live. In 1733, an executive residence was funded by an act, and was almost completed by Governor Thomas Bladen when suddenly construction was halted following a dispute between Governor Bladen and the House of Delegates over the cost. As a result, the building remained unfinished until after the Revolution, when it was then turned over to the newly chartered St. John's College.

A search continued for a suitable residence resulting in the acquisition of the Jennings House on what is now part of the United States Naval Academy. This house was leased by Governor Horatio Sharpe and later purchased in 1769 by Governor Robert Eden. Following Eden's return to England at the beginning of the Revolution, the house and grounds were confiscated by the State. In 1866, the property was conveyed to the United States Government as part of a bid agreement to keep the Naval Academy in Annapolis. In 1868, a plot of land was acquired between State and Church Circles in Annapolis, and construction began on a new executive residence. This house, a mid-Victorian brick structure, was ready for Governor Oden Bowie and his family in 1870, but took another six years before the mansion and grounds were completed.

In 1935, Governor Harry W. Nice made extensive renovations. Using the main body of the old house as a central block, the mansion was converted to a five-part Georgian country house by adding two adjoining corridors, known as hyphens, and two wings. This work was completed in 1936. Governor Nice believed that the renovations he made would last for a hundred years. Upon his term as governor ending, Governor Nice moved out and the new governor, William Preston Lane moved in. Governor Lane, in 1947, discovered that extensive remodeling was needed. Again, forty years later in 1987, Governor William Donald Schaefer discovered that major renovations were again necessary. In 1995, the name of the Governor's Mansion was changed to Government House, its original name, under Governor Glendening.

Today the Government House reflects a number of decorative themes representing Maryland, past and present. Visitors are welcome, and a ramp was installed in recent years to facilitate access to the house by the disabled. The public rooms of the Government House are open to the public, by appointment.

Government House

Anne Arundel County also has many other areas of historic interest. These include: All Hallows Episcopal Church, located on Rt. 2 & Brick Church Road, Davidsonville, built in 1710, was the pastorate of Mason Locke Weems, biographer of George Washington; Benson-Hammond House, Aviation Boulevard & Andover Road, Linthicum, this early nineteenth century farmhouse was built by Thomas Benson. This house features four period rooms, a museum and gift shop and is on the National Register of Historic Places; Historical Electronics Museum, 1745 W. Nursery Road, Linthicum, features military and space exhibits, WWII radar systems, a working telegraph, and research library; Captain Salem Avery House, 1418 E. West Shadyside Road, Shady Side, is a restored watermen's home and museum on the West River, and is operated by the Shady Side Rural Heritage Society; Fort George G. Meade Museum, Building 4647, Fort Meade, this museum traces the evolution of the fort and the First U.S. Army from WWI to present. Established in 1917, Fort Meade was named in honor of the Civil War general.

St. James Parish, 5757 Solomons Island Road, Lothian, was built in 1763 and its graveyard contains the two oldest known tombstones in Maryland; and the Londontown Publik House & Gardens, 839 Londontown Road, Edgewater, is an eighteenth century tavern and inn on the banks of the South River. This is the only remaining structure of a once thriving seaport. Now a museum, surrounded by ten acres of woodland gardens, the site features self-guided garden and museum tours, school tours and educational programs.

Other attractions in Anne Arundel include the Maryland State Archives, Hall of Records, 350 Rowe Boulevard, Annapolis. This is the historical agency and permanent records repository for the State of Maryland. Collections include original public and church records, newspapers, photographs, and maps. A public searchroom for family history and historical research is available. Exhibits, books and gifts are available in the lobby; Scenic Overlook, Rt. 450, at the northern end of the Severn River Bridge, offers a spectacular view of Annapolis; and the Thomas Point Lighthouse, located at the mouth of the South River, was erected in 1875 and is one of the few surviving offshore lighthouses, and is listed on the National Register of Historic Landmarks.

Anne Arundel County's population in 1990 was 427,239. By 1994 the population was 456,171, and increase of 6.8% since 1990. In 1998, the population rose to 468,365, and the projected population by the year 2000 is 480,200.

Form of Government: Charter (1964)

State House, Annapolis, Maryland

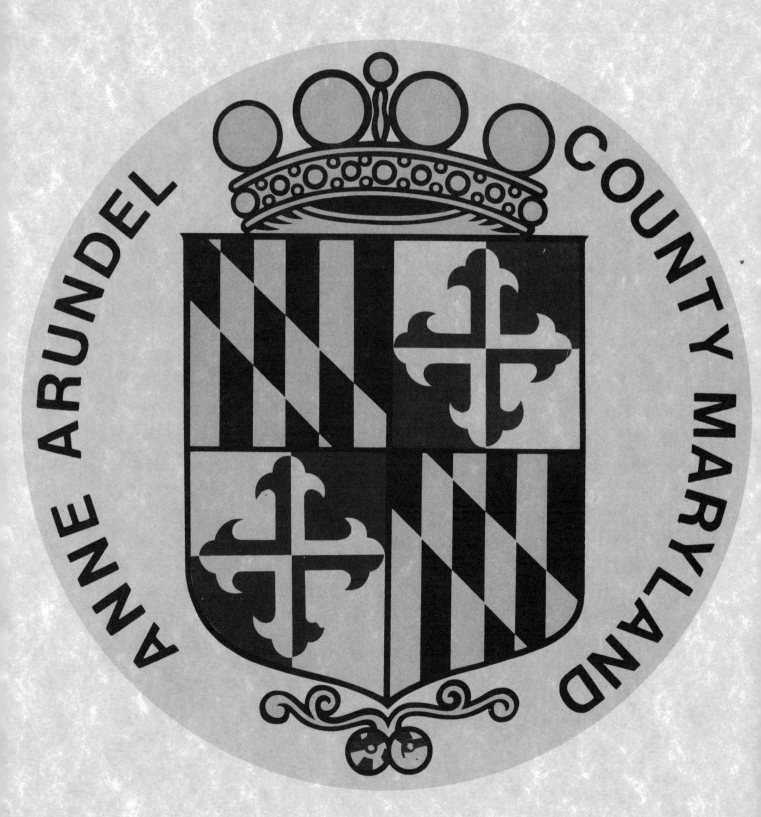

Map of Anne Arundel County

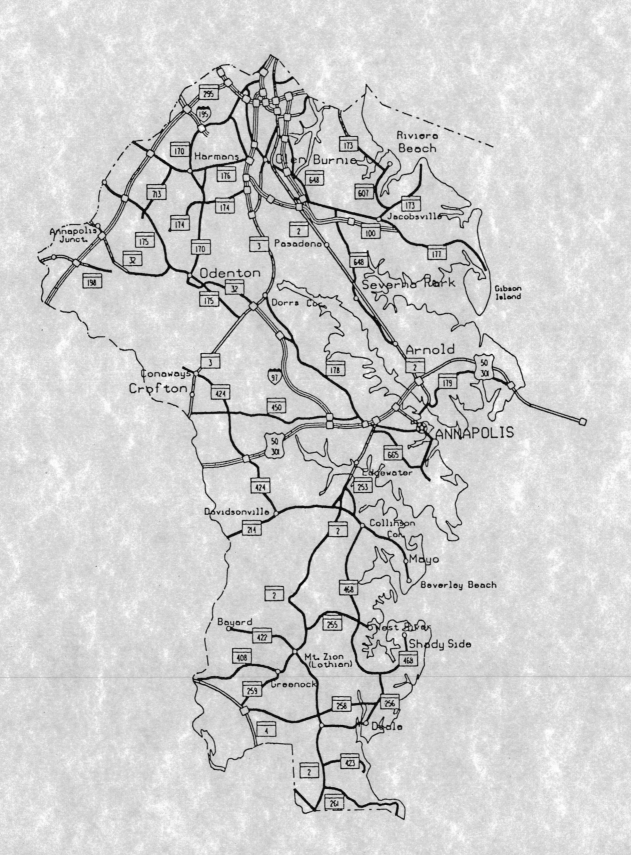

BALTIMORE CITY

Baltimore City was incorporated in 1797 (Chapter 68, Acts of 1796). As a governmental unit, the City separated from Baltimore County in 1851. The City's name was derived from the Proprietary's Irish Barony.

Baltimore's City's Seal was adopted in 1827. The seal is black and gold in color, and contains the emblem of the Battle Monument in the center. Around the monument are inscribed the words, "City of Baltimore," and below the monument is the date, "1797."

The original town of Baltimore was established in 1729, with the Maryland Assembly's "Act for Erecting a town on the north side of Patapsco, In Baltimore County, and for laying out into lots sixty acres of land..." This act recognized that Baltimore was a good place to load, unload, and sell various trade items. These lots were laid out in 1730, on sixty acres of land purchased from Charles and Daniel Carroll. By 1732, ten additional acres were added.

By 1790, the population of Baltimore was 13,503. In 1816 the northbound boundary was extended to what is now North Avenue. Growing rapidly, it increased to 169,054 by 1850, and was made an independent city by the Constitutional Convention the same year. In 1888, it consisted of more than seventeen square miles to the north and west of the old city, and in 1918, fifty square miles were added. By 1990, the population of Baltimore City was 736,014. In July 1994 the population dropped to 703,057, a decrease of 4.5%. In 1998, the population again dropped to 663,110, and by the year 2000, they expect the population will drop to 643,300.

Baltimore Town

Along the rivers of northern Maryland, and on the Western Shore, many farms and plantations began to appear. This part of Maryland, since 1659, was known as Baltimore County. Its first county seat was on the Bush River, a small village known as Old Baltimore. During the early days of the county, its seat location was changed several times. In 1709, a courthouse was built on the Gunpowder River, and soon the town of Joppa grew, the first of northern Maryland's real towns. As Joppa became a busy river port, the village of Bush River died out.

During this time the laws of England allowed colonists to only load foreign-bound ships at areas called ports of call. This was done so that the king was able to collect a tax. Many farmers lived great distances from these ports. As a result selling their crops was hard for them unless they could get small boats, load them, and then travel to the nearest port of call. During colonial times, seagoing ships could sail directly up to Joppa, as the Gunpowder River was much deeper than it is today. In Joppa, the townspeople, wanting their town to grow, passed an unusual law. The law allowed that all people paying debts with tobacco, needed to pay only nine-tenths of what they owed, if they sold their tobacco at Joppa and settled all their debts at the same place. Because of this, the town of Joppa became the busiest in the country, as men from farms near and far brought their tobacco here.

The old town of Joppa no longer exists, but one road that led there, Joppa Road, still exists today. For some time so much tobacco came into Joppa that it was thought it would turn into a large city. However, a rival settlement, not far away, was also continuing to grow.

They were also raising crops of corn and tobacco along the branches of the Patapsco River. As years passed, larger numbers of ships anchored at the port of entry on the Patapsco, near Whetstone Point. It was here that farmers received their supplies from England, and where they loaded their crops of corn and tobacco, for the return trip, to be sold in England. As business increased, the farmers along the upper branch of the Patapsco decided that they needed a port of entry nearer to them. To accomplish this, sixty acres of land was purchased from Charles and Daniel Carroll on December 1, 1729, and Baltimore Town was born.

This new village called Baltimore Town was the third such town in Maryland using Baltimore as its name. The first was Old Baltimore, on the Bush River that eventually dwindled to just a few houses, and the second on the Eastern Shore that was planned but never actually became a town.

One first settler was Jonathan Hanson who settled on the opposite bank of the Jones Falls, which was the eastern boundary line of Baltimore. Here he built a mill on the falls. Baltimore Town had three major things in its favor for the farmers, travelers and traders. First, there were the rich farmlands along the three branches of the Patapsco River, and the safe harbors opening into the Chesapeake Bay. Second, was the Great Eastern Road from Philadelphia that crossed Jones Falls, passing very close to Baltimore Town. This road also went to Georgetown and Annapolis, which would prove a great asset in the future. Third, was the Jones Falls itself, used to turn the wheels of the mills that the settlers needed for the grinding of grain.

Within a short time, a bridge was built connecting Baltimore Town with another older settlement known as Jones Town. As both grew, Jones Town became part of Baltimore Town in 1745.

Although the Joppa law made it cheaper for the people to pay their debts in Joppa, many farmers, were bringing their tobacco to Baltimore Town, as it was a better port, and often closer than Joppa. Although Baltimore Town was now a busy port, it had very few people living there. By 1752, it had only twenty-five houses, one church, and two taverns, to handle the needs of the travelers, and traders.

Jones Falls

People From Other Parts of the World

German farmers needed Baltimore, as the port of entry was closer than Annapolis. Baltimore offered a good harbor and water transportation where the Patapsco River branches and empties into the Chesapeake Bay.

German-speaking people from Pennsylvania were among the first settlers to come to Baltimore and establish farms. The first German settlement was at Monocacy, in 1734, near the present city of Frederick. Before a road was built, when there was only a rough trail, the Maryland Germans began to send goods to the port of Baltimore. As a result, Germans soon began to live in Baltimore. This history of the many German families has a special significance to me. Many Germans came from Rhineland, Switzerland, Alsace and other European areas. In tracing my own family history, I found that my ancestors were among the first to live in Baltimore at this time. They, along with others, established the first Evangelical Lutheran Congregation in 1755. This church was the center of German cultural activity for many years in Baltimore. In 1785 the name was changed to Zion Lutheran, its present name and is at Gay and Lexington Streets in Baltimore. For many years, the Baltimore Germans lived principally in the northeast section of the city. One section of Belair Road, near what is now Perry Hall, was known as "German Town." Additionally, others, in the 1880s lived in Cordova and Preston on the Eastern Shore.

A family bible, from 1794, passed down from generation to generation indicated that my ancestors namely, Walter Johan Michael Marck; Johann Georg Marck and Heinrich Marck, from St. Leonhard in Basel, Switzerland, and Uftenheim in Anspach, Deutschland in Franken (County of Franken in Germany) were among the first to settle in Baltimore.

Cover of Family Bible

Translation:
Sermons
about
freely (randomly)
chosen texts
held
by
Andreas Battier
Minister at St. Leonhard
in
Basel

Second Edition
Basel
by Joh. Heinrich Decker
1794[1]

Predigten

über

freygewählte Texte

gehalten

von

Andreas Battier,

Pfarrer bey St. Leonhard

in

Basel.

Zweyter Band.

Basel.

Bey Joh. Heinrich Decker.

1794.

---

[1] *German translation by Gudrun Brown, Joppa, Maryland.*

Examples of handwritten text from Marck family bible, 1794.

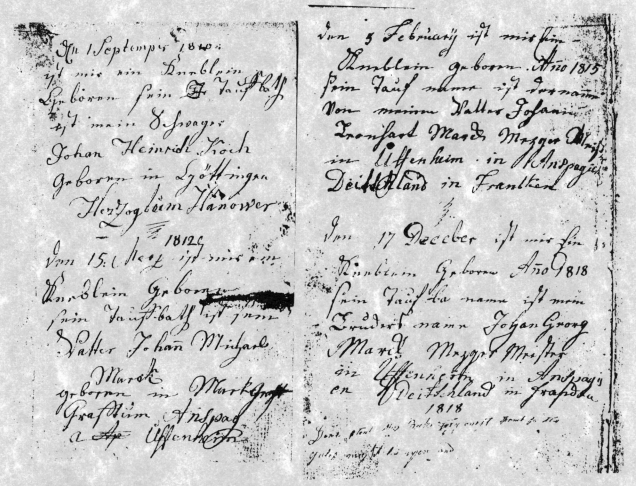

Other examples of German settlers who helped Baltimore grow are: Charles and Louis Dohme, who founded the drug manufacturing company; August Hoen who built one of the finest lithographic companies in the country; Henry Mencken, who became a well-known writer and editor; and Ottmar Mergenthaler who invented the Linotype machine, which set type to print newspapers and books. Persons of German descent were not the only ones responsible for helping Baltimore and Maryland grow. Other examples are the Greeks, Czechoslovakians or Bohemians, African-Americans, Italians, Jews, Lithuanians, Poles, Ukrainians and French.

Greeks

In 1900, many Greeks came to Baltimore in large numbers. Settling in Highlandtown and Lexington Market neighborhoods, they worked in restaurants, confectionery stores, bakeries, florist and tailor shops. Today their descendants are found in various trades and professions. They were strongly attached to the Greek Orthodox Church, and founded the Greek Orthodox Church of the Annunciation, now called the Greek Orthodox Cathedral of the Annunciation, at Maryland Avenue and Preston Street, which is still active today. Although patriotic Americans, the Greeks celebrate March 25, (also Maryland Day) the date in which Greece won independence from Turkey. One well-known Marylander of Greek descent is Spiro T. Agnew, who became Governor of Maryland, and later vice-president of the United States under President Nixon.

Bohemians

The first Bohemian resident of Maryland was Augustine Herrman, who in 1673 published a map of the colony for the Second Lord Baltimore. In return for this work, the Second Lord Baltimore gave him five thousand acres of land in Cecil County known as "Bohemia Manor." After Herrman, other persons of Bohemian descent settled in the neighborhoods of Fells Point, and the area around Saint Wenceslaus' Catholic Church, at Collington and Ashland Avenues. Many Bohemians became excellent tailors and cabinetmakers. Bohemian Hall, at Gay and Preston Streets was the center of their many activities. Some of their clubs and societies joined to form the United Czechoslovakian Societies of Baltimore, which held annual picnics on October 28, known as Czech Day. On this day they would also hold special church services, followed by activities held at Patterson Park. Some well-known Baltimore descendants are August Klecka, a newspaper editor and politician; Frank Novak, a contractor; and Dr. Frank Otenasek and Dr. William Supik, surgeons.

African-Americans

The first blacks came to Maryland shortly after the colony was settled, although not willingly, but as laborers or slaves. Slavery remained lawful in Maryland until 1864. For two hundred years blacks were the main laborers on farms and plantations in Southern Maryland and the Eastern Shore. In 1760, the Quakers and Methodists began to protest slavery, and soon some people began to free their slaves. By the year 1790, more than eight thousand of Maryland's slaves were living free. Although laws prohibited them from certain jobs, they began to farm or work in stables, hotels and inns. Over the years they were able to save enough money to buy their own farms.

During the Civil War, Maryland was represented by six African-American regiments who fought for the Union Army. By 1870, blacks had won the right to vote, and by 1900, more than 30,000 black farmers lived in Maryland, two thousand of whom owned their own farms, and approximately two thousand who worked as fishers and oystermen on the Chesapeake Bay. Most blacks during this time remained poor, and they were not allowed to attend public elementary schools until 1867, nor high schools until 1889. One important event in the progress of blacks was the beginning of the Centennial Biblical Institute in 1867, which later grew into Morgan State College, now Morgan State University. In 1890, a well-known Negro man named John H. Murphy founded the *Afro-American* newspaper, which became a leader in the Negro drive for more rights and freedom. Additionally in the 1890s, Negroes established the Provident Hospital, located now in a modern building on Liberty Heights Avenue.

Several well-known African-American Maryland or Baltimore persons are: Matthew A. Henson, who along with Admiral Perry went to the North Pole in 1909; Benjamin Banneker, who taught himself mathematics, astronomy, and clock making. He also helped survey the District of Columbia, and in 1792 published an almanac each year for ten years; Harriet Tubman, who was born in Dorchester County, made many trips to lead slaves to freedom during the Civil War; Frederick Douglass, born in Talbot County, who became a well-known writer for his speeches and books against slavery, and became the editor of the abolitionist newspaper; and Thurgood Marshall, born in Baltimore, who became an outstanding lawyer, winning many equal rights cases, and whom President Lyndon Johnson appointed as Associate Justice of the United States Supreme Court.

Italians

The first Italians who came to Baltimore about 1820 were sailors. Finding life in Baltimore profitable, they settled in the neighborhood of Exeter and Stiles Streets, known today as "Little Italy." By 1890, larger numbers arrived, settling in areas around Lexington and Belair markets. They worked as tailors, bakers, shoemakers, bricklayers, stonemasons and fruit dealers. Soon they published their own newspaper, printed in Italian. The young Italians attended public schools as well as classes at either Saint Leo's or Saint John the Baptist Church. They celebrated and continue to celebrate October 12, Columbus Day as a holiday, as do others. Two well-known persons of Italian descent are: Thomas D'Alesandro, Jr. and his son the III, both of whom became mayor of Baltimore.

Jews

Dr. Jacob Lumbrozo, who lived in the colony from 1656 to 1666, was the first known Jew in Maryland, who was a physician who traded with the Indians and worked as a farmer. For the next hundred years, there is no record of any other Jews being Maryland residents. In 1773, Benjamin Levy settled in Baltimore, and became its first Jewish resident, who operated a small general store. Following the Revolutionary War, numbers of Jewish people came to Baltimore. They settled in a neighborhood at High and Exeter Streets and along Broadway. Because their religion was different, most were unliked by many other people. They were looked upon as non-citizens and were not permitted to vote, or hold office. In 1826 they finally won civic equality. As religion was very important, they built the Lloyd Street Synagogue as their place of worship. Many became successful businesspeople, moving to better homes in the neighborhoods of Hanover, Lexington and Fayette Streets. By 1870, the wealthiest moved to areas on Madison Avenue and Eutaw Place.

Several more prominent Jews are: Jacob Blaustein, who founded a well-known oil business; Mendes Cohen who for many years was president of the Maryland Historical Society; Jacob Epstein who started a dry goods wholesaling business; Isidore Rayner who became a United States senator from Maryland; Simon Sobeloff, a lawyer who became Solicitor General of the United States; Ephraim Keyser, a well-known sculptor, and several members of the Friedenwald family who became famous physicians.

Lithuanians

Many Lithuanians came to Baltimore in 1880 and settled in neighborhoods around Hollins Market, and built Lithuanian Hall at Hollins and Parkin Streets. This hall contained meeting rooms, a library, bowling alleys, an auditorium and a gymnasium. Their religious activities centered around Saint Alphonsus' Catholic Church, at Park Avenue and Saratoga Street. It was here that they operated a school for their children. Dr. William F. Laukaitis, was well-known as one of their first leaders. Another well-known Baltimorean of this descent is Johnny Unitas, former quarterback of the former Baltimore Colts professional football team.

Poles

Polish people began settling in Baltimore in 1885, and made their homes in Canton, Curtis Bay and Locust Point. Because most of them were uneducated farm laborers in Poland, they found it difficult to find jobs. Many men worked in the port of Baltimore, loading and unloading ships. Others found jobs in factories or steel mills, while others worked as crop pickers, harvesting fruits and vegetables on various Maryland farms, while Polish women worked in tailoring shops or packing plants. By tradition, they would turn over all money earned by any family member to the family. Sons, would do this until they turned twenty-one years old, and daughters until they married. Because all family members worked so hard to earn enough money to buy their homes, many found getting a good education difficult. Because of this, the Poles were slow in learning the American way of life.

The Poles formed societies, like many other immigrant groups. They formed this society to help each other in buying a home, or to help the sick, and to help any Polish newcomer to the state. Most of the Poles were Catholic, centering their religious activities around three churches: Saint Casimir, Saint Stanislaus, and Holy Rosary. A special day celebrated by the Poles is October 11, the death of Count Casimir Pulaski. Count Pulaski was a Pole who was killed while helping the Americans in the Revolutionary War. One well-known Baltimore descendant is Dr. Arthur G. Siwinski, a surgeon.

Ukrainians

The first Ukrainians came to Maryland in 1890, and settled in Chesapeake City in Cecil County. They were farmers who grew crops for a Ukrainian convent in Philadelphia. Others found work on the Chesapeake and Ohio Canal. Many Ukrainians settled in Baltimore, in the neighborhoods of Curtis Bay, Dundalk, and Locust Point. Most were uneducated farm workers in Ukraine, and found it difficult to secure jobs in an industrialized city like Baltimore. Many became tailors, window washers, or tavern keepers. They joined to form "The American Citizens of Ukrainian Origin." They also attended the Ukrainian Catholic Church of Saint Peter's and Paul's in Curtis Bay, and Saint Michael's, on Wolfe Street. The Ukrainians celebrate January 7 as their Christmas, observing the old calendar.

French

In 1735, the British conquerors of Nova Scotia sent several hundred Frenchmen to Maryland. Some settled in Baltimore, and others in counties along the Chesapeake Bay. One settlement called Frenchtown in Cecil County was burned by the British during the War of 1812, and by the 1860s had completely vanished. In 1793, other French people, fleeing the island of Santo Domingo during a revolution, settled in Baltimore, in neighborhoods around Charles and Lombard Streets. Although no longer there, for years it was referred to as Frenchtown.

Others

Many other groups came to Baltimore, although in much smaller numbers than the groups previously mentioned. Chinese came and lived in the areas around Park Avenue and Mulberry Street. Others such as Cuban, Spanish, Japanese, and Latin American also came to Baltimore. Today, just about every country of the world is represented. All these groups contributed greatly to the growth of Baltimore and Maryland.

Places of Interest

Baltimore City has many wonderful, interesting, and historical places to visit. These include:

<u>B & O Railroad Museum</u>: Located at 901 W. Pratt Street, (at Poppleton Street), at the old Mount Clare Station. Featured here are the Baltimore & Ohio Railroad's extensive collection of more than one hundred American steam and diesel locomotives, both originals and replicas, dating from 1829. The museum's focal point is the round house's dome, which covers a turntable surrounded by twenty-two stalls that contain cars and locomotives. Excursion trains run on weekends. Also found here is the Museum Shop and a Research Library. Admission charged.

<u>Baltimore Streetcar Museum</u>: Located at 1901 Falls Road, this museum features a rolling history of the streetcars in Baltimore.

<u>Baltimore City Fire Museum at Old Engine House #6</u>: Located at Gay and Orleans Streets, this magnificent 1799 structure is one of the country's oldest fire stations. In 1853, a Florentine bell tower was added. This No. 6 firehouse features exhibits of antique fire apparatus, photographs and memorabilia.

Eubie Blake National Museum and Cultural Center: Located at The Brokerage, 34 Market Place. This museum is dedicated to the life and music of Baltimore-born jazz musician Eubie Blake. The Cultural Center showcases the talents of community artists and offer performing arts classes.

Babe Ruth Birthplace/Baltimore Orioles Museum: Located at 216 Emory Street, off Pratt Street, comprising four adjoining rowhouses, including the birthplace of Ruth, the "Sultan of Swat." The museum includes many photographs, paintings and memorabilia associated with Babe Ruth (1895-1948), as well as other Maryland baseball greats and the Baltimore Orioles. They show film clips of Ruth along with highlights of the Baltimore Orioles World Series games. Upon entering the museum, a computer-controlled figure of Babe Ruth greets visitors, and the furnishings are 1895 period. Admission charged. In June 1995, a statue honoring Babe Ruth was unveiled in front of Oriole Park at Camden Yards.

Baltimore Arena: Formally called the Baltimore Civic Center, located on Baltimore Street, between Howard Street and Hopkins Place, has a seating capacity of 14,000, and is used for conventions, cultural events, concerts, exhibitions and sporting events. Admission for non-scheduled events is free.

Baltimore City Hall: Located at 100 N. Holliday Street contains the offices of the Mayor of Baltimore City and the City Council. The building itself has some finest examples of architectural iron work in the country. Built in 1867 and completed in 1875, it has been restored in sections to provide a working environment for the Mayor and City Council. The building has a 100-foot rotunda, a courtyard, galleries and various exhibits relating to the city's history. Tours of the Victorian chambers and offices are provided by appointment only, and they require security checks.

Baltimore City Life Museums: These include six attractions in downtown Baltimore. Four of the six are: Carroll Mansion, the Center for Urban Archaeology, the Courtyard Exhibition Center, and the 1840 House, all called the Courtyard Sites and are part of Museum Row in historic Jonestown, northwest of the Inner Harbor. The remaining two, the Peale Museum and the H.L. Mencken House are elsewhere in the city.

(1) Carroll Mansion: Part of the Courtyard Sites, at 800 East Lombard Street, was the last home of Charles Carroll of Carrollton, one of the signers of the Declaration of Independence. The home is considered one of Baltimore's finest, built in 1812. It contains Empire furnishings, paintings from the late eighteenth century to 1840 and many decorative arts. A winding staircase leads from the marble-floored hall to the formal rooms on the second floor.

(2) Center for Urban Archaeology: Located at 800 East Lombard Street, it houses an extensive display of artifacts from the eighteenth and nineteenth centuries, including glassware and ceramics. Here visitors can watch archaeologists studying artifacts.

(3) Courtyard Exhibition Center: also at 800 East Lombard Street, it offers an exhibit that traces the changes in Baltimore since the 1930s called "Rebuilding an American City: Baltimore Today." This exhibit shows how citizens, business people and government leaders worked toward urban revitalization.

(4) 1840 House: Located at 800 East Lombard Street, it brings history back to life in a reconstructed nineteenth century rowhouse. Visitors are taken back in time through a series of dramatic participatory programs.

(5) H.L. Mencken House: Located at 1524 Hollins Street, was the home of the famous literary critic for more than sixty-eight years, until his death in 1956. This nineteenth century rowhouse appears much the same as it did in Mencken's lifetime. Slide shows and displays depict Mencken's various stages of life.

(6) Peale Museum: Located at 225 Holliday Street, near City Hall. The museum consists of three floors of exhibits: the Orientation Gallery, the Assessions Gallery, and the Lecture Gallery. Included are samples of artwork, and exhibits that trace Baltimore's history through architectural styles, economy, culture, and technology. Another exhibit called "The Peales: An American Family of Artists in Baltimore" features Victorian furnishings and paintings from the Peale Collection.

Baltimore Museum of Art: Located on Art Museum Drive, near North Charles and 31st Streets. Designed by John Russell Pope, who later designed the National Gallery of Art in Washington, D.C., the museum displays paintings by old masters; eighteenth and nineteenth century American paintings, sculptures, furniture, silver, art from Africa, early Christian mosaics and many other objects. The Alan and Janet Wertzberger Sculpture Garden contains examples of twentieth century sculpture by European masters, with emphasis on the human figure. Admission charged.

Basilica of the Assumption of the Blessed Virgin Mary: Located at Cathedral and Mulberry Streets, this is the oldest cathedral in the United States. Planned by Bishop John Carroll, and designed by Benjamin Henry Latrobe, the basilica was dedicated in 1821. Its highlights include nine stained-glass windows and the south tower's clock and bells, which sound the "Angelus" at 6:00 a.m., noon and 6:00 p.m. Open daily and guided tours are available.

Druid Hill Park: Located in Northwest Baltimore, this 674-acre park is one of the country's largest natural city parks. It contains the Baltimore Zoo, which comprises 150- acres, housing more than one thousand two-hundred birds, reptiles and mammals. Admission charged. Also contained in Druid Hill Park is the Conservatory, known locally as "The Palm House" for its large collection of tropical plants. There are three major displays each year: chrysanthemums in November; poinsettias in December; and spring flowers at Easter. Admission is free.

The Baltimore Zoo's Mansion House

Built in 1801, the present Mansion House is the third such house built on the estate known as Druid Hill Park. Fire in 1796 destroyed the second home, which was designed and built by Colonel Nicholas Rogers in the late 1700s. While their new house was being constructed, the Rogers' moved into a temporary home in downtown Baltimore. However, in 1801, fire destroyed this temporary residence, whereby the family then moved into their new home, before it had been completed. Two wings, which had been planned on each side of the Mansion House were never built. The Mansion House consisted of a basement, which housed the kitchen and storage areas, and on the first floor is a drawing room, salon, and dining room interconnected along the rear of the house, with a central hallway dividing the master bedroom and study. The second floor housed five bedrooms.

In 1860, Lloyd Nicholas Rogers, the son and heir of Colonel Nicholas Rogers, reluctantly sold his four hundred seventy-five-acre estate to the City of Baltimore for $121,009 in cash and $367.027 in city stock. Lloyd Rogers left the Mansion House the day following the inauguration of Druid Hill Park. He died several weeks later, having never returned to the Mansion. In 1863, under the direction of Mayor John H.B. Latrobe, the Mansion House was converted into a public pavilion. The original entrance was removed and a twenty-foot-wide open porch was added around the entire Mansion House. The interior was "Victorianized" with Gothic arches, ornate ceilings, and an elaborate staircase on the second that led to a cupola.

In 1935, another renovation was completed, by which the porch was enclosed. Soon afterwards the Mansion enjoyed fame as a restaurant, although short-lived, most-likely because the restaurant did not have a liquor license. During its heyday, it featured curb service, a modern Milk Bar, a doughnut-making machine and dining on the veranda. In advertisements, they billed it as "every man's country club in the very heart of Baltimore," and that "All Roads Lead to the Mansion House."

During the mid-1940s, the building was used as a day school for the Young Men's and Women's Hebrew Associations, and later housed the Zoo administrative offices. In the mid-1950s, when the Hall of Jewels exhibit, which featured exotic birds and small animals, opened on the Mansion porch, the building became informally known as the Bird House, and operated as such for almost thirty years. In 1978, renovations again began to restore and modernize the Mansion House. They moved the Bird exhibit throughout the Zoo, and the building was used exclusively for administrative offices and educational programming. By the mid-1990s, the Mansion House fell into a state of disrepair. Funded by a million-dollar allocation in the State of Maryland's capital budget, a rehabilitation project began in the summer of 1996, which focused on the exterior of the one hundred ninety-five-year-old building. They recessed the front entryway, rotting woodwork and broken windows were replaced, and the porch and much of the first floor were enhanced by new paint, carpet and lighting fixtures. Today, the building is restored to much of its original grandeur. It continues to house the administrative offices, and serves as a popular rental for corporate parties, weddings and other special events.

The Mansion House, and the Homewood estate, on the campus of Johns Hopkins University, are considered the only two remaining Federal-style country houses in Baltimore. They display furniture from the original Mansion House/Rogers home at Homewood and the Maryland Historical Society. Descendants of Rogers' family still live in the Baltimore area.

    <u>Fort McHenry National Monument and Historic Shrine:</u> Located near Baltimore's Inner Harbor, E. Fort Avenue, Fort McHenry was constructed between 1798 and 1803. The fort has seen action in every American War through World War II. During the War of 1812, it was here that Francis Scott Key wrote the lyrics to "Star-Spangled Banner." The fort has been restored to its pre-Civil War appearance. Its flag, which flies twenty-four hours a day, three hundred sixty five days a year, is in the same location as the original. Fort McHenry can be reached by car or by boat from tours originating at the Inner Harbor. Admission charged.

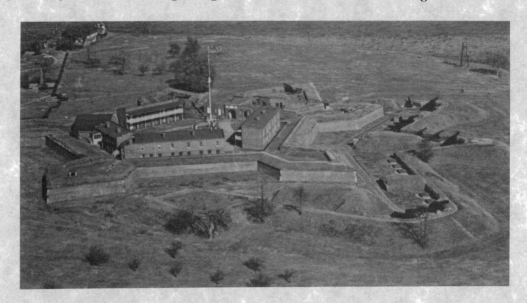

    <u>Greek Orthodox Cathedral of the Annunciation:</u> Located on Preston Street at Maryland Avenue, it was built in 1889 as a Reformed Church by architect C.E. Cassell. It is a notable example of Romanesque style. In c.1958, an addition was added to the church, being a Educational and Social Center. Additionally, in the late 1970s, the Annunication Orthodox Center was build across the street from the Cathedral. All areas are in use today.

1893

Present Day

<u>Johns Hopkins University</u>: Located at 3400 North Charles Street, this private liberal arts university and Medical School, located on Broadway, was founded in 1876. Today it contains one of the nation's finest medical schools. The 140-acre campus was originally the estate of Charles Carroll, Jr., the son of Charles Carroll of Carrollton, one of the signers of the Declaration of Independence. Homewood House, located on the campus, was a wedding gift to Charles Carroll, Jr., from his father in 1801. This restored 1801 Federal-style mansion was built by Charles Carroll, Jr., and includes the Carroll family furnishings. The house has been fully restored to its original nineteenth century look. Admission charged. The Homewood Gift Shop is also located here.

In 1873, Johns Hopkins, a wealthy Baltimorean merchant and banker gave a large sum of money to the city to establish the university named for him. In his plans for the university was a school of medicine, where physicians and surgeons were to be trained. He also gave another large sum of money for a hospital, to be carried on in connection with the school of medicine. His total gift to the city was more than $7 million. Throughout its long history the university has given a great deal of knowledge to the world through the work of its teachers and students. Men and women from all parts of the world come to the university and medical school to study. They have made many important medical and surgical discoveries here, as well as the treatment of thousands of sick.

Homewood House

Charles Carroll of Carrollton

<u>Lacrosse Hall of Fame Museum</u>: Located at 113 W. University Parkway, on the Johns Hopkins University campus, next to Homewood Field, this national museum of America's first sport spotlights 350 years of lacrosse's greatest moments through artifacts, photographs, and art. Vintage equipment and uniforms, a multi-image show and an interactive game are also featured. Admission charged.

<u>Maryland Historical Society:</u> Located at 210 W. Monument Street at Park Avenue, is the Museum and Library of Maryland History. Among the many exhibits on Maryland's history is the original manuscript of Francis Scott Key's "Star-Spangled Banner." There is also a collection of portraits by American artists such as Gilbert Stuart, Thomas Sully, and James and Rembrandt Peale. The museum has a nineteenth century silver collection of Samuel Kirk, and eighteenth century costumes and accessories, including Revolutionary War uniforms. A gift shop and book store are off the lobby. Admission charged.

<u>Maryland Science Center, IMAX Theatre and Davis Planetarium:</u> Located at 601 Light Street in the Inner Harbor. Offers live science demonstrations, exhibits and films relating to science. Features an exhibit on the Chesapeake Bay, as well as a science arcade and displays on energy and computers. They offer multimedia presentations in the Davis Planetarium. Inside the IMAX Theatre, a five-story screen takes you on an adventure soaring over the Grand Canyon, or rolling down the tracks of a roller coaster. Admission charged.

<u>National Aquarium:</u> Located at 501 Pratt Street, on Pier 3 at the Inner Harbor. The seven story structure is divided into three major areas: first, exhibits four stories high consisting of marine mammals; second, a series of ring tanks for sharks; third, a simulated Amazon rain forest. Containing more than one million gallons of water, the aquarium is home to more than five thousand creatures. There is also an outdoor seal pool, and marine mammal shows take place daily. Admission charged.

Pimlico Racetrack: Located at Belvedere and Park Heights Avenues, Pimlico is Maryland's oldest racetrack and is home to the Preakness and Pimlico Cup, as well as other races held in the spring. Also found here is the National Jockey's Hall of Fame, which is open during racing season.

Shot Tower: Located at East Fayette and Front Streets. Built in 1828, and used until 1892, this restored brick shaft is two hundred thirty-four feet high, and is said to be the oldest shot tower in the United States. Shot was made by dropping molten lead down the shaft into tanks of water, hardening into round pellets as it fell. Visitors are shown a sound, light and slide display show depicting the tower's history.

Edgar Allen Poe House and Museum: Located 203 N. Amity Street off Lexington Street. This is the Clemm family house where Poe began his writing career and lived from 1832-1835. It contains period furniture, Poe artifacts, exhibits, and a video presentation. Restored as part of a public housing project, it is operated as a museum by the Edgar Allen Poe Society. Admission charged.

Edgar Allen Poe Grave: Located in Westminster Churchyard at Fayette and Greene Streets. Poe was first buried in the rear of the yard, but in 1875 was moved to the present location complete with a large monument in his honor. Additionally, the Westminster Presbyterian Church was built in 1852 on top of the old Western Burying Ground. The Greene Street Gates were designed in 1820 by Maximilien Godefroy, who also designed the Battle Monument. Many famous Baltimoreans are buried here, and the unusual Egyptian-style tombs date from the 1820s.

Sherwood Gardens: Located on Stratford Road, east of St. Paul Street, the gardens consist of seven acres, planted with thousands of tulips, azaleas, English boxwoods, dogwoods and other plants. Open daily dawn to dusk, with peak season being mid-April to mid-May. Admission is free.

Star-Spangled Banner Flag House: Located at 844 East Pratt Street. This was the home of Mary Pickersgill, who at this house, made the fifteen star & stripe flag that flew over Fort McHenry during the bombardment in 1814. This flag was the one that inspired Francis Scott Key to write "Star-Spangled Banner." On the grounds is an interesting map of the United States, composed of stones from each state. They commemorate the War of 1812 in an adjacent museum, which includes a receipt for $405.90, the price of the original flag. Admission charged.

R. McGill Mackall's painting of a little-known moment in American history - which took place in a Baltimore brewery, where the stars were put on the flag that inspired Francis Scott Key to write our national anthem.

Top of the World Observation Level & Museum: Located on the twenty-seventh floor of the World Trade Center at the Inner Harbor. Contained here are exhibits pertaining to Baltimore's harbor, and its cultural and economic development. An observation floor provides for a spectacular view of the city and harbor. Admission charged.

Mount Clare Mansion: Located in Carroll Park at Monroe Street and Washington Boulevard. This is the only pre-Revolutionary War mansion within the city limits. The one hundred seventy-year-old Georgian-style house was the home of Charles Carroll, barrister and Revolutionary hero, and his wife Margaret Tilghman. Charles Carroll was born in 1723. Mount Clare was built in 1756, and this eight-hundred acre Patapsco River plantation once supported wheat fields, an orchard, racing stables, flour mills, brick kilns, a grist mill on the Gwynn's Falls, and a shipyard on the Middle Branch of the Patapsco River. Within the walls of Mount Clare, many famous guests were entertained, including George and Martha Washington. During the time of the American Revolution, Charles Carroll made many contributions. He wrote Maryland's Declaration of Independence, and was a member of the committee that drafted Maryland's first State Constitution. One of Maryland's first senators, he served in this capacity until his death in 1783. In 1831, his heir, James Maccubbin Carroll, donated the land north of Mount Clare to the Baltimore & Ohio Railroad. Mount Clare Depot, which now is the center of the B&O Railroad Museum, was the first passenger station in America. At Mount Clare, during the Civil War, the Union Army established Camp Carroll, which was used to recruit troops and to protect rail access to Washington, D.C.

Mount Clare was the first historic museum house in Maryland, opening in 1917. It is a registered National Historic Landmark, and a cherished part of Maryland's history. The house contains period furnishings, of which many are original. A visit here truly reveals an intriguing look at the life in eighteenth and nineteenth century America. Admission charged.

<u>U.S.S. Frigate Constellation</u>: Located at Constellation Dock, Pratt Street, Pier I, at the Inner Harbor, this is the oldest warship in the United States. First launched as a frigate in 1797, it saw action in Tripoli in 1802 against the pirates, as well as against the British in 1812. In 1853-1854, it was rebuilt as a Sloop of War, and again saw action in the Civil War. Admission charged. (The U.S. Frigate Constellation is in dry dock for a complete restoration. It is scheduled to be completed in 1999).

<u>Pier Six Concert Pavilion</u>: Located at the Inner Harbor, this pavilion was built in 1981. Under the control of the Baltimore Center for the Performing Arts, it has a seating capacity of four thousand three hundred. With fantastic staging and permanent ancillary buildings, it offers fabulous music under the spectacular tent at the water's edge.

<u>Evergreen House</u>: Located at 4545 N. Charles Street, this house is owned by The Johns Hopkins University.   Situated on twenty-six wooded acres and built in the 1850s, this magnificent forty-eight-room Italianate mansion displays exceptional fine and decorative arts, rare book collections consisting of thirty-five thousand volumes, Tiffany glass, Japanese and Chinese porcelains and artwork, and Baltimore's only private theater. From 1878 to 1952, Evergreen House was the home of Ambassador John Work Garrett, and his wife, Alice Warder Garrett. Following a full-scale restoration, the house was reopened in 1990. Admission charged.

<u>Enoch Pratt Free Library</u>: Central Branch, at 400 Cathedral Street, is one of the nation's largest public libraries, and features special collections on Poe and Mencken.

<u>Mother Seton House</u>: Located at 600 North Paca Street, this house and chapel were the locations where the first American-born canonized saint founded a girls' school and in 1809, received her first vows.

    Memorial Stadium: Located on 33rd Street, and dedicated in 1954, Memorial Stadium for years was the home of the Baltimore Colts Professional Football Team, and the Baltimore Orioles Professional Baseball Club. In 1983, the Baltimore Colts moved out of Baltimore, and the Baltimore Orioles moved to their new stadium in 1992. In 1993 and 1994, the Canadian Football League Baltimore Stallions made Memorial Stadium their home. In 1996, Maryland again received a professional football team in the NFL, The Baltimore Ravens. The Ravens played their 1996 and 1997 seasons here. They played the last ever professional football game at Memorial Stadium on December 14, 1997, when the Ravens defeated the Tennessee Oilers in their last home game of the 1997 season. For the 1998 season, the Baltimore Ravens will move to their new stadium located directly across from Oriole Park at Camden Yards.

  On the front of Memorial Stadium
  is written the following:

MEMORIAL STADIUM

Erected By The
CITY OF BALTIMORE

1954
Dedicated By

The Mayor and the City Council
And The People Of Baltimore City
In The State Of Maryland

AS A MEMORIAL TO ALL
WHO SO VALIANTLY FOUGHT
AND SERVED IN THE WORLD
WARS WITH ETERNAL
GRATITUDE TO THOSE WHO
MADE THE SUPREME
SACRIFICE TO PRESERVE
EQUALITY AND FREEDOM
THROUGHOUT THE WORLD

TIME WILL NOT DIM THE GLORY OF THEIR DEEDS

    Oriole Park at Camden Yards: Located at 333 W. Camden Street. Opened in April 1992, Oriole Park at Camden Yards is the new and present home of the Baltimore Orioles Professional Baseball Club. This old-fashioned ballpark seats forty-six thousand, and incorporates intricate architectural detail with modern amenities.

THE BALTIMORE COLTS
1953-1983

Won-Lost Record, 1953-1983

YEAR	W	L	T	PCT	Finish	Head Coach
1953	3	9	0	.250	5th	Weeb Ewbank
1954	3	9	0	.250	6th	Weeb Ewbank
1955	5	6	1	.458	4th	Weeb Ewbank
1956	5	7	0	.417	4th	Weeb Ewbank
1957	7	5	0	.583	3rd	Weeb Ewbank
1958	9	3	0	.750	1st	Weeb Ewbank (1)
1959	9	3	0	.750	1st	Weeb Ewbank (2)
1960	6	6	0	.500	4th	Weeb Ewbank
1961	8	6	0	.571	3rd	Weeb Ewbank
1962	7	7	0	.500	4th	Weeb Ewbank
1963	8	6	0	.571	3rd	Don Shula
1964	12	2	0	.857	1st	Don Shula (3)
1965	10	3	1	.750	2nd	Don Shula (4)
1966	9	5	0	.643	2nd	Don Shula
1967	11	1	2	.857	2nd	Don Shula
1968	13	1	0	.929	1st	Don Shula (5)
1969	8	5	1	.607	2nd	Don Shula
1970	11	2	1	.821	1st	Don McCafferty (6)
1971	10	4	0	.714	2nd	Don McCafferty
1972	5	9	0	.357	3rd	Don McCafferty/John Sandusky
1973	4	10	0	.286	4th	Howard Schnellenger
1974	2	12	0	.143	5th	Howard Schnellenger /Joe Thomas
1975	10	4	0	.714	1st	Ted Marchibroda (7)
1976	11	3	0	.786	1st	Ted Marchibroda (8)
1977	10	4	0	.714	1st	Ted Marchibroda (9)
1978	5	11	0	.313	5th	Ted Marchibroda
1979	5	11	0	.313	5th	Ted Marchibroda
1980	7	9	0	.438	5th	Mike McCormack
1981	2	14	0	.125	4th	Mike McCormack
1982	7	8	1	.437	5th	Frank Kush
1983	7	9	0	.438	4th	Frank Kush

(1) NFL Champions
(2) NFL Champions
(3) Lost NFL Championship Game
(4) Lost Western Conference Championship Game
(5) Conference Title Winners
(6) SUPER BOWL CHAMPIONS
(7, 8, 9) Lost Division Title

Baltimore Colts Fight Song

LET'S GO YOU COLTS

Let's go you BALTIMORE COLTS,
And put that ball across the Line
So, Drive on you BALTIMORE COLTS
Go in and strike like lightning bolts
FIGHT, FIGHT, FIGHT
Rear up you COLTS and let's fight,
Crash thru and show them your might
For BALTIMORE and MARYLAND

Johnny Unitas in 1958 Championship Game

NAACP National Headquarters Building: Located at 4805 Mt. Hope Drive, this headquarters includes a library and conference room. Featured is the Dorothy Parker Memorial Garden, named for the noted writer, who left her estate to Dr. Martin Luther King, Jr.

St. Vincent de Paul Church: Located at 120 North Front Street, this is Baltimore's oldest Catholic parish. They list this Georgian-style church on the National Register of Historic Places.

Fell's Point: Located on the waterfront near the Inner Harbor, Fell's Point is one of Baltimore's most exhilarating portside communities, dating from 1730. More than two hundred of the area's brick homes date to before the War of 1812, and more than one hundred homes before the Civil War. Fresh fruit and vegetables are featured at Broadway Market and the area has many local pubs with live bands and fine seafood restaurants.

Pride of Baltimore II: A Baltimore Clipper Ship, commissioned in October 1988, and docked at Baltimore's Inner Harbor, is a replica of the Pride of Baltimore. The Pride of Baltimore was commissioned in May 1977, and was lost at sea in May 1986.

Great Blacks in Wax Museum: Located at 1601 East North Avenue, this museum is committed to the early study and preservation of the African-American history. There are more than one hundred life-size wax figures of those who had a significant impact on events in ancient Africa, the middle passage, the Civil War, Reconstruction, Harlem Renaissance, and the modern civil rights movement. Also on display is a full model slave ship depicting the four hundred year history of the Atlantic Slave Trade, and a Maryland Room. Contains a Museum Shop. Admission charged.

Baltimore Maritime Museum: Located at Pier III, Pratt Street, at the Inner Harbor. On display here is the U.S. Coast Guard Cutter *Taney*, which is the only ship still afloat that survived the attack on Pearl Harbor. Also the *U.S.S. Torsk*, a Tench Class Submarine, which sank the last Japanese combatant ships of WWII, and a 1930's floating lighthouse, which guided sailors in the bay for many years. Admission charged.

Baltimore Museum of Industry: Located at 1415 Key Highway, this museum is housed in an 1870 oyster cannery on the harbor.. This museum is dedicated to instilling and preserving pride in Baltimore's unique role in the Industrial Revolution. Visitors experience the sights and sounds of a belt-driven machine shop, garment loft, print shop, and the historic 1906 steam tugboat, the *S.S. Baltimore*. It features "hands-on" cannery activity, motorworks, and a assembly line for children. Admission charged.

Baltimore Public Works Museum & Streetscape: Located at 715 Eastern Avenue, (Inner Harbor East), this museum is housed in a historic pumping station. The museum has exhibits and media presentations on public works history and urban environmental history of Baltimore. Featured here are "What's Beneath the Streets," and "The Rotten Truth About Garbage." Admission charged.

Baltimore Children's Museum at the Cloisters: Located at 10440 Falls Road, Brooklandville. Featured here are "hands-on" exhibits, art activities, workshops, and participatory performances that make learning a fun experience. The historic castle enchants both children and adults, and houses a portion of the Parker collection. Admission charged.

Lovely Lane Museum: Located at 2200 St. Paul Street, this is the Mother Church of American Methodism. Its congregation was founded in 1772, and the present structure was built between 1884-1887. Designed by Stanford White, it is one of America's architectural treasures. Featured are exhibits, portraits, papers and artifacts from United Methodist history. Admission is free.

Nine North Front Street: Located at 9 North Front Street in Museum Row, this c.1790 house was the home of Baltimore's second mayor, Thorowgood Smith. Restored and maintained by the Women's Civic League, it features a colonial kitchen, and video docudrama of Mayor Smith. The art gallery highlights the Shot Tower, and the Federal parlor is a tourist information center. Admission is free.

Old Otterbein United Methodist Church: Located at Sharp and Conway Streets, this is the oldest church in continuous use in Baltimore, built in 1785. The first church on this site was built in 1771.

Cylburn Arboretum: Located at 4915 Greenspring Avenue. This one-hundred-seventy-six-acre estate features gardens, trails, a hands-on nature museum, a bird museum with dioramas, (a three-dimensional miniature scene with painted modeled figures and background) and a horticultural reference library.

Robert Long House: Located at 812 S. Ann Street in Fell's Point. This is Baltimore's oldest surviving urban residence. Built in 1765, this house has been restored and furnished with period antiques.

St. Jude Shrine: Located at Paca and Saratoga Streets, this 1873 church and 1941 shrine are a nationwide center for St. Jude devotions.

St. Alphonsus Roman Catholic Church: Located at 114 W. Saratoga Street at Park Avenue. This beautiful Gothic church was built in 1842 and is where St. John Nuemann and the blessed Frances Seelos served as pastors.

Peabody Conservatory of Music: Located at One East Mount Vernon Place, this is the oldest music school in the United States. It is an outstanding example of neo-Renaissance architecture. The adjacent library contains a rare book collection and features an atrium bounded by six stories of wrought-iron stacks.

S.S. John W. Brown: Located at Pier I, Clinton Street. This ship is a restored WWII Liberty Ship, one of only two still in existence.

Baltimore Convention Center: Located at One West Pratt Street, Baltimore's Convention Center recently completed its multimillion dollar expansion. It has exhibition space to 300,000 square feet, and a meeting space of more than 87,000 square feet. It features a special presentation room incorporating advanced technology for sound, lighting and audiovisual capabilities. It also has full banquet facilities. Tours are available by appointment.

Baltimore International Culinary College and Cooking Demonstration Theater: Located at 206 Water Street, this ninety-seat, state-of-the-art theater showcases step-by-step, ninety-minute, cooking demonstrations covering an array of culinary topics. These demonstrations are taught by the college's chef instructors and special guest chefs.

Harborplace and The Gallery: Located at Pratt and Light Streets. These are the twin glass pavilions of Harborplace along The Gallery, connected by a skywalk, that offer some of the city's best shopping and dining. The Harborplace Amphitheatre offers ongoing entertainment during the day, and concerts in the evening.

Hopkins Plaza: Located at Charles and Baltimore Streets, this area features the France Memorial Fountain, the Mechanic Theatre, the Mercantile Building, musical events, art exhibitions, and ethnic festivals.

Market Center: Bounded by Franklin, Liberty, Baltimore, and Greene Streets, this culturally diverse, colorful collage features more than four hundred merchants, offering unusual discounts, ethnic foods, specialty shops and Lexington Market.

Baltimore's Monuments

<u>Washington Monument:</u> Located on North Charles Street in an area known as "Mount Vernon Place." The first architectural monument erected to George Washington, it was begun in 1815 and completed in 1824. Enrico Causici was the sculptor. It was designed by architect Robert Mills, who also designed the Washington Monument in Washington, D.C. years later. The column is one hundred seventy-eight feet tall, containing two hundred twenty-eight steps. Colonel John Eager Howard donated the land for the monument itself, whose estate "Belvidere" encompassed the neighborhood. In 1827, his heirs gave more land for the four parks around the monument. The east-west section is Mount Vernon Place, and the north-south is Washington Place. Popularly we know these four sections together as Mt. Vernon Place.

<u>Maryland Line Monument:</u> Located on Mt. Royal Avenue at Cathedral Street. This monument was built in 1901 in honor of the Maryland troops in the Revolutionary War. The first Maryland Regiment, under Colonel William L. Smallwood, saved the American Army from destruction at the Battle of Long Island in 1776, by a desperate and costly rearguard action. Brigaded with other Maryland units under the general name of "The Maryland Line," it fought throughout the War. They commended John Eager Howard as a regimental commander at the Battle of Cowpens. A.L. van der Bergen was the sculptor.

Francis Scott Key Monument: Located on Eutaw Place at Lanvale Street. Erected in 1911 by sculptor Jean M.A. Mercie, as a gift to the city from Charles L. Marburg, it is a tribute to the author of the National Anthem.

Battle Monument: Located on Calvert Street at Fayette Street. Begun in 1815 by architect Maximilien Godefroy, it was dedicated to those slain in the famous Battle of Baltimore, both at North Point and Fort McHenry, and is the first true War Memorial in the United States. The only names to appear on the monument are those of the hero dead, along with the sculptor, Antonio Cappellano. In 1827, the monument was adopted as the emblem for the City Seal, and it appears on the City Flag. In 1964, a small park was constructed around the monument.

Wells - McComas Monument: Located at Gay & Monument Streets. Begun in 1850 to honor Daniel Wells and Henry McComas, two youths killed at the Battle of Baltimore in the land action east of Patterson Park. They credit them with the shooting of British General Robert Ross.

The Death of General Robert Ross

Civil War Monuments: Two of the many monuments dedicated to the Civil War are the Union Soldiers and Sailors Monument unveiled in 1909, and the Lee and Grant Monument, which was sculpted by Laura Garden Fraser and was erected in 1948. Both monuments are within a short distance from each other in Wyman Park.

Korean War Monument: Although it has been called the "Forgotten War," the Korean War is remembered by the people of Baltimore and Maryland. This unique circular memorial contains the names of every Baltimore and Maryland soldier killed in the conflict.

Frederick Douglass Monument: This monument of the Great Abolitionist looks out from the campus of Morgan State University. It is a reminder of both the African American fight for freedom, and the importance of education to maintaining that freedom. (See also page's 418-420)

William Wallace Monument: This monument is dedicated to Scottish hero William Wallace, on behalf of the Scottish descendants from Maryland. This statue of "Braveheart" is found in Druid Hill Park.

Thurgood Marshall Monument: This magnificent bronze sculpture honors the first black Justice of the United States Supreme Court. This statue is at the corner of Pratt Street and Hopkins Plaza, and is the work of Reuben Kramer who received the commission in 1977.

War Memorial Monument: This monument, located at 101 Gay Street, across from City Hall, was erected in honor of the one thousand seven-hundred fifty-three Marylanders who gave their lives and services in World War I. It was designed by Laurence Fowler in 1922, and dedicated in 1925.

War Memorial Building and Plaza: Located at Lexington and Gay Streets, this building was designed as a tribute to those citizens who gave their lives and services during World War I, then rededicated for World War II, Korean, and Vietnam servicemen. It features exhibits and events.

Holocaust Memorial and Sculpture: Located at Water, Gay and Lombard Streets, this memorial and sculpture, erected in 1980, stand as an austere reminder of the six million Jews murdered by the Nazis in Europe between 1933 and 1945.

Casimir Pulaski Monument: Pulaski was one of America's greatest Revolutionary War heros, who fought to free Poland from Russia and fought along side George Washington in the fight to free the American colonies from Britain. He became known as the "Father of the Calvary." This calvary was recruited by him from men in Baltimore. This monument shows Pulaski leading a calvary charge at the siege of Savannah. The statue was sculpted by Hans Schuler and A.C. Radziszewsk, and was unveiled in 1951. It is located in Patterson Park.

Babe Ruth Monument: As Baltimore is the birthplace of baseball great George Herman "Babe" Ruth, this monument is dedicated in his honor. This seventeen-foot statue was sculpted by Susan Luery and is called "Babe's Dream." It is located in front of Oriole Park at Camden Yards, and is a short distance from the Babe Ruth Museum.

O'Donnell/Fells family Monuments: These two monuments are dedicated to three of Baltimore's historical figures, Captain John O'Donnell and Edward and William Fell. Captain O'Donnell founded the Canton community after coming here from China, and the Fells bought the land that became Fells Point. When Baltimore became incorporated in 1797, this consolidated Fells Point, Jonestown and Baltimore Town. Through their pioneering spirit and business sense, they provided two wonderful areas for the people in Baltimore to live. The O'Donnell Monument was sculpted by Tylden Street of Baltimore and was erected in 1980. The Fell memorial is located on the original Fell Family burial ground.

Simon Bolivar Monument: This monument dedicated to Simon Bolivar is located in Guilford, and was given to Baltimore by the Venezuelan Government in 1961.

Mothers' Garden Monument: This is a five-acre garden laid out with terraces and a central pavilion in Clifton Park. It was the idea of William I. Norris, President of the Park Board, and honors the mothers of Baltimore City and the State of Maryland. It was originally dedicated in 1926 and presented to then Mayor Howard W. Jackson. Since then it was restored and rededicated in 1984 in honor of Tululu Schaefer, mother of then Mayor William Donald Schaefer. It was again rededicated in 1997 by Mayor Kurt Schmoke.

Latrobe/Wiley Monuments: Dedicated to Mayor Ferdinand Latrobe, who during his seven terms as mayor, planned the construction of some of Baltimore's best known buildings. These are Johns Hopkins, Enoch Pratt Library, and City College. This monument is located at Baltimore and Broadway Streets. The Wiley monument is dedicated to Thomas Wiley, who brought the first Odd Fellows Lodge to the United States, in Baltimore. The Wiley Monument was created by Edward Durang, and is located at Baltimore and Fayette Streets, one block from the Latrobe Monument.

D'Alesandro/McKeldin Monuments: Although from different political parties, both Thomas J.D'Alesandro and Theodore R. McKeldin shared a love and vision for Baltimore City. As mayors of Baltimore, between them they served for eighteen years. The D'Alesandro Monument was sculpted by Lillie and was completed in 1987. It is located overlooking Charles Plaza. McKeldin Square, which includes the Meyerhoff Fountain, attracts millions of visitors a year, and is located at the Inner Harbor.

Marquis de Lafayette Monument: This statue was erected on the south side of the Washington Monument, at Washington Place, and was unveiled September 6, 1924. President Calvin Coolidge took part in the ceremony. It was sculpted by Andrew O'Connor.

Other Revolutionary War Monuments in Baltimore City are: Sons of the American Revolution at Federal Hill Park; Howard Monument, at Washington Place, was erected in 1904 and sculpted by Emmanuel Fremiet; Mount Washington War Memorial, located at Falls Road and Kelly Avenue. It was erected in 1951.

Other Monuments in Baltimore City dedicated to the Civil War are: George Armistead Plaque, located at Old St. Paul's Cemetery, which is encircled by Redwood Street, Martin Luther King Boulevard, Lombard Street and Cider Alley. Other famous people buried here are John Eager Howard (1752-1827); Tench Tilghman (1744-1786); Thomas Chase (d.1779); Samuel Chase (1741-1811); Charles Carroll, the Barrister (1723-1783); Nicholas Rogers (1753-1822), a colonel in the Continental army; Richard K. Heath, a major at the Battle of North Point; and Edward Johnson (1767-1829) and Jacob Small (1772-1851), who were mayors of Baltimore. Confederate Women Monument: located at University Parkway and Charles Street, it was erected in 1918 and was sculpted by J. Maxwell Miller; Eppley Monument, at Greenmount Cemetery; Grand Army of the Republic Sundial Monument, erected in 1933 and is located at Federal Hill; Gleeson Monument, erected in 1866 and located at New Cathedral Cemetery, 4300 Old Frederick Road.

Additionally, Loudon Park Cemetery and Loudon Park National Cemetery include many monuments dedicated to the Civil War. At Loudon Park, these include: Confederate Dead Monument, erected in 1870 and sculpted by Frederick Volk; Confederate Mothers and Widows Monument, erected in 1906; Confederate Women Monument, erected in 1913; Johnson Monument, erected in 1901; and the Murray Association Monument. Those at Loudon Park National include: Artillery Monument; Confederate Prisoner of War Monument, erected in 1912; Dodge Post Statue (GAR Monument), erected in 1898 and sculpted by A.C. May; Loyal Sons of Maryland Naval Monument, erected in 1896; Rigby Monument, erected in 1891; Sons of Maryland Monument, erected in 1884; and the Unknown Dead Monument, erected in 1885.

Baltimore City also has other monuments dedicated to the memory of those who served in World War I and World War II. These include: 5th Regiment Armory Monument, erected in 1925. It was sculpted by Hans Schuler and is located at 29th Division Street; Baltimore City College War Memorial, located at Baltimore City College, at Howard Street, and erected in 1920. It was sculpted by J. Maxwell Miller; Carroll Park Monument, erected in 1920; Flag Pole, erected in 1923 in Patterson Park; Flagstaff, erected in 1920 at Wilkens Avenue & Gilmore Street; Hamman-Costin Plaque, erected in 1939 at Howard & Preston Streets; Mount Washington War Memorial, at Falls Road and Kelly Avenue, erected in 1951; Servicemen's Memorial, at Herring Run Park at Belair Road and Shannon Drive. It was erected in 1921 and sculpted by Edward Berge; Memorial Stadium Facade, erected in 1954; and Druid Hill Park that contains the Grove of Remembrance, erected in 1919, and the Memorial Grove Pavilion, erected in 1927.

Baltimore By Sea

Baltimore Defender & Guardian: A Fort McHenry/Fell's Point shuttle service departing from the Inner Harbor's Finger Piers; Baltimore Patriot II & III: Departing daily from Constellation Dock, it provides one-and-a-half-hour narrated tours of the harbor; Clipper City/Baltimore's Tall Ship: Provides two and three-hour sailing tours, departing from Harborplace; Spirit of Baltimore: Harbor cruise ship featuring lunch, dinner and moonlight cruises, with two live bands and a Broadway revue; Harbor Belle, Inc: A replica of a turn-of-the-century steam boat paddle wheeler, offering lunch and dinner cruises; Minnie V.Skipjack: Offers tours aboard historic Chesapeake Bay oyster boats; Harbor Shuttle: Offers year-round shuttle service in weather-protected boats.

Baltimore's Beginning, A Look Back

A Chronology of Early Events From 1668-1929

1668
John Howard patented a tract of land which included a large part of South Baltimore between the Middle and Northwest branches of the Patapsco.

Thomas Cole took five hundred and fifty acres known as Cole's Harbor which was bounded by what is now Paca, Mulberry, High and Lombard Streets.

1698
James Todd obtained a warrant for Cole's Harbor and had it surveyed. A patent was granted on June 1, 1700, under the name of Todd's Range. This patent was later void.

1706
Whetstone Point was made a point of entry by an Act of the Legislature, and was the first within the city's limits.

1711
Jonathan Hanson acquired thirty-one acres and erected a mill, at the point where Bath and Holliday Streets intersect.

1723
Iron ore was discovered at Whetstone Point, and the tract of land was resurveyed and passed into the hands of the Principio Furnace Company, on March 29.

1729
On August 8, an Act authorizing the "erection" of Baltimore Town was passed.

1730
The town Council met and officially surveyed sixty acres on January 12.

1732
Jones Town, located east of Baltimore Town was laid out on November 22.

1739
The Protestant Episcopal Parish Church built on the site afterwards occupied by St. Paul's Church, at the corner of Charles and Saratoga Streets was completed.
Construction had begun in 1730.

1745
Baltimore and Jones Town consolidated and incorporated as Baltimore Town.

1751
A subscription of £100 was made by citizens on April 23, for the building of a market house and town hall. This was erected ten years later at the northwest corner of Gay and Baltimore Streets.

1753
Thirty-two acres known as "Hall's addition," was annexed to Baltimore Town.

1754
Mount Clare House was erected by Charles Carroll, Barrister.

1756
Acadian exiles settled in Baltimore.

1768
Baltimore was made the county seat, and a courthouse was erected on the site where the Battle Monument now stands.

1769
The Mechanical Company was organized and a fire-engine purchased.

1772
The first umbrella to be used in the United States was brought to Baltimore from India.

1773
A Baptist Church was erected at the corner of Front and Fayette Streets on the site where the Shot Tower now stands.

The first issue of the first newspaper, the *Maryland Journal and Baltimore Advertiser*, established by William Goddard, was published on August 20.

The first stage route to Philadelphia was opened.

In November, the First Methodist meeting-house in Baltimore was built in Strawbeery Alley.

1774
Lovely Lane Methodist Meeting-House was erected in October.

1775
Baltimore Town contained 564 houses and had a population of 5,934.

1776
The Continental Congress held its sessions in Congress Hall, located at the corner of Baltimore and Liberty Streets, from December 20 to January 20,

1777
The first notable riot occurred when William Goddard of the *Maryland Journal* was attacked in his office by excited members of the "Whig Club," who took exception to an article in his paper complimenting King George and Parliament on March 25.

1778
Count Pulaski organized his corps in March.

1780
The first Custom House was erected.

1781
Baltimore began paving its streets.

The first brick theatre was erected on East Baltimore Street, opposite the Second Presbyterian Church.

1782
The theatre opened with the play, "King Richard III," on January 15.

1783
The first regular stage line to Fredericktown and Annapolis was established.

1784
The first Baltimore policemen were employed.

Oil lamps were first used as street illumination.

The Methodist Episcopal Church in the United States was organized in December.

1785
The Methodist Church on Light Street and Wine Alley began in August, and was dedicated by Bishop Asbury on May 21, 1786.

1791
St. Mary's College was established.

1791
A Presbyterian Church was erected on the northwest corner of Fayette and North Streets. This structure was later demolished to give place to the United States Courthouse in 1860. The courthouse was torn down in 1908 to make way for an extension to the Post Office.

The Bank of Maryland was organized.

1794
A yellow fever epidemic hit Baltimore from August to October.

1795
The Bank of Baltimore was incorporated on December 24.

1796
The first directory of Baltimore Town and Fell's Point was published.

On December 31, an Act was passed for the laying out and establishment of a turnpike from Washington, D.C. to Baltimore Town.

1797
Baltimore Town was incorporated as a city.

A marine observatory was established on Federal Hill.

On January 20, The Library of Baltimore, which merged with the Maryland Historical Society, was incorporated.

1798
On September 8, the Maryland Society was formed which promoted the abolition of slavery, and the relief of free Negroes and others unlawfully held in bondage. This was the fourth such organization formed in the United States.

1799
The Baltimore American and Daily Advertiser was first issued on May 14. This was the successor to the *Maryland Journal and Baltimore Advertiser*.

1799
On December 15, news of the death of General Washington reached Baltimore, and on January 1, 1800, commemorative funeral rites were held. The militia, including the regulars from Fort McHenry, and citizens, formed a procession beginning at Baltimore Street, where an address was delivered by Rev. Dr. Allison. The procession ended at Christ's Church, where a bier was carried into the edifice. Funeral services were conducted by Rev. Dr. Bend.

1800
President Adams passed through Baltimore on June 15. The Mayor and City Council delivered him an address of welcome.

1804
Union Bank of Maryland was organized.

1806
The Mechanics' Bank was incorporated.

The corner-stone of the Roman Catholic Church was laid on July 7.

1807
Water was first supplied to Baltimore through cast-iron pipes in May. The water used was taken from Jones Falls.

1809
The courthouse on North Calvert Street, at the corner of Lexington was completed and occupied. Construction had begun in 1805. This building was later torn down to make place for the present marble structure.

1812
The office of the *Federal Republican* was destroyed by a mob on July 27.

1813
The "New Theatre," opened on May 10. It was later called the "Holliday Street Theatre."

The first steamboat built in Baltimore, the *Chesapeake*, was constructed by William McDonald & Company.

1814
British forces under General Ross advanced against Baltimore on September 12. Later this day he was killed in the engagement at North Point. Fort McHenry was bombarded by the British fleet on September 12 and 13. The "*Star-Spangled Banner*" was composed by Francis Scott Key while on board the U.S. ship *Minden*, during the bombardment.

1814
"Star-Spangled Banner," was printed in the *Baltimore American and Daily Advertiser* on September 21.

1815
The corner-stone was laid for the Washington Monument on July 4. The monument, 180 feet high was completed on November 25, 1824.

The corner-stone was laid for the Battle Monument on September 12. The monument was completed on September 12, 1822. It was erected in honor of Baltimoreans killed defending the city in 1814.

1816
The annexation of precincts increased the population of Baltimore to 16,000.

The Maryland Hospital was incorporated on January 29.

The Medical Society of Maryland was incorporated on February 1.

1817
The Jones Falls overflowed its banks, placing a part of the city known as the "Meadows," under 10 to 15 feet of water.

1819
President James Monroe visited Baltimore.

1822
A disastrous fire destroyed three lumber yards and thirty buildings, most of which were warehouses, on June 23.

1824
General Lafayette visited Baltimore from October 7 to 11.

The Washington Monument, the first to be erected in honor of George Washington, was completed on November 25.

1825
Mrs. Ellen Moale, the first white child born within the town of Baltimore, died in March.

The erection of Barnum's Hotel was begun.

1826
The first exhibition of the Maryland Institute was held November 7.

1827
Subscription books for the stock of the Baltimore & Ohio Railroad were opened on March 20. In seven days, $4,178,000 was raised by 22,000 subscribers.

1828
The first banking house was opened by Evan Poultney on Baltimore Street in June.

1828
The foundation stone of the Baltimore & Ohio Railroad was laid on July 4, by the Masonic Grand Lodge of Maryland, assisted by Charles Carroll of Carrollton.

The Shot Tower, (belonging to the Phoenix Company), which is 234 feet high, circular in shape, and constructed of brick, was built without scaffolding. It was completed on November 25.

1829
The centennial anniversary of the founding of Baltimore was celebrated on August 8.

The cornerstone of the Baltimore and Susquehanna Railroad, later known as the Northern Central Railroad, was laid on August 8.

The first public school in Baltimore was opened on September 24.

1830
The first steam car was run on the Baltimore & Ohio Railroad on August 28.

1832
Charles Carroll of Carrollton, the last survivor of the signers of the Declaration of Independence, died at Baltimore on November 14, at the age of 95.

1834
The Bank of Maryland failed on March 24.

The Baltimore and Washington Railroad opened on August 25.

1835
A riot, growing out of the failure of the Bank of Maryland took place in August.

1837
The first issue of the *Baltimore Sun* was published on May 17.

Nine lives were lost in a sudden overflow of the Jones Falls on July 14, resulting in Harrison and Frederick Streets being ten feet under water.

1838
The *City of Kingston*, the first steam vessel to sail from Baltimore to Europe left port on May 20.

1839
The Baltimore College of Dental Surgery, which was the first dental college, and for many years the only dental college in the world, was chartered.

1842
The steamer *Medora*, exploded killing 27 and injuring 40 on April 15.

1843
Francis Scott Key, author of "*Star-Spangled Banner*," died on January 11.

1844
The Historical Society of Maryland was organized on January 27, with General John Spear Smith as its first president.

The first omnibus line was established in May.

1848
The Maryland Institute for the promotion of the mechanics' arts was organized on January 12.

A fire, originating in a cotton factory on Lexington Street destroyed sixty dwellings on May 28.

1849
Baltimore Female College opened in 1848 was chartered.

Edgar Allan Poe died in Baltimore on October 7, at the age of 40.

1851
The corner-stone of the Maryland Institute at Baltimore Street and Marsh Market Space was laid on March 13, and the building was opened on October 20. This building was destroyed in the Baltimore fire of 1904. A new building was erected in 1907 at what was known as Center Market.

1852
Loyola College, Calvert Street near Madison, opened on September 15.

The remains of Junius Brutus Booth, arrived at his home in Baltimore on December 9, from Louisville, Kentucky, where he had died on December 2.

1853
Loudon Park Cemetery was dedicated on July 14.

1854
The water-works were purchased by the city.

1855
The first trial steam fire-engine seen in Baltimore, the "Miles Greenwood," arrived on February 2.

1855
The erection of the First Presbyterian Church, at the corner of Park Avenue and Madison Street began in July.

1856
St. Paul's Protestant Episcopal Church, which burned on April 29, 1854 was rebuilt and dedicated on January 10.

An election riot took place on November 4, between the Democrats and the Know-nothings.

1857
A disastrous fire at 37-41 South Charles Street killed 14 on April 14.

1858
The first steam fire-engine, the "Alpha," to be owned by the Baltimore Fire Department, arrived on May 18.

1858
A destructive flood occurred on June 12.

An ordinance was passed in September providing for a partial paid fire department.

The Peabody Institute, which was endowed by George Peabody in 1857 with $1,300,000, was incorporated on March 9, and the corner-stone laid on April 16, 1859.

The police and fire-alarm telegraph system was placed in operation on June 27.

1859
The first car was placed on the City Passenger Railroad tracks on Broadway and the line was opened on October 27.

1860
The Baltimore police force was placed under State control on February 2.

Druid Hill Park, purchased by the city in September, 1860, opened to the public on October 19.

1861
While the Sixth Massachusetts and the Seventh Pennsylvania Regiments were attempting to pass through the city on their way to Washington, D.C., on April 19, they were attacked by Southern sympathizers resulting in 12 citizens and 3 soldiers being killed, and 23 soldiers and several citizens wounded.

General B.F. Butler took military possession of the city on May 13.

1865
The corner-stone was laid for St. Martin's Roman Catholic Church, at the southeast corner of Fulton Avenue and Fayette St. on July 9.

1866
The Maryland State Normal School opened.

The Peabody Institute was dedicated on October 25.

1867
The corner-stone was laid for the new City Hall on October 18.

1868
The most disastrous flood in Baltimore occurred on July 24. A street car floated down Harrison Street; the water reached to the second story of buildings, and most of the bridges over the Jones Falls, including the heavy iron bridge at Fayette Street were swept away.

1871
Ford's Grand Opera House opened on October 3, with Shakespeare's play, "As You Like It."

1872
The initial issue of the *Evening News* was published on November 4.

1873
The Protestant Episcopal Church of the Ascension was destroyed by fire on May 12.

The first passenger train passed through the Baltimore and Potomac tunnel en route to Calvert Station on June 29. Construction on this tunnel, which is one and one-half miles long started in June, 1871.

1873
The largest fire to occur in Baltimore to date started in a planing-mill on Park Avenue and Clay Street on July 25, destroying 113 buildings, including 2 churches and 3 schoolhouses.

Johns Hopkins died on December 24, at the age of 79.

1875
The *Morning Herald* was established.

City Hall was dedicated on October 25. It was constructed at the cost of $2,272,135.64

The monument to Edgar Allan Poe erected in the Westminster Presbyterian Church-yard, at Fayette and Greene Streets, was unveiled on November 17.

1876
The Johns Hopkins University, which was incorporated on August 24, 1867, opened.

1877
Following a strike on the Baltimore & Ohio Railroad, a riot occurred at the Sixth Regiment Armory, in which eleven persons were killed and several wounded. The trouble continued to the end of the month before they were quieted. On July 30, railroad travel was partially resumed.

1886
The Enoch Pratt Free Library, founded in 1882 by Enoch Pratt, opened to the public on January 5.

A fire occurred in Hopkins Place on September 2, killing seven firemen and wounding six.

1889
The Johns Hopkins Hospital opened on May 7.

1895
At the Front Street Theatre, a panic occurred during a Yiddish performance, killing 23.

1898
Governor Lowndes approved the Act of the General Assembly which granted a new charter to the City of Baltimore on March 24.

1904
The great Baltimore fire started in the cellar of the John E. Hurst & Company building, Hopkins Place, Redwood (then German) and Liberty Streets on February 7. It burned for three days, destroying eighty-six blocks, covering one hundred forty acres in the heart of the city. The estimated loss was $125,000,000.

1906
The "Greater Baltimore Jubilee," celebrating the rehabilitation of the City, began September 10.

1908
William Pinkney Whyte, who had been State Comptroller, Mayor of Baltimore, Governor of Maryland, United States Senator, and a leading member of the Bar, died on March 17.

1910
Electric current, generated at McCall Ferry, Susquehanna River, was introduced in Baltimore on October 14.

1911
F.C. Latrobe, who was seven times Mayor of Baltimore, died on January 18.

The Key Monument was unveiled on May 15.

1911
The fifteenth anniversary of the ordination of Cardinal Gibbons, and the twenty-fifth anniversary of his elevation to the rank of Cardinal was celebrated on June 6.

The steamship, *Friedrich der Grosse*, which sailed from Baltimore for Bremen on June 28, was the largest steamer to visit this port up to that date.

1912
The high-pressure fire pipe line was placed in service on April 23.

1914
The one hundredth anniversary of the writing of "*Star-Spangled Banner*" was held in Baltimore, September 6 to 13.

The Municipal Flag of Baltimore was adopted by the Flag Commission of Baltimore on December 2.

1915
A new road called the Fallsway was constructed over the Jones Falls as a flood control measure and opened to traffic.

The new filtration plant at Lake Montebello was dedicated and put into service on September 13.

1916
The German submarine *Deutschland* arrived at Baltimore on her first trip across the Atlantic on July 10. The vessel brought dyestuffs and merchandise to Baltimore, and carried out rubber, bandages and war relief goods.

During the years 1915 and 1916 Baltimore's industrial expansion far exceeded that of any like period in its history. The greatest single industrial development was at Sparrows Point, where the Bethlehem Steel Corporation began improvements costing $50,000,000 and employed 20,000 persons. Railroads during this period included the construction of the Baltimore & Ohio Railroad Company's coal pier at Curtis Bay, and the new export pier at Locust Point, at a cost of $2,150,000. The Pennsylvania Railroad built the new coal pier at Canton and rebuilt the grain elevator, which was burned, at a total cost of $3,500,000. The Western Maryland Railroad erected a concrete grain elevator and storage bins at Port Covington, costing $1,000,000.

1917
The new Hanover Street Bridge opened to street car traffic on January 17.

1918
The Maryland Legislature passed, the new Annexation Act for Baltimore City in March. It became effective January 1, 1919, increasing the City's area from 32.05 to 91.93 square miles.

1919
A bronze tablet in memory of William Fell, a founder of Baltimore Town, was unveiled at William Fell School, Ann Street, near Fleet Street on November 1.

1920
The merit system became effective in the Municipal Government on April 1.

1921
French Marshall Foch broke ground for the War Memorial on November 22.

1922
The Congressional Monument at Fort McHenry was unveiled on June 14.

A fire destroyed two grain elevators and several piers at Locust Point

1922
Terminal, owned by the Baltimore & Ohio Railroad Company on July 2. The blaze was started by a bolt of lightning, and was the largest fire since 1904.

The new Baltimore Stadium was opened for use with the playing of the Army-Marine football game on December 2.

1923
The corner-stone of the War Memorial was laid on April 29.

The new one-branch City Council held its first meeting May 24. The body was composed of a president and three members from each of the six councilmanic districts.

1924
New traffic regulation became effective on June 21.

The bronze statue of Marquis de Lafayette, erected on the south side of the Washington Monument, was unveiled on September 6. President Calvin Coolidge took part in the ceremony.

The Baltimore & Ohio Railroad Company's new grain elevator at Locust Point was placed into operation on September 19.

The Army-Navy football game was first held at the new Baltimore Stadium on November 29.

1925
The Old Shot Tower at Fayette and Front Streets became the property of the City on January 12.

The War Memorial at Lexington, Gay, Fayette, and Frederick Streets was dedicated on April 5.

1926
A new building was erected by the City of Baltimore for the Police Department at a cost of over $1,000,000. This structure occupied the entire block bounded by the Fallsway, Lexington, Frederick and Fayette Streets.

1927
Municipal ambulance service, under the direction of the Fire Department began on June 15.

The Memorial Plaza, facing City Hall in the east, was dedicated on Armistice Day, November 11.

1928
The site for Baltimore's Municipal Airport was selected on the waterfront in the Dundalk-Soller's Point section adjacent to Logan Field in January.

The new City College building was completed in January and occupied in February.

President Coolidge signed a bill in April, authorizing an expenditure for the restoration of Fort McHenry to its original design, and making it a national shrine. The dedication services were held on September 12.

Baltimore's Flag House, located at 844 East Pratt Street, was made a national shrine on November 12.

1929
Construction of Baltimore's airport began in March.

The Glenn L. Martin Company, purchased twelve hundred acres of land at Middle River on March 14, for the erection of a plant for the manufacture of airplanes.

BALTIMORE CITY SEAL

CITY OF BALTIMORE

1797

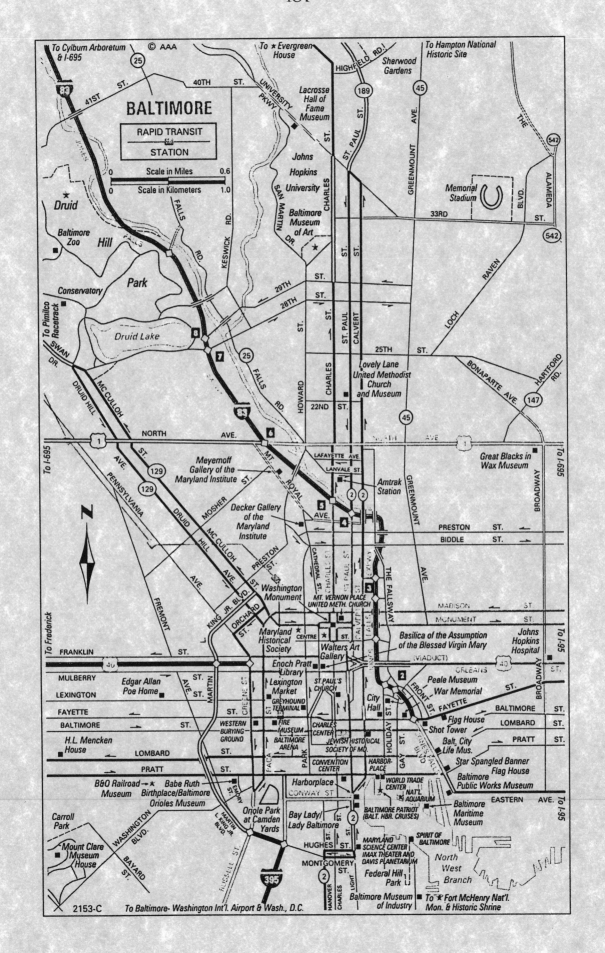

BALTIMORE COUNTY

Baltimore County's legal origin is not known; however, it was in existence by January 12, 1659, when a writ was issued to the sheriff of the county. The County name was derived from the name of the Proprietary's Irish Barony.

Baltimore County's Seal, referred to as The Baltimore County Common Seal, was passed by the first County Council under the Home Rule Charter form of government and signed into law on June 10, 1957. The seal features the Calvert and Crossland Coats of Arms (Identical in style and color to the Maryland State Flag), and seven stars, representing the seven councilmanic districts. The Baltimore County Common Seal was designed by Adelaide M. Haspert, a Towson, Maryland resident.

Old Baltimore County, was the sixth county to be established by the colonial assembly in 1659, and was the first in the northern part of Maryland. The original area of Baltimore County was much larger then its present size. Originally it included parts of what are now Cecil, Harford, Carroll, Howard, and Kent on the Eastern Shore. Its first county seats were Old Baltimore on the Bush River and Joppa on the Gunpowder River, both of which are in Harford County today (See Baltimore City).

Baltimore County today is the third largest county, with an area of six hundred thirty-eight square land and water miles. Only Frederick and Garrett counties are larger. It extends northward to the Pennsylvania Line, which is part of the historic Mason-Dixon Line. On the south it encloses Baltimore City on all but the southeastern border of the city. To the east lies the Chesapeake Bay, and to the north Harford County. To the west is Carroll County, and to the south are Howard and Anne Arundel counties.

Baltimore County is unique in that it contains no incorporated municipalities. In 1790, its population was almost 39,000 (including approximately 13,000 from Baltimore City) and in 1860 rose to 54,000. By 1960, the population was almost 500,000, and in 1990 was 692,134. In 1994, the population was 711,783, an increase of 2.8% since 1990. In 1998, the county population rose to 725,060, with a projection to 732,700 by the year 2000.

Baltimore County contains some of the largest unincorporated areas in the United States, such as: Dundalk, Essex and Catonsville. In all there are eighteen unincorporated areas in the County.

Areas of interest in Baltimore County are: <u>Towson</u>, the county seat since 1854. The community of Towson got its name from the tavern of Ezekiel Towson in 1750. The name Towson was made famous, not by Ezekiel, but by his grandson, Nathan Towson, an artillery commander in the U.S. Army. Captain Nathan Towson gained prominence in the War of 1812, fighting the British on the Canadian border. Throughout the war, he was continuously commended for his bravery. This Baltimore County native would later serve as Paymaster General of the U.S. Army and was breveted as a major general before his death in 1854. Nathan was born on January 22, 1784, on a small farm in Baltimore County, where he helped his father until 1801, when at the age of seventeen he was sent to Kentucky to farm land to which his father had a claim. Finding in Kentucky that the land was owned by another he went to Natchez, returning to Baltimore County in 1805, where he continued farming until just prior to the outbreak of the War of 1812, when he was appointed captain of the artillery in the U.S. Army. Following the United States declaration of war on the British, Nathan's artillery company was sent to the Canadian border, to Black Rock on the Niagara River. It was here that his company was assigned to protect the U.S. vessels being fitted for service on Lake Erie. Involved in many encounters, Nathan was a part of the first U.S. victory of the great lakes in October, 1812.

Throughout the war, Nathan Towson helped capture and secure the British vessel, <u>Caledonia</u>, resulting in the seizing of furs having a value of $200,000. He also was involved in the Battle of Queenston, and during the time the British were attacking Washington and Baltimore in 1814, Towson was busy commanding the artillery during the capture of Fort Erie, as well as the victories at Chippewa and Lundy's Lane. It was noted that Towson's battery emitted a stream of light through its constant firing. The British, as a result nicknamed Towson's battery, "The Lighthouse." Following the war, Nathan Towson returned to Maryland as a lieutenant colonel, and was offered a job of Sheriff of Baltimore, which he refused, preferring to stay in the army. He then accepted a position as commandant of the army troops in Boston harbor. While there he met and married Sophia Bingham in 1816. In 1819, upon the death of the Paymaster General of the U.S. Army, Nathan was appointed to this position, and moved to Washington D.C. Nathan held this position as Paymaster General until his death on July 25, 1854. Nathan Towson is buried in Oak Hill Cemetery, Georgetown, along with his wife, Sophia Bingham, who died in 1852.

<u>Cockeysville</u>: Named for the Cockey family and noted for the marble obtained from its nearby quarries; <u>Lutherville</u>: First developed around the Maryland College for Women, chartered in 1853, through the efforts of two Lutheran clergymen, J.G. Norris and D.B. Kurtz. First called the Lutherville Female Seminary and later named Maryland College for Young Ladies, it burned in 1911 and was later rebuilt; <u>Timonium</u>: Known for the Timonium Fairgrounds, which hold horse races, and where the annual fair is held; <u>Pikesville</u>: Settled

before the Revolutionary War, but was not named until after the War of 1812. Dr. James Smith owned much of the land in this area, and named the first village for his friend, Brigadier General Pike of New Jersey, who was killed during the siege and burning of York, Canada. Near the center of town is located the former <u>Maryland Line Confederate Soldiers' Home</u> built in 1819 by the Federal Government as a United States Arsenal. The veterans who once occupied this site were moved to private homes in 1932, and the buildings then turned over to the county. Today it is headquarters of the Maryland State Police.

<u>Druid Ridge Cemetery</u>: In this cemetery lie the graves of: <u>Mary Washington</u>, the wife of Colonel L.W. Washington (1825-1871), a great-grandnephew of George Washington. Colonel Washington was held hostage at Harpers Ferry in 1859 by John Brown; and William Benton Marck, my great-great grandfather, who served in the 30th Infantry, Company C, Army of Northern Virginia, who was wounded at Dunker Church during the Battle of Antietam, September 17, 1862, as well as other of my ancestors; and also at the cemetery is the <u>Queen Victoria Monument</u>, built in 1901 by the St. George's Society of Baltimore, and said to be the only monument to England's famous queen in the United States.

<u>Grey Rock</u>: Built about 1700 and remodeled in 1890, this large gray stone house was the birthplace of John Eager Howard (1752-1827), who served with distinction in the Revolutionary War. At Cowpens, seven British officers surrendered their swords to him, after which he was awarded a Congressional medal. He went on to serve as governor of Maryland, and as a United States senator from Maryland.

<u>Hereford</u>: Located between Monkton and Shepperd's Corners on what once was My Lady's Manor, a tract of land the third Lord Baltimore bestowed in 1713 upon his fourth wife, Margaret. It has since been subdivided into many farms. The first covered bridge built over the Gunpowder Falls was at Bunker Hill Road, about a mile northwest of Hereford. It was built in 1880 and survived until 1961 when it was destroyed by fire. It was rebuilt, but was destroyed by vandals in 1971, and was not replaced. Also located in Hereford are the <u>Old Gorsuch Tavern</u> and the <u>Hurst House</u>. The tavern was built in 1810 by Captain Joshua Gorsuch, and it was here he stored silks, spices and other goods and materials he brought from his voyages to the East. The stone barn on the grounds was used by his son, Edward Gorsuch, who was a slave-trader, to house the slaves.

In September 1851, two of the Negro slaves escaped with the help of the Underground Railway, and made their way to Lancaster, Pennsylvania. In an attempt to retake them from their protectors, Edward was killed, and his son Dickerson, along with others were wounded. This incident is known as the Christiana Massacre. The Hurst

House, was once the Milton Academy, where John Wilkes Booth and his brother Edwin received their early education. Founded in 1847, it was known as the Lamb's School, after John E. and Eli M. Lamb. They ran the school until 1877. In 1885, the school was moved to Baltimore here it stayed in operation until 1899.

Bonnie Blink: Overlooking Hunt Valley Mall is a Masonic Home, establish in 1932 as a home for the aged; Hayfields: Built in 1808, by Colonel Nicholas Merryman Bosley. When Lafayette visited Maryland in 1825, he presented Bosley with a silver tankard for having the best tilled farm in the State. This was also the home of Lieutenant John Merryman. During the Civil War, the Chief Justice of the United States issued a writ of habeas corpus, for Lieutenant Merryman, that the military authorities ignored; and Hampton National Historic Site: Located at 535 Hampton Lane, off Dulaney Valley Road. This Georgian House was begun in 1783 by Charles Ridgely. It is the best known house of the Ridgely family, and occupies a 60-acre site with nineteenth century gardens, greenhouses, icehouse, stables, and a restored orangery. Now a National Historic Site, it is maintained by the National Park Service. Open daily 9-5. Admission free. The Ridgley family also owned Northampton, a great iron works, now the site of Goucher College.

The oldest building in Baltimore County is Fort Garrison. It is located on Stevenson Road, south of Green Spring Valley Road. It was designed and built as a lookout for possible Indian attacks, and housed a captain and six rangers. It was built in the 1600s, and later remodeled in the nineteenth century. This remodeling included the addition of a second story, which was removed years later. Although no Indian attacks ever occurred here, the fort stayed in use until about 1698. Today the fort is in its original state, without the second story.

One of the notable persons from Maryland, and Baltimore County is Benjamin Banneker, America's first black man of science. He was born on November 9, 1731 into a free black family. He was raised on a hundred-acre tobacco farm which contained a one-room log cabin. It was located in Catonsville, about a mile from the Patapsco River.

Benjamin's father, Robert, was born in Africa and had been a slave. His mother was Mary Banneky, the daughter of Bannka, a freed Negro slave, and an indentured Englishwoman named Molly Welsh. After fulfilling her servitude, Molly established a small tobacco farm nearby and hired two slaves to help her work the farm. She gave these two slaves their freedom, and eventually married one of them, who was Bannka.

Benjamin's father, having no surname of his own, took his wife's surname of Banneky, upon their marriage, and changed it to Banneker. It was through Robert's hard work that enabled him to first purchase a twenty-five acre farm, and later the hundred acre farm on which Benjamin was born. The log cabin in which Benjamin was raised was built by his father. Benjamin lived in this house his entire this life.

Not having the opportunity to obtain an ordinary education, he was taught to read and write by his grandmother, using a Bible, the only book in the house. When time permitted away from his farm duties, Benjamin would travel the considerable distance to the country school where he met Peter Heinrich, the only teacher. Although he was only able to attend this school for two years, off and on, he did advance quickly in mathematics with the help of Heinrich. He received no other formal education. Banneker also enjoyed reading, and with only a few books that he could either borrow or sometimes purchase, he taught himself in literature, history, and further mathematics during the few leisure hours that he had away from his chores. He had a natural gift for mathematics, and at a young age created mathematical puzzles. At the age of twenty-two he accomplished an astounding feat by completing all aspects of construction on a chiming wooden clock, without ever having seen one before. There were no books or clockmaking in the area; however, he did see a pocket watch at one time. He undertook this project as a mathematical challenge, calculating the proper ratio of the rears and wheels, and then carving them from wood with a pocket watch. The clock properly operated for more than forty years.

In 1759, Benjamin's father died, and he continued to work the farm while living with his mother and three sisters. As time passed his sisters married and left home, but stayed in the vicinity. About 1775, his mother died, and Benjamin continued to live alone on the farm. His sisters would come by frequently and handle his housekeeping needs.

The major event in Benjamin's life occurred about 1771, when five Ellicott brothers, who were Quakers from Bucks County, Pennsylvania, bought the large tract of land that adjoined his farm. The Ellicott brothers developed this land into a major center for the production of wheat and the milling of flour. Within a few years it had developed into the community of Ellicott's Lower Mills, with flour mills, saw mills, an iron foundry, and a general store. Benjamin visited the Mills often, and became friend with George Ellicott, a son of one of the founding brothers. George Ellicott had an interest in the sciences, and it was from him that Benjamin derived an interest in astronomy, from having observed George make astronomical presentations at the Mills. In 1789, George loaned Benjamin several of his books on astronomy, as well as several instruments. Benjamin, on his own, taught himself astronomy, and learned to calculate an ephemeris and to make projections for lunar and solar eclipses. He complied an ephemeris for the year 1791, with was incorporated into an almanac. Although submitted to several printers, it was never published. Meanwhile, he continued his self-studies and learned how to astronomical and surveying instruments.

Early in 1791, President George Washington appointed George Ellicott's brother, Major Andrew Ellicott to undertake the survey of a ten-mile square known as Federal Territory (now the District of Columbia), in which a new national capital was to be established. Banneker was chosen to assist Andrew in this work by making surveying calculations from astronomical instruments. Banneker worked with Andrew for about a month, until Andrew's two brothers could join him. This experience furthered his interest in astronomy, so upon his return home, he calculated an ephemeris for the following year. With the help of George Ellicott and his family, it was brought to the attention of the Pennsylvania and Maryland abolition societies. With their help and support, it was published in Baltimore by Goddard & Angell, and titled, "Benjamin Banneker's Pennsylvania, Delaware, Maryland and Virginia Almanack and Ephemeris, for the Year of Our Lord, 1792; Being Bissextile, or Leap-Year, and the Sixteenth Year of American Independence, which commenced on July 4, 1776."

Shortly after its publication, Banneker sent a copy to Thomas Jefferson, who was then the Secretary of State, with a letter urging the abolition of slavery of the Negro. He compared the situation of slavery to the former enslavement of the American colonies by the British Crown. Jefferson acknowledged his letter, and further sent a copy of the letter and his ephemeris to the Marquis de Condorcet, secretary of the Academie des Sciences in Paris, as an example of a unique achievement by a black man. It unfortunately arrived on the eve of the French Revolution, and was not acknowledged nor sent to the Academy. However, the exchange of letters between Banneker and Jefferson were published by the abolition societies, which helped the sale of his almanac.

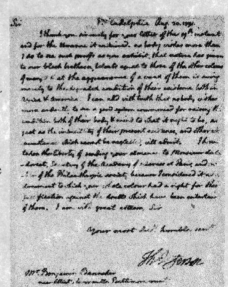

Jefferson's acknowledgement letter to Banneker, addressed: To Benjamin Banneker, near Ellicot, lower mills, Baltimore county; dated August 30, 1791

Over the next few years, Banneker continued to published his almanacs. In 1797, the publication of Banneker's almanacs terminated, with this being the last year, most likely due to diminishing interest in the abolition movement. Still, Banneker continued to compute ephemerides for almanacs each year until 1804.

Until the end of his life, he continued frequent visits to Ellicott's Lower Mills, and was a familiar figure at the Ellicott Store. On October 9, 1806, Benjamin Banneker died, a month short of his seventy-fifth birthday. He was buried two days later in the family burial plot on his farm. While the funeral was in progress, and with all his family members in attendance at the grave, his house caught fire and burned to the ground, along with al its contents. Most of Benjamin's possessions, including his clock, books and writings were destroyed. Fortunately, prior to his death, he had left instructions that all the books, instruments and an old table that had been loaned to him by Ellicott, be returned to him. Before the funeral began, Benjamin's nephew gathered these items, placed them in a wagon, and returned them to George. Some of the items saved by this removal were his commonplace book in which he had made entries of his accounts, as well as some astronomical notes, and his manuscript for his astronomical journal. This journal today is housed at the Maryland Historical Society.

Due to the fire, the exact site of Banneker's house and grave in the little town of Oella, Maryland have been lost and can no longer be identified. In 1854, a marker honoring Banneker was erected at the Westchester Elementary School in Oella Historic Mill Town, Maryland. In 1970, Banneker Circle, adjoining L'Enfant Plaza in Washington, D.C., was named in his honor.

In 1985, Baltimore County purchased more than forty-two acres of the Banneker farm. The Friends of Benjamin Banneker Historical Park was established to offer assistance in supporting the park. Research was conducted over a three year period by the Maryland Historical Trust, whereby a number of artifacts dating back to Banneker were located.

Baltimore County Churches

Religion in Maryland and Baltimore County has played an important role, especially following the Revolution of 1688. Maryland proprietors, the Calverts, were Catholics, but did permit other denominations to exist. Some of the churches of historical significance in Baltimore County are:

St. John's Valley Episcopal Church, located on Butler Road in Glyden was built in 1816. It was destroyed by fire on Christmas Day 1867. The present church was rebuilt in 1869. Mt. Paran Presbyterian Church, located on Liberty Road at Lyon's Mill Road in Harrisonville, began in 1784. It was remodeled in 1883, and again in 1924. Its original random-width floorboards and pews remain today. The parish of St. John's at Kingsville, dates back to a church built in Cecil County in 1697. In 1724, the church moved to Joppa, and in 1817, moved to Kingsville. It was enlarged in 1850, and the tower added in 1870. Sater's Baptist Church off Falls Road in Lutherville dates from 1742. It is regarded as the Mother Church of Maryland Baptists. It is named for Henry Sater, an English immigrant who donated the land. St. James Episcopal Church in Monkton was built in 1755. It was first called the "Chapel of Ease." It was originally made of brick cast in English molds and laid in Flemish bond. Additions were added in 1791 and again in 1871. On June 2, 1941, lightning struck the tower, which caught on fire and burned. The bell in the tower fell, and had to be recast. In the process it lost three hundred pounds changing its resonance.

The earliest meeting house for the <u>Society of Friends</u> in Baltimore County still in existence in located on Beaver Dam Road. It was build in 1773. <u>Chestnut Grove Presbyterian Church</u> on Sweetair Road in Phoenix was built in 1825, in the Long Green Academy. The present church was built in 1842. Located in Parkville is the <u>Hiss Methodist Church</u>, built in 1839 and named for Dr. William Hiss. The original was replaced in 1895, and was remodeled in 1954. The oldest religious structure in Pikesville is the <u>Mettam Memorial Baptist Church</u>. It was built in 1834, and is named for its first pastor, Joseph Mettam. On Bellona Avenue in Ruxton is located the <u>St. John's African Union Methodist Protestant Church</u>. It began as a log building in 1833, constructed by Reverend Aquilla Scott, a Falls Road area blacksmith. The original structure burned in 1886 and was rebuilt. It was restored in the 1970s and placed on the National Register of Historic Places in 1980. On Westchester Avenue in Oella, Maryland is located the <u>Mt. Gilboa African Methodist Episcopal Church</u>. It began on May 27, 1860, and was built by free blacks. In 1861, two churches in Towson, the Towson Methodist Episcopal Congregation and the Methodist Protestant Church were divided over the cost of installing an organ. Consequently, they merged in 1958 to form the <u>Towson United Methodist Church</u>, located on Hampton Lane. These are just a few of the historic churches located in Baltimore County.

Another place of interest dating back to the time of the Calverts is <u>Ballestone Manor</u>. In 1659, Cecilius Calvert, second Lord Baltimore, granted four hundred-fifty acres of land on Back River Neck to William Ball, George Washington's maternal great-great-grandfather. William Ball, who lived in Virginia, never built nor visited this land, but rather looked at it as an investment. In 1780, the land was purchased by the Stansbury family who were the first to built; a two and one-half story flemish-bond brick house. In 1819, the estate was sold to the Leakin family, who expanded the house by adding a one and one-half story addition. Again in 1850, the estate was sold to Edward Miller who continued to expand the house. Over the next thirty years until 1880, he raised the roof to a full two story structure and added a columned portico. The house, which was built over a period of one hundred years, eventually began to deteriote, over time, and through the elements and vandalism. The house was saved and then restored by the Heritage Society of Essex and Middle River, and furnished throught the help of the Maryland Historical Society. These furnishings throughout are from the Federal, Empire, and Victorian periods. The house is open from June to August on Sundays from 2:00 to 5:00 p.m., and at other times by appointment. It is located at Rocky Point Golf Course in Essex.

A sort distance from Ballestone Manor is the <u>Heritage Society of Essex and Middle River</u>, located at 516 Eastern Boulevard. It is housed in an 1920 fire house, and the museum features replicas of a general store, candle and music shop, toy store, schoolroom, pharmacy, workshop and jail cells. Included also are archives and thousands of artifacts dealing with local history.

Other historical and interesting attractions in Baltimore County are:

The <u>Fire Museum of Maryland</u>, located at 1301 York Road in Lutherville is a nationally renowned collection of historic fire fighting apparatus and memorabilia. In the collection are over fifty fire-fighting vehicles dating from 1822, and an impressive collection of support equipment. The museum was founded by Stephen G. Heaver in 1971. It is open from May through October on Sundays, from 1:00 to 5:00 p.m.

One of the few remaining covered bridges in Maryland is the <u>Jericho Covered Bridge</u> located on Jericho Road in Kingsville. This long single-span bridge crosses the Gunpowder River and is open to traffic.

Baltimore County is also the home to two of Maryland's finest vineyards.

<u>Boordy Vineyard</u> is located at 12820 Long Green Pike in Hydes. Founded by Philip Wagner, he first attempted to cultivate California varieties of grapes to make wine in the early 1920s. Wagner, who was a reporter with the <u>Baltimore Sun</u> was sent to France during World War II with fellow correspondent H.L. Mencken. While there, Wagner persuaded the French farmers to give him cuttings of their hybrid grapes. Upon his return home to Riderwood, he tried these cuttings, which, proved ideal for the Maryland climate. Being successful with this, he opened a winery and also sold the French hybrids to other vintners across the country. Wagner's Boordy Vineyards became acclaimed throughout the country for its outstanding wines. Looking for more land on which to plant, Wagner asked his friends, the Defords, to plant grapes on their Long Green Farm in Hydes. In 1980, upon Wagner's retirement, Boordy Vineyards was purchased by the Defords. Today, Boordy Vineyards remains in the hands of the Defords, who also use a number of farms in different regions of Maryland. By using different regions, they are able to stagger the harvests. From all sources, Boordy produces eighteen thousand gallons of wine a year. They make five white, three rose, and three red wines. For several occasions Boordy has won the top prize for its various wines. Tours and wine tastings are available throughout the year.

<u>Woodhall Vineyards and Wine Cellars</u> are located at 15115 Wheeler Lane in Sparks. Available here are wine tastings and tours of the vineyard and winery. They are open Saturdays and Sundays from 10:00 a.m. to 5:00 p.m., and by appointment.

Old Baltimore County had many wealthy and famous families. The Carrolls owned Doughoregan Estate, now in Howard County, as well as Homewood, where Johns Hopkins University now stands. The Eager family had large estates in this area, one being the Belvedere Estate, now a part of Baltimore City. John Eager Howard inherited this through his mother, as well as other land from his father's family. These estates were the centers of culture, and social life centered on them. Today, fox hunting and horse racing are still part of the enthusiasm characteristic of early colonial times.

Form of Government: Charter (1956)

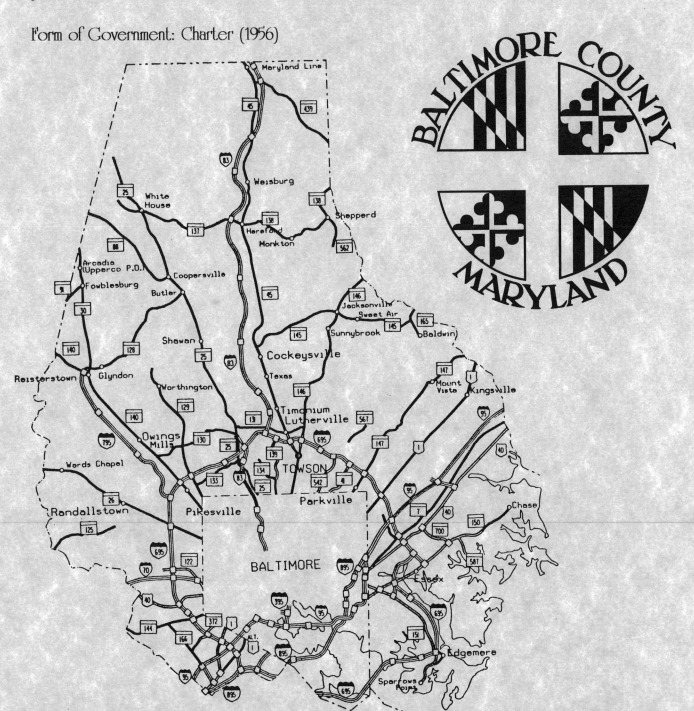

CALVERT COUNTY

Calvert County was established by an Order in Council of 1654, the fourth county to be built, and called Patuxent County until 1658. The County name derives from the family name of the proprietary, the founding family.

The Seal was designed and adopted as the official Calvert County seal in 1954. It shows a Tobacco Leaf, Calvert's leading product; a Horn of Plenty symbolizing fertility and hospitality of Calvert County; an Oyster Shell portrays the bountifulness of Calvert's Seafood Industry and Rope and Anchors which symbolizes the nautical tradition of our forefathers which continues to be perpetuated today.

Calvert is the smallest of the Maryland counties, with a total land and water square area of two hundred forty-four miles. Located on the western shore of the Chesapeake Bay, it is a peninsula approximately thirty-five miles long with a width of nine miles. Its western boundary is the Patuxent River, and its only land contact is Anne Arundel County to the north. Almost surrounded by water, Calvert County is an upland plain with its majority being one hundred twenty-feet above sea level.

Settled by English colonists and their Negro slaves, it had a population of 8,652 in 1790, and one hundred seventy years later in 1960, it had only grown to a population of 15,826. By 1990, the population was 51,372. By 1994, the population grew to 62,179, an increase of 21% since 1990. In 1998, the population rose to 70,570, and by the year 2000, the population is projected to rise to 75,000.

Tobacco was grown in colonial times, almost to the exclusion of food crops. As a result, an early enactment of the colonial legislature required that two acres of corn be planted for every person in each family for sustenance. Today, tobacco is still the chief money crop raising almost 20 percent of Maryland's total tobacco production, although it is by far the smallest of the five tobacco producing counties (Anne Arundel, Calvert, Charles, Prince George's and St. Mary's). Besides tobacco, corn, barley, wheat, soybeans, oats and rye are raised. For example, in the 1960s, Calvert County farmed 7,273 acres of land, producing 6,849,893 pounds of tobacco. In contrast, Anne Arundel County farmed 6,353 acres, producing 6,466,703 pounds; Charles County farmed 8,198 acres, producing 7,709,099 pounds; Prince George's 7,893 acres, producing 7,139,276 pounds and St. Mary's 7,437 acres, producing 7,400,906 pounds.

Calvert's leading industries are boat building and oyster packing, while fishing, oystering, and forestry are important activities. It ranks fifth in the State in sales of forest products.

In Calvert County there are three old churches of historic interest: <u>All Saints</u>, located on Routes 2 and 4 in Sunderland. This Flemish bond brick structure, founded in 1692 and built in 1775, replaced the first church built in 1700, which burned in 1775; <u>Christ Church</u>, located on Broomes Island Road (Rt.264) dates from 1672. The present structure was built in 1772 and remodeled in 1906. The church features a garden of biblical plants and a one-room schoolhouse; <u>St. Peter's Church</u>, located in Soloman's, is a typical fisherman's chapel of board and batten, dating from 1872. <u>Middleham Chapel</u>, located on Route 4 in Lusby. This is the oldest cruciform-designed church in Maryland. Founded in 1684, as a Chapel of Ease in Christ Church Parish and named for Middleham, Yorkshire, England. This site has been used for worship since the founding, and the present building was rebuilt in 1748. The Bell, given by John Holdsworth, is dated 1699.

Middleham Chapel

Calvert County is the home of the oldest structure of its type on the Chesapeake Bay, the Old Cove Point Lighthouse. This brick tower lighthouse has been in continuous service since 1828. Two other famous old houses are the Charlesgift (1651) and the Taney Place (1682).

Solomons Island, at the southern tip of the county, is a most interesting place, established in 1867. Originally called Bourne's in 1680, then Somervell's Island in 1740, it became known as Solomon's Island in 1867, because of Isaac Solomon's oyster packing facilities located here, and shipyards were developed to support the island's fishing fleet. The famed "Bugeye" sailing craft were built here in the nineteenth century. The deep, protected harbor has been a busy marine center ever since. During the War of 1812, Commodore Joshua Barney's flotilla sailed from here to attack the British vessels on the Chesapeake Bay. The causeway that connects the island with the mainland was built in 1870. Here on the island is located the Chesapeake Biological Laboratory. At this laboratory they make scientific studies of fisheries, game, forestry and other related biological problems. On the Patuxent side of Solomon's Island is a two mile-wide harbor, having a depth of more than one hundred feet.

Other places of interest in Calvert County are: Calvert Cliffs Nuclear Power Plant Visitors Center: Located on Route 4 South, ten miles south of Prince Frederick. Visitors can take a walk through the ages, from the wooly mammoths of years ago to the technology of the twentieth century. Calvert Marine Museum and Lighthouse: Located in Solomons, visitors can explore the wonders of the Bay through fascinating fossil exhibits, the "Estuarium" and maritime history. Special attractions at the museum include the Wm. B. Tennison, the oldest Coast Guard licensed passenger-carrying vessel on the Chesapeake Bay. Built in 1899, this nine-log chunk-built bugeye served as an oyster buyboat until 1978. The Drum Point Lighthouse, located just east of the museum is one of only three remaining screwpile lights which served on the Chesapeake Bay at the turn of the century. This cottage-style, hexagonal lighthouse has been restored to its original appearance. This lighthouse marked the entrance to the Patuxent River from 1883 until 1962. Located south of the museum is the J.C. Lore Oyster House, where visitors can learn about the region's commercial seafood industries, and touch the tools and gear used by local watermen to harvest fish, soft-shelled clams, eels, crabs and oysters.

Chesapeake Beach Railroad Museum: Located on Route 260 in Chesapeake Beach, it is here that visitors can relive the golden days of the Chesapeake Beach resort of the early 1900s, and learn about the railway that made it possible; <u>One-Room Schoolhouse:</u> Located in Port Republic, this authentically restored one-room schoolhouse is filled with memorabilia of school days gone by.

<u>Oyster Fleet:</u> Visitors get a close-up look at working oyster, crab, and fishing boats at Broomes Island, Chesapeake Beach and Solomons Island; <u>Battle Creek Cypress Swamp Sanctuary:</u> Located in Prince Frederick, this is the northernmost naturally occurring Cypress Swamp in America, containing giant bald cypress trees, wildflowers, wildlife, and indoor exhibits.

<u>Calvert Cliffs:</u> Features thirty miles of towering fossil-embedded cliffs that rise hundreds of feet above the Chesapeake Bay; <u>Calvert Cliffs State Park:</u> on Route 4 South, fourteen miles south of Prince Frederick, this 1460-acre wooded park has facilities for fishing, camping, and picnicking.

<u>Jefferson Patterson Park and Museum:</u> Located at 10515 Mackall Road in St. Leonard, this 512-acre cultural and environmental preserve is listed on the National Register of Historic Places. The Park and Museum were created through a gift from Mrs. Jefferson Patterson to the State of Maryland in 1983. It is the largest historic property ever given to the state. Visitors can walk the Nature Trail as well as the Archaeology Trail. During the months of June through August, visitors can watch the ongoing excavation of artifacts from 7500 BC to the nineteenth century AD.

<u>Flag Ponds Nature Park:</u> Located on Route 4, ten miles south of Prince Frederick. At Flag Ponds, the natural wonders of the Chesapeake Bay are preserved in this 327-acre park. It offers three miles of hiking trails, observation platforms overlooking two ponds, a wetlands boardwalk, a beach and fishing pier on the Chesapeake Bay, and a visitor's center with wildlife exhibits. From the early 1900s until 1955, this area was a sheltered harbor on the Chesapeake Bay. It featured a "pound net" fishery supplying croaker, trout and herring to Baltimore's markets. Today the only remaining structure of the Flag Ponds fishing complex is "Buoy Hotel Number Two," which houses an attractive exhibit on the bay's old-time fishing industry. Within the park visitors will discover quite a variety of wildlife. These include, muskrat, otter, whitetail deer, turkey, fox, and the pileated woodpecker. The flora varies from hardwood trees to the native Blue Flag (iris) from which Flag Ponds Nature Park got its name.

Major areas in Calvert County include: Dunkirk, Owings, North Beach, Chesapeake Beach, Huntingtown, Prince Frederick, Port Republic, Broomes Island, St. Leonard, Sunderland, Lusby, Lower Marlboro, and Solomons.

Calvert County is a very interesting and beautiful place and continues to retain its old-time charm of an unspoiled rural area.

Form of Government: County Commissioners

Map of Calvert County

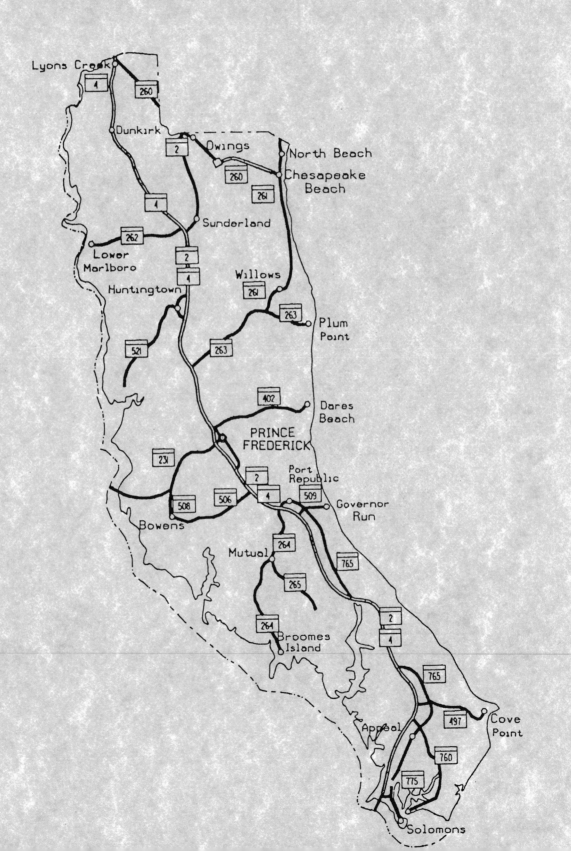

CAROLINE COUNTY

Caroline County was created in 1773 from Dorchester and Queen Anne's counties. (chapter 10, Acts of 1773). The county's name is derived from Caroline Eden, daughter of Charles Calvert, Fifth Lord Baltimore, and the wife of Sir Robert Eden, Maryland's last colonial governor.

The Great Seal of Caroline County was discovered in the Maryland State Archives as a seal that was used on county legal documents by the Clerk of the Court in Denton from c.1814 to 1856.

The Great Seal features parts of the Calvert coat of arms assigned to George Calvert of Yorkshire, England. The belt around the Caroline County Seal is a recent adornment added by an Annapolis genealogist and heraldic researcher in 1953. The scroll and motto in Latin, "Terra Dulcis Vivendum" means "Land of Pleasant Living," representative of Caroline County's welcome to all. The "Land of Pleasant Living" phrase was developed by the late Arthur Deute, who made Maryland and Baltimore City his adoptive home upon his purchasing the National Brewing Company.

The six vertical pieces (or pales) of the seal, into which the Calvert Shield is divided, represent palings or palisades, and constitute the heraldic symbol of a stockade or fort, which would be appropriate to one who had fortified a town or successfully stormed a hostile fort. The diagonal band, or bend, was held to represent either a swordbelt or a scaling ladder. The crown above the shield is an earl's coronet. The Lords of Baltimore could use the earl's coronet only in relation to their American colony, which according to their charter had the rank of a county palatine. The rank of county palatine is equivalent to that of an earl. The full-face position of the helmet above the earl's coronet symbolizes the exercise of government by an absolute ruler over a free state or country. Above the helmet is a ducal coronet from which rises two spears or lances with pennons attached. The pennons display the Calvert colors, gold and black.

The Caroline County Great Seal was officially adopted by the Caroline County Commissioners on July 3, 1984. The flag of Caroline County is composed of the county seal on a medium green background, symbolizing Caroline County's heritage and future in agriculture.

Caroline is the only county on the Eastern Shore that is not bordered by either the Chesapeake Bay or the Atlantic Ocean. With a land area of three hundred twenty miles, it's bordered on the east by the State of Delaware, and on the west and northwest respectively by Talbot and Queen Anne's counties, and on the south by Dorchester County.

Its surface is level with rolling hills but there are also steep slopes bordering some of the largest streams, especially along the Choptank River, the largest Eastern Shore stream which flows through the center of Caroline County, and along the Marshyhope Creek. Caroline's boundaries were not decided until 1760 because of the confusion regarding the Maryland-Delaware border, which was established in 1773.

Denton, the county seat, was named for Sir Robert Eden and was formerly called Eden-Town in honor of him. Eden was the last colonial governor and was an ancestor of Sir Anthony Eden, former prime minister of Britain. The name was later changed to Edenton and then shortened to Denton.

The first settlers were English, many of whom were religious refugees. Others were Quakers from Virginia and New England, attracted by the Toleration Act of 1649. Most of the early settlements were built along side streams which were easy to navigate.

In 1790, Caroline County had a population of 9,506, ranked eighteenth among Maryland counties. By 1910, the population rose to 19,210; but only to 19,462 by 1960. By 1990 the population was 27,035 and in 1994 rose to 28,720, an increase of 6.2% from 1990. In 1998, the population is 29,920, and by the year 2000, it is projected to be 30,600.

Although Denton, with a population of approximately 1800 is the county seat, the largest city is Federalsburg, with a population of 2,050. Federalsburg was founded in 1789, under the name Northwest Fork Bridge. In 1812, the Federalist Party met there, thus its name was changed. Prior to the Civil War the town was known for its boat building, and an old tavern there was the center for slave trading.

Other towns include: <u>Greensboro</u>, which is one of the oldest towns on the Eastern Shore, having been settled in 1732. It was originally named Bridgetown, in honor of the first bridge to cross the Choptank River, and then changed to Head of Choptank, then Choptank Bridge, to finally Greensboro in 1791. <u>Ridgely</u>, was named after Rev. Greenbury W. Ridgely who convinced the railroad to build there in the 1800s. <u>Goldsboro</u>, was named after Dr. G.W. Goldsborough, a popular land owner. The town was originally named Oldtown, until 1867 when the Delaware & Chesapeake Railroad arrived and the townspeople wanted a modern name, changing it to Goldsboro. <u>Marydel</u>, located on the Maryland and Delaware borders, used the combination of the two states names for its name. Originally named Halltown after William Hall, the name was changed in 1853; and <u>Hillsboro</u>, named after a relative of the Lords Baltimore, Lord Hillsboro. Located across Tuckahoe Creek from Queen Anne's County, Hillsboro was once the home of the famous Maryland artist Charles Wilson Peale.

Once a chief tobacco grower, Caroline County's main industry today is poultry and poultry products, as well as dairy production.

In earlier days, the chief transportation was by boat on the many streams. Today, the Pennsylvania Railroad has two branch lines which cross the county, and five State Highways provide the chief transportation, for both travelers and transport.

The oldest grist mill in the United States, called Linchester Mill, is located near the town of Preston on Hunting Creek. It began its operation in 1681. During the Revolutionary War it was known as Murray's Mill, supplying provisions for the Continental Army. George Washington, in 1777 received corn meal, flour, meat and molasses from Linchester via schooner to the head of the Elk River, and overland to Valley Forge. In 1962, the Maryland Historical Society placed a marker at the site commemorating the old mill and its history.

Other old buildings of historical interest are: <u>Daffin House</u> (1710); <u>Castle Hall</u> (1781); <u>Oak Lawn</u> (1783) and <u>Patty Cannon House</u>, built in the early nineteenth century but rebuilt in 1885.

<u>The Neck Meeting House</u>: In 1798, Quakers living near Denton asked the Third Haven Meeting House for the entitlement of holding preparatory meetings and building a Meeting House. On May 8, 1804 their request was granted. One and one-half-acres of

land was purchased in Tuckahoe Neck from William Wilson, from land called Controversy. Upon paying the sum of four pounds, ten shillings, the deed was delivered to the trustees of the Neck Meeting House. They were: Samuel Troth, Solomon Kenton, James Wilson, John Dawson, William Emmerson and Trustam Needles.

This religious order dates back to earlier times when these people referred to themselves as "Nicholites," following the strict teachings of Joseph Nichols. It was Nichols who began to form his beliefs and hold meetings in Maryland's Eastern Shore and Delaware in the 1760s. In 1797, these "Nicholites" began to join the Quaker religion.

The Neck Meeting House has a long history. In addition to being used as a Meeting House, it was used as a private school by Miss Eliza Heacock of Philadelphia in 1856. More recently, a well-known teacher from Denton, Miss Rachel B. Satterwaite also used the Meeting House for a school. Just prior to the outbreak of the Civil War in 1861, the Meeting House was used for abolitionist meetings with speakers of national fame. During the Civil War, Union troops made camp in and around the building. Interestingly, on Sunday mornings, the Union troops withdrew, allowing the Friends to hold their meetings as usual.

In 1890, the Neck Meeting House was closed as a place of worship for lack of funds. At this time, Edward Tylor, the half brother to the teacher Miss Satterwaite, secured legislation to purchase the land and protect the spot where his parents lie buried by erecting an iron grate. Upon his death in 1916, the Meeting House became the property of Edward Scott Tylor. In 1928, it was purchased by Wilson M. Tylor and sold again in 1929 to Elizabeth White Dixon. Through the efforts of Mrs. Dixon and Wilson M. Tylor, a fund was established for perpetual care of the Meeting House. As a result the crumbling Meeting House was partially restored, painted, and new benches were installed. Following the death of Mrs. Dixon, the grounds became overgrown and the house abandoned. In 1949, the property was purchased by the Choptank Electric Cooperative, from the heirs of Mrs. Dixon. It was sold with the explicit agreement that the graves be maintained. The Cooperative cleared the overgrown brush and whitewashed the building. Through the help of several individuals and the Historical Society, the building survives today.

Caroline County is the home of two of Maryland's State Parks. Martinak Park, located in Denton off Route 404, was opened to the public in 1964. The park derives its name from George Martinak, who deeded the land to the State of Maryland in 1961. Mr. Martinak wanted the location preserved as a recreational facility for those who enjoyed its natural beauty, just as he had. History has revealed that there once was a Native American village located down the river from the park. The inhabitants belonged to the Algonquian Nation, who were hunters, farmers, and fishermen. On display in the park nature center is a section of a wooden work boat, believed to be a pungy, retrieved from Watts Creek. Vessels such as the pungy were instrumental in the development of the Choptank River area. Features of the park include camping, whereby sixty campsites are available for tent or trailer camping, as well as picnic areas, fishing and boating. A cabin which can accommodate up to four persons is available for year round rental.

The second park in Caroline County is <u>Tuckahoe State Park</u>, located seven miles west of Denton. Land acquisition began in 1962 and has continued since. The park now spans an area of about 3500 acres. Tuckahoe Creek, which runs the length of the park, forms the dividing line between Caroline and Queen Anne's Counties. In the park are four camping sites, each accommodating up to twenty-five persons. Featured are fishing, boating, and picnicking. There are three miles of surfaced walkways as well as other trails. These include Piney Branch Trail, the Overcup Oak Self-Guided Nature Trail, the Physical Fitness Trail and the Lake Trail. Hunting is allowed in certain designated areas only. Generally, although exceptions exist, the hunting season runs from October 15th through February 15th.

Caroline County's incorporated towns are: Denton, Federalsburg, Preston, Greensboro, Ridgely, Hillsboro, Goldsboro, Marydel, Henderson and Templeville.

Caroline County is a beautiful, rural area of the state. For natural beauty, boating, fishing, and camping, Caroline County is the place to visit.

Form of Government: Code Home Rule

Map and Great Seal of Caroline County

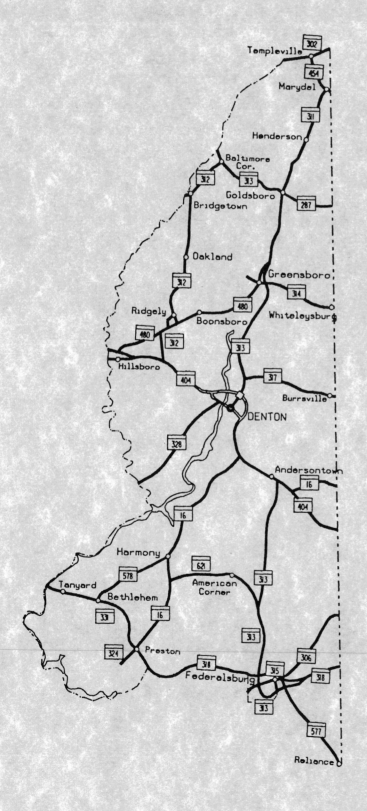

CARROLL COUNTY

The land comprising Carroll County was originally part of Baltimore County, created by the proprietary government in 1659. Carroll County was created from Baltimore and Frederick Counties by an Act of the Maryland Legislature, Chapter 256, Acts of 1835, confirmed by Chapter 19, Acts of 1836 on March 25, which was passed January 19, 1837. The County was named for Charles Carroll of Carrollton (1737-1832). Carroll was a Marylander who was the last surviving signer of the Declaration of Independence, dying in 1832 at the age of 95.

The Carroll County Seal was provided for in the minutes of the Commissioners of Tax for Carroll County on June 5, 1837, and became the county's official seal on July 1, 1977. The seal consists of "three concentric circles, with the inscription 'Carroll County Maryland' inserted between the inner and middle circles also having two stylized six-leaved blossoms located, one each, on opposite sides of the same space between the inner and middle circle, also within the inner circle is a replica of the four-horse freight wagon with the year 1837 imposed above the wagon." When legislation was enacted effective July 1, 1977, there was no mention of colors for the seal, although the colors used are red, white, blue and brown.

Carroll County is bordered by the State of Pennsylvania to the north, and the south by Howard County. To the west is Frederick County, and to the east Baltimore County. Its size is four hundred fifty-three square miles, and extends twenty-seven miles in both width and length at its greatest dimension.

The county's topography is hilly, dissected by streams flowing through narrow valleys. Two elevations known as Dug Hill and Parr's Ridge, extending northeast and southwest, make up the "backbone" of the county. These form a divide between the streams. Streams to the east of the ridges flow in a southeastward direction, while those on the other side flow southwest. The elevations range from three hundred to one thousand feet above sea level. The first settlers were English Quakers, followed by Germans from Pennsylvania, other English from the Annapolis area, and Scotch-Irish from the Tidewater region of Maryland and Pennsylvania.

In 1960 the population of Carroll County was 52,785, growing to 69,006 in the '70s. By 1990 the population was 123,372. By 1994, the population increased by 10.6% to 136,443. In 1998, the population rose to 145,300, and by the year 2000, it is projected to be 149,300.

The largest city is Westminster, the county seat, although not incorporated until 1838. Other incorporated towns are: Taneytown, Sykesville, Manchester, Uniontown, Union Bridge, New Windsor, Hampstead, and Mt. Airy, which encompasses both Carroll and Frederick counties. The original town of Westminster was comprised of about one hundred acres known as White's Level. It was bought by Englishman William Winchester in 1754 for 150 Pounds sterling, or about $4.50 per acre. When William Winchester officially registered the town, he picked the name "Westminster" after his English birthplace. At times, among the local people, the town was referred to as "Winchester's Town," but officially was always Westminster. With the creation of Carroll County in 1837, Westminster was the logical choice for the county seat due to its central location.

Westminster quickly became a trading center, serving the needs of local farmers and within a short time was an overnight stop for those carrying wagon loads of goods from Central Pennsylvania to the Port of Baltimore. The principal industry was tanning, joined by a variety of merchants and craftspeople. During the War of 1812, banks began appearing, when Baltimore's bankers fled to the safety of rural Carroll County. One of the bankers, who stayed in Westminster, offered Maryland rye whiskey with each transaction, in an attempt to gain customers. Westminster at one time had seven hotels, which catered to the travelers heading west from Baltimore.

Historical sites in Westminster include: City Hall, which was built by Colonel John K. Longwell in 1842. Originally called "Emerald Hill," this mansion was the residence of Longwell who was a key figure in the history of both Westminster and Carroll County. The city purchased this building in 1939. The Carroll County Courthouse, built in 1838 is still in use and is considered "one of the most beautiful in the United States," by the American Bar Association. Located on Court Street, the courthouse originally cost $18,000 to build. Across the street from the courthouse is the Ascension Episcopal Church, built in 1844.

Western Maryland College, was chartered in 1866, and began in 1868 under the jurisdiction of the Methodist-Protestant Church. It was the first co-educational institution of higher learning south of the Mason-Dixon Line.

The Carroll County Farm Museum, was initially the County Almshouse, in use from 1852 to 1965. The museum today depicts late nineteenth century rural life.

The Historical Society of Carroll County, is located at 206 and 210 East Main Street. The society occupies the buildings known as the Sherman-Fisher-Shellman and Kimmey Houses. These buildings were the homes of several leading citizens of Westminster. The society is nationally famous for its doll collection and research library.

Westminster During The Civil War: After more than 130 years, The Civil War, or the War Between the States as it is known in the South, remains a defining event in American History. Maryland's close proximity to the Federal and Confederate capitals made battles on her soil inevitable. Confederate and Union troops passed through Westminster during the three major Maryland campaigns, and on one occasion, blue and grey cavalrymen clashed on Main Street. During each visit local residents often had an opportunity to see a family member, friend or an acquaintance who was serving in one of the opposing armies.

Confederate soldiers occupied Westminster during General Robert E. Lee's first Northern invasion in the fall of 1862. Cavalrymen led by Colonel Thomas Lafayette Rosser rode into town on the evening of September 11th and quickly established picket posts to prevent word of their arrival from reaching the Federal authorities. Their visit generated considerable excitement and anxiety, however, the troopers were well behaved and generally respected private property and the citizenry. The meeting place of the Carroll Guards, a prewar militia organization, did not fare as well. Cavalrymen demanded the keys to the Odd Fellows Hall (140 E. Main Street) and, according to a New York newspaper article. "destroyed the framed muster roll of the Carroll Guard, which was hanging on the wall of the Armory, broke all the lamps, carried off a drum and a United States flag which had been put up in front of the hall." The soldiers also destroyed the enrollment books for the anticipated draft, much to the delight of Southern sympathizers. Colonel Rosser spent the night in the home of John Brooke Boyle (79 W. Main Street) while his troopers bivouacked on a pasture near the center of town.

The Confederates left in the morning and were later engaged in the severe battle along Antietam Creek near Sharpsburg, Maryland, on September 17th. Undaunted by this unsuccessful Antietam Campaign, Lee launched a second invasion in the early summer of 1863. A small detachment of Union cavalrymen, approximately one hundred members of Companies C and D of the 1st Delaware Cavalry, entered Westminster on the morning of June 28. Their mission was to guard the important rail and road junction at Westminster. On the following afternoon news of an approaching force of Confederates reached town. These men turned out to be more than five thousand cavalrymen under the command of General J.E.B. Stuart. The Delaware cavalrymen under the command of Captain Charles Corbit gallantly attacked the head of the Confederate column as it entered the western edge of town from the Washington Road (Route 32). Although repulsed at first, the Confederates quickly overwhelmed Corbit and his men. The brief skirmish left two Confederate officers and two Federal enlisted men dead; Captain Corbit and the majority of his command were prisoners of war. The body of Confederate Lieutenant John W. Murray still rests in the small cemetery behind the Ascension Episcopal Church where he was buried along with the other casualties.

General Stuart and his cavalrymen remained in Westminster overnight and departed on June 30th. The Confederates fought another skirmish at Hanover, Pennsylvania, and eventually arrived at Gettysburg on July 2 at the height of the battle. Union troops of the Sixth Corps under the command of General John Sedgwick occupied the town shortly after the Confederates left. Union forces secured the strategic railroad and made Westminster a supply center during the Gettysburg Campaign. At the time of the battle there were approximately ten thousand Union soldiers, five thousand army wagons and thirty thousand mules in Westminster. A letter written by an Ohio man to his family described the Union occupation: "The teamsters' aides and stragglers are the very dregs of the army. One went to Sister Anna and demanded the key to her stable, took her fine horse, Stonewall Jackson. The match, Jeff Davis, was fortunately out of reach and is safe. The fine meadow (now the site of the American Legion Carroll Post 31), only separated by an alley from her garden, unmowned, had one hundred horses on it."

In the aftermath of the battle thousands of wounded and Confederate prisoners were entrained in Baltimore. Among the wounded were Union General Winfield Scott Hancock and General John Gibbon. General Hancock, who had commanded the 2nd Corps, had been severely wounded in the thigh. General Gibbon, who had initially commanded the 2nd Corps, also received a severe wound.

Both men were in Westminster on July 4th. Ironically, General Gibbon was cared for at the home of his wife's aunt, Mrs. Abner Neal (71 E. Main Street). Mrs. Neal was a southern sympathizer who had two sons in the Confederate army. The brothers, Harry and Frank Neal, had been arrested as Southern supporters on August 28, 1862, and upon release had joined the Confederates. Attached to Stuart's cavalry, they visited their mother following the cavalry skirmish on June 29, 1863.

The third and final occupation of Westminster by Confederate forces took place in July 1864. Confederates under the command of General Jubal Early had moved toward Baltimore and Washington, D.C., in an effort to relieve pressure on Lee's forces in Virginia. The Confederates defeated a Union force at Monocacy Bridge near Frederick, Maryland, on July 9th. Early immediately dispatched General Bradley T. Johnson to cut communications between Baltimore and Philadelphia. Colonel Harry Gilmore, a member of Johnson's command, led a force of Confederates into Westminster on the evening of July 9th. Several hours after their arrival a courier brought orders from General Johnson for Colonel Gilmore to secure 1,500 suits of clothes from the city.

Colonel Gilmore had established his headquarters in the home of Mrs. Katherine Shellman (206 E. Main Street). Her daughter Mary later recalled that Westminster was "threatened with destruction" if the city failed to supply the demanded clothing. Mayor Jacob Grove apparently could not locate enough city councilmen to discuss the matter but the Confederates dropped their demand. According to Miss Shellman, Colonel Gilmore and General Early decided the fate of the city while enjoying a bottle of whiskey "raided" from a local distillery. The Confederates soon departed; Westminster remained well within the Union territory for the remainder of the war.

While Westminster fortunately bears no scars from the war, the conflict left its mark on the community. The home where Colonel Rosser stayed in 1862 is known as Rosser's Choice Apartments. A historical marker at the intersection of East Main Street and Washington Road marks the site of Corbit's charge. The home where Colonel Gilmore and General Johnson met has been restored as a house museum administered by the Historical Society of Carroll County. The history of this most turbulent period in American and local history still evokes great interest and strong emotions more than a century later.

The area known today as Taneytown, was once the area on which the Tuscarora Indians hunted deer, otter, wolves and wildcats, which were once quite abundant. Such local names as Otterdale, Bear Branch, Beaver Dam and Monocacy bear witness to this early heritage.

At the outbreak of the Revolutionary War, Taneytown was an established community on part of a sixty acre plot commonly known as "Maryland's backwoods." Technically, this land was recorded as "Brothers Agreement." Original title to this land was issued to John Diggs on April 14, 1744. Records indicate 1754 as the date of one of the area's first land grants, when 7,900 acres were granted to Edward Diggs and Raphael Taney under a patent designated as the Resurvey of Brothers Agreement. As a result, lots were laid out and the first deeds were registered in 1762. Raphael Taney, who at this time lived in St. Mary's County, laid out the town and gave it its name, although there is no evidence that he ever lived here. A popular misconception is that the town was named for Roger Brooke Taney, a U.S. Supreme Court Chief Justice. Although Judge Taney was an ancestor of Raphael Taney, he was not born until 1777.

In these early years there were many disputes over the boundary lines between Maryland and Pennsylvania. One tragedy rising from these disputes was the fatal shooting of Dudley Diggs, brother of Edward and son of John Diggs. These disputes continued until finally, two experienced surveyors, Charles Mason and Jeremiah Dixon were sent from London to America. The result of their work is known today as the Mason-Dixon Line.

Sykesville, is named after James Sykes, originally of Baltimore, who in 1825 bought one thousand acres of land from his business associate, George Patterson. One tract of this land was on the south side of the Patapsco River and contained an old combination saw and grist mill. James Sykes replaced it with a newer and stronger building and constructed a five story hotel to accommodate the tourist trade from Baltimore. Soon thereafter the Baltimore & Ohio Railroad extended its "Old Main Line" through Sykesville in 1831.

Other additions and improvements soon followed. In 1865, Dr. Orrelana H. Owings built a large two story stone store on Main Street for his son-in-law, Harry Miller. Today this old stone store is St. Barnabas Episcopal Parish House. Overlooking the town, on a hill was built St. Joseph's Catholic Church. It was from this location that townspeople watched in horror as the lower portion of Sykesville was swept away by the raging Patapsco in the great flood of 1868. In 1883, the B & O Railroad Station was built on the eastside of Main Street along the Patapsco River. This Queen Anne structure designed by E. Francis Baldwin, became the property of the town in 1988.

St. Paul's United Methodist Church, which was originally built on the Howard County side of the Patapsco River was moved to Sykesville in 1889. This white, weatherboard church with stained windows faces Main Street. In 1890, J.H. Fowble, an architect and contracting builder came to Sykesville. It was Mr. Fowble who was responsible for the designing and building of most of downtown Sykesville, such as; the McDonald block, two brick bank buildings, the Wade H.D. Warfield building, the Arcade, and Kate McDonald's home on Main Street, which is the present Sykesville Town House.

The town of Manchester was laid out by Richard Richards and began in 1760, through the compatible efforts of persons from English and German cultures. This beginning is indicated by the English name of the town and by the old tombstones in the cemetery inscribed in German. Manchester developed through the atmosphere of local pride and cooperation. This allegiance is evident today through such enterprises as the volunteer fire department, the community swimming pool and "Christmas Tree Park." At one time, north of Manchester near Melrose, an iron mine opened. This mine had such promise that a railroad line was built to the site. Over the years, the mine proved unprofitable, and soon the mine and rail line disappeared. The town managed to stay in existence through its agricultural trade. Tobacco was once a major crop, and Manchester was once the home of an extensive cigar manufacturing business. One of the attractions in the town is the large White Oak Tree, the symbol of Manchester.

Uniontown, which dates back to the eighteenth century is the second oldest town in Carroll County. It is located on a tract of land once known as "The Orchard," which was granted to an Englishman named Thomas Metcalf on April 6, 1799. In 1802, Metcalf deeded the remaining land not sold on the north side to Erhart Cover, who had the land laid out in lots by a local surveyor named John Hyder on May 27, 1824.

Uniontown's original name was "The Forks," named for the Buffalo Road and Hagerstown Pike that came together at the western section of the town. Upon Carroll County being formed from parts of Frederick and Baltimore Counties, "The Forks" changed its name to Uniontown, hoping this new name would lead to it becoming the county seat. But this did not happen, as Westminster was made the county seat due to its central location.

Prior to the Civil War Uniontown was once prosperous, having several taverns, a hotel, and many shops including; a millinery shop, tin shop, printing shop, blacksmith shop, newspaper, tannery and a post office. But this prosperity did not last as the Western

Maryland Railroad came to Carroll County, but bypassed Uniontown. As a result, many townspeople as well as those living nearby were forced to go to railroad towns to transact business formerly done in Uniontown.

Today, the oldest section of Uniontown has several large brick homes built in the early 1800s. These homes were once the taverns and hotel, and are in a good state of preservation. Located at the west side of town, they are occupied today by private citizens. Also featured is a unique bank, a one-room schoolhouse, and a continuously opened general store.

Uniontown's post office, established in 1885, was one of the offices along the mail route from Baltimore to Hagerstown, then on to Pittsburgh. This office became the distribution point for other small mail routes in surrounding towns and villages in the county.

The town was also quite active during war time. During the War of 1812, a meadow located in back of Main Street was used as a drilling ground for the militia. On June 29, 1863, during the Civil War, the 2nd Corps of the Union Army occupied Uniontown on its march to Gettysburg. At this time, General Winfield Hancock occupied the residence of the town's doctor, J.J. Weaver. This house today remains in good condition.

Uniontown remains the quaint, peaceful village it always was, with few changes since the nineteenth century. In 1970, the Uniontown Historic District was created and is one of the few entire towns to be listed on the National Historic Register.

Another of Carroll County's interesting towns is Union Bridge. The town received its name from two settlements, located on both sides of Little Pipe Creek. The townspeople from both settlements decided to build a bridge, connecting the two villages to form one. When deciding on a name, they chose Union Bridge, identifying the merger for their united effort. The town was originally settled prior to the Revolutionary War by the Farquhars from Pennsylvania, and chartered by the Maryland General Assembly on May 2, 1872. The glorious shade trees which line the streets today are offspring from two sugar maples originally brought from Brownsville, Pennsylvania by Mrs. Elizabeth Farquhar Wright. Union Bridge has grown slowly over the years, maintaining its quiet charm of yester years.

Several inventions have come from Union Bridge; they include the world's first reaping machine, designed and assembled by Jacob R. Thomas in 1811. The site where this reaping machine was first assembled is now occupied by the Farmers and Mechanics Bank. Another is the "knuckle," a railroad coupler invented because of a need of the Western Maryland Railroad.

Union Bridge is also the birthplace of one of the country's preeminent sculptors, William Rinehart. William Henry Rinehart (September 13, 1825-October 28, 1874) was born on a small farm near Union Bridge. William was the fifth of eight sons born to Israel and Mary (Snader) Rinehart, whose family had established themselves as farmers. William's schooling included "Quaker Hill" near Union Bridge which at this time was a log school, then "Priestland" near Linwood, and finally at Calvert College, a New Windsor high school.

At the age of twenty-one he became an apprentice to Baughman & Bevan, the largest stone-cutters in Baltimore. Within two years he was a foreman, with a studio of his own, and soon accepted private commissions. To supplement his practical training he took night courses at the Maryland Institute. In 1851, he received a gold medal from the institute for a copy in stone of Teniers' "Smokers."

The earliest publicly exhibited work (1853) was a bust of the Reverend Dr. John G. Morris, and a reclining figure, "Faith." In 1855, Rinehart traveled to Rome where he remained for a short time, and while there executed two bas-reliefs, "Night" and "Day." Upon his return to Baltimore, he opened a studio and received orders for several works including the fountain for the old Post Office in Washington, D.C., and figures of an "Indian" and a "Backwoodsman," which once supported the clock of the House of Representatives.

Other famous works include the Bronze Doors of the main entrance to the Rotunda, East Front of the United States Capitol, as well as the Bronze Doors to the House and Senate wings, also in the United States Capitol.

One of his most famous sculptures located in Maryland is the seated portrait of Chief Justice Roger Brooke Taney, in Annapolis, as well as a replica of this sculpture in Mount Vernon Square, Baltimore. Many other of Mr. Rinehart's works can be seen at the Peabody Institute, which houses an extensive collection, and the Metropolitan Museum of Art in New York as well as the Corcoran Gallery of Art in Washington, D.C. At the east side of Union Bridge is a sign which designates Mr. Rinehart's birthplace.

Union Bridge is also the home of Hard Lodging, built in the first decade of the nineteenth century, and today is the property of the Historical Society of Carroll County. At 41 N. Main Street, also in Union Bridge, is the Western Maryland Railroad Museum, located in a completely restored Victorian train station. Also here is the EnterTRAINment Line, where visitors may ride on special excursions in vintage cars. Dinner and dancing trips are featured on weekends; and the Old Pipe Creek Friends Meetinghouse, which overlooks Union Bridge. This Quaker church was built in 1772, and is still in use.

New Windsor, located on Route 31, was first known for its Sulphur Springs baths (1790), Dielman Inn (1864) originally called Atlee's Tavern, and a church sponsored college (1846). Today the springs of years ago have lost their charm, and the college, after undergoing changes in sponsorship under different religions, finally moved into a merger with a Virginia institution. The original campus and buildings today are the home of the New Windsor Service Center and International Gift Shop. The name, "New Windsor, USA," is known throughout the world because of relief and response efforts. Many forms of worldwide assistance are provided through the center, including clothing and medicines shipped to areas of political or natural disasters. New cloth is cut into garments for babies and children who would otherwise go unclothed. The International Gift Shop offers museum quality handcrafts from forty countries, and features a nonprofit status resulting in fair prices for producers and customers.

Another area of interest in New Windsor is the Robert Strawbridge Home, located at 2650 Strawbridge Lane. This replica of the 1760 Methodist meeting house was the birthplace of American Methodism.

In 1786, the town known today as Hampstead, was laid out by Christopher Vaughan, an Englishman, who was the son-in-law of the founder of Manchester. Hampstead is located on two tracts of land originally in Baltimore County, formally known as "Spring Garden," patented to Dustane Dane in 1748, and "Landorf." For a number of years, this village was known as "Coxville," named after John Cox, the first settler of the land. In 1879, the population of the town increased through the completion of the railroad to the town. Important factors in the development of wealth in the community were flour making and canning.

Today, the old tradition of community spirit remains. Citizens take great pride in maintaining their properties, retaining the small town atmosphere. Most of this atmosphere centers around the several churches and volunteer fire companies. For over the past sixty years, the town's annual celebration has been the firemen's carnival. More recently, a newer event "Hampstead Day," has attracted thousands of visitors. Hampstead became an incorporated town in 1888.

Mt. Airy was formed following the founding of Baltimore in 1727, when the Old National Pike was built to transport produce and other trade goods to and from the city. Within a short time after the Old National Pike was completed, the first settlements were formed along the road. These were Parrsville and Ridgeville. Located on Parr's Ridge, these two areas served travelers providing food and lodging as well as other necessities.

In 1827, the Baltimore & Ohio Railroad, the first common carrier railroad in the United States, began building its lines west, to compete with the Old National Pike. By 1831, the tracks extended to Ridgeville, where a series of four inclined planes were constructed to negotiate the menacing heights of Parr's Ridge. Steam engines were constructed with enough power to handle the ridge, and thus became more practical. Prior to this, horses and mules were used to power up the ridge, using sails with the help of the winds, but this practice was short lived. To avoid the inclines, another route was laid out with a stop which would become Mt. Airy. By 1839, Mt. Airy was an important station on the Old Main Line.

In 1901, reconstruction of the railroad occurred and again it went through Ridgeville, however this time through the longest tunnel in the B & O system. While the railroad was completing the tunnel, other construction was underway which would become a Mt. Airy landmark. This was a twin arch to carry tracks over the road and headwaters of the Patapsco River. Consequently, the Old Main Line, which had been a source of trade and growth to Mt. Airy, returned to Ridgeville. Within twenty years, the Old National Pike became Route 40, and Ridgeville prospered while Mt. Airy became stagnant. Eventually, automobiles and trucks superseded the once very important railways.

The history of the Mt. Airy post office is an interesting one. First established in Ridgeville on June 30, 1827, it was moved to Parrsville in March, 1830. On July 23, 1845, it moved to Mt. Airy, where it remained until June 6, 1861. At the beginning of the Civil

War, the Army Provost Marshal took control of the post office and moved it back to Ridgeville. Following the war, it was moved back to Mt. Airy where it has remained since.

The Ridge Presbyterian Church was built in 1846 and also served as a private school, held in the basement until the Civil War. During the War, the church was occupied by a New Jersey regiment whose duty was to guard the roads and rail lines in Mt. Airy and Ridgeville. In 1863, during the Gettysburg campaign, the VI Corps under Major General John Sedgwick moved through Ridgeville, Mt. Airy, New Windsor, Westminster, and Manchester, where they were used to support the Double Pipe Creek defense line. Upon the outbreak of the battle of Gettysburg, the VI Corps joined the battle.

Mt. Airy became an incorporated town in 1896. In 1914 the first electric company was franchised, and in 1919 the roads were paved, street lighting was established, and the water systems installed by 1924. The town's actual expansion began with the construction of a sewer system in the late 1960s.

In the late 1970s, a Mormon temple was erected to round out the church representation which included Methodists, Episcopalians, Baptists, Lutherans, and others. In 1986, Mt. Airy elected its first woman mayor. Some of the attractions in Mt. Airy are the Pine Grove Chapel (1846) and Cemetery (1895), and the Baltimore & Ohio Railroad Station (1868-1882).

Considered one of Maryland's better agricultural counties, Carroll once raised tobacco, but has now turned to crops such as corn, wheat, oats, barley, soybeans, hay, and vegetables. Livestock and dairying also provide for a major part of the agricultural income. Today, through a program, Carroll County has set aside 40,000 acres of land, preserved and dedicated strictly for agricultural activities.

Industries in Carroll County are quite diversified. These products include electric tools, motor components, clothing, shoes, floor coverings, roofing, as well as cured meat and fresh vegetables. At one time, the most unusual industry in the county was the distilling of oil from vermifuge, which was grown in better quality in southwest Carroll County than in any other place. This oil was used effectively in combating intestinal worms (hookworm) in both man and animals, and its sale once added a significant amount to the county's income. This industry ended in the 1940s.

A Carroll County original enterprise, the Western Maryland Railroad, as well as the former B & O and Pennsylvania once provided the county's rail service. President Lincoln used the Western Maryland Railroad on his way to deliver the Gettysburg Address. Today the Maryland Midland Railroad runs through Carroll County.

The town of Keysville, in the northeastern part of the county is the birthplace of Francis Scott Key. Key was born in a house called "Terra Rubra," which means "redlands", named for the red soil on the land. Partially destroyed in 1850, it has been restored; however, much of the original house remains. The American flag flies here twenty-four hours a day, three hundred sixty-five days a year, as it does over his grave in Frederick and Fort McHenry in Baltimore. Today the house is occupied as a private residence.

Located seven miles north of Westminster on Route 97 is <u>Union Mills</u>. Since 1797, this complex has been the home of six generations of Shrivers. The main house at Union Mills is a weathered gray clapboard dwelling, which overlooks the Big Pipe Creek. This old building began with four rooms in 1797, during the time George Washington was President. Looking from the main house stands a tall brick grist mill, started by Andrew and David Shriver. It was here that the families thriving milling business began, followed by the tannery and canning enterprises. The flourishing grist mill attracted people from all parts. As a result, the area became the center of activity, hosting meetings and political functions, essential to the elections in the 1800s. It also served as a post office, wayside inn, and schoolhouse at various times in its history.

During the Civil War, as the battle of Gettysburg was approaching in 1863, both Union and Confederate troops were headed into Pennsylvania. Union Mills was directly in the path of the Union Army of the Potomac as it traveled north to intercept the Confederate Army. Additionally, Union Mills was in the path of the Rebel cavalry as it circled through Maryland. On their way J.E.B. Stuart's Cavalry stopped at Union Mills, followed later by the Union's Fifth Corps Command for overnight stays. The Homestead was loyal to the North and "The Mills" across the lane was sympathetic to the South. Interestingly, soldiers from both sides were fed from the huge kitchen of the Homestead, although on different days. As the battle of Gettysburg raged on from July 1st to 3rd, the families at Union Mills could hear the distant thunder of cannons. In the days that followed the battle, these families watched as wagon trains loaded with the wounded moved past. Interspersed with the wagon trains were Confederate prisoners. Many stopped at the Homestead, to take water from the pump. Although the family was divided by the war, they again came together after the war to concentrate on business. The tannery won awards at the Centennial in 1876, and was in use until 1890 when a storm blew down its brick smokestack. The water-powered grist mill, restored as a mill museum, operated until 1947, and the canning business until 1976.

This historic landmark was also the site where Washington Irving would sit before a fire and talk late into the night and where James Audubon often visited. Everything at Union Mills is much the same as when the Homestead was in daily use. Relics dated back to Jefferson's time can be seen. Union Mills is a very interesting place, rich in history, and well worth a visit.

Carroll County is also the home of Piney Run Park and Cascade Lake. Piney Run Park, located on Martz Road in Sykesville, features a five hundred acre woods with a three hundred acre lake. Boating, fishing, tennis and picnicking are characteristic. Cascade Lake, located at 3000 Snydersburg Road in Hampstead, is a beautiful six acre, spring-fed lake nestled among twenty-five acres of hills and woods. The area offers picnicking, swimming, and fishing.

Another area of interest, the Pennsylvania Dutch Farmer's Market in the Crossroad Square Shopping Center offers such items as handmade amish quilts, antique dolls, on-site potter and stained glass artists, fine china, clothing, crafts and brooms, and fresh produce, home baked goodies, flowers and more.

Carroll County was the first complete county to have rural free delivery service of U.S. Mail. A plaque in the county reads, "In The United States Was Inaugurated By The Post Office Department On December 20, 1899 Covering The Whole Of Carroll County And Small Parts of Adjacent Counties With Westminster As The Central Distributing Point".

One interesting story of historical interest from Carroll County is the incident involving Alger Hiss and Whitaker Chambers, commonly referred to as the Pumpkin Patch Papers. Alger Hiss was a native of Baltimore and began working for the State Department in 1936. He also had been Secretary of the Dumbarton Oaks Conference in 1944 that formed the groundwork for the United Nations. At the time of the House Un-American Activities Committee hearings, Hiss was president of the Carnegie Endowment for International Peace in New York.

Whitaker Chambers was born Jay Vivian Chambers on April 1, 1901 in Philadelphia, Pennsylvania. He changed his name to avoid being humiliated by his classmates, and picked Whitaker as this was his mother's name. In 1920, he entered Columbia College, and in 1925, disenchanted with college he left and joined the communist party. It was here that he met Alger Hiss, and worked along side him in the communist underground. Disillusioned with the communist party, Whitaker quit in 1939.

At the House Un-American Activities Committee hearings, Hiss testified that he had never belonged to the communist party, did not know Whitaker Chambers, nor could he identify Chambers from the pictures presented. Chambers, on the other hand, testified that Hiss did know him, and that he had passed documents to him intended for the Russians. Hiss continued his denials. Hiss challenged Chambers to make the same charges outside the committee hearings, so he could sue him. Two days later, Chambers made the same charges on a Baltimore radio station, and Hiss sued him for $75,000 charging slander. A deposition followed whereby Chambers produced government documents that Hiss had supplied him. He claimed that microfilms had been produced from the government documents, and then returned to the State Department before they were missed. As a result, the members of the committee staff went to the Chambers farm located near Westminster. At the farm, Chambers led the staff members to a hollowed out pumpkin in a field and fished out the microfilm of State Department documents.

These documents were presented to a Grand Jury in New York, and although the statue of limitations had expired on a charge of espionage, Hiss was indicted on two counts of perjury. Prosecutors were able to prove that the documents found had been typed on a machine owned by Hiss. Two trials followed with Chambers testifying at both. Hiss was convicted and sentenced to five years, but served only 44 months. His civil suit against Chambers was also dismissed.

In 1988, the National Park Service designated the farm a National Historic Landmark. Hiss had maintained his innocence ever since the incident, in two volumes of memoirs, and at the time declined to comment about the landmark designation. Whitaker Chambers died in 1961. President Reagan awarded him a Medal of Freedom posthumously in 1984.

Chambers' Medfield Farm is well-known for the microfilm being hidden in a hollowed out pumpkin, and thus is referred to as the Pumpkin Patch Papers. The Medfield Farm is located two miles back Bachman Valley Road at Saw Mill Road, approximately ten miles north of Westminster. Today, the farm is owned by retired Senator George Della. Senator Della built his house over the remains of the original residence of Whitaker Chambers, which was destroyed by fire in 1957.

Form of Government: County Commissioners

THE
FIRST COMPLETE COUNTY
RURAL FREE DELIVERY SERVICE

IN THE UNITED STATES WAS INAUGURATED BY THE POST OFFICE DEPARTMENT ON DECEMBER 20, 1899 COVERING THE WHOLE OF CARROLL COUNTY AND SMALL PARTS OF ADJACENT COUNTIES WITH WESTMINSTER AS THE CENTRAL DISTRIBUTING POINT.

STATE ROADS COMMISSION

Map of Carroll County

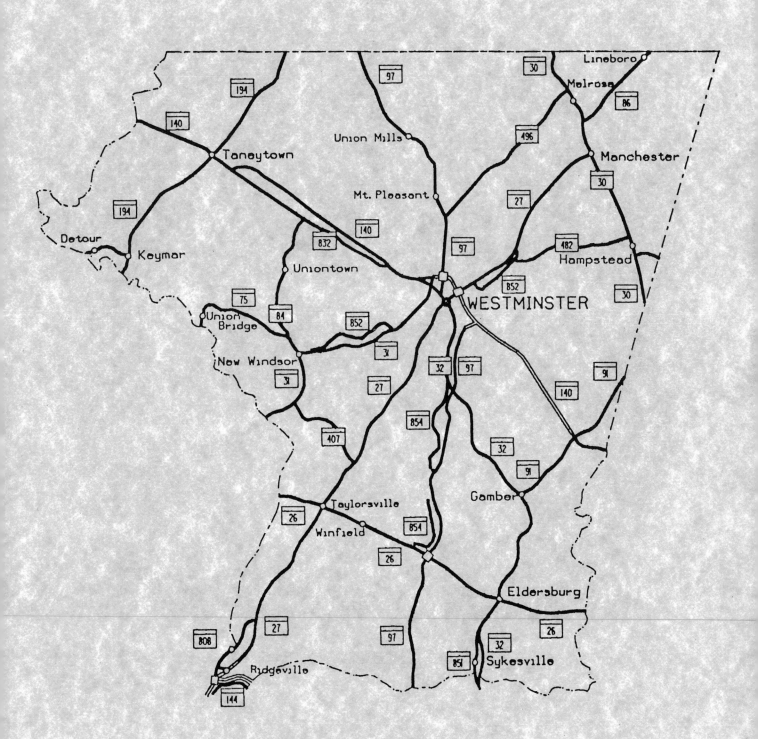

CECIL COUNTY

Cecil County was created in 1674 from Baltimore and Kent counties by proclamation of the Governor. The County was named for Cecil Calvert, Second Lord Baltimore, founder of the Maryland colony.

Cecil County is bordered by the State of Delaware on the east, and the State of Pennsylvania on the north. Visited by Captain John Smith in 1608, Cecil is Maryland's northeastern-most county, and the tenth to be established.

Having a land area of three hundred fifty-two square miles, and a water area of thirty-four square miles, Cecil County has two distinct regions which make up this area. To the north it is part of the Piedmont Plateau, but to the south it lies in the Coastal Plain. Agriculture is still an important industry, with corn, grains, soybeans, livestock and dairy production being the most important.

In 1880 the population was 27,108, but it dropped somewhat each year to a population of only 23,612 in 1920. By 1940, it had increased to 26,407, but has maintained an upward trend since, having a population of approximately 71,347 in 1990. By 1994, the population was 77,037 an increase of 8.0% since 1990. In 1998, the population rose to 81,420, and by the year 2000, it is projected to be 83,700.

The seal of Cecil County was adopted by the Board of County Commissioners on June 11, 1968. The seal consists of a river scene which will reflect the water itself, together with a scene of the sky. On the sky is a male mallard duck in flight, and underneath the male duck is a female mallard duck, also in flight. To the left of the heads of the ducks in flight is a cluster of cattails and reeds.

Cecil's largest city and also the county seat is Elkton, with a population of 6,500. Elkton was first called Elktown and Head of Elk, so named for its location near the Elk River. Built on a tract of land called Friendship, Elktown was incorporated in 1787, after the county seat was moved there from Charlestown. For many years before 1938, Elkton was known as the marriage capital of the east coast. Before the passing of the Maryland law which instituted a waiting period for marriage after applying for a wedding license, the city was quite active with wedding ceremonies. Many couples eloped from areas such as New York, Pennsylvania and other points north and east to be married, as their States during this time imposed a waiting period. In Elkton, one could obtain an almost instant marriage. Elkton during these years was known as the "Gretna Green of the East."

The second largest incorporated town in Cecil County is Perryville, with a population of about 2,200. Other incorporated towns in the county are: North East, named after the Northeast River by explorers searching for the Northeast Passage; Chesapeake City, named after the existence of the Chesapeake & Delaware Canal; Port Deposit, named because it was a shipping point and an active "port of deposit" for lumber and other products. Earlier names were Rock Run, Smith's Falls and Smith's Ferry after Captain John Smith and Cresap's Ferry after Thomas Cresap who established the first ferry across the Susquehanna to Lapidum in 1725, and Creswell's Ferry after Colonel John Creswell who succeeded Cresap; Rising Sun, named after observing the sun rising over the horizon on a shingle outside the Sunrise Tavern; Charlestown, named for Charles Calvert, the fifth Lord Baltimore in 1742; and Cecilton, named for Cecilius Calvert.

The Chesapeake & Delaware Canal, one of the most important waterways in the United States, cuts across 14.7 miles of the Maryland-Delaware isthmus. Ships from Baltimore come up the Elk River, and enter the canal several miles west of Chesapeake City. This most valuable connecting link between the Chesapeake Bay and the Delaware River was first started in 1804, and completed in 1829, at a cost of $2.25 million. In the following years, it has been widened and deepened. In 1919, the canal became the property of the United States Government and is used by approximately 50 percent of the arrivals and clearances at the Port of Baltimore. Ships using the canal can reduce their voyage to Baltimore from eastern United States ports by almost twenty hours, and from Baltimore to European ports by a minimum of ten hours. As a result, ships not only save valuable time, but also thousands of dollars by using the canal.

The C & D Canal Museum in Chesapeake City, centers on the history and operation of the one hundred sixty-three year-old canal which joins the Chesapeake and Delaware Bays. The Upper Bay Museum, located in North East contains a large collection of Chesapeake Bay area hunting, fishing, and boating artifacts.

Cecil County is also the home of one of the nation's most beautiful forests and parks. Elk Neck State Park, containing some two thousand two hundred acres is maintained by the Department of Natural Resources, and is equipped with cabins and fireplaces, as well as facilities for camping and picnics. The park is located on a peninsula between the Bay and the Elk River. Hunting is permitted in-season in the forest areas.

Forming the western boundary is the Susquehanna River. Spanning the river is the Conowingo Dam, one of the largest hydroelectric dams in the United States. Covering an area four thousand five hundred forty-eight feet long and one hundred five feet high, the dam provides electricity for a number of areas. Not far down the river is located the town of Port Deposit. It is here that the Bainbridge Naval Station is located, which at one time maintained over 30,000 officers and men. No longer a naval station today, it is used mainly as a center for several service schools.

Historical tradition is widespread in Cecil County, dating from the Colonial and Revolutionary War days. Some historical buildings and places of interest are: The Hermitage, located at 323 Hermitage Drive, Elkton, was built in 1735 and was the home of Robert Alexander, a delegate to the Continental Congress in 1775. It was here that General Washington was entertained on August 25, 1777 and was the headquarters for General Howe on August 28, 1777. This estate was confiscated and sold by Patriots in August, 1777. Old Hollingsworth Tavern, located at 207 W. Main Street, Elkton, was built in 1750. Also known as Holly Inn, and according to tradition was visited by both General Washington and General Howe in August 1777.

Partridge Hall, was built in 1768 by Colonel Henry Hollingsworth, who raised the Elk Battalion of Militia in 1775. Colonel Hollingsworth also fought at Brandywine, and became Quartermaster and Commissary of the Eastern Shore. He furnished munitions, food and transportation for the Colonial Army. The home is named for James Partridge, who married the colonel's daughter. The house is located at 129 W. Main Street, Elkton. Gilpin Manor, was built in 1760 by Joseph Gilpin. It was here at Gilpin's Bridge on Gilpin Manor that Colonel Henry Hollingsworth was wounded at the Gilpin Manor Skirmish. The manor is located on Route 316, near Route 279. Holly Hall, built in 1820 is the site of the Holly Hall Tree, which was designated the official Bicentennial Tree in 1975, and is located on Route 40, east of Route 213. The Mitchell House, is an elegant town house built in 1769. This house was built for Dr. Abraham Mitchell, a well-known physician and patriot. The house was used by Dr. Mitchell during the Revolutionary War as a hospital for wounded soldiers. Lafayette once visited this house, which is located at 131 E. Main Street, Elkton. Graymount, located on Route 281, 1.8 miles east of Elkton. The earliest section of this house was built in 1769. From here General Washington watched Howe's Army as they disembarked for their march on Philadelphia in August, 1777.

Also located in Elkton is the Historical Society of Cecil County, located at 135 E. Main Street. Here one can see exhibitions, an early American Kitchen, country store museum, early Fire House, Log school house, a research library and the Sheriff John F. DeWitt Military Museum. This museum contains memorabilia from the American Revolution through Desert Storm.

Other areas in the county of historical interest are: Belle Hill, which was the birthplace of Michael Rudolph, who served with Lee's Legion in the Revolutionary War. Later, Michael was reputed to be the controversial "Marshal Ney." Belle Hill is located on Route 316, one mile north of Route 279. Dysart Tavern, was originally Longwell's, then later as Fox Chase, but more popularly as Seven Stars. It dates from the eighteenth century and has been rebuilt several times. It was located at the northwest corner of Route 273 and Route 316. Red Ball Tavern, was a favorite place for drovers in the eighteenth century. This stone house is the first one on Route 273, west of Big Elk Creek, at the Historical Marker for New Munster Tract. Mitchell House in Fair Hill, was built in 1764 as the summer home of Dr. Abraham Mitchell. Lafayette also visited here, and sent the cherry trees found here as a gift. It is located at the southeast corner of Route 273 and Route 213. Blue Ball Tavern, is located on the northeast corner of Route 273 and Route 545, and was built in 1710 by Andrew Job. Thomas Job was the son of Andrew, who married Elizabeth Maxwell, niece of Daniel Defoe, who came to America as a redemptioner.

The Quaker Brick Meeting House (East Nottingham Friends Meeting), is located on old Route 273, west of Route 272 at Calvert. This present building was built in 1724, and enlarged in 1752. It was here that the wounded soldiers of General Smallwood's Continentals were hospitalized during the Revolutionary War. Those soldiers who died are buried near the south door. In 1781, Lafayette's troops camped in the Meeting House woods on their way to Yorktown.

Cross Keys Tavern, was a stagecoach stop, midway between Baltimore and Philadelphia, and was built in 1744. Located just south of the Quaker Brick Meeting House, on Calvert Road; Located 1.5 miles west of Rising Sun on Route 1 is Richard's

Oak, a 500 year old tree. It was under this tree that Lafayette camped on April 12, 1781. The tree is so named because it stands on land originally granted to the Richards family.

Bald Friar Ford & Ferry, is the site of ferry and ford used by Lafayette's troops and Rochambeau's artillery on their way to Yorktown, and is located one-half mile northwest of Pilot. Octoraro Mansion, was the home of Colonel Elihu Hall of the Susquehanna Battalion, Maryland Militia. Located on Route 338, one-half mile south of Conowingo. Lafayette is said to have also been received here; On Route 276, south of Harrisville is the Grave of Leonard Krauss, who fought under General Washington, whom he greatly admired. In 1802, Krauss built the Cross Keys Tavern, where celebrations of Washington's birthday were a great annual event.

Midway between Rising Sun and Port Deposit at Battle Swamp is Cummings Tavern. It is here that Rochambeau's baggage and artillery detachments bivouacked in 1781. More technically it is located off Route 276 at Woodlawn, near Dr. Jack Road. Anchor & Hope Tavern, located on Route 276 near Port Deposit served as a stagecoach and ferry ticket office. It is believed that General Washington used this ferry in 1775 on his way to the Continental Congress in Philadelphia, when he was chosen as Commander-in-Chief of the American forces. Brookland, was acquired by George Gale in 1781, who was a wealthy patriot who served in the Continental Army. Brookland is located on St. Marks Road, west of Route 222. Rodgers Tavern & Lower Ferry, is located in Perryville, on the old Post Road, at the eastern terminus of the Lower Susquehanna Ferry. The tavern was visited many times by George and Martha Washington, VonClausen, Lafayette, and Madison. The tavern was named for its proprietor Colonel John Rodgers, who served in the Revolutionary War, and who was the father of John Rodgers, a naval hero of the War of 1812.

Perry Point Mansion & Mill, is a beautiful eighteenth century mansion which was recently restored. Located on Route 7 at the Susquehanna River, it is now the residence of the Director of the Veterans Hospital. It is said that the beech trees located here were a gift from the Marquis de Lafayette when he visited here, accompanied by General Washington. The old grist mill marks the mouth of the Susquehanna River. Principio Furnace, located on Route 7, two and one-half miles east of Perryville, was the first iron works in Maryland erected c.1715, by British Iron Masters. George Washington's father owned one-twelfth interest in this company which supplied cannon balls during the Revolutionary War.

Carpenter's Point, is located at Mountain Hill Road and Carpenter's Point Road, south of Route 7, and was the first permanent settlement in Cecil County. It was founded by William Carpenter in 1658. Captain Jeremiah Baker of the 30th Susquehanna Battalion of the Cecil County Militia made his home here. Authorized by the General Assembly in 1742 is Stone Wharf, which served as a supply depot for the Continental Army during the Revolutionary War, and is located in Charlestown on Route 267.

Also in Charlestown is the Hamilton House and the Indian Queen & Red Lyon Tavern. The Hamilton House is one of the oldest buildings in the town, and was named for Reverend John Hamilton, rector of North East Parish. The Indian Queen & Red Lyon Tavern is a two hundred year old inn and tavern originally owned by Zebulon Hollingsworth, one of the original town commissioners of Charlestown. It contains many fascinating architectural details, a log kitchen, stone fireplace, beamed ceiling, well-house and smoke house. Next to this site is the Revolutionary War home of Lieutenant Colonel Nathaniel Ramsey, a delegate to the Maryland Convention in 1775 and 1776. It was Lt. Colonel Ramsey who led the 3rd Maryland Regiment that saved the Continental Forces at the battle of Long Island.

Located in and around Elkton and North East is Greenhill, built in c.1780 by Thomas Russell, the British Ironmaster of Principio Furnace, who turned over the output of the furnace to the Continental Army. Although the house is not the original one, some original slave quarters are still standing. Oldfield Point, was named for George Oldfield, who purchased the property in 1684. This was the home of John Ford, a Captain of the Militia in the Revolutionary War. Elk Landing, was the Port of Elkton, formerly called Head of Elk. This was the birthplace of Colonel Henry Hollingsworth, who raised the 1st Company of Militia in 1775, and who furnished munitions, supplies and transportation for the Continental Army. During the Revolution, American and British forces in the Chesapeake Bay landed here.

The site of Harmony Hall, on Oldfield Road, is where Millicent Hyland, the daughter of Captain John and Martha Tilden Hyland of Harmony Hall, married Captain John Ford. Millicent's brother, Colonel Stephen Hyland, of Revolutionary War fame, entertained Lafayette and the officers of the French fleet here. Court House Point, is where the court moved from Ordinary Point in 1719, and is located on Court House Point Road, west of Route 213, opposite Oldfield Road. Elk Ferry connected this area with Oldfield Point, and on August 27, 1777, a detachment of Howe's troops under Knyphausen and Agnew carried off the county records. <u>Brick House</u>, built in the eighteenth century served as the temporary quarters after the Court House at Court House Point was burned. The Brick House is located on the northwest corner of Route 310 and Route 342.

Located in Cecilton is <u>Mount Harmon</u>, <u>Rose Hill</u>, and <u>Worsell Manor</u>. Mount Harmon, overlooking the Sassafras River is an old tobacco plantation consisting of 1200 acres. The house is a exquisite Georgian brick mansion, beautifully restored, and on the grounds is a boxwood garden. Designated a National Trust Home it is located on Grove Neck Road, four miles west of Cecilton. Rose Hill is also located on Grove Neck Road, five miles west of Cecilton. The original house was built in 1683. Major Thomas Marsh Foreman, a distinguished member of General Washington's staff, inherited this estate from his grandfather. Major Foreman is buried on the grounds. Worsell Manor, is a attractive old brick house of Charles I type architecture. General Washington and his step-son visited Worsell Manor, according to an entry made by General Washington in his diary for May 14, 1773. The manor is located on Route 282, east of Cecilton.

<u>Cherry Grove</u> is another interesting place of historical interest in Cecil County. Located on Cherry Grove Road, off Glebe Road, west of Route 213, this mansion was built in 1697 by John Veazey. His grandson, John, was Deputy-Surveyor for Cecil County and colonel of Bohemia Battalion in 1776. His grandson was Thomas Ward Veazey, Governor of Maryland in 1836, the youngest son of Captain Edward Veazey, who fell at the battle of Long Island, August 27, 1776. Governor Veazey is buried in the family burying ground near the house.

Cecil County is also the home of several interesting churches. <u>St. Mary Anne's Episcopal Church</u>, 317 S. Main Street, North East, was erected in 1742. Located in the churchyard are fieldstone grave markers said to mark Indian graves. Also buried here are Captain John Baker, a Revolutionary War patriot and Thomas Russell, the British Ironmaster of Principio Furnace. <u>St. Stephens Episcopal Church</u> is a Sassafras Parish established in 1692, and dedicated in 1705. This beautiful nineteenth century building houses such items as eighteenth century silver, a sundial crafted in 1718, and a bell presented to Queen Anne. The first Negro south of the Mason-Dixon Line was ordained here in 1834. St. Stephens is located on Route 282, three miles west of Cecilton, at the intersection of Glebe Road. <u>St. Francis Xavier (Old Bohemia Mission) Roman Catholic Church</u> is one of the earliest permanent Catholic foundations in the colonies. Charles Carroll of Carrollton, a signer of the Declaration of Independence and John Carroll, the first Catholic Bishop in the United States attended the Academy, which was established in 1745. Kitty Knight is buried in an adjoining cemetery. A Museum is located in the former rectory. St. Francis Xavier is located two miles north of Warwick on Bohemia Church Road. St. Augustine Episcopal Church was built in 1838, on the site of Manor Chapel, c.1692. Today it has been beautifully restored. In the cemetery is the grave of Colonel Edward Oldham of the Continental Army. The church is located on Route 310, at the corner of Route 342. Rock Presbyterian Church, was organized in 1720. The present building was erected in 1761, and has been remodeled several times since. The Early Session House housed the Rock Academy. Rock Church is located on the northwest corner of Route 273 and Rock Church Road.

Another well-known church is the West Nottingham Presbyterian Church & Academy. In 1974 the church celebrated its 250th anniversary. The present buildings were completed in 1803 with money obtained from the lottery authorized by an Act of the Legislature. The Academy was founded in 1741 by Reverend Samuel Finley, minister of the church. The original site was located in Rising Sun, and today is located on Route 276, south of Route 269. Richard Stockton and Dr. Benjamin Rush, two signers of the Declaration of Independence were students of the Academy.

Cecil County is also the center of equestrian activity in Maryland, thanks in part to the Fair Hill Natural Resources Area, located north of Elkton. This five thousand acre tract is home to two national equestrian organizations, as well as a wide variety of equestrian activities. Highlighting the horse events at Fair Hill are the Fair Hill Races. Run in the spring and fall, these races attract crowds of 10-15,000 people. Offered are a varied program of turf, hurdle, and timber races, along with full parimutuel wagering facilities. Avid racing fans as well as the casual spectator can enjoy top-quality steeplechase racing here.

Augmenting Fair Hill racing is a series of year-long training events produced by the Fair Hill Equestrian Events (FHEE). These range from one to three day events, with cross country and stadium jumping. Each year in October, the Fair Hill International three day event is held. This world-class competition attracts riders and horses from the highest echelon of the sport. Many of these competitors have represented their respective countries in the Olympic Games.

Another interesting sightseeing area is Schaefer's Canal House and Restaurant in Chesapeake City. Here visitors may dine and also watch the ships pass through the canal.

Cecil County today maintains a mostly serene rural existence. The county's slogan is "We'd Love Your Company."

Form of Government: County Commissioners

Map of Cecil County

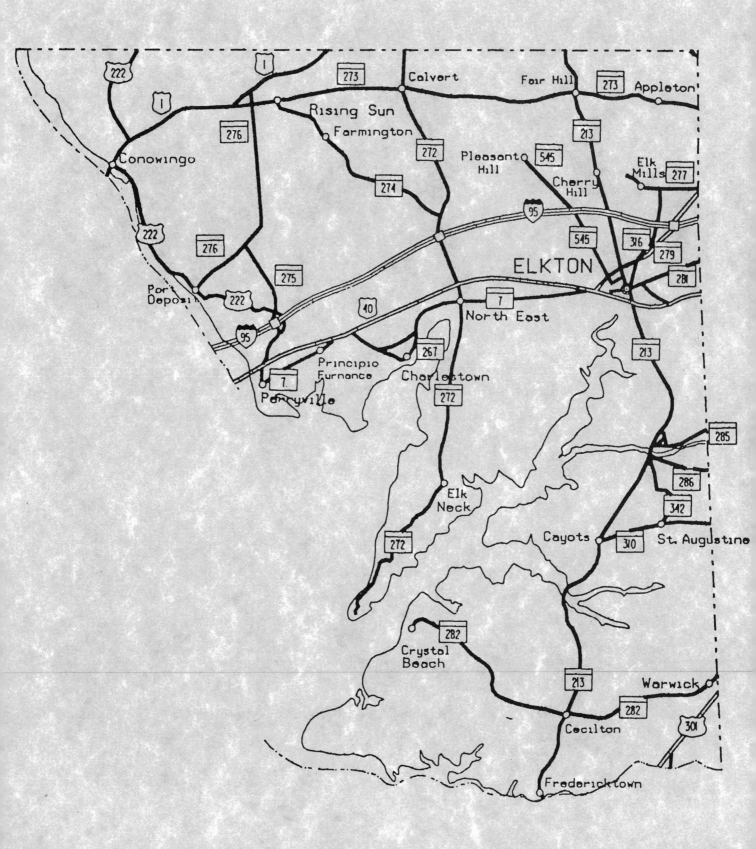

CHARLES COUNTY

Charles County was created by an Order in Council of 1658. It is not to be confused with an earlier Charles County (1650-1653) known as Old Charles County. The County was named for Charles Calvert, Third Lord Baltimore, son and heir of Cecil Calvert, Second Lord Baltimore.

Charles County is well-known as historic tobacco land, and today carries out many customs of centuries ago. Charles County has a total area of five hundred two square miles; four hundred fifty-eight land and forty-four water. Its boundary extends to Prince George's County on the north and northeastern corner, and below that the Patuxent River and the northwestern section of St. Mary's County. To the South and West its boundary is the Potomac River, including the river itself to the Virginia shore. Generally the land surface is flat, ranging from one hundred to two hundred twenty feet above sea level.

In 1669, the General Assembly passed an act to prevent servants from running away. This act required that "there be a Seale devised and provided for Each County Court... with which Seale all writs and process of the Said Several and Respective County Commissioners and all passes for people departing out of the Said Counties for Foreign parts shall be sealed."

As Charles County did not have a seal from its beginning in 1658, it is speculated that one must have been acquired shortly after the passage of this act. To this day, no one has been able to locate an impression of this first seal. Evidence that the County Seals were changed when Maryland became a royal colony is found in the following item recorded in the Proceedings of the Governor and Council in 1692. It read, "Sir Thomas Lawrence humbly moves the Board for their advice and opinion what Seals to provide each County of the Providence, Resolved that the King's Arms with the names of the County inscribed be made for each County."

Impressions of this seal are found on the transcripts of records of two cases appealed from the Charles County Court to the Provincial Court in 1707 and 1712.

Presumably, the use of the royal seals was discontinued after Maryland was restored to the Lord Proprietary, for the Seal affixed to a transcript made in 1721 bears the coat of arms of Lord Baltimore. It is likely this seal was the same or similar to the one in use before the royal seal was adopted.

By the year 1752, the Charles County Court was using another seal, that bears the Lord Baltimore coat of arms, but was slightly different in size and detail of the ornamentation. History indicates that this was the seal in use at least until the Revolution, when the colonists developed an aversion to all things British and devised other seals.

The present seal of Charles County was designed by Frederick Tilp, using the Great Seal of Maryland as the main motif. The seal is described as: "An earl's coronet on which the shield was surmounted borne by the Lords Baltimore only in relation to their American Province, to which was accorded by royal charter the rank of County Palatine." A description of the coronet is a silver gilted band, covered with yellow lacquer. Five spheres atop the crown are plain silver balls. Between the silver balls are gold strawberry leaves. The white ermine between the crown and the shield has the characteristic black spots. The red and white colored cross in the shield symbolizes the arms of the Crossland family of the mother of the first Lord Baltimore. The date "1658" on the bottom of the County Seal is the date of the order of erection by the Colonial Governor, with the assent of the Council at the urging of the Proprietary.

Interestingly, in 1650, there was another Charles County in Maryland instigated by Lord Baltimore, which was located on the south and west shores of the Patuxent River, and included parts of what are now St. Mary's, Charles, and Prince George's Counties.

First settled by the English, much of the population's ancestry can be traced to the English or to the slaves who worked in the tobacco fields in its pre-Civil War days. Until 1920, most of its population was Negro. By 1950, the population rose to 23,415 and in 1990 was 101,154. By 1994, the population was 109,295, an increase of 8% over 1990. In 1998, the population rose to 118,340, and by the year 2000, it is projected to be 123,200.

LaPlata is the county seat, being established in 1895, with a then population of only about three hundred thirty. Its population has been slow to rise, totaling only one thousand two hundred fourteen by 1960.

Tobacco growing, has always been the predominant activity, being grown on about

90 percent of the farms. Corn, wheat, soybeans, potatoes, and sweet potatoes are also grown, while some dairying and beef cattle are also present.

One of many interesting places in Charles County that is rich in history is Port Tobacco, once a thriving seaport in 1790. The town of Port Tobacco was not named for the tobacco weed as some may assume, but for the "Potobac" Indians who inhabited the area. "Potobac" means "a jutting of the water inland." From 1650 to 1895, Port Tobacco was the county seat, and the center of the business and culture in Maryland in colonial times and for years following this period. It became the second largest seaport in Maryland, as much of the tobacco sent to England was loaded here. At one time the Maryland Assembly christened the settlement Charles Town, but the name never caught on, local residents insisting that the name stay as Port Tobacco. The harbor of Port Tobacco, which was once the most important in Maryland, became filled with silt and gradually died out, turning it into a ghost town. Today Port Tobacco consists of a village with many of its former buildings having been restored. These include a Federal-style courthouse, which houses the Charles County Museum of Port Tobacco, two restored eighteen-century houses (Catslide House and One-room School House), one reconstructed nineteenth century home and the Salt Box (1700), a restored home on Cheapside Street.

Additionally, Charles County has some of the finest examples of Colonial and Southern architecture in Maryland. These include: Thomas Stone National Historic Site. This plantation, called Habre de Venture, was built by Thomas Stone, a well-respected lawyer and one of Maryland's four signers of the Declaration of Independence. Both Stone and his wife and buried on the site. In 1977 a fire gutted the central block and severely damaged the West wing. Reconstruction is being done. St. Ignatius Church (1798) From this church, one has a majestic view of the Port Tobacco River. Also here is located a Civil War tunnel which runs under the cemetery to the river. West Hatton (1790); LaGrange, home of Dr. James Craik, Surgeon General of the Continental Army; and Rose Hill (1730), the home of Dr. Gustavus Richard Brown, physician to George Washington.

Mulberry Grove, is the home of John Hanson, considered the first "President of the United States," under the Articles of Confederation. Called "Our Forgotten First President" Hanson was born at Mulberry Grove Plantation in Port Tobacco, Maryland on April 3, 1721. As he got older, Hanson moved from Charles County to Frederick and became a delegate to the Second Continental Congress. John Hanson and Daniel Carroll were the two from Maryland who signed the Articles of Confederation on March 1, 1781, Maryland representatives being the last to sign. On November 5, 1781, Hanson was elected the "President of the United States in Congress Assembled," this being done under the newly adopted Articles of Confederation, because with the surrender of Cornwallis, the people began to realize that the new United States was a reality. Because of this reality, on the last day of their meeting on November 3, 1781, the Second Continental Congress turned over all public matters to the "United States in Congress Assembled." This body then elected John Hanson the first "president" on November 5, at Independence Hall, Philadelphia. From a technical standpoint, Hanson was our nation's first president if you add the words, "in congress assembled." George Washington became the first President of the United States under the present Constitution of the United States, having taken office on April 30, 1789. John Hanson served the nation for many years, and in retirement while visiting his nephew at Oxon Hill Manor, died on November 22, 1783. Hanson is buried at Oxon Hill. His grave lies on a hill above the Woodrow Wilson Bridge in Prince George's County. The John Hanson Highway, completed in 1960 is named in his honor.

Another historic house in Charles County is <u>Smallwood House</u>, a restored home located in Smallwood State Park in an area known as Smallwood's Retreat. This was the home of the Revolutionary War hero, William Smallwood. Each year a Christmas Candlelight Tour is held which depicts a Colonial Christmas at General Smallwood's Plantation Home, where visitors can enjoy the sights, sounds, and smells of an eighteenth century Christmas. <u>The Mudd House</u>, outside Waldorf is famous as the place where Dr. Samuel Mudd, a local country doctor, set the broken leg of John Wilkes Booth on April 15, 1861, the morning after Booth assassinated President Abraham Lincoln. Guided tours and a gift shop are available.

A small town on the Patuxent River, known as Benedict, was the site where General Ross landed his British army in 1814, for an attack on Washington, D.C., which resulted in the burning of the Capitol and the White House.

Other areas of interest in Charles County include; The Afro-American Heritage Museum, which depicts the life and history of Afro-Americans who lived in Charles County; Christ Church, is one of the original Episcopal Parishes established in 1692. The church was moved by ox cart to its present location from Port Tobacco; Christ Church, Durham, established in 1732 and located on Rt.425, west of La Plata, is an early Episcopal church. Featured here is an ancient sundial near the front gate and graves dating from 1695; Mt. Carmel Monastery, founded in 1790 is the first religious community for women established in the United States, and is a priceless relic of early religious life; Friendship House, located on the La Plata campus of the Charles County Community College. Founded in 1680, this reconstructed colonial home is reminiscent of the life and architecture of Maryland's early settlers; Maryland Indian Cultural Center, is a museum which attempts to educate the non-Indian public to the diversity of People who are known as "American Indian." Exhibits reflect their geographic locations, tribal structure and art.

Other recreational areas in Charles County include Cobb Island, bordered by the Potomac and Wicomico Rivers. This island is a sanctuary for fishing, boating, and seafood lovers. Doncaster Forest, Gilbert Run Park, Myrtle Grove Wildlife Management Area, Popes Creek and Zekiah Swamp are other areas. Doncaster Forest, located on Route 6, thirteen miles west of La Plata in Doncaster contains one thousand four hundred forty-five acres featuring hiking, hunting and picnicking. Gilbert Run Park, located on Route 6, seven miles east of La Plata is a one hundred eighty acre wooded park with a sixty acre fresh water lake. Featured here are fishing, row and paddle boating, hiking and picnicking. Myrtle Grove Wildlife Management Area includes eight hundred twenty-four acres for hunting, fishing and hiking, and a gun range. Located on Route 225, seven miles west of La Plata, this area is considered a prime location for bird-watching and nature photography. Popes Creek, along the shores of the Potomac River is known for its homey atmosphere and good crab houses, and Zekiah Swamp is a twenty mile long, three-quarter mile wide wooded bottomland swamp, originating near Cedarville Natural Resource Center, and flowing through the county to the main headwaters of the Wicomico River.

Charles County is also the home of many interesting annual events. Each year in early spring the Tobacco Auctions are held. These interesting, colorful and aromatic tobacco auctions are held Monday through Thursday, beginning at 9 a.m. Other events include a Patchworker Quilt Show, farmers markets, antique shows, Trail Ride-Equestrian, Southern Maryland Wildlife Festival, Charles County Fair, Balloon Fest, Lobster Festival, Pumpkin Jubilee, and the Festival of Trees.

Today Charles County, along with Calvert and St. Mary's, is still considered "Old Southern Maryland." It is in these counties that the original life of the tobacco communities of 1650 remains, that of basic and quiet. Some areas over the years have become more urbanized such as Waldorf, St. Charles City, Indian Head and LaPlata, with its continued construction of family dwellings; as well as restoration in Port Tobacco.

Form of Government: County Commissioners

"Chandlers Hope" built in 1658 by Job Chandler, Port Tobacco, Maryland. This was Charles County's first Manor House, home of the First Settler, by the late Messrs. Judson Sydnor Bohannan and Henry Vroom DeMott. Job's Grave is located in the center of the Box Wood enclosure.

Map of Charles County

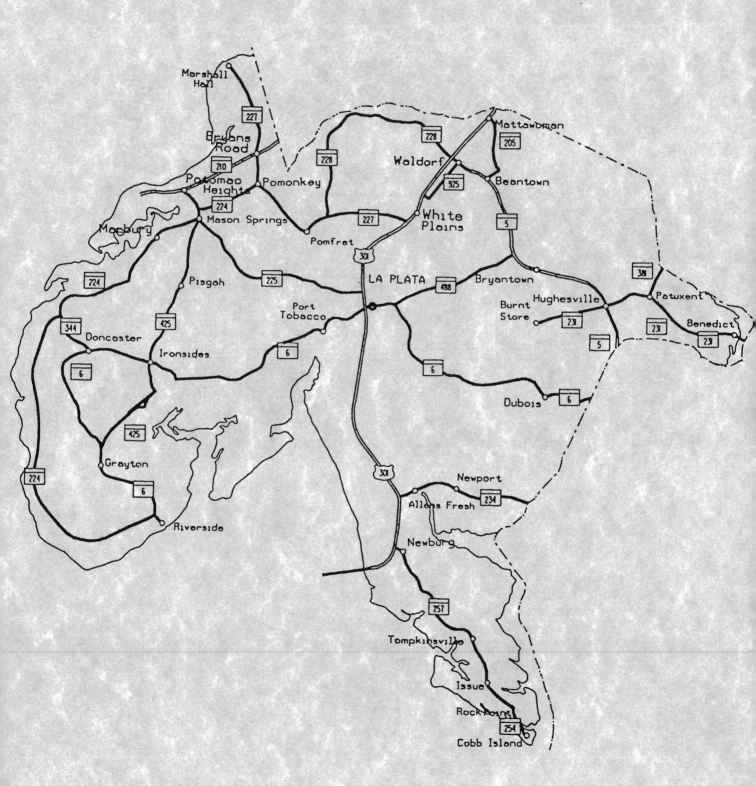

DORCHESTER COUNTY

Dorchester County's legal origin is not known, although it was in existence by February 16, 1668, when a writ was issued to the county sheriff by the Lord Proprietary. The County was named for the Earl of Dorset, a family friend of the Calverts.

The Dorchester County Seal was adopted by the County Commissioners officially in 1967, and was designed by Andrew Tolley, a South Dorchester High School student. The seal is described as; a waterman, holding a pair of oyster tongs and a crab pot, faces a farmer, holding a cornstalk and a pitchfork. At the top is the popular "blue crab." The center shield is divided to show county interests, sailing, religious heritage, industry and shorelines. In the background is a map of Dorchester County surrounded by blue water, although the county is not completely surrounded by water. On the small banner under the shield are written the words "Populus prope deum habitans." Translated, this means, "people living under the care of God." The gold banded border of the seal is imprinted with the County's name and 1669, the year it became a unit of government.

Dorchester County, located on the Eastern Shore, is the largest of those counties. It has an area of five hundred eighty square land miles and one hundred eight square water miles. The county's greatest width from east to west is thirty miles and its greatest length, northeast to southwest is thirty-three miles. It extends into the Chesapeake Bay as a broad peninsula, almost surrounded by the waters of the Bay and the Choptank and Nanticoke Rivers. It is bordered to the north by Talbot County across the Choptank River, and to the east by Caroline County. To the southeast across the Nanticoke River is Wicomico County and to the extreme east it borders the State of Delaware.

Dorchester lies entirely within the Atlantic Coastal Plain, divided into three areas: the uplands; the low, flat land; and the tidal marshes. These areas of mostly level land lie about fifty-five feet above sea level. The first settlers who were of English descent came to this area with their slaves.

The population has seesawed over the years, being approximately 28,006 in 1940, falling to 27,815 in 1950, and rising to 29,666 in 1960. In 1990 the population was 30,236, and in 1994 was 30,424, and increase of 0.6% over 1990. In 1998, the population dropped to 30,210, however; is projected to rise again to 30,350 by the year 2000.

The largest city, Cambridge, founded in 1684 is the county seat. It is located on the Choptank River and contains over 40 percent of the county's total population. Its name was inspired from its first residents of aristocratic Englishmen, after the University of Cambridge.

Other communities in Dorchester County are: Hurlock, named after John Martin Hurlock and incorporated in 1892. The town began from a Dorchester/Delaware Railroad station built in 1867. John M. Hurlock owned the land on which this station was erected and in 1869, built the first grocery store and warehouse. Hurlock is the second largest town in Dorchester County. Vienna, whose name origin is quite unusual, and is one of the oldest settlements in Maryland. In the 1600s an Indian village called Emperor's Landing stood on the same land as Vienna does today. The Indians were named Nanticokes, and their leader was called the "Emperor." When the English and the Virginians began settling the area, their leader was called Vinnacokasimmon. Eventually, the early settlers abbreviated the Emperor's name as "Vnna." It later became Vienna, being pronounced as Vee-Anna. Through shipbuilding, tobacco farming, trade and commerce, the town of Vienna prospered. During the American Revolution, Vienna was used as a source of supplies for the Continental Army, and was raided five times by British war ships. The British again fired on the town during the War of 1812. A Breastwork was constructed from a ship's ballast, and can be seen today.

Secretary, began during the time of the proprietary governorships of Maryland in 1661, and is named after Secretary Sewall's Creek, (now Warwick River). Lord Henry Sewall owned many acres of land, and served as Secretary to the Province of Maryland under Governor Charles Calvert. For reasons unknown, the name of Sewall was dropped from Secretary's Sewall's Creek, and thus the town and creek became Secretary. East New Market, founded in 1669, and originally called "Crossroads" for its location, then New Market after the New Market House, later changing its name to East New Market. The town was formed on the North-South Choptank Indian Trail, and in 1767 an Indian trading post was erected. It is here in the historic district that many examples of beautiful eighteen and nineteenth century homes can be found, many of which are original. During the American Revolution, East New Market was a supply center for the Continental Army, and in the 1780s was the center for American Methodism. East New Market today is a registered National Historic District. <u>Church Creek</u>, founded in 1692 and originally named Dorset, Old Dorchester Town, White Haven, and finally Church Creek as a result of the community being formed around the Protestant Episcopal Church. <u>Eldorado</u>, was originally called The Ferry, after a ferry which crossed the Marshyhope Creek to Brookview. After the ferry was no longer used, the name of Eldorado was decided, named after a nearby farm.

Dorchester's economy comes mostly from food producing and processing. Chief crops are barley and soybeans, of which Dorchester leads Maryland in production, and corn, wheat, and rye are also grown. The county is also ranked high in its production of vegetables such as tomatoes, cucumbers, snap beans, peas, melons, peppers, broccoli, asparagus and spinach.

The Pennsylvania Railroad provides a means of transportation, using two branches that cross at the town of Hurlock. Boating is another means of transportation as well as recreation. Many streams are navigable and boating regattas are common on the Choptank. The Cambridge Yacht Club is famous for its many sailing contests. Under the Department of Natural Resources, the State of Maryland owns thousands of acres of land, used as wildlife refuges and management areas.

Dorchester County has many old homes of historical and architectural interest. These include: <u>Shoal Creek House</u>, built in 1750 as was the home of Governor Charles Goldsborough in 1818; <u>Old Trinity Church</u>, dating from 1690, is the oldest Episcopal Church in continuous use in the United States. Located on Route 16, six miles south of Cambridge, the church contains a silver chalice from a communion set donated by Queen Anne in the year 1700, and has a graveyard containing the graves of many Maryland Revolutionary War soldiers, as well as Anna Ella Carroll, the silent member of President Lincoln's cabinet. <u>Friendship House</u>, built in 1790 in East New Market is a good example of early colonial architecture; <u>Glasgow House</u>, (1760); <u>Jordan House</u> and <u>Sycamore Cottage</u>, dating back before the Revolutionary War, located in Cambridge; and <u>Dorchester Court House</u>, built in 1853. Also found in Cambridge is: <u>Wallace Mansion</u>, and <u>LaGrange or Muse House</u>, both dating back to the early 1700s.

Dorchester County is the home of many fascinating historical figures. Two of these are Annie Oakley and Harriet Tubman. The <u>Annie Oakley House</u>, is located at 28 Bellevue

Avenue, on Hambrooks Bay in Cambridge. It was designed and built by the Wild West Sharpshooter Annie Oakley, when she and her husband, Frank Butler retired to Cambridge in 1912. The house is typical of the period except for two unusual features. The first is that the roof line was altered to allow Annie to step directly out of the upstairs windows, so that she could shoot incoming waterfowl over Hambrooks Bay, and the second was the lack of closets in the house. Throughout her entire adult life, Annie had traveled extensively and lived out of trunks and suitcases. Upon building her house, she forgot that she would need closets in retirement. One interesting story reveals that a neighbor of Annie's complained to her that his walnut tree failed to produce a single nut. The following day, Annie delivered a basket of walnuts along with an apology. She explained to the neighbor that the tiny brown nuts swaying in the breeze made targets too difficult to resist, so she shot every one.

The Birthplace of Harriet Tubman is located approximately one and one-half miles down Green Briar Road. Harriet Tubman was commonly called the "Moses of her People," for her tireless efforts in the Underground Railroad freeing over three hundred slaves. Harriet, who was a slave herself, ran away only to return to Delmarva nineteen times to free others. During the Civil War, she served the Union Army as a nurse, scout and spy. The Underground Railroad: Harriet Tubman Museum and Gift Shop is located at 424 Race Street in Cambridge. Featured here is a resource area for Harriet Tubman, and the gift shop offers items from all nations, including Kenya and Nigeria. The Bazel Church, located on Bestpitch Ferry Road, one mile south of Green Briar Road. This small wooden church is where Harriet Tubman worshipped in the mid 1800s. Services are held each year in July to honor Harriet Tubman. Following the Civil War, Harriet was active in the Women's Suffrage and temperance movements. She also helped form the African Methodist Episcopal Zion Church and homes for the needy.

Dorchester County is the home of an interesting legend; the legend of Big Liz. Big Liz was a slave on a bucktown plantation. On her owner's request, she accompanied him to Green Briar Swamp where they stashed his gold in a burial vault. The owner, fearful that she would betray his secret, drew his sword and slashed off her head, burying her remains with the treasure. According to legend, the ghost of Big Liz appears at the burial vault with her head in her hands to shock and terrify would-be thieves.

Other areas of interest in the county are: Cartegena (My Lady Sewall's Manor), was built by Lord Henry Sewall. Located in Secretary, on Willow Street, the house was once magnificent. Today only one section of the original house remains, but it gives an idea of the vast rooms and enormous chimneys and fireplaces. Presently this historic house is owned by Our Lady of Good Counsel Catholic Church.

The Patty Cannon House, (Johnson's Corner Tavern) was the home of Murderess and Slave Trader Patty Cannon. Interestingly, the house was built on the Maryland/Delaware line so she could escape arrest by fleeing into the next state whenever the law came for her.

Although the tobacco plantations, lumber mills and shipyards of years ago are now gone, Dorchester County's life remains much the same as it did over three hundred years ago.

Form of Government: County Commissioners

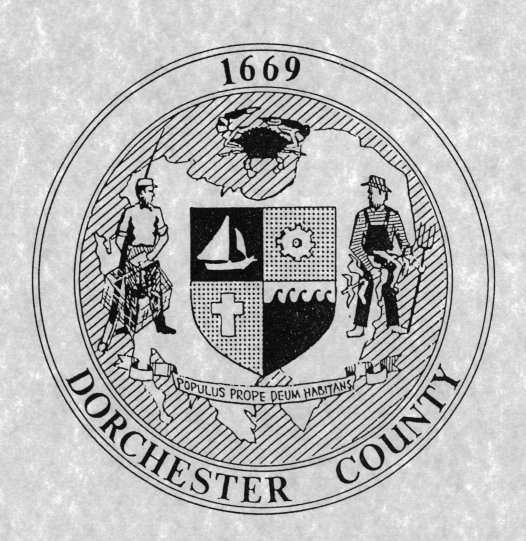

Map of Dorchester County

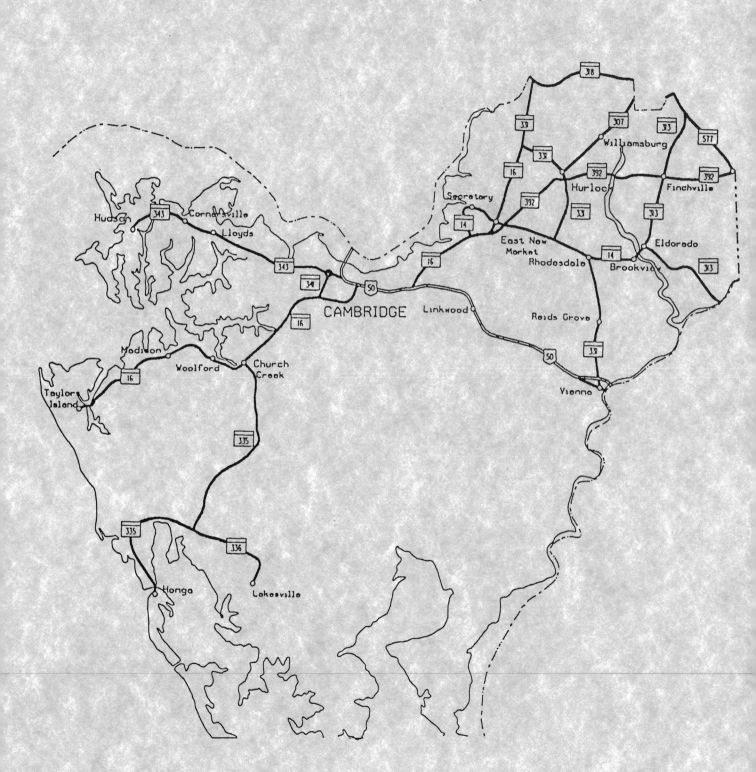

FREDERICK COUNTY

Frederick County was created in 1748 from Baltimore and Prince George's counties (Chapter 15, Acts of 1748). The County was named for Frederick Calvert (1731-1771), sixth and last Lord Baltimore.

The original Frederick County Seal, dating back into the mid to late 1800s depicted a nude farmer holding an ancient spike-toothed harrow and a single-shovel plow. The redesigned, May, 1957 version of the Seal emphasizes agriculture and agribusiness, industrial development, and the historic character of Frederick County.

Frederick is the largest of all the Maryland's counties, having a land area of six hundred sixty-four square miles, with six square miles of water, for a combined total of six hundred seventy square miles. Being almost equal in distance from Baltimore and Washington, Frederick County extends from the Potomac River to the Pennsylvania State line. To the east it is bordered by Carroll County, and to the southeast by Howard and Montgomery Counties and to the west by Washington County. Frederick is part of the Appalachian Region and Piedmont Plateau. This division falls in the middle of the county.

Originally Frederick County was much larger, but over the years was reduced in size to create the adjacent counties, the last of which was Carroll in 1836. Founded in 1730, its early settlers were Germans who came from Pennsylvania. Following the Germans came English and Scotch-Irish, then Germans and Irish directly from Europe.

Frederick is rich in its history. During the Civil War, Frederick was occupied by both Union and Confederate troops several times. During the Confederate invasion in 1862, as the Rebels were marching through Frederick on their way to Sharpsburg and the Battle of Antietam, Barbara Fritchie, a 96 year old Frederick resident stood in defiance of the Rebels, waving the Union flag. She dared the Confederates to shoot her to stop her waving the flag. This act by Fritchie inspired the controversial poem by John Greenleaf Whittier.

Barbara Fritchie

by John Greenleaf Whittier

Up from the meadows rich with corn, clear in the cool September morn,
The clustered spires Frederick stand green-walled by the hills of Maryland.
Round about them orchards sweep, apple and peach trees fruited deep,
Fair as the garden of the Lord to the eyes of the famished rebel horde,
On that pleasant morn of early fall when Lee marched over the mountain-wall;
Over the mountains winding down, horse and foot, into Frederick town.
Forty flags with their silver stars, forty flags with their crimson bars,
Flapped in the morning wind: the sun of noon looked down, and saw not one.
Up rose old Barbara Fritchie then, bowed with her foursome years and ten;
In her attic window the staff she set, to show that one heart was loyal yet.
Up the street came the rebel tread, Stonewall Jackson riding ahead.
Under his slouched hat left and right he glanced; the old flag met his sight.
"Halt!" - the dust brown ranks stood fast.   "Fire!" - out blazed the rifle blast.
It shivered the window, pane and sash; it rent the banner with seam and gash.
Quick, as it fell, from the broken staff dame Barbara snatched the silken scarf.
She leaned out the window-sill and shook it forth with a royal will.
"Shoot if you must, this old gray head, but spare your country's flag," she said.
A shade of sadness, a blush of shame, over the face of the leader came;
The nobler nature within him stirred to life at that women's deed and word:
"Who touches a hair of yon gray head dies like a dog! March on!" he said.
All day long through Frederick street sounded the tread of marching feet:
All day long that flag tree tost over the heads of the rebel host.
Ever its torn folds rose and fell on the loyal winds that loved it well;
And through the hill-gaps sunset light shone over it with a warm good-night.
Barbara Fritchie's work is o'er, and the Rebel rides on his raids no more.
Honor to her! and let a tear fall, for her sake, on Stonewall's bier.
Over Barbara Fritchie's grave, Flag of Freedom and Union, wave!
Peace and order and beauty draw round thy symbol of light and law;
And ever the stars look down on thy stars below Frederick town!

Barbara Fritchie is buried at Mt. Olivet, and a reconstruction of her home is located at 154 West Patrick Street. It was here that the legendary confrontation between Barbara and Confederate General Stonewall Jackson occurred in 1862. The museum is an exact replica of the original Fritchie home, which was destroyed by a flood. This house was built in 1926, and contains many articles of historical interest, including the original moldings, mantels, floors and hardware. Also on display are clothes, furnishings and personal effects of Barbara Fritchie.

Barbara Fritchie House

Early in 1864, Confederate General Jubal Early forced the city of Frederick to pay $200,000 ransom to save the town from destruction. This loan granted by the local banks cost the city of Frederick $600,000 in principal and interest when it was finally repaid in 1951, after nearly a century of amortization.

Frederick is also known for two former residents: Francis Scott Key, author of "Star-Spangled Banner," and Chief Justice Roger Brooke Taney who wrote the Dred Scott Decision. Incidently Taney was married to Key's sister, Anne. Both men are buried in Frederick. Francis Scott Key is buried in Mt. Olivet Cemetery as are several other well-known persons; Thomas Johnson, the first governor of Maryland; Jane Contee Hanson, wife of the president of the first Congress of the United States; and Dr. Samuel Hansen, a Revolutionary War surgeon. Over Francis Scott Key's grave, the American Flag flies twenty-four hours a day, three hundred sixty-five days a year, by Presidential proclamation. Chief Justice Taney's grave is located in St. John's Catholic Cemetery.

In 1790, Frederick had the largest population of any Maryland county with 30,791. By 1960, the population rose to 71,930 and in 1990 the population was 150,208. By 1994 the population rose to 171,274, an increase of 14% since 1990. In 1998, it increased to 192,060, and by the year 2000, it is projected to be 203,200.

The county seat is the city of Frederick, the county's largest. It was established in 1748. Frederick ranks sixth in size among Maryland's incorporated municipalities. Some larger towns in Frederick County are: Brunswick, Buckeysville, Emmitsburg, Middletown, New Market, Thurmont, and Walkersville. Part of the town of Mt. Airy is also located in Frederick County.

Frederick is one of the top ranking agricultural counties in the State, ranking third in its farm products sold. The county has more farms than any other in Maryland, and leads in production of milk and dairy products. Also corn, small grains, alfalfa, timothy and clover are raised in large quantities, and are largely used as feed crops for the dairy farms. Fruits and vegetables are also grown.

Frederick County has over six thousand acres of beautiful land in several parks. Cunningham Falls and Gambrill State Park are operated by the Department of Forests and Parks. Some of Gathland State Park is also located in Frederick County.

Two of the oldest Catholic colleges in the United States are at Emmitsburg. These are: Mount Saint Mary's for men, the county's oldest and St. Joseph's for women. Other colleges in the county are Hood College, Frederick Community College, and Frederick Academy of the Visitation. Located nearby in the Catoctin Mountains is the famous presidential resort, formerly known as "Shangri-La," named by President Franklin D. Roosevelt, but more recently known as Camp David. Although Frederick County is still an agricultural community, it has, as years go by become more of an urbanized community, especially because of its location near both Baltimore and Washington, D.C.

There are many fascinating historical attractions in the City of Frederick. These include: Mount Olivet Cemetery: Located at the end of Market Street, and established in 1852, this cemetery contains the graves of many of Frederick's prominent people. These include Francis Scott Key, Barbara Fritchie, and Thomas Johnson. Mt. Olivet is also the final resting place for over eight hundred Union and Confederate soldiers who died in the battles at Antietam and Monocacy, and who are buried along the western edge of the cemetery.

Hessian Barracks: Located at 101 Clarke Place, on the grounds of the Maryland School for the Deaf, these accommodations were built in 1777 to house two battalions of soldiers. The Barracks soon became a repository for Hessians, (mercenaries fighting for England) who were captured in the battles of Saratoga and Bennington. English troops were also detained here, and all prisoners were released in May, 1783. In 1802-03, the Barracks were used as an organizing point for the Lewis and Clark Expedition. Since it was built, the building has been in steady use. During the Civil War it was a general hospital, and since as classrooms for the Maryland School for the Deaf. Open by special appointment only, visitors will see relics from the Revolutionary and Civil Wars.

Rose Hill Manor: Located at 1611 North Market Street, this was the home of Maryland's first elected governor, Thomas Johnson. This pristine example of Georgian Colonial architecture has been restored to its original nineteenth century splendor. A blacksmith and a log cabin are also on the grounds. Hands-on displays are of interest to children. Many historical festivals are held here each year. Thomas Johnson was also the one who nominated his personal friend George Washington for the post of Commander-in-Chief of the Continental Army. Here visitors can obtain a better understanding of home life two hundred years ago.

<u>Historic Saint John's Cemetery</u>: This cemetery has entrances on East 3rd and East 4th Streets. Established in 1845, the cemetery contains the graves of members of the Jesuit Novitiate (1805-1904), Father John McElroy, the founder of Boston College, Chief Justice Roger Brooke Taney, Governor Enoch Lowe, John Boisneuf, one of those who condemned Marie Antoinette to the guillotine, and soldiers from the Revolutionary and Civil Wars.

<u>Historical Society of Frederick County</u>: Located at 24 East Church Street, this 1820 Federal-style mansion house offers a collection of Frederick County artifacts. These include special exhibits, a reference library and a genealogical research facility. Guided tours are also available. The Society, which was formed in 1888, opened the mansion to the public in 1960.

<u>The Delaplaine Visual Arts Center</u>: At 40 South Carroll Street, this regional center is housed in a historic flour mill founded in 1850, which features national and regional exhibitions.

<u>Roger Brooke Taney Home/Francis Scott Key Museum</u>: Located at 121 South Bentz Street, this was the home of Chief Justice Roger Brooke Taney and his wife Anne Key, and was built in 1799. Anne's brother was Francis Scott Key, who was a frequent visitor to the home. As a Supreme Court Justice, Taney administered the oath of office to President Lincoln and six others. As a lawyer, his partner was Francis Scott Key. Here visitors will learn about two of most influential men in United States history. Taney, was the drafter of the majority opinion for the Dred Scott Decision, and Key, the writer of "Star-Spangled Banner." Personal effects of these men and their families are on display.

Home and Museum of Judge Roger Brooke Taney • Frederick • Maryland

Schifferstadt Architectural Museum: This unusual manor house was built in 1756 and is the oldest dwelling in Frederick City and features fine German-American construction. Schifferstadt provides an indication of what life was like in the 1750s. Included in the house are a vaulted cellar, and a five-plate jamb stove, as well as exposed hand-hewn oak beams and original hardware. This historically accurate dwelling is located at 1110 Rosemount Avenue, and the grounds also highlight an eighteenth century garden. Here visitors will see one of the most interesting examples of German colonial architecture in the country. One exhibit not to be missed is the "Bible In Iron."

Monocacy National Battlefield: Located at 4801 Urbana Pike, Monocacy Battlefield is the home of one of history's little-known Civil War encounters, which may have been the battle which saved Washington, D.C. This battle placed General Jubal Early and his army of eighteen thousand Confederates against Union General Lew Wallace and his force of five thousand. Although Early won the battle, Wallace detained him long enough to allow Union troops to strengthen positions at Fort Stevens, pushing the Confederates back. This farm land is virtually unchanged since the battle which took place on July 9, 1864. Of special interest is the electronic map presentation which details the battle, as well as many artifacts on display. Five monuments on the ground honor the fallen soldiers.

New Market: Located on historic National Pike, west of Frederick, this small town was an important stop for early nineteenth century travelers. During the Civil War, New Market was patrolled by Confederate troops under the command of General Fitz Hugh Lee at the time of General Lee's invasion of Maryland in September 1862. Also J.E.B. Stuart and his Confederate cavalry escaping from Union forces passed through New Market on their return trip after raiding Pennsylvania. New Market today has a wonderful historic district containing many antiques and crafts.

Frederick County is also the home of seven Historic Landmarks. These are Catoctin Furnace, Jug Bridge Monument Park, Legore Bridge, Memorial Park, National Shrine Grotto of Lourdes, Point of Rocks Railroad Station, and the War Correspondents Memorial Arch.

Catoctin Furnace is located off Route 15 on Route 806, south of Thurmont. Constructed in 1774 by Governor Thomas Johnson, the furnace produced iron for the Revolutionary and Civil Wars, including plates for the Union's ironclad "Monitor."

Jug Bridge Monument Park in Frederick, off I-70 at the East Patrick exit, is a roadside park showcasing a historic stone demijohn from the original jug bridge. Also featured is a monument commemorating Lafayette's visit to Frederick. Legore Bridge is located off Route 194, on Legore Bridge Road at the Monocacy River. This magnificent stone bridge's construction began in 1898 and opened to the public in 1900. James William Legore, one of Frederick's civic leaders, was the driving force behind the creation of this bridge. The bridge measures three hundred forty feet in length, twenty-seven feet wide and sixty-four feet high.

Memorial Park is dedicated to all veterans from Frederick County. It features memorials to World War I, World War II, Korean War, and Vietnam. The park is located on the corner of West Second and North Bentz Streets in Frederick. National Shrine Grotto of Lourdes is the oldest replica of the Grotto of Lourdes in the western hemisphere. It is on the grounds of Mount Saint Mary's College, Emmitsburg. Point of Rocks Railroad Station is located at Point of Rocks, on U.S. 15 South to Md 28. Built in the 1880s, this is a superb example of a Victorian railroad station. Today the station is used by the MARC passenger trains.

War Correspondents Memorial Arch, at Crampton's gap, in Gathland State Park. This location was an important site of fighting during the Battle of South Mountain during the Civil War. It was built in 1885 by George Alfred Townsend, famous author and war correspondent of the Civil War. Gath was the pen name of Townsend, from which Gathland originates. This Arch is the only monument in the world erected to the memory of the work of War Correspondents.

Form of Government: County Commissioners

Map of Frederick County

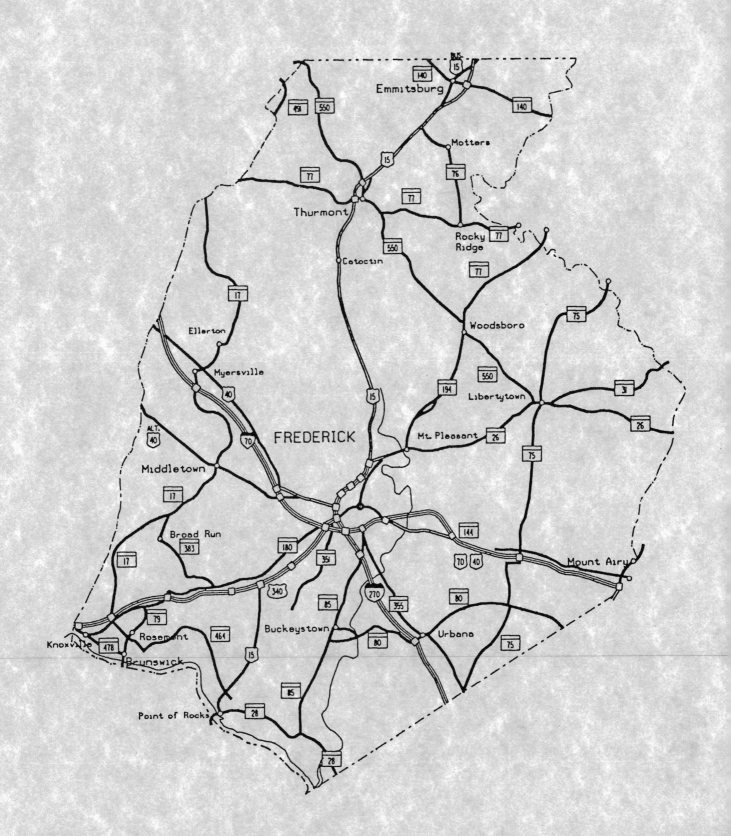

GARRETT COUNTY

Garrett County was created from Allegany County in 1872 (Chapter 212, Acts of 1872). The County was named for John Work Garrett (1820-1884), railroad executive, industrialist, and financier.

Garrett County is located in the extreme northwestern corner of Maryland, and is bordered on the east by Allegany County, and on the west and south by the Potomac River and State of West Virginia. To the north is the State of Pennsylvania. It has a land area of six hundred sixty-two square miles and a water area of six square miles. Seventy-five percent of the county is mountainous with the remaining twenty-five percent being a rolling plateau. The highest mountain ridge is Backbone Mountain reaching a height of three thousand three hundred sixty feet above sea level. Three other mountain ranges comprise the other main elevations: Meadow Mountain and Winding Ridge which range to approximately nine hundred feet and Big Savage Mountain at three thousand feet.

On December 15, 1977, the seal of Garrett County went into effect by virtue of Resolution #7. The seal is described as elliptical, with the name "Garrett County" inscribed above the upper fourth of the ellipse, and "Maryland 1872" inscribed below the lower fourth of the ellipse. The seal depicts the seasons, winter, spring, summer and fall. Winter is illustrated by a large snowflake. Spring and fall by the oak leaves and conifer representing the County's mountains, and water and sailing for summer. The colors are blue for the water and sky, with kelly green dividing the blue and white background. The date 1872 depicts the year that Garrett County was founded.

The first settlers in Garrett County were English, German and Irish, most of whom came from Pennsylvania. Many present residents are descendants from these groups. The population of Garrett County in 1940 and 1950 was below 20,000. After 1960 the population rose to 20,420, and in 1990 was 28,138. The population in 1994 was 29,372, an increase of 4.4% since 1990. In 1998, it rose again to 30,170, and by the year 2000 it is projected to be 30,650.

Garrett County was the last of Maryland's Counties to be created. Unless the constitutional provision requiring an area of at least four hundred square miles for each new county is amended, there will be no new counties formed in the future. In naming the county, "Laurel" was the first chosen, but local sentiment was overwhelmingly in favor of Garrett, in honor of John W. Garrett, who during this time was President of the Baltimore & Ohio Railroad.

The manner in which Garrett County was created is unique in Maryland history. A permissive clause for the creation of a county in the area now included in the bounds of Garrett County was inserted in the constitution of 1851 (Article 8, Section 2). No action was taken about the matter until 1872 after two subsequent constitutions, 1864 and 1867, which provided that any new county must have an area of at least four hundred square miles and have a population of a least ten thousand. Significant turmoil for another Western Shore county began after the creation of Wicomico County on the Eastern Shore by the constitutional convention of 1867.

By 1871, it was conceded that all constitutional requirements had been met, and the Assembly created Garrett County by an act on April 1, 1872 (Acts of 1872, Chapter 212). This act set the bounds as follows: "That all that part of Allegany County lying south and west of a line beginning at the summit of the Big Backbone, or Savage Mountain, where the mountain is crossed by Mason and Dixon's line, and running thence by a straight line to the middle of Savage River, where it empties into the Potomac River; thence by a straight line to the nearest point or boundary of the State of West Virginia; then with the said boundary to the Fairfax stone, shall be a new county, to be called the County of Garrett; provided the provisions of this act as to taking the census of the people and the area of said new county, and the sense of the people therein, shall be complied with in accordance with the constitution of this state." These boundaries consisted of three straight lines of the west, north, and east and the Potomac River on the south. The southern boundary of the county lies on the right bank of the north branch of the Potomac River, whose waters are accordingly within the limits of Garrett County. The northern boundary is fixed by that part of the Mason-Dixon line which had no permanent markers, and was not known exactly until the resurvey of this line was done by the states of Maryland and Pennsylvania some years later. The eastern boundary was long in dispute due to the difficulty in surveying the line required by the act. The western line, which also marks the common boundary of Maryland and West Virginia, could not be drawn exactly until the boundary dispute between these two states was settled. When all the boundary lines were finally fixed, Garrett County was found to have an area of six hundred sixty-two square miles, making it the second largest county in the state.

The history of Garrett County is an interesting one. Although no battles were fought here, many great events and forces of American history played an important role in the growth of the county, with the development of several significant roads. It was these roads which served to open the county to settlers. In some cases, these roads were originally Indian trails which were widened to improve travel.

One such case was Nemacolin's Path, which passed through the northern part of the county. In 1755, General Braddock's army followed this route and cut the first wagon road from Fort Cumberland through the wilderness to the Great Meadows near Uniontown, Pennsylvania. It was on this road that the opening battle of the French and Indian War occurred, when the young Colonel George Washington was defeated at Fort Necessity. Following the French and Indian War, this old road remained in use for many years.

Other roads important to Garrett's development were the Old State Road (Winchester-Morgantown-Clarksburg Road) built in 1789 through the county. This road was used by settlers going to the newly formed lands opened by the Louisiana Purchase.

The first great highway joining the eastern and western sections of the United States was the Cumberland Road. This highway passed through the northern section of Garrett County near the old Braddock Road, and was built between 1811 and 1819 by the Federal Government. It soon became known as the National Road and today is part of Route 40. As a result of the highway, the town of Grantsville was formed, named after Daniel Grant of Baltimore. Another well-known east-west route is the Northwestern Turnpike, which crossed the southern part of the county. This turnpike was proposed by George Washington and surveyed by Crozet, who was a soldier in Napoleon's army in Egypt, then an engineer for Virginia. The turnpike today is part of U.S. Route 50.

Prior to the Revolutionary War, only a scant number of settlers came into Garrett County. The first permanent settlement was established by John Friend, Sr., along with his brothers in 1765. This settlement was called "Friends Fortune," and was located at the mouth of the Youghiogheny River, and is presently the town of Friendsville.

Having a greater effect on the development of Garrett County was the building of the Baltimore & Ohio Railroad through the mountains in the 1850s. Following the construction of the railroad in the southern part of the county, new farm lands were cleared, timber and coal resources were generated, and new towns built along the route.

Oakland was one such town which was laid out in 1849 near the little settlement of McCarty's Mill. Bloomington was also laid out the same year as a coal mining center, and the town of Swanton grew up as a shipping point for timber. Garrett County, after having been a part of Allegany County for eighty-three years was formed in 1872.

Another factor in the growth of Garrett County was the work accomplished by John Work Garrett. Under his presidency of the Baltimore & Ohio Railroad, the railroad built large summer resorts in Deer Park and Oakland. Deer Park eventually became a resort for the affluent before 1900. In 1886, President and Mrs. Cleveland spent a week of their honeymoon at the resort. Also in 1881, the town of Mt. Lake Park was organized as a summer religious and cultural center.

After 1900 the county's popularity as a summer resort declined, but this trend reversed with the coming of Deep Creek Lake and the State Parks.

The county seat is Oakland, and lies in part of what was the westernmost of Lord Baltimore's manors. It was founded in 1849, twenty-three years before Garrett County was established, and incorporated in 1861. In 1851, the main line of the Baltimore & Ohio came through Oakland, encouraging the community's development. Located near Mountain Lake Park and Deep Creek Lake, Oakland has a population of 1,750. Other incorporated towns and their populations are: Accident (350), located on Route 219, approximately five miles north of Deep Creek Lake is a scenic farming town dating back to the 1800s. The oldest known structure, the Drane House has been restored. In Zion Cemetery and St. Paul's New Cemetery are two stone markers indicating the former sites of the earliest frame structures used by the Lutheran congregations for church services. The historic Kaese's Mill, on Bear Creek-Fish Hatchery Road still stands, appearing much the same as it originally did in 1868; Deer Park (420); Friendsville (575) is the site of the first settlement (whereas Selbysport is the oldest town). Friendsville was named for John Friend, Sr., who came to this area in 1765, and who bought the land from the Indians. In 1890, upon the building of the Chesapeake & Ohio Railroad, the town became an important shipping point for lumber.

Grantsville (500) is located two miles south of the Mason-Dixon Line on Route 40. Grantsville contains the oldest and most historic section in Garrett County. These include the Casselman River Bridge, Casselman Hotel, Stanton's Mill and Penn Alps; Kitzmiller (275), Loch Lynn Heights (465), and Mountain Lake Park (1,941). Between 1882 and

1912, Mountain Lake Park had twenty-eight hotels and boarding houses. Thousands of visitors from all over the world would visit the park each year to partake of the cool, clean mountain air and the numerous cultural, educational, and recreational activities. Wealthy families who owned their own houses would spent an entire summer here, bringing with them their servants, animals, and in later years automobiles, via the B & O Railroad. President Taft, William Jennings Bryan and Billy Sunday were just three of the well-known people who visited the park, and who would speak before huge audiences.

Although mostly mountainous, Garrett County still has agricultural areas in valleys, and on the plateau. Dairying and livestock, as well as the growing of corn, wheat, rye, alfalfa, timothy and clover hay. One of the leading industries is the production of maple syrup, responsible in large part for most of the State's supply. Garrett is also ranked high in the production of forest products and mineral production. The town of Jennings is one example of a developing mining center. Coal, stone, sand and gravel are major productions and the only natural gas fields in the State are located here. Coal and lumber are important industries in the communities of Kitzmiller, Shallmar, Vindex, Kempton, Crellin and Friendsville. The towns of Grantsville and Accident have remained mostly agricultural centers.

The Baltimore & Ohio Railroad crosses the county, and the Western Maryland Railroad follows a branch of the Potomac River. The State of Maryland owns more land in Garrett County than in any other county. This land is concentrated in such areas as Deep Creek Lake State Park, Garrett State Forest, Potomac State Forest, and Savage River State Forest.

Deep Creek Lake State Park is a major recreational facility. The largest freshwater lake in Maryland, it is twelve miles in length with a shoreline of sixty-five miles, covering three thousand nine hundred acres. The lake was built in 1925 by the Youghiogheny Hydroelectric Power Company, and was purchased by the Pennsylvania Electric Company in 1942. In 1980, the lake and buffer strip were leased to the Maryland Department of Natural Resources to be managed as a public recreational resource. Today it is managed by the Maryland State Forest and Park Service. Deep Creek Lake's elevation is two thousand four hundred sixty-two feet. The average depth is twenty-six and one-half feet, with a maximum depth of seventy-two feet. Used in both summer and winter, Deep Creek has many good motels, restaurants, cottages and camps to rent, as well as public swimming and boating.

Garrett State Forest is comprised of seven thousand four hundred acres of mountain forests, streams, and valleys. In 1906 the Garrett brothers gave the State of Maryland two thousand acres of forest land with the provision that a state forestry department be established. This land was originally named Swallow Falls State Forest. In 1976 the name was changed to Garrett State Forest in honor of the donors. Within Garrett State Forest are two of the oldest State Parks in the State of Maryland. These are Swallow Falls and Herrington Manor. Within Swallow Falls State Park are three beautiful waterfalls: Muddy Creek Falls, Maryland's largest; Swallow Falls, and the smallest, Tolliver Falls.

Potomac State Forest contains twelve thousand four hundred acres of trees, streams, and wildlife. The terrain here is rough with elevations ranging from one thousand eight hundred feet along the Potomac to two thousand nine hundred sixty feet on Backbone Mountain. Several of the larger streams in the area are Schell, Laurel, Lostland Run, and Crabtree Creek.

Savage River State Forest is the largest of Maryland's State Forests containing fifty-three thousand acres of forestland, streams and wildlife. This forest forms part of the Appalachian Plateau and also contains two State Parks, New Germany and Big Run.

In addition to Garrett County's outstanding beauty, it also has many historic sites and attractions. These include the Casselman River Bridge and the Casselman Hotel. The Casselman River Bridge is the oldest stone arch highway bridge in the United States and is located near Grantsville on Route 40 east. The Casselman River Bridge was built in 1813, and at the time of its construction was the largest single-span stone arch bridge in the United States (eighty feet). This bridge was built with native Western Maryland stone, and served traffic on the nation's first Federal highway. As a part of the National Pike, which ran between Cumberland and Wheeling, West Virginia, this bridge improved the method of transportation for freighters, drovers, wagoners, horsemen, stagecoach passengers, and pedestrians when the western frontier was the Alleghenies.

As people watched the construction of the bridge, many believed that it would collapse when the supporting timbers were removed. On the night before the opening day celebration, the contractor, to avoid an audience should the bridge collapse, loosened the supports to check the bridge. All went well, so the next day during the opening celebration, as the supports were removed, the contractor stood under the bridge to prove its worthiness. This charming stone arch has stood the test of time for over the past one hundred eighty years as one of Garrett County's most photogenic as well as historic sites. The bridge was closed to traffic in 1953, and restored with funds made available by the State of Maryland. In 1964, the bridge was designated a Registered National Landmark by the Department of the Interior. Today, a picnic area with fireplaces and other facilities are available along the bridge.

The Casselman Hotel, also in Grantsville, was first opened as a drover's inn in 1824. This hotel, located on Main Street, is still in operation today. Many of its original features have been preserved. This hotel, which has been in operation for over 170 years is one of Garrett County's finest landmarks.

Grantsville is also the home of Stanton's Mill and Penn Alps. Stanton's Mill, was built in 1795 by Jesse Tomlinson and is one of Garrett County's oldest grist mills. In 1856 the mill was rebuilt by Perry Schultz and deeded to William Stanton in 1862. Stanton's son, Eli, operated the mill for forty-three years. Stanton's Mill is still in operation today, and is located at Little Crossings on Route 40. Penn Alps is a log building which was built in 1818 as a stagecoach stop on the National Road. It was originally called "Little Crossings Inn," and today serves as a restaurant and craft shop. Next to Penn Alps is the Spruce Forest Artisan Village which consists of four log cabins, a plank shed and several other buildings, including one from the Revolutionary War, 1920 log houses, and the 1835 Miller House, built by an Amish patriarch of the Casselman Valley.

Other areas of historical interest are: the Baltimore & Ohio Railroad Station. Located in Oakland, this is one of the oldest stations in the United States. In 1884, this Queen Anne-style station was built after the B & O Railroad had developed a resort clientele for Oakland. The ground that the station stands on was first used by the B & O Railroad as early as 1851. Now a member of the National Registry, the Oakland Station is distinguished by its incised brick, artistic massing and the mixing of building styles from long ago. The station was built by a Baltimore based firm of Baldwin and Pennington, who also built a similar station in Laurel, Maryland in 1884. The Church of the Presidents in Oakland is where three presidents preferred to attend services over any other place of worship. It was here that Presidents Grant, Harrison and Cleveland would come to services while they were on vacation, as Garrett County was their favorite vacation retreat. For many years it was not used, but today is open to the public and occupied by St. Matthew's Episcopal Congregation. On Center Street, also in Oakland is the

<u>Garrett County Historical Museum</u> which first opened in 1969 and is operated by the Garrett County Historical Society, Inc. The museum contains many artifacts important to the historical and cultural development of Garrett County. A section of the museum is dedicated to Indian and military artifacts from the <u>USS Garrett County</u>.

Located east of the town of Accident is the <u>Drane House</u>. Built in the late 1700s, it is one of the few original frontier plantation homes remaining on Maryland's Tableland. It provides a living history of the tobacco growing days in the uplands. Today the house has been restored and is available for tours.

Another interesting town in Garrett County in <u>McHenry</u>, located north of Deep Creek Lake. This settlement was originally called "Buffalo Marsh," by the first white men who visited the area and found the carcass of a large buffalo in the mud. The town was later named for Colonel James McHenry of Baltimore, who was an aide to General George Washington during the Revolutionary War. McHenry was also a physician, a signer of the Constitution, and Secretary of War under two Presidents. Fort McHenry in Baltimore was also named for this same man in his honor. On Route 219, overlooking Deep Creek Lake, a memorial plaque was erected honoring Dr. McHenry. Today, McHenry is the site of Wisp, Maryland's only downhill ski slope. In the northern part of the county lie several campsites used by the men of General Braddock's army on their way to Fort Duquesne in 1755.

Garrett is a county of great beauty offering a large number of natural resources and recreational facilities.

Form of Government: County Commissioners

Map of Garrett County

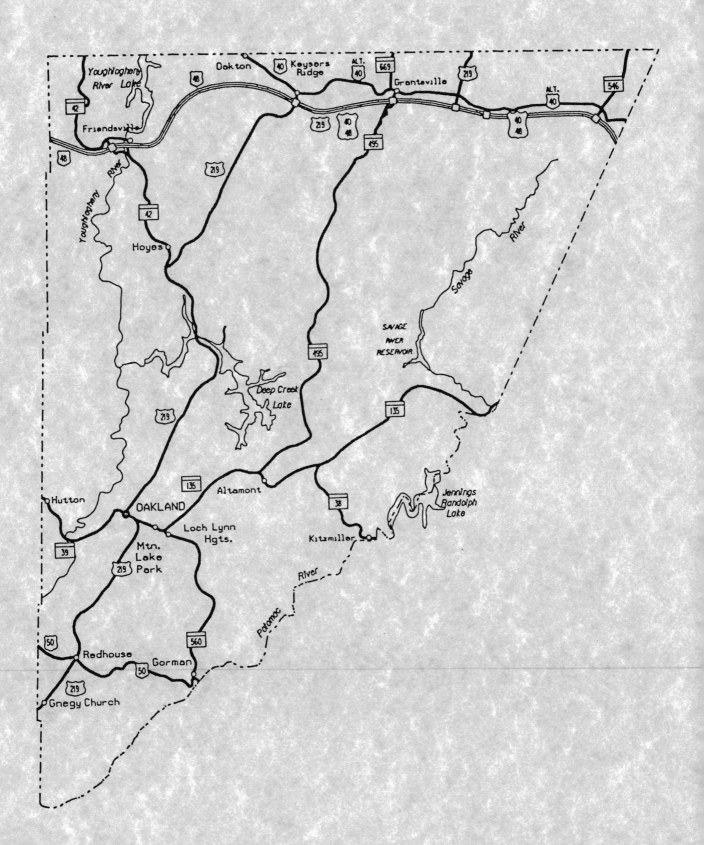

HARFORD COUNTY

Harford County was separated from Baltimore County in 1773 (Chapter 6, Acts of 1773). The County was named for Henry Harford (1759-1834), last proprietary of Maryland. He was the son of Frederick Calvert, Sixth Lord Baltimore, but because of his illegitimate birth did not inherit his father's title.

The Harford County Coat of Arms was designed by George Van Bibber and adopted by the County Commissioners on September 28, 1964. In the accepted design the shield is gold to symbolize the wealth of the county and the richness of its fields. Across the shield are waving bends of blue signifying three major county streams - Deer Creek, Bynum Run, and Winters Run. The crest is a two-handed forearm with the right hand holding escrivant (heraldic for "writing"), a white quill symbolizing the pen used by those who wrote and signed the Bush Declaration. The left hand holds a sword as if presenting into the right hand of the nation the skills of reproducing defense materials, emanating from Edgewood Arsenal and Aberdeen Proving Ground. The "motto "At the Risque of our Lives and Fortunes" comprises the last eight words of the Bush Declaration and preserves the same spelling for "risk" that is used in that document.

Harford County lies between Pennsylvania and the Chesapeake Bay, bordered by the Susquehanna River on the east, separating it from Cecil County. Most of its western border is the Gunpowder River, and on the other side is Baltimore County.

The County was originally settled by the English, followed by those from Virginia and North and South Carolina. The northern areas of the county lie in the Piedmont Plateau, and have an elevation of two hundred to seven hundred fifty feet above sea level. The southern areas are part of the Coastal Plain and range from forty to two hundred feet above sea level.

Harford is mostly an agricultural county. Dairying is an important industry as well as the raising and cultivation of corn, grains, and hay. Farming is a major part of Harford County life, with the growing of various vegetables. Raising horses is an important activity in Harford County, especially race horses of which Harford County has produced many major race winners.

The first major industrial plant was Bata Shoe Company, located in Bel Camp. It was established by Czech refugees just prior to World War II, and for years supplied many jobs to local residents. Other industrial products from Harford County include: concrete, iron railings, adhesives, aluminum core honeycomb, flooring, cabinets, sodium sulphate, liquid chlorine, clothing, carbonated beverages and canned corn.

Probably the two most important factors in Harford's economy were the Aberdeen Proving Ground and the Edgewood Arsenal. Aberdeen Proving Ground was first used primarily for the testing of ordnance and Edgewood Arsenal for the U.S. Army chemical warfare station, where various types of gases were developed for military use. Training is also carried on in offensive and defensive chemical warfare. Located on the reservation at Edgewood Arsenal was Fort Hoyle, a field artillery and ordnance battery headquarters, and also used as a summer camp of the U.S. Army Field Artillery Reserve. First opened in 1922, Fort Hoyle was used until 1940. In July 1971, Edgewood Arsenal merged with the Aberdeen Proving Ground, and was renamed Edgewood Area of Aberdeen Proving Ground. Today these areas are used for various military functions. These two areas have provided hundreds of jobs contributing greatly to the economic stability of the county.

The State of Maryland owns several small areas of the county: Rocks State Park, covering six hundred acres; Susquehanna State Park, two thousand five hundred acres; and approximately seven hundred seventy-seven acres of the eleven thousand acres of Gunpowder State Park.

Rocks State Park, located eight miles north of Bel Air, is an area characterized by natural beauty and massive rocks and boulders. Featured in the park is a throne-like rock formation known as the King and Queen Seats, where according to legend, Indian chieftains sat in tribal council.

Located in what is now Rocks State Park is the second largest vertical drop falls in Maryland (The Largest being Muddy Creek Falls in Swallow Falls State Park in Garrett County). Opened to the public in October 1993, Falling Branch Falls (also called Kilgore Falls) is located on Falling Branch stream, a little known area, surrounded by thick forests and vines. Prior to 1993, the falls was located on private property until March, when the State of Maryland, Department of Natural Resources purchased the land and made it a part of Rocks State Park.

The stream got its name from a series of rock cliffs located about a mile above its mouth, which make the water fall thirty feet, spraying ancient logs. This natural thirty foot waterfall is where the original Americans would come to bathe. Near the falls are the remains of stone steps, perhaps constructed by the Susquehannock Indians. Just below the falls there once stood a mill and dwelling house, owned by a man named Isaac Jones. Once at the falls, it is also interesting to note the huge rock walls which enclose the area on three sides.

Falling Branch Falls is a beautiful, remote, tranquil, historic area worth the visit. As it is managed by the Rocks State Park, picnicking and swimming are permitted, but open fires are prohibited. To get there you follow Route 24 through Rocks State Park, past Route 165, to St. Mary's Road. Turn left on St. Mary's Road and follow to Falling Branch Road. Follow Falling Branch Road (a gravel road) to a parking lot, located at the home of the park ranger. From this point there is a walking path to the falls, which is an approximate fifteen minute walk.

Falling Branch Falls

Susquehanna State Park is located north of Havre de Grace, off Route 155 on the west bank of the Susquehanna River. Main attractions in the park are the Carter Mansion, Jersey Toll House and the Rock Run Mill, which has been completely restored. Also in the park is the Steppingstone Museum, located in farm buildings, housing a collection of 13,000 pieces of authentic Americana, focusing on the rural household and life between 1880-1920.

Gunpowder State Park is an eleven thousand acre park, located on the Harford-Baltimore County Line, of which over seven hundred acres are in Harford County. Featured is the Jericho Covered Bridge (circa 1865) which crosses the Little Gunpowder on Jericho Road. The Jerusalem Mill (1772), located near the bridge features a rare vertical shaft mill design.

Harford County today has an area of four hundred forty-eight square land miles and twenty-seven square water miles. Harford has three incorporated towns: Aberdeen, Havre de Grace, and Bel Air, the County Seat.   Bel Air was first planned in 1780 by Aquilla Scott on a portion of his inheritance named Scott's Improvement Enlarged, and more commonly called Scott's Old Fields.   In this early planning there were forty-two lots consisting of one-half acre, fronting on Main Street. The first lot sold was to Daniel Scott of Aquilla who paid thirty pounds in gold and silver. Other purchasers soon followed including county officials, attorneys, innkeepers, and merchants. Some of the more prominent first buyers were: John Love, Esq. who was a Delegate to the Annapolis Convention June 22, 1774; Gilbert Jones, an innkeeper; Benjamin Bradford Norris, a signer of the Bush Declaration and Edward Robinson a tavern owner.

In 1782, Daniel Scott, also a signer of the Bush Declaration, laid out the plans for the court house. By this time the town limits extended to both sides of Main Street, from about seventy-five feet north of the Methodist Church to about three hundred feet beyond Baltimore Pike on the south, and from Bond Street on the west to Dallam Place on the east.

Scott's Old Fields was chosen as the County Seat in 1782. The Act of 1784 conferred certain powers to the County Commissioners who decreed that henceforth Scott's Old Fields should be known as "Belle Aire." By 1798, Belle Aire had been changed in spelling to the present Bel Air. In this year Bel Air had only about one hundred fifty inhabitants, a Methodist Church and Meeting House, four inns, a courthouse, jail, two blacksmith shops, two joiners, one tailor, chairmaker, shoemaker, and wheelwright, and three stores. According to the 1798 tax assessment list, there were twenty-five houses of which twenty-three were made of wood, two of brick and one of stone. Additionally, there were fourteen stables, four meat houses and one spring house. Sixty years later, in 1858, the number of buildings on Main Street rose to seventy. Office Street and Courtland Street (formally named Leeds Street) had been cut through to Bond Street.

Following the Civil War, Bel Air felt a building boom. Houses were built along the east side of Main Street, along Gordon Street and on the west side of Broadway, a prominent area of the town. By 1886, the "Hays Addition" was added, when George A. Hays and William F. Hays developed the areas west of Bond Street to include Thomas, Archer, Hays, and George Streets.

Bel Air is rich in history with many interesting buildings both past and present. These include: Bel Air Volunteer Fire Company: First incorporated in 1924, it evolved from the Bel Air Fire and Salvage Company. The first headquarters was on Courtland Street, and the first engine was a 1923 Model T. In 1924, it moved to Main Street and the main engine was a 1924 Seagraves. As they continued to grow they again moved to an alley area between Main and Bond Streets, next to the Methodist Church. The first ambulance was a converted hearse, acquired in 1938. In 1956, the Central Fire Alarm System was started; it coordinated all fire companies in the county. In 1964 they moved to their present location on Hickory Avenue at Churchville Road; Dallams Hotel: Prior to 1874, the Dallams Hotel, also called the Dallam's Harford House was located on Main Street adjacent to what used to be the Commercial & Savings Bank. Later renamed the Vaughn Hotel, Dallam's was used as a stagecoach terminal to Baltimore and Magnolia.

The Harford Mutual Insurance Company, was established in 1824 as the Mutual Fire Insurance Company in Harford County, it is located on Bond Street at Gordon Street and is in operation today. In 1842 it was granted a charter which empowered it to make insurance on all kinds of property. It is one of Bel Air's permanent fixtures; Kenmore Inn: Located on the southwest corner of Main Street and Baltimore Pike, this house was originally the home of Dr. Wakeman, and for a brief time his daughter and son-in-law, Dr. and Mrs. William T. Munnikhuysen. In 1909, Colonel H.D. Hanway made an addition and thus established the Kenmore Inn. It was later managed by C.C. Hanway, followed by various other managements over the years. A popular stopping place for travelers between

Washington and New York, and also a local meeting place, the inn was demolished in 1962 to make way for the Safeway Food Store. Other businesses are present at this site today.

Bel Air has been the home of hundreds of businesses, both past and present. Some popular founding businesses are: <u>Hirsch's Men Store:</u> Originally located on Main Street at Lee Street, this was one of Bel Air's first tailoring and haberdasheries. Founded by Benjamin Hirsch in 1924, it moved to 9 South Main Street in 1926, where it is located today. In 1938, the store came under the management of David Cohen, son-in-law of Mr. Hirsch; <u>F. Bond Boarman:</u> Located on Main Street at Courtland Street. In 1918, F. Bond Boarman purchased the Gover Hotel and converted it into a hardware store under his name. Following his death in 1923, the business became the F. Bond Boarman Company, operated by Horace Boarman, Sr. After the death of Horace, the F. Bond Boarman Company became <u>Courtland Hardware</u> under the partnership of Horace Boarman, Jr., and W. Eugene Graybeal. It remained in operation at this location for years, and is presently located on Bond Street; <u>Klemper's Drugstore:</u> Founded in the early 1900s by Dr. Klemper, the drug store is located at 23 S. Main Street. At his death, the store was purchased by Dr. Boyd and Mr. A.M. Fulford, and became Boyd and Fulford. In 1952, Dr. Edwin Maisenhalder bought the drugstore from Mrs. Fulford and managed it under the same name. Today it is still in operation on Main Street.

KENMORE INN
BEL AIR, MARYLAND
C. C. Hanway, *Manager*

Phone—No. 4 Bel Air. Most modern inn on State Road between New York and Washington. Every comfort for the tourist. Rooms— single and ensuite with bath. Running water in every room. Clean and sanitary. Garage in connection.

The Kenmore Inn as it appeared in the early 1900s.

F. Bond Boarman as it appeared in the early 1900s at Main & Courtland Streets.
This building eventually became Courtland Hardware.

Many other stores and persons helped form the businesses of Bel Air to make it the thriving community it is today. Others were: Charles L. Lutz, establishing his business in 1927; McComas Brothers, a lumber, coal and hardware store established in 1905; John S. Richardson who founded Richardson's Drug Store, formerly at Main Street and Pennsylvania Avenue; Corbin Ice and Coal Company, established in 1915, producing ice and coal; Getz Clothing Store, established in 1895 by Mr. and Mrs. Soloman Getz, originally located at 26. S. Main Street. After moving several times it returned to 26 S. Main where it remained for many years. This location is now used by descendants for the Getz Law Firm; Guercio's Meat Market, founded in 1921 by Paul and Josephine Guercio; Bauer's Bakery, founded in the early 1900s and once located at 18 South Main Street; Keithley's Jewelry Store, founded in 1929 by Edmund and Pearl Keithley, once located at 24 Office Street; and Walker's 5 & 10 Store, established in the early 1900s and formerly located on Main Street. These are just a few of the many early businesses which helped in the forming of Bel Air.

Bel Air, throughout its history, like other communities, has had its share of disasters, whether by heavy snow, winds, floods, fires or explosions. Some best remembered fires and explosions are: In 1900 the <u>Enterprise Carriage Company</u> caught fire resulting in a major blaze. In 1930, Coale's Store on Main Street caught fire destroying the building. In 1931 the dry cleaning portion caught fire in Hirsch's Haberdashery on Main Street. On March 11, 1936, the Bel Air Presbyterian Church burned, damaging the entire interior, leaving only the stone structure. In 1942, another major blaze destroyed the tavern operated by Helen Magness Archer, at the corner of Main Street and Churchville Road. Again in 1942 a fire on Main Street destroyed the Acme Store, where the Hub was formerly located, and did some damage to Hirsch's Men's Store.

On February 2, 1972, a major fire hit Bel Air, wiping out six businesses and leaving many apartment dwellers homeless. The overflowing of a fuel oil tank being filled and subsequent ignition of the oil by a gas water heater caused a two million-dollar fire which raged for four hours before finally being controlled. Lost in the fire were the Red Fox Restaurant, The Bel Air Recreation Center, Bel Air Office Products, Smithson's Barber Shop, Talles Jewelry Store, and the Main Street Market. The apartment complex located in the former Vaughn Hotel was also destroyed. Over two hundred twenty-five firefighters in twenty-five fire units answered the 8:13 a.m. alarm. The Red Fox Restaurant did rebuild, and is located in the same basic area today. Other businesses did not rebuild. Those that did, are located in other sections of the town.

Two explosions hit Bel Air over the years. The first was on December 10, 1953 when a jet plane from the Glenn L. Martin plant in Middle River exploded about a mile in the air above Bel Air. Burning parts of the plane landed on many areas of the town. One man died in the crash, while three other passengers survived. The second explosion came on March 23, 1970 when a car blew up enroute from Bel Air. The early morning explosion came when the car exploded on Route 1, at Tollgate Road, in front of the old Toll House. This incident was based around the upcoming trial of H. Rap Brown, who had been charged with several criminal violations, including inciting to riot in Cambridge, Maryland. Believing that he could not receive a fair trial in Cambridge, a change of venue was granted, to Bel Air. In preparation for but prior to the date of trial, times in Bel Air were tense. Threats had been received relating that the courthouse would be bombed. As a preventive measure, the Maryland State Police, along with other law enforcement officials placed a twenty-four-hour guard on the courthouse and its proximity. A curfew was placed in force for several days, due in part to racial tension and as a preventive measure. On March 23, 1970, two African-American males drove into Bel Air, armed with a large amount of C-4, commonly called plastic explosive. Their intent was to bomb the courthouse. Upon arriving in the area of the courthouse they observed that it was heavily guarded. Being unable to complete their mission, they headed out of the town, south on Baltimore Pike. As they approached the intersection of Tollgate Road, the C-4 detonated in the right front passenger area of the car. The explosion was so intense that it blew a hole in Baltimore Pike, destroying the car, killing both occupants immediately, and blew out the windows of the Toll House at this intersection. The blast was seen and heard for miles. This incident was both the culmination and beginning of a series of racial incidents, keeping times in Bel Air tense. No further major incidents occurred, and soon Bel Air returned to business as usual.

Two other places of historical interest in Bel Air are the Hays House and Liriodendron. The Hays House, built in 1788, today sits quietly on Kenmore Avenue. Getting the house here was not an easy task. Thomas Archer Hays, Sr. (1780-1861), was the Bel Air lawyer who owned the house from 1813 to 1861. Although there were other owners of the property and house, Mr. Hays owned the house for the longest period of time, thus its name. The original Hays House property was part of two tracts of land know as "Scotts Improvement Enlarged" and "Burr." Both of these tracts were acquired by Daniel Scott in the early eighteenth century. On July 30, 1731, a patent was issued to Daniel Scott for three hundred ninety acres of "Scotts Improvement Enlarged." This tract of land was a resurvey of two former tracts patented to Scott. These were known as "Scotts Friendship" acquired in 1705, and "Scotts Improvement" in 1728. The tract of land known as "Burr," was originally patented to James Carroll, who gave this property to Michael Taylor through his will. Taylor, deeded one hundred acres of this land to Daniel Scott in 1730. Daniel Scott in his will, bequeathed the tracts of land known as "Scotts Improvement Enlarged" and "Burr" to his son, also named Daniel, in March 1744. Daniel, the second, deeded this land to his son, James, on November 5, 1745. James owned the land until his death. In his will, in 1762, he bequeathed to his son, Aquila, "the Plantation whereon I now live, being the remaining parts of Scotts Improvement Enlarged and also part of a tract called Burr adjoining the same." There was another part of "Scotts Improvement Enlarged" that James left another son, Benjamin. This land, acquired by Aquila Scott in 1762 and later called Scotts Old Fields, would eventually become the town of Bel Air.

During the years from 1788 to 1813, it is not exactly clear as to who may have occupied the house, known today as the Hays House. It is possible that the house was occupied by persons other than the owner. It is known that the house was occupied by a Josias Smith in 1798.

The exact date that the house was built is unknown, but records indicate that it was circa 1788. Aquilla Scott sold one acre of land to John Bull on April 3, 1788, lot numbers 39 and 41, where the house originally stood. From this time there were various owners of the Hays House property. Deed records indicate that John Bull sold the property to Frederick Yeiser on September 23, 1789. The succession of ownership that followed is: Thomas Gibson, November 27, 1794; Elizabeth Gibson, wife of Thomas, September 6, 1796; John Churchman Bond, January 3, 1809; Arnold Richardson, June 5, 1810; and Thomas Archer Hays, Sr., on April 12, 1813.

Thomas A. Hays was the single largest land owner in Bel Air. Thomas married Betsy Jones, who was the granddaughter of William Jones, and the daughter of Gilbert Jones, a well-known tavern keeper in Bel Air, located at Main Street and Baltimore Pike, on the northwest corner. Thomas and Betsy had seven children: Sally Galloway, Mary Giles, Frances Fulford, Elizabeth Jacobs, Harriet Whaland, Pamelia Hays, and Thomas Hays, Jr. Records exhibit that Thomas Sr., lived in the house and also that he lived there with his daughter Pamelia at the time of his death in 1861. In his will, probated August 5, 1861, Thomas A. Hays Sr., bequeathed the house, property, furniture, and inventory to his daughter, Pamelia H. Hays. Pamelia never married, and continued to live in the house until her death on January 14, 1875. As she had no direct heirs, she left the house, property, and inventory to her sister, Elizabeth A. Jacobs. This was a provision of her father's will. Elizabeth owned the property from 1875 to August 20, 1893. From this time, the house stayed in the Jacobs family until September 11, 1957, when Joseph S. Jacobs and his wife Sarah M. Jacobs sold the property to Anna Irene McCleary. Anna held the property until May 20, 1960, when it was sold to Safeway Stores, Inc., for the purpose of building a Safeway grocery store.

In April 1959, Anna advised the Historical Society of her intentions to sell the property, and offered the house to the Historical Society. Upon Safeway Stores, Inc., purchasing the property, they had no use for the Hays House, and offered to give it to the Historical Society, providing it was moved. A course of events followed, which included the tireless efforts of many people, including Mrs. Sharpless Ewing, Miss Alice

Wilson, Mrs. William Howard, Mrs. Paul Beatty Harlan, Mrs. Richard Wysong, Mrs. Benjamin H. Adams, Mrs. J. Glasgow Archer, Jr., Mr. Sydney Peverley and Mrs. C. Holden Rogers. It was Mrs. Adams who suggested moving the house to the Bel Air High School grounds; Mr. Peverley who contacted the then superintendent of schools, Dr. Charles W. Willis; and Mr. John Baumgardner, whose company moved the house.

On July 22, 1960, the house was raised and moved to its present location on Kenmore Avenue. At this time there still was no final agreement with the School Board, but through the efforts of Senator William S. James, the School Board was persuaded to finally sell the property on which the house stood. In August, 1961, the Historical Society paid $845.60 for the lot. Under the terms of the contract, the lot was deeded to the Board of County Commissioners, which in turn gave the Historical Society a twenty-five year lease at $1.00 per year. In May of 1966, this lease was cancelled and a new one executed for seventy-five years.

The Hays House is a frame, two-story house with a gambrel roof. Originally, the house was built in two stages, having a stone section, two stories high, built by Thomas Hays between 1825-1840. This section was demolished in 1960, when the house was moved to its present location.

The Hays House today is an interesting place to visit. Containing period furniture, it reflects the nineteenth century lifestyle of its namesake. In the parlor, the fireplace mantel is in the design of a side view of a table, modeled after another Hays-Heighe House. A fireback added years later contains information on the Jones, Hays, and Jacobs families. Thomas Archer Hays, Sr. is buried in the Hays-Jacobs lot in Rock Spring Cemetery. Also buried in this lot is Elizabeth Hays, wife of Thomas Sr., as well as Pamelia and Thomas Hays, Jr.

Located on West Gordon Street in Bel Air, is Liriodendron, a nineteenth century mansion which was the summer home of its owner, Dr. Howard Atwood Kelly. The estate was named Liriodendron by Dr. Kelly after the tulip poplar trees that shade the beautiful mansion grounds. Liriodendron is the botanical name for these tulip poplars.

The property was purchased on October 19, 1897 by Dr. and Mrs. Howard Atwood Kelly who paid $12,000 for the two hundred acres. They then hired the architectural firm of Wyatt and Nolting of Baltimore to design the house. This same firm had also designed the Baltimore Court House, Fifth Regiment Armory, and the Emmanuel Episcopal Church in Bel Air.

The house was laid out in a "T" shape. As you enter the front doors, you arrive in the center hall, which is twenty-six feet wide, and faces an extraordinary grand staircase, which ascends to seven bedrooms on the second floor and household quarters on the third. To the left of the center hall is the drawing room, and to the right, the dining room. The "T" of the house forms the service area and contains a three story stair atrium. Additionally, a separate servant stairs, music room, library, kitchen, servant dining room and butler's pantry are located there. The house is equipped with a working elevator, which was skillfully concealed by Fritz Kelly and his brother Howard in later years to accommodate their mother's failing health. There are fireplaces in every room except one, and back to back fireplaces grace the drawing room and center hall. Each fireplace is faced with imported Italian marble except the one in the center hall. Through repeated use, the center hall fireplace marble facing cracked and was replaced by Fritz Kelly with sandstime that came from Aquia Creek Quarry outside Alexandria, Virginia, which at one time was owned by Dr. Kelly. To give an idea of the quality of this stone from Aquia Creek, the Capitol Building, as well as others in Washington, D.C., were built from this same type. One of the more outstanding features of the mansion is the skylights and the natural air conditioning of three of its rooms on the first floor. To accomplish this, duct work was run from the deep stone wells under the porches, which drafts cool air into the rooms.

In 1935, Dr. Howard Kelly had passed ownership to his son, Fritz, who maintained the residence until his death in 1980. Through an agreement made in 1972, upon the death of Fritz, the property came under the ownership of Harford County Parks and Recreation, as part of "Heavenly Waters Park." Today, the Liriodendron Foundation, a non-profit corporation aids in administration.

Howard Atwood Kelly was born in Camden, New Jersey on February 20, 1858. His father, Henry Kuhl Kelly was a captain in the 118th Pennsylvania Volunteers during the Civil War. His mother, Louise, moved to Chester, Pennsylvania with their three children to await his return from military service. Following the Civil War, Howard entered the University of Pennsylvania in 1873. In 1880, poor health interrupted his studies, and in an attempt to restore his health, he moved west and became a cowboy. The fresh air and exercise helped, so in 1882, he returned to graduate from the College of Medicine of the

University of Pennsylvania. In the years that followed he specialized in abdominal surgery, and pioneered radium treatment of cancer, and developed anti-toxins and established his own clinic for women on Eutaw Place in Baltimore. Due to his area of specialization in gynecology, he was asked to join with Dr. William Henry Welsh, Dr. William Osler, and Dr. William S. Halstead in the founding of the Johns Hopkins Medical College. Dr. Kelly traveled over the years, for the sake of learning and furthering his professional knowledge. These travels placed him in the company of celebrated personages such as Madam Curie and Dr. William Mayo of the Mayo Clinic. In 1889, he married Laetitia Bredow in a cathedral in Danzig, Germany. It was said that Liriodendron was Laetitia Kelly's triumph and Howard's solution to his wife's homesickness for European vacations. Dr. Howard Atwood Kelly died in January, 1943, preceding his wife's death by six hours. Neither was aware the other was dying.

Today Liriodendron is the center for Harford County history and cultural arts. Its large rooms, wide covered porticos and exquisite reception areas offer outstanding facilities for government, business and civic groups. The mansion is open free to the public every Sunday from 1:00 to 4:00 p.m., and is well-worth the visit.

Located outside Bel Air, in Fountain Green is <u>Tudor Hall</u>, the home of <u>Junius Brutus Booth</u>, and birthplace to <u>Edwin Booth</u> and <u>John Wilkes Booth</u>, assassin of Abraham Lincoln.

Side view of Tudor Hall, showing the balcony off John Wilkes Booth's room, where he used to practice his acting skills.

Aberdeen is the site of Aberdeen Proving Ground, a 75,000-acre military base, established in 1917. One of its main purposes was for the testing of ordnance, shells, air bombs, mines, and other military material under simulated combat conditions. Outdoor displays on the reservation include U.S. Artillery and tanks. Also on the grounds is the U.S. Army Ordnance Museum, which contains small arms, artillery and tanks from many nations. Through various displays the history and development of twentieth century weaponry are traced. Open Tuesday through Friday noon-4:45 and Saturday and Sunday 10-4:45. Free.

Also of interest in Aberdeen is the Old Wesleyan Church, erected in 1826; and Medical Hall, the birthplace of Dr. John Archer (1741-1810). In 1768, he received the first medical diploma issued in America from the Philadelphia Medical College. Dr. Archer was also a signer of the Bush Declaration of Independence, in which the men of Harford County indicated their readiness to fight for independence. Dr. Archer became a member of Congress in 1802, and founded the Medical and Chirurgical (Surgical) Faculty of Maryland. Aberdeen is also known as the birthplace and residence of Baltimore's baseball family, the Ripkens. Calvin Ripken, Sr., spent over thirty years with the Baltimore Orioles, most notably as manager and coach. Billy Ripken played for the Orioles and Texas Rangers, returning to the Orioles in 1996. Cal, Jr., (the "Iron Man") has played with the Baltimore Orioles since 1982, and is considered baseball's finest shortstop. Among his many records are AL Rookie of the Year, 1982; AL Most Valuable Player, 1983-1991; AL All Star, 1983 thru 1996; AL Gold Glove, 1991-1992, and all time home run leader as a shortstop. On September 5, 1995, Cal tied Lou Gehrig's long standing record of 2,130 consecutive games, reached by Gehrig on May 1, 1939. On September 6, 1995, Cal broke Gehrig's record, playing in his 2,131 consecutive game. On June 13, 1996, Cal tied Hiroshima Carp star Sachio Kinugasa's international record by playing his 2,215th consecutive game, breaking this record on June 14th with his 2,216th consecutive game.

Havre de Grace, located on the Susquehanna River, is an old-fashioned town rich in history. Settled in 1658, it was developed as a stop on the old Post Road and was originally known as Susquehanna Lower Ferry. Incorporated in 1785, its present name of Havre de Grace was first used in a letter that same year by Lafayette to Washington. During the Revolutionary War Rochambeau's troops camped out twice at the Havre de Grace Racetrack, on their way to Yorktown in September 1781, and on their return after Cornwallis' surrender. During the War of 1812, on May 3, 1813, Lieutenant John O'Neill commanded the town militia. It was during this attack that the British burned and plundered most of the town's buildings.

Other historic places of interest in Havre de Grace are: The Ferry House: Built in 1760 it is a two-and-a-half-story structure at the end of the old Susquehanna Bridge, later turned into the Lafayette Hotel; The Rodgers House: Located at 226 W. Washington Street, was the home of Colonel John Rodgers, built in 1774. Colonel Rodgers commanded a militia in the Revolutionary War. During the War of 1812, in the British attack of 1813, the house was damaged by fire, but later restored; St. John's Protestant Church: Located on the corner of Union and Congress Avenues. In 1832 it replaced an earlier church; City Park: Located on South Union Avenue, also called Bayside Park, is a seventeen acre bay-front area with yacht anchorage; St. Francis Villa: Located on the east end of the City Park, was established as a home for retired Sisters of St. Francis, and formerly was the Hotel Bayou.

The Havre de Grace Lighthouse: Located on Concord Point, at Concord and Lafayette Streets. It was built in 1827 and was in continuous operation for over one hundred fifty years. This lighthouse was one of eight built by John Donahoo of Havre de Grace in the northern bay area. It was part of the navigational improvement effort which enhanced the flow of goods down the Susquehanna River to the ports of Baltimore and Philadelphia. During the War of 1812, John O'Neill, in appreciation for his gallant stand against the British was the lighthouse's first keeper. Since then the keepers had always been his descendants. On the water side is located the cannon used by John O'Neill in this defense of Havre de Grace.

The Havre de Grace Lighthouse

Havre de Grace Yacht Club: located near the lighthouse is the home of annual regattas; Oakington Farms: the estate of Millard E. Tydings, former U.S. Senator from Maryland.

Havre de Grace Decoy Museum: Located next to the Bayou Hotel at Market Street and R. Madison Mitchell Place, the building which houses the Decoy Museum was acquired in 1981 from the Bayou Hotel, which earlier was used for the hotel's swimming pool and boiler room. Established in 1982, the museum is a private non-profit organization, run by a Board of Directors, and started through private contributions. The Decoy Museum's foundation was created to preserve the cultural and historical legacy embodied in the waterfowl hunting decoy and to perpetuate the folk art tradition of the hunting decoy as it was practiced in the Susquehanna Flats. It also seeks to educate and promote the conservation, preservation, and restoration of waterfowl and their natural habitats. In November 1986, the museum was open to the public two days a week. Today the museum is open seven days a week, three hundred sixty days a year, being closed on major holidays.

The Havre de Grace Decoy Museum is visited each year by over 25,000 people from all parts of the United States, England, Germany, New Zealand, Japan, Sweden, as well as other parts of the world. Upon entering the museum, visitors will see beautiful, extensive collections of waterfowl decoys, largely from the upper Chesapeake Bay region. In addition to decoys, the museum collects carving tools and equipment used in the creation of decoys including: chopping blocks, paints, patterns, molds and templates. Each Saturday and Sunday, visitors may view volunteer carvers demonstrating their craft. Throughout the vast displays of decoys, several of the more prominent carvers are featured, not only through their collections but also by a life size figure likeness of the carver, the most prolific being Robert Madison Mitchell (1901-1993), or Madison as he liked to be called. During his lifetime he produced over 100,000 decoys, using cedar or white pine. His use of sharp clean lines and intricate paint patterns made his decoys a standard by which all others are measured. Mr. Mitchell is featured in three displays, each with a different figure likeness, as well as a program using his voice. Other displays include the works of Charles "Charlie" Bryan, Jr., of Essex, Maryland, Robert Litzenberg of Elkton, Maryland, and James Currier (1886-1969). Each year the museum holds a variety of events, including the Decoy Festival, Carver's Appreciation Day and the Duck Fair. The Duck Fair includes such activities as duck and goose calling, carving and painting contests, and retrieving and firearms demonstrations.

Also in Havre de Grace is the <u>Susquehanna Museum of Havre de Grace, Inc at the</u> <u>Lockhouse</u>. Located at Erie and Conesto Streets, this museum is in the Locktender's house at the Southern terminal of the Susquehanna & Tidewater Canal. This 1840 house, which is listed on the National Register of Historic Places, is furnished with period pieces, and contains the Locktender's office. A reconstructed pivot bridge across the canal's outlet lock and a video describing the operation of the canal are featured. The Museum is committed to the continuing development of archives which record local history and the display of artifacts in the restored Lockhouse which interpret the earlier life of the city.

<u>The Havre de Grace Maritime Museum</u> is located at 100 Lafayette Street, and was incorporated in 1988. Historically, the city of Havre de Grace was a major hub for water-related commerce and recreational activities on the Upper Chesapeake Bay. On display are artifacts, memorabilia, and photographs from these interesting eras. The museum also features annual boat shows, guest lectures, small boat exhibits, and educational programs and displays on local maritime history. The <u>Steppingstone Museum</u> at 461 Quaker Bottom Road in Susquehanna State Park is a private, non-profit museum which preserves and demonstrates the rural arts and crafts of the 1800-1920 period. The collection of tools was started by J. Edmund Bull and has been augmented by local gifts over the years. This museum was once a working Harford County farm, and tours include the formal sitting room, sleeping quarters, and kitchen containing a woodburning stove and ice box.

One of Harford County's most beautiful tourist attractions, located in Monkton on Jarrettsville Pike, between Madonna and Jacksonville is <u>Ladew Topiary Gardens</u> and <u>Pleasant Valley House</u>, the home of Harvey Smith Ladew. Harvey Ladew was born in New York in 1886, the son and heir to his family business making leather belts. Not the leather belts a person might wear, but the ones used in factories to operate various types of machinery. As a result of the family business, Mr. Ladew became a millionaire, and never had to work, and never really did. His plan was to enjoy life while he was young, and begin work when he was fifty years old. As Harvey said, "There is so much to see, to do, I thought I'd reverse life's patterns - play, then work." A mischievous boy, and a man of great humor, he was raised under the good, fashionable life in New York. Traveling many times in his youth to Europe, his favorite trick was sitting on the thrones in castles. By the time he was fifteen, he had sat on more thrones than all of Queen Victoria's vast family put together. At the outbreak of World War I, Harvey took the first boat that was available home; which happened to be Kaiser's confiscated yacht.

Following the war, where he served as an Army liaison officer, he decided to retire from the family business, and pursue one of his passions, fox hunting. Having hunted for twenty-one seasons, not only in Maryland, but also in England, Ireland, and France, he once set an international fox hunting record by riding to hounds on both sides of the Atlantic in a seventy-two hour period. This was accomplished by crossing the Atlantic in an amphibious plane. It was this passion for the fox that led him to Maryland.

In 1929 he moved from his home on Long Island, to Maryland, and purchased Pleasant Valley House, because the hunting was good and the fences weren't made of wire, as they were in Long Island. When Harvey purchased this house it was in terrible condition. In 1929, at age forty-three, Harvey was to some degree starting over. Here was a man who was used to living in mansions, and manor houses, and who stayed at various castles in Europe, and who came from a fine house on Long Island, which had magnificent flowers and greenhouses about. Pleasant Valley had none of these things he was used to, not even plumbing or electricity. The only flowers on the property was a dying lilac bush which was "promptly put out of its misery" he once said. But as hunting was his passion, he needed a house in which to live so he could do the hunting in Maryland, mostly for convenience.

Upon purchasing Pleasant Valley House in 1929, he started to re-do the house. The house was originally built in c.1770, and over the next forty-seven years he added on the house, as well as perfected the many gardens within its two hundred acres, to what they are today. As one walks through the house, you get the feeling that you are a guest of Mr. Ladew, rather than just a visitor touring the home. Everything that you see within the house is the same as when Harvey lived there. Throughout the house, the most notable theme is the fox and hound, from the stuffed fox heads on the walls, to the many paintings both canvas, and on the windows. Although Harvey was the genius behind the renovations, it was his friend and architect, James O'Connor who made it all possible.

Upon entering the drawing room, one will notice the architectural details of the broken pediments and molding which were copied from the Hammond-Harwood House in Annapolis due to Harvey's love of the State of Maryland. The paneling in the drawing room is a rare Elizabethan type, which he found in London, and the ceiling plasterwork was copied from a period design by New York craftsmen. The ceiling plaster was white in color, but Harvey felt that it looked too new, so using the fireplace in the room, he would make a fire, then close the flue, allowing the black smoke to fill the room, darkening the ceiling, creating the "old look." Hanging on the walls in the drawing room are two Chippendale-style mirrors, quite unique with the fox and hound theme on the gilt frame.

As you enter Mr. Ladew's office, you will see that it is filled with hunting memorabilia. Also throughout the house are many photographs as well as letters displayed. Two letters of particular interest are one from the then Prince of Wales, later King Edward VIII, thanking Harvey for loaning him his favorite horse, named "Ghost" for a hunt on Long Island. The second letter to Mr. Ladew is from T.E. Lawrence. Mr. Ladew had an oval Chippendale partners desk, but did not know where to put it in the house. He asked a friend for advice, and the friend said why not build a room around it? And so he did, again with help from James O'Connor. Harvey called this room his circulating library, which contains over three thousand volumes, many first editions. In the library are many bookcases, of which one swings out much like a door. Behind this bookcase is a small closet-like area, which leads to an exterior door. As the story goes, Harvey, upon getting bored with his guests, would slip out through the bookcase to the outside. In the entrance hall, at the foot of the stairs leading to Mr. Ladew's bedroom, is a newel post inset containing a silver dollar dated 1847. This was done by the original owner to indicate the year the mortgage was finally paid off.

Perhaps the best known of this estate are the Topiary Gardens., In all the grounds contain thirty-one different types of gardens covering twenty-two acres. From April through October these magnificent gardens contain hundreds of beautiful flowers, plants, and trees. The names of some of the gardens are the Woodland, Victorian, Berry, Pink, Rose, Yellow, Water Lily, White, Garden of Eden and the Topiary Sculpture. Never without humor, it was in the Garden of Eden, which contains apple trees that Harvey placed a statue of Adam and Eve. Inscribed in the three steps which lead to this garden is written, "If you would be happy for a week, take a wife. If you would be happy for a month, kill your pig. But if you would be happy all your life, plant a garden."

Throughout the grounds one will see the topiary designs of swans, and of course the fox and hounds, along with the horse and rider. One of the most beautiful views is looking from the Sculpture Garden across the Great Bowl toward the house. The Great Bowl is a large oval pool, ten feet deep, with a fountain, once used by Mr. Ladew for swimming. Today this large area surrounding the Great Bowl is the setting for concerts as well as other events. The grounds also contain a Croquet Court, which originally was a tennis court, converted by Mr. Ladew. Each December the Topiary Gardens holds its annual "Christmas at an English Country House" celebration. For this celebration, the manor house, and the topiary hounds on the lawn are lavishly decorated. On the grounds is also a gift shop which carries hundreds of items, as well as a cafe. Continuous tours of the manor house and grounds are held each day from 11 a.m. to 3:30 p.m.

During Mr. Ladew's lifetime he received many awards. He was the Master of the Elkridge Harford Hunt for seven years. In 1971, about the time the Topiary Gardens opened to the public, he received the Distinguished Service Medal of the Garden Club of America for his "great interest in developing and maintaining the most outstanding topiary in America, without professional help." Mr. Ladew died in 1976, at the age of ninety. Today the twenty-two acre gardens, with their world famous topiary figures and hedges are still considered the most outstanding topiary gardens in America by the Garden Club of America. The house and gardens are a place that all should visit.

Harford County has grown considerably in the last several decades. Having a population of 182,132 in 1990, the county continues to grow with new housing and new businesses each year, and major roads have been built to assist with this growth. By 1994 the population increased to 201,985, an increase of 10.9% over 1990. In 1998, the population is 219,600, and is projected to be 226,600 by the year 2000.

Having a mix of historical areas of interest, agriculture, industry and businesses, Harford County still is beautiful, retaining many of its delicate charms of years past.

Form of Government: Charter (1972)

Map of Harford County

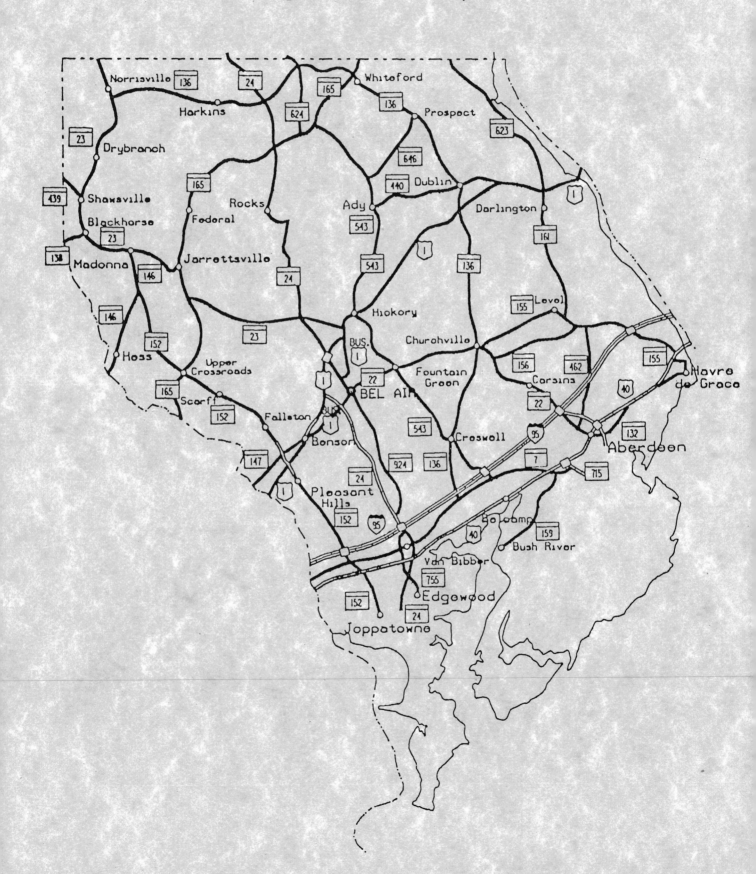

HOWARD COUNTY

Howard District was created from Anne Arundel County by Chapter 22, Acts of 1838 (confirmed by Chapter 50, Acts of 1839). Although unrepresented in the General Assembly, the District enjoyed the status of a county. Formed in 1851 (Const. 1851, Art. VIII, sec. 1), the County was named for John Eager Howard (1752-1827), Revolutionary War officer, Maryland Governor, United States Senator and statesman.

The original Howard County seal dates back to 1840. A renowned seal designer of the time, Edward Stabler, was commissioned to produce the seal. His design included typical elements of the area: tobacco plants and a shock of wheat - important early crops; necessary farming implements, a plowed field, and rolling hills in the background. From time to time the plants in the foreground changed over the years; however, in November 1973, the original design as done by Stabler was adopted as the official county seal.

Located in central Maryland, Howard County is bordered by Carroll County to the north, Baltimore County to the northeast, Anne Arundel to the southeast, Montgomery and Prince George's Counties on the south, and Frederick County on the west. The county's topography is rolling hills, except the areas of the Patapsco River on the north and Patuxent River on the south. The elevation varies from fifty feet on the extreme east to about eight hundred fifty feet in the western sections. Most of the county's elevation averages between three hundred and seven hundred feet above sea level.

In 1960, Howard County had a population of 36,152, and grew to 118,443 by 1980. By 1990 its population was 187,328, and in 1994 rose to 212,976, an increase of 13.7% over 1990. In 1998, the population increased again to 239,310, and by the year 2000, it is projected to be 253,500.

An agricultural county, corn, wheat, oats, barley and alfalfa are raised. Dairy farming, as well as cattle and hog feeding are important industries to the county. Most farms also raise vegetables and fruit; also some turkey raising.

Howard County has played a role in both United States and Maryland history. One prominent resident was Charles Carroll of Carrollton, the last surviving signer of the Declaration of Independence. His home, <u>Doughoregan Manor</u> is several miles west of Ellicott City. Built in 1727, this house was once the manor of a 13,000 acre estate.

This two-story house is three hundred feet long with two ells or wings, the whole of which exemplifies axial symmetry of the eighteenth century. The south ell contains the servants quarters of which the north ell is a Roman Catholic chapel. The central section of the house is surmounted by a railed roof platform and octagonal cupola. From the roof promenade a great part of the original estate can be seen. The interior is paneled with oak and decorated with various paintings of hunting scenes and family portraits.

Charles Carroll of Carrollton was the third of his name in America, born in Annapolis, Maryland on September 19, 1737. His grandfather was a land agent for Lord Baltimore and had acquired thousands of acres of land in the colony, including the manor of Carrollton in Frederick. As a young man, Charles spent several years in France where he completed his education, then went on to London where he studied law. At the age of twenty-eight he returned to America, but found himself barred from practicing law because of the restrictions surrounding Roman Catholics.

During this time there was much unrest in the colonies, and Charles involved himself in politics. As time went on his role became increasingly important. In 1768, Charles married his cousin, Mary Darnell. A delegate to the Maryland convention in 1776, Charles was instrumental in effecting the resolution of separation from England and on July 4, 1776, signed the Declaration of Independence as a member of the Continental Congress. Following the Revolutionary War, he was a Senator from Maryland in the first Federal Congress.

Charles was a shrewd business man and a brilliant and talented lawyer. He was involved in various commercial enterprises, being a member of the Potomac Company, and its successor the Chesapeake and Ohio Canal Company. As the director of the Baltimore & Ohio Railroad, combined with his vast land holdings he was the wealthiest man in America at the time of his death in 1832. Charles is buried in the chapel at Doughoregan Manor. After the death of Charles Carroll of Carrollton, the manor was occupied by John Lee Carroll, governor of Maryland from 1876-1880. The present estate is now approximately three thousand acres. Each year on Thanksgiving Day, the members of the Howard County Hunt Club attend a prehunt service here, an English custom of blessing the hounds.

Other historical houses are: Burleigh Manor, located near Doughoregan Manor. Built in 1785 by Colonel Rezin Hammond, this two-and-a-half story late Georgian Colonial structure is notable for its beautifully carved marble mantels; <u>Glenelg Manor</u>, was built about 1700, and was later known as Governor George Lowndes Estate. This house is a two-story U-shaped Gothic-Revival structure, with a three-story crenelated tower at the left wing. The house is ivy-covered and is surrounded by giant hemlock and locust trees; <u>Oakdale</u>, built in 1838 and formerly the home of Governor Edwin Warfield. Located on one thousand three hundred acres, the house is a three-and-a-half-story brick structure with Classic portico. The interior is decorated with ancestral portraits. On the grounds stands a kiln where the bricks for the house were made.

<u>Waverly</u>, located at 2335 Marriottsville Road in Marriottsville, was built in 1750, and is a two-story L-shaped structure that was the home of Governor George Howard, the son of John Eager Howard of Revolutionary War fame. On the grounds are the overseer's house and a slave jail, complete with barred windows and iron fetters. In the yard is the gravestone of the governor's son, John Eager Howard the Younger, whose body now lies in Frederick.

The original owners and builders of Waverly were Nathan Dorsey and his wife Sophia Owings, who had received the land as a wedding gift from Nathan's father, John Dorsey of Edward, in 1756. The original portion of the house was built between 1756 and 1764. Due to the remote location of the house, building became difficult. As a result, Nathan soon encountered financial difficulties so severe that the house was taken over by his brother Edward. In 1786, Edward sold the house and its four hundred fifty acres of land to Colonel John Eager Howard. Colonel Howard bought the property mainly as an investment, renting it for many years to tenants who farmed the land. In 1811, Colonel Howard's son, George, married Prudence Gough Ridgely, the daughter of Charles Carnan Ridgely of Baltimore County. Once again, Waverly became a wedding gift as Colonel Howard gave it to his son shortly after his wedding.

Upon receiving the house, George and Prudence began to modernize it. They demolished the free-standing two-story kitchen and built a new service wing, connecting it to the main house by means of a hyphen (wing). They also built a large dining room, and removed two small fireplaces, building a larger one in its place. This dining room is the one still in use today. During their residence, Waverly was the scene of many formal parties, as George served as governor of Maryland from 1831 to 1833. He and his wife also raised eight of their fourteen children who survived infancy at Waverly.

Following the death of George in 1846, and Prudence in 1847, Waverly was owned by many different people. George's son, George Howard, Jr., held the property until 1858. Following this it was purchased at public auction by Joseph H. Judick, who lived there until 1881. From 1881 to 1964, Waverly was owned by the Frederick Brosenne family, who farmed the land during the eighty-three year ownership. In 1964, the Brosennes sold the house and property to a real estate company. They in turn conveyed the house and three and one-half acres surrounding the house to the Society for the Preservation of Maryland Antiquities (SPMA), the only non-profit, state-wide organization devoted to the preservation of Maryland's architectural heritage.

After acquiring Waverly, the SPMA, along with the Federated Garden Clubs of Howard County, the Waverly Committee, and others, completed an extensive restoration and landscaping project, resulting in Waverly's "re-birth." Today, the Society maintains this historic site for use by individuals, clubs, corporate groups, and civic associations, for meetings, wedding or other receptions. Facilities available are the formal dining room, the paneled parlor, and the museum kitchen. There is also a fully equipped modern kitchen for use by caterers. One popular feature is the "Bride's Chamber," a special room located one-half story removed from the house. Here brides and their attendants may gather privately before and after receptions. The first floor of the house can accommodate up to one hundred and fifty people.

Located on the extreme eastern border of the county is Ellicott City, the county seat. In 1772, Joseph, Andrew and John Ellicott of Bucks County, Pennsylvania, purchased seven hundred acres once known as "The Hollow," on the banks of the Patapsco River. This land was purchased at $3.00 per acre for a grist and flour mill. Following this, they brought by ship to Elkridge Landing, workers, most of whom were Quakers. They also hauled machinery, mostly of their own invention overland to what is today Ellicott City. By 1774, the grist and flour mills were established in time for the harvest that year. Prior to this, tobacco had been the principal crop, but with the backing of Charles Carroll of Carrollton, the Ellicotts made wheat so successful that they were the largest initial force in dethroning tobacco. The mill produced Patapsco Flour, a popular flour for many years used throughout the country. The first rail line of the Baltimore & Ohio Railroad extended from Baltimore to Ellicott City in 1830, and the original station still stands. Following the building of the Cumberland Road westward and the railroad in 1830, the town grew rapidly. The Ellicotts erected a furnace and rolling mill, ironworks, schools, a meeting house, stores, and houses made from beautiful granite. By 1840, Ellicott Mills, as it was then called was one of the most important manufacturing towns in Maryland, with a population of two thousand. Later this same year, Ellicott Mills was made the site of the court house for the newly formed district. In 1864, Ellicott Mills was used to care for the wounded from the Battle of Monocacy, until they could be transported to Baltimore. In 1867, a city charter was secured for Ellicott Mills, and the name changed to Ellicott City. Over the years Ellicott City has been ravaged three times by dreadful floods. The first was 1868 resulted in the loss of fifty lives. In 1972, Tropical Storm Agnes, and Eloise in 1975, leveled much of the area.

Other areas of historical interest in Ellicott City are: The Howard County Historical Society, which was built in 1892 and was previously the First Presbyterian Church. The Historical Society became organized and incorporated in 1957; The Howard County Courthouse was built in 1841 on top of Capitoline Hill, also referred to as Mt. Misey. The wing to the rear of the Courthouse was originally the home of Edwin Parsons Hayden, built in 1840; off of Court House Road is the Early Quaker stone schoolhouse, built in c.1790; located behind the Quaker schoolhouse is the Howard County Jail, built in 1878 and was originally known as Willow Grove, and has quite a unique architectural design.

On Church Road is the Emory Methodist Church, built in 1837 and remodeled in the 1880s, and Mount Ida, the last home to be built by an Ellicott in 1828. Located a short distance from Mount Ida on Church Road was the site of the Patapsco Female Institute, now in ruins. Designed by Robert Cary Long, Jr., it officially opened on January 1, 1837, and served as a finishing school for well-to-do ladies. It was originally built on lands donated by the Ellicott brothers and others. Today the land is being used by the Howard County Government for a future historic garden park.

The Firehouse Museum, located at 3829 Church Road was built in 1889. This firehouse museum was the town's first fire station. On Columbia Pike is Tongue Row, built in the 1840s by the widow Ann Tongue. Today it is occupied by a number of specialty shops.

Main Street in Ellicott City has a number of interesting, historical places. In what is today the public library was once the site of the Old County Fire Department, built in 1896; Disney's Tavern, operated by Mrs. Deborah Disney; The Howard House, built in 1850 and once a thriving hotel; Ellicott Country Store, a fine Early American house, displaying an extensive line of art objects, gifts, and antiques; New Town Hall, which became a movie theater. Located near the railroad tracks is the former site of the Patapsco Hotel, a popular lodging stop during the development of the Baltimore & Ohio Railroad. Across the street from this site is the Baltimore & Ohio Railroad Terminal, the first terminus of the first railroad in the United States, and today is registered as a National Historic Landmark. Located here today is the Baltimore & Ohio Railroad Station Museum. Directly across the railroad tracks are the sites of the original Ellicott Lower Mills, 1774, and the residences of George Ellicott, 1789, now in ruins, and Jonathan Ellicott, which was destroyed by the flood during Agnes in 1972. On New Cut Road is St. Paul's Catholic School, which was built in 1830 and was once the Patapsco Bank.

Other historical points of interest in Howard County are: Old Quaker Burial Ground and West River Friends Meeting House: The house, built in 1798 was one of the largest in the province. In addition to a meeting house, it also served as a war hospital and a school. In the burial ground is the marked grave of Captain James Dooley, who had been a Friend but carried on privateering during the War of 1812, and continued the practice after the treaty of peace, when it then became piracy, and the graves of John and Andrew Ellicott, as well as some of their descendants. Also of interest are the Old Town Hall and the Angelo Cottage, a turreted castle.

The first curved stone-arch bridge in America located over the Patapsco River, near Elkridge is another unusual structure. Named the Thomas Viaduct, it was built over one-hundred years ago. It supported the Baltimore & Ohio Railroad cars, both in earlier times and the heavier trains which came later. Also in Elkridge, at 6555 Belmont Woods Road is Belmont Mansion. This exquisite eighteenth century house offers overnight facilities, situated on eighty-two acres.

Savage, located in the southern section of Howard County, is the home of Historic Savage Mill and the Bollman Truss Railroad Bridge.

Savage Mill was founded in 1820, when Amos Williams and his three brothers borrowed twenty thousand dollars from their friend, John Savage to start a textile weaving business on the banks of the Patuxent River. The machines that wove the cloth were powered by water from the river which flowed over an enormous thirty foot water wheel. The business was named Savage Mill, after their friend due to his generosity. The mill operated from 1822 through 1947. The main product produced at the mill in the 1800s was canvas. This material was used in making sails for the clipper ships that sailed in and out of Baltimore harbor. During the Civil War, the canvas was used for making tents, cannon covers, and other supplies for the various armies. From 1890 to 1900, this material was painted and used as backdrops for the first silent movies made in Hollywood. During World War I and II, the canvas was again used for making tents, truck covers, cots, and transport bags used by United States soldiers.

Following World War II, the Mill had grown to twelve different buildings by 1950. At this time the Mill was bought by Harry Heim, who converted the entire complex into a Christmas Display Village. He would dress as Santa Claus, and was known as Santa Heim by those who visited the village. Featured were reindeer who grazed in the orchards, and a miniature B & O train which transported the visitors to and from the parking lots. Also featured was a one-ring circus, with elephants, trapeze artists, and a carousel. Although the village did rather well, Heim's plans were bigger than his pocketbook, and he went bankrupt late in 1950. Today, the Mill no longer weaves material. A three-phase renovation process was undertaken in 1985 and completed in 1992. Through this project, the Mill was transformed into a specialty shopping marketplace. Savage Mill consists of twelve buildings which date back to 1820. The Mill no longer owns the mill houses which surround the complex, which are privately owned. These private houses were included in the complex as part of its Historic Landmark status. In 1974, Savage Mill was placed on the National Register of Historic Places.

The Bollman Truss Railroad Bridge is a semi-suspension bridge which spans the Little Patuxent River. It was brought to this location in 1860 when the B & O Railroad serviced the Mill. The design for this type of bridge was used all over the United States and Europe. It was made of wrought and cast iron which rusted out in the case of all the other bridges except one. One of two of the last standing Bollman Truss semi-suspension bridges in the world is located here at Savage Mill. It is recognized as a national treasure. The other such bridge is located in Washington County.

Howard County is the home of several parks, lakes and recreation areas. Two such areas are Patapsco Valley State Park, of which about three thousand acres of land lie in the county and two hundred forty-five acres of Patuxent River State Park. These are maintained by the Maryland Department of Natural Resources.

Other areas include, Brighton Dam, which includes the Azalea Garden and Picnic area, located in Brookeville; Cedar Lane Park and Lake Kittamaqundi in Columbia;

Centennial Park, in Ellicott City; Rockburn Branch Park, in Elkridge; Savage Park, in Savage; Schooley Mill Park, in Highland; and Scotts Cove, in Laurel.

In 1966, the James Rouse Company unveiled plans for a new city in Howard County called "Columbia." Columbia is now a thriving city containing many residential "Villages," shopping centers, schools, hospitals, industries and recreation. The Merriweather Post Pavilion presents many popular concerts in the summer months. Also the Columbia Festival of Arts, held in midsummer features local and international performing talent, craft shows, and performances for children. Also in Columbia is the Howard County Center of African American Culture. Located at 1 Commerce Center, this museum features rotating exhibits that preserve the history of African-American Culture in Howard County and Maryland.

One fascinating event in Howard County is the Afternoon Tea at Historic Oakland. Henry James once said in Portrait of a Lady, "There are few hours in life more agreeable than the hour dedicated to the ceremony known as afternoon tea."

This interesting pastime is recreated in the 1811 mansion known as Oakland, located at 5430 Vantage Point Road in Columbia. Afternoon tea originated in early nineteenth century England when Anna, the Duchess of Bedford, summoned her kitchen staff to prepare a light repast of sandwiches and pastries with tea. The Duchess began inviting friends to share the occasion, and the ritual of good food and good conversation evolved.   Oakland offers a three-course repast, accompanied by entertainment, which include fashion shows, music or art displays. Oakland may also be used for special meetings in a separate room during tea. Open the first and last Thursday of each month, Oakland has been restored by the Columbia Association to reflect the value of preserving the past on the midst of contemporary society.

Howard County's major cities and towns include, Ellicott City, the County Seat, Columbia, Elkridge, Savage, Jessup, Dorsey, Laurel, Scaggsville, Fulton, Highland, Clarksville, Dayton, Lisbon, West Friendship, Cooksville, Lawyers Hill, and Mt. Airy.

Form of Government: Charter (1968)

Map of Howard County

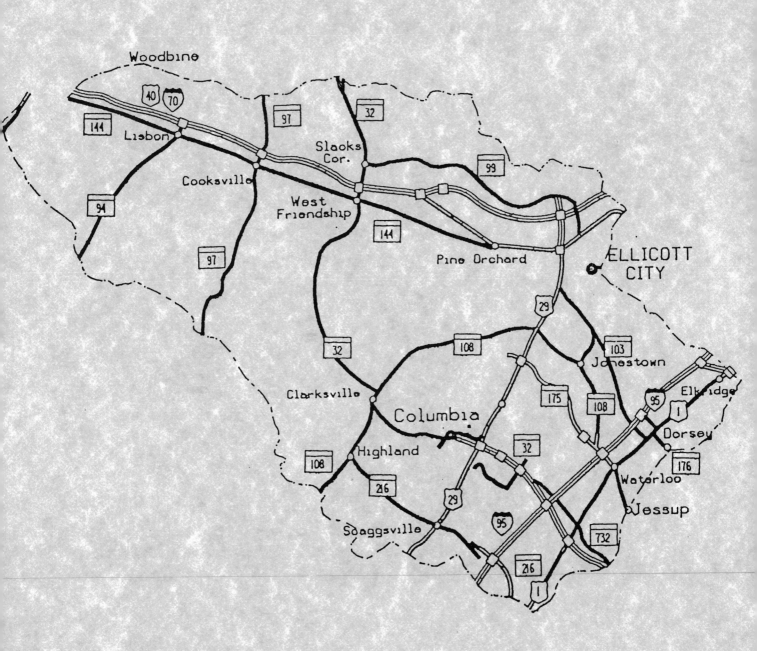

KENT COUNTY

Kent was first mentioned as a county in 1642, when the Governor and Council appointed commissioners for the Isle and County of Kent which was named for the English county of the same name.

The shield is generally described as bearing the full blazonry of the House of Stuarts. Within the center is a lion rampant of the paternal shield of Nassau, denoting the House of Orange. The inclusion of the Heraldic symbols of the House of Stuart and Orange signify the joint sovereignty of William of Orange and of Mary of the House of Stuart at the time the seal was adopted, on May 21, 1692.

Located on the northern part of the Eastern Shore, Kent is the second oldest county in Maryland. It is bordered on the north by the Sassafras River, which separates it from Cecil County, and on the west by the Chesapeake Bay. To the south it is bordered by the Chester River, which flows between it and Queen Anne's County, and to the east by the State of Delaware. Its elevation ranges from sea level to eighty feet above sea level, and its land area is two hundred eighty-four square miles.

When Kent was formed as Maryland's second county in 1642, it was the Eastern Shore. As years passed and new legislation was enacted, Kent County was slowly divided and chiseled away to form the other eight Eastern Shore counties. As a result, Kent today is the smallest county on the Eastern Shore.

The first settlers were English, who came to Kent County to grow tobacco, and in the early times only tobacco. The flat terrain, and navigable streams made Kent County an ideal area in which to grow and ship tobacco. The first port of entry, and the first county seat was called New Yarmouth, at the mouth of Gray's Inn Creek. As tobacco trade continued and prospered, a more accessible port was needed. Chestertown was thus established. Founded in 1698 as New Town, it was renamed in 1780 as Chestertown. Although Kent County no longer raises any tobacco, it still prospers today as a major agricultural county. Corn, wheat, oats, rye, hay, soybeans, and various vegetables such as sweet corn, snap beans, asparagus and spinach are raised. Over 80 percent of the county is used as farmland. Commercial fishing and trapping of raccoons, opossums, skunks, otters, muskrats, red and gray foxes and rabbits for their pelts was also at one time a major industry.

Chestertown, the county seat, was first called Port of Chester, and was officially founded in 1706 replacing New Yarmouth. As one of the Maryland's oldest seaports, its only competition in the eighteenth century was Annapolis. Becoming Chestertown in 1780, it was named after the Chester River. The original act establishing the port was made in the name of Her Most Sacred Majesty Queen Anne and its purpose was to advance trade in the Province of Maryland. Nine local port Commissioners were appointed by the Governor to purchase land, survey, stake out and design the streets and waterfront area on one hundred acres of land. The port prospered for nearly two centuries until the automobile and rail system began to replace the convenience of the Chester River as a means of transportation.

In 1774, the citizens of Chestertown became enraged over England's tea tax, and threw tea brought into their port by the brigantine Geddes overboard. Today the town commemorates these acts during their annual Chestertown Tea Party Festival in May. Chestertown is also the home of Washington College, incorporated in 1782, as the successor to the Kent County Free School, the first institution of higher learning in the State, named after George Washington who was a member of its Board of Visitors and Governors. Although St. Mary's College is generally considered the successor to King William's School established in 1696 it was not chartered as a college until 1784, two years after Washington College's incorporation.

In Chestertown there is an area referred to as Old Chester Town. It is here that many historical structures can be seen. These include: The Hynson-Ringgold House, located at the corner of Cannon & Water Streets. This house was constructed in two stages on land which was originally owned by Dr. Nathaniel Hynson in 1735. In 1743, Dr. William Murray purchased the lot from Hynson and built the front section of the house, which features an impressive hip roof and all-header bond facade. In 1767, Thomas Ringgold, purchased the property and allowed his son, Thomas, Jr., and his wife, Mary Galloway Ringgold to reside there. The large back wing along Cannon Street was constructed in 1772, just prior to the father's death. During this same time period, William Buckland, a well-known architect was commissioned to design the unusual antler staircase. Buckland had worked on several other Maryland houses, including Tulip Hill, the home of Mrs. Ringgold's parents. The interior of the east room in the older front section was removed to the Baltimore Museum of Art in 1932. In 1944, the house was purchased by Washington College and has served as the residence of the presidents of the college.

The Customs House: Originally, the Customs House was a one story building (which no longer stands) on Water Street. The present building was build in 1746, and was only partly used for customs purposes in connection with the original house. The remainder of the building, as well as the addition, was used as a private residence. Built in 1770, it faces the river. Near this location on May 23, 1774, citizens angry over the closing of the Port of Boston following its "Tea Party" boarded Port Collector William Geddes's brigantine of the same name and threw its cargo of tea into the Chester River.

Anderson-Aldridge House: at 103 Water Street is a fine example of an eighteenth century house. It was originally two stories high. This original structure was laid out in Flemish bond with a wing. In the late nineteenth century the house was remodeled, adding a third story in American bond. Visible today are the original nails that fastened the wire lath to the brick.

River House, at 107 Water Street was built between 1784 and 1787 by Richard Smythe of "Widehall." This three story house was built in Federal style using Flemish bond brick on the street side and American bond on the two sides. This house is characteristic of Philadelphia town houses, as well as others on the Eastern Shore which are one room deep with no windows on the sides, except in the attic. In 1926 the woodwork from a second floor room was removed to Winterthur Museum near Wilmington, Delaware, and is called the "Chestertown Room." This house was owned by the Maryland Historical Trust from 1967 to 1993.

Also located on Water Street are the Watkins-Bryan House at 109, the Frisby House at 110 and the Perkins House at 115. The Watkins-Bryan House was built about 1740. This Flemish bond brickwork formal merchant's home is one of Chestertown's finest. The Frisby House was built in 1770 as a town house of the Frisby family. It is distinguished by its wide chimneys with interesting cap detail, as well as all-header bonding and curvilinear window arches. The Perkins House is built with an all-header-bond facade and Flemish-bond with glazed header pattern. The house has been restored to its original eighteenth century splendor.

Located at 101 Church Alley is the Geddes-Piper House, the home of the Historical Society of Kent County. This three and a half story structure was owned by several Chestertown merchants, including the port's Customs Collector, William Geddes. The house has several interesting features including the vestigal buttresses on the four corners of the original structure as well as the original kitchen, which is still in the basement. On display in the house are a unique collection of eighteenth century Chinese import tea pots as well as local artifacts.

Queen Street, in Chestertown is an attractive, narrow street which contains many houses from the eighteenth and nineteenth centuries. Among these is the Nicholson House, located at 111, which was built in 1788 by Captain John Nicholson of the Continental Navy. Captain Nicholson was the youngest of the Nicholson brothers, James and Samuel, all of whom were Continental Navy Captains. John Nicholson was skipper of the sloop of war Hornet and sometime skipper of the Continental frigate Deane, when his older brother Samuel was not aboard. The Deane took the last naval prizes of the American Revolution, and was the only frigate held by the Navy at the end of the war. The Nicholson House is one of many of Federal style in Chestertown.

At the corner of Queen and High Streets is the Buck-Bacchus House. John Buck of Bideford, Devonshire, England purchased the lot and built the house in 1735. Buck was memorialized in the Church of St. Mary, Bideford with the following inscription: "John Buck, Esq., was a great merchant in this town and three times mayor thereof. He died the 3rd of April 1745..." Although doubtful that John Buck even actually lived here, the structure was probably a store for the merchandise he shipped from various parts of the western world. Historians say that there is no doubt that the front room was used as a store from 1820 to 1830. Based on the memory of older residents of the town, a store was continued until 1922 by William Bacchus, when upon his death, his widow sold the building, which was converted to a private residence.

Other structures of interest include the William Barroll House (1743); Wickes House (1832); Molloy House (early nineteenth century); Masonic Building (1827) and the Palmer or "Rock of Ages" House.

Emmanuel Episcopal Church, at Cross Street and Park Row was erected between 1767 and 1772. It was built as a chapel of ease for Chester Parish, with the mother church being Christ Church I.U. On November 9, 1780, the rector of Chester Parish and future founder of Washington College in 1782, the Reverend Doctor William Smith, presided over a convention that adopted the name of the Protestant Episcopal Church in the United States. Reverend Smith had been elected to become Maryland's first Episcopal Bishop in 1784, but his name was later withdrawn due to his controversial nature. In the 1860s, Emmanuel Episcopal Church underwent changes when it was remodeled to adjust to the Victorian style of the day. The second story was removed as were the box pews and the stained glass windows were substituted for the original clear panes.

The White Swan Tavern, located at 231 High Street was built in 1733 by Joseph Nicholson as a residence. Nicholson purchased the property from John Lovegrove, a local tanner, whose original frame structure still stands at the rear of the tavern. In 1790, the building was enlarged into a tavern and remained active until the 1850s when it became a general store. In 1981, the Tavern was restored to its 1795 appearance and reopened as a bed and breakfast.

At the corner of Spring and High Streets is the Methodist Meeting House, built between 1801 and 1803. This was the first permanent Methodist Church in Chestertown. In his letters, Francis Asbury, the first Methodist Bishop of America, refers to this church. This structure has not been used as a church for many years, and nothing remains of the interior woodwork. It has been said that on a digression, Bishop Asbury found Chestertown "a very wicked place."

At Washington College on Washington Avenue are the Middle, East and West Halls, which are brick structures dating from 1845. These structures stand on the site of the original college edifice of Washington College, which was built between 1783 and 1788. The original buildings were destroyed by a fire in 1827. The college's namesake, George Washington, served as one of its first Visitors and Governors and was present for the meeting that determined the design of the building as well as the lottery that would finance much of the construction. Washington was responsible for the sale of these lottery tickets in Alexandria, Virginia in 1784. The nation's tenth oldest institution of higher learning (1782) and Maryland's first, Washington College provides visitor's with an architectural tour of great variety.

There are many other historical sites in Kent County: Caulk's Battlefield located near Tolchester is where the British under Sir Peter Parker were defeated on August 31, 1814 and their commander killed. Today the site is marked by a granite monument.

Higman's Mill built in 1764, is one of the six mills once located here that gave the town of Millington its name.

Rock Hall in colonial times was the interchange point on the road to Philadelphia and New York. Travelers would cross the Bay from Annapolis and board a stage at Rock Hall. It was also known as the seafood capital for about three hundred years, and got its name for the abundance of rock fish in the area.

Old St. Paul's Church built in 1713, is one of the oldest in continuous use in Maryland. Originally established in 1650, the pew rent was paid in tobacco and for one thousand pounds a permanent pew could be purchased. One pew purchased in this manner by Michael Miller is still used today by his descendants; Shrewsbury Church: Named for the Earl of Shrewsbury, the present church was the third such built on this site in 1832. The churchyard contains headstones of burials from centuries ago, making it one of the oldest in the country.

Kent County has many excellent colonial homes. These include: Comegys Bight, built in 1768; Godlington Manor, 1637; Trumpington, 1658; Hinchungham, 1659; Great Oak Manor, 1656; Hendrickson House, 1700; and Kitty Knight House in Georgetown, north of Galena, which was saved from burning by the British in May 1813.

Another house called Shepherd's Delight, built in 1682 on a part of the Camelsworthmore tract, was the home of Reverend Sewell S. Hepburn, pastor of the I.U. Church and grandfather of Katharine Hepburn, the actress. The walls of the house, with brick nogging are clapboarded, but are only six inches thick. The hall is paneled with vertical random-width boards, and the living room has a mantel carved by hand with nineteen sizes of auger bits, and a chair rail with five thousand handmade holes. The kitchen's hand-hewn rafters are still visible. The brick floor has since been covered with flooring and the fireplace has been bricked up. Looking across the land you can see Hebron owned by the Hebron family (also called Hebrone and Hepburn) and built by James Corse, the Quaker son of Colonel Henry DeCourcy, secretary of Maryland in 1660. The names Hepburn, Hebron and Hebrone, evidently refer to the same family in this area.

Regarding Shepherd's Delight, I contacted Miss Katharine Hepburn, and she was kind enough to communicate the following:

Katharine Houghton Hepburn

I - 12 - 1995

Dear John T. Marck -

    Yes, Shepherd's Delight was my
grandfather's house - and I used to
go there often as a kid - My
grandfather was the minister of the
church nearby - and we used to ride
over on horse and buggy - It's a
charming spot - I'm glad you liked
it too - Thank you for telling me -

Katharine Hepburn

    Other towns in Kent County and their origin include: <u>Betterton</u>, located on the Sassafras River, and named for the wife of resort developer Richard Turner, the former Elizabeth Betterton. <u>Fairlee</u>, was first known as Bel Air. The name was changed in deference to the more prominent town in Harford County. The residents settled on the former name of Fair Lea, which evolved to Fairlee. <u>Galena</u>, named for a type of silver called galena found near the town in 1813, but never mined for fear that the British would confiscate it. <u>Georgetown</u>, founded in 1736, and named for the royal prince King George III.

Gratitude, was first known as Deep Landing but was later named Gratitude after a steamboat of the same name which regularly docked there in the late 1800s. Hanesville, named for the settlement's first postmistress, Mary A. Hanes in 1878.

Millington, founded in 1794 by Thomas Gilpin on a tract of land known as London Bridge. It was named for Richard Millington, who owned a farm and mill on land where the town was built. Millington was also known as Bridgetown and Head of Chester in earlier times. Morgnec, located east of Chestertown, was originally known as Morgan's Neck, named after Henry Morgan, Sheriff of the Island of Kent. Over time it was changed to Morgnec.

Sassafras, named after the Sassafras River, was originally called Head of Sassafras. Still Pond, named for the Still Pond Creek. Formally known as Four Corners, as the town is located at the intersection of several roads, south of Betterton, and Tolchester, located west of Chestertown, and named for William Tolson, a seventeenth century surveyor and the Chester River. By combining the two names, Tol and Chester, the name was formed.

The population of Kent County has changed over the years, seesawing back and forth. In 1930 it was 14,242, dropping to 13,465 by 1940 and 13,677 in 1950. By 1960 it had risen to 15,481, and 16,680 in 1980. In 1990 the population was 17,842, and in 1994 it had increased by 4.7% to 18,687 since 1990. In 1998, the population is 19,120, and by the year 2000 it is projected to be 19,350.

Kent County and its once busy seaport of Chestertown, is a beautiful, tranquil place, with rich farmland symbolizing basic Eastern Shore characteristics, making it a unique, interesting and attractive area of Maryland.

Form of Government: Code Home Rule (1970)

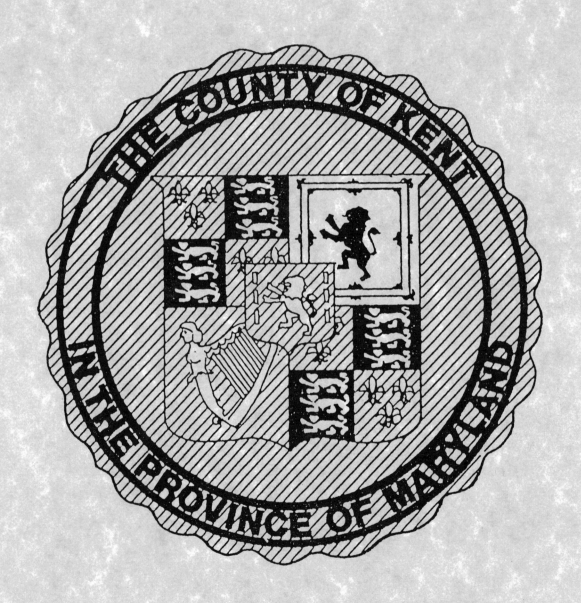

Map of Kent County

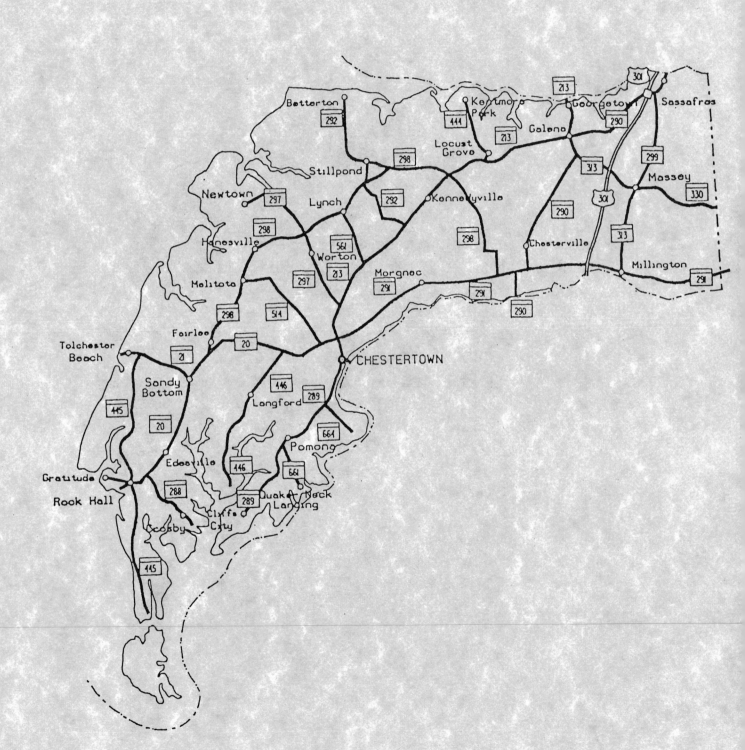

MONTGOMERY COUNTY

Montgomery County was created from Frederick County by resolve of the Constitutional Convention of 1776 and named for Revolutionary War General Richard Montgomery (1738-1775), an Irish officer who had served in the British Army during the French and Indian War and later settled in New York State. General Montgomery was killed on December 31, 1775, at the age of thirty-seven, leading an attack on Quebec. Benedict Arnold succeeded his command.

The Great Seal of Montgomery County uses some elements of the family arms of General Richard Montgomery. It was designed and approved by the College of Arms in London, England, and officially adopted by bill 38-76, enacted by the County Council on October 5, 1976 at the request of the County Executive.

The gold fleur-de-lis in the two quarters of the seal are reminders of the French ancestry of the Montgomery family. The gold rings with blue gemstones in two quarters of the seal proclaim royal favor and protection and are also found in the Montgomery family coat of arms. Below the bottom two quarters is written, "Gardez Bien" which translated means, "Guarded Well". To the left side of the bottom quarters is written "17" and to the right side, "76", depicting 1776, the year in which the county was created. Circular in shape, the seal also contains the words, "Montgomery County" along the top edge, and "Maryland" along the bottom edge.

Montgomery County lies directly northwest of the District of Columbia, once a part of Maryland. It has a land area of four hundred ninety-four square miles and water area of twelve square miles. It is bordered on the south and southwest by the Potomac River and the northwest by Frederick County, and northeast by Howard County. To the east is Prince George's County. It has an elevation of one hundred fifty feet along the Potomac to eight hundred feet above sea level in the northern sections of the county.

The first settlers in the county were English, Scotch and Irish, starting small settlements in Barnesville, Brookville, Laytonsville and Poolesville, which today still have relatively small populations.

Since 1777 Rockville has been the county seat of Montgomery County. First called Montgomery Court House and later Williamsburg, it took its present name of Rockville in 1804. During the Civil War, Rockville was frequently raided by Confederate troops in search of horses. After General Lew Wallace's defeat at Monocacy, General Jubal Early's forces passed through on their way to and from the attack on Washington. Today Rockville is a beautiful city, the fourth largest in Maryland with many large trees surrounding attractive homes.

Some interesting places to visit in Rockville are: Self-guided tour: A walking tour of Rockville is available at City Hall, on Maryland Avenue at Vinson Street, and at the Rockville Library, at 99 Maryland Avenue.

Beall-Dawson House: Located at 103 W. Montgomery Avenue, this home is restored in period furnishings. The Federal-style exterior of this house, built in 1815, complements the interior, designed in neoclassical style. Also located in this site is the Montgomery County Historical Society (MCHS). The MCHS operates the Beall-Dawson House, which also contains the Stonestreet Medical Museum, which focuses on nineteenth century medicine and a research library, as well as the Museum Shop. Open Tuesday - Saturday, noon-4 p.m. and First Sunday 2 to 5 p.m. Admission charged.

The Doctor's Museum: Located on the grounds of the Beall-Dawson House, and built in 1850, exhibits nineteenth century medical instruments.

The Research Library: Located in the Beall-Dawson House, the library offers a collection of books, maps, documents, and photographs pertaining to Montgomery County history. Admission charged.

Glenview Mansion at Rockville Civic Center Park: This pillared, neo-classical mansion was built in the style of an early nineteenth century plantation house. It overlooks Rockville's one hundred fifty-three acre Civic Center Park.

Old Red Brick Courthouse: Built in 1891, this is the third courthouse to occupy this site since 1779. In use today, the courthouse is open during business hours. It contains fine examples of wood, windows, and original hardware.

Baltimore & Ohio Railroad Station: Located on Old Baltimore Road, and built in 1873, this station is an excellent example of Railroad gothic architecture. The station was placed on the National Register of Historic Places in 1974. Also in Rockville are the graves of F. Scott and Zelda Fitzgerald. They are located at St. Mary's Church Cemetery, at the corner of Veirs Mill Road and Rt. 355.

Montgomery County has many historical cities and towns. These are: Takoma Park founded in 1883, and is Washington, D.C.'s first commuter suburb, Takoma Park features examples of period architecture, and today is on the National Register of Historic Places.

Gaithersburg, founded in 1722. Located here is the National Geographic Member Services, which features exhibits and a book/map store in a park-like setting. Also in Gaithersburg is the Potomac Horse Center, whose focus is monthly shows, lessons and training, and the Gaithersburg Heritage Museum. This museum offers exhibits on life in a small agricultural railroad town from 1870 to 1930. Available are tours of the B & O Station, outdoor rail car exhibits, as well as information on Olde Towne Gaithersburg restaurants, brewpub, antiques and stores.

Chevy Chase, founded in 1890. Here is located the Chevy Chase Historical Society which features a collection on the history of Chevy Chase from 1890 to the present day.

Kensington, established in 1890, this historic community is listed on the National Register of Historic Places. Located here on Stoneybrook Drive is the Mormon Temple Visitors Center. This site features a stunning architectural design, beautiful gardens and vivid exhibits. It is open daily from 10 a.m. to 9 p.m.

Garrett Park, which was founded in 1898. The entire town of Garrett Park is registered as an "historic district" in the National Register of Historic Places. Washington Grove, also listed on the National Register as a historic district. Here at McCathran Hall is located the Washington Grove Heritage Committee Archive, which maintains an archival collection. Brookeville, which was established in 1794, is one of the country's earliest settlements with the Caleb Bentley home in 1779 and the Brookeville Academy in 1815. Brookeville also had the distinction of being the "U.S. Capital for a day," when President James Madison fled here while the British were burning Washington, D.C. in the War of 1812.

Glen Echo, where the "Clara Barton National Historic Site" on Oxford Road is located. Clara Barton was instrumental during the Civil War for her work in locating missing soldiers, obtaining medical supplies, and nursing care for the wounded. She also founded the American National Red Cross in 1881. Her home is operated by the National Park Service. Located on MacArthur Boulevard and Goldsboro Road is Glen Echo Park, which was established in 1891. An amusement park in the first half of the century, Glen Echo has become a unique arts and cultural center with an original Dentzel Carousel (1921) still in operation from May to September. The former Chautauqua meeting ground now features artists at work and instructional classes. During the summer months, potters, puppeteers, dancers, painters, and a children's theatre are featured.

The town of Olney was founded in the early 1800s as a community of artisans, traders and merchants. Olney was formerly "Mechanicsville." The Montgomery County History Consortium, Inc. is located here. This network is comprised of eight individual historic museums and historical societies. Together their nearly 500,000 artifacts constitute Maryland's largest historical and cultural collections. Beallsville, established in 1798, is a small crossroads community having a rich heritage. It includes the site of an eighteenth century "chapel of ease" - the Monocacy Chapel - whose current building in the Monocacy Cemetery dates from 1912. Beallsville was also the site of much Civil War activity. In Boyds is located the Boyds Negro School House - Boyds/Clarksburg Historical Society. Open by appointment only, the Historical Society maintains a restored one-room schoolhouse (1896-1936) complete with period furnishings and literature on the school and community.

Poolesville, established in the 1700s, has several areas of historical interest. Located here is the John Poole House, built in 1793. This structure was the first building in Poolesville, built by the town's founder John Poole II. Today it contains a museum with a Civil War room and information center. On River Road is Kunzang Palyul Choling, a beautiful peaceful Tibetan Buddhist Temple, located on a seventy-two acre wildlife refuge. Featured are walking trails, contemplative gardens, twenty-four hour meditation room, and an unusual giftstore.

The Seneca Schoolhouse, established in 1865 is a reminder of the early days of public education. Today it is a museum with a scenic picnic area on the grounds. In downtown Poolesville are located the Town Hall and St. Peters Episcopal Church, established in 1847 and the Dr. Thomas Poole House (1835).

Riley's Lockhouse in Seneca, was established in 1833 and is the only original lockhouse open to the public in Montgomery County.

Sandy Spring is another historical area containing charming rustic homes. Here are located the Sandy Spring Meeting House (1817) and the Sandy Spring Museum. The Meeting House is a Colonial Church with original benches and unique wavy-paned windows. It was a place of worship for the Society of Friends and is an important part of Quaker history. White's Ferry, located on MD Rt. 107 at White's Ferry Road is the last working ferry on the river, and has been a widely used means of crossing the Potomac River between Maryland and Virginia since its inception. Today, commuters use the ferry daily. It has a capacity of fifteen cars per trip.

The largest communities are unincorporated, but fall under county government jurisdiction. These are: Silver Spring, named for the mica flakes that gleamed on the bottom of nearby springs. Located here is the Seventh Day Adventist World Headquarters, containing a religious and educational complex, with a visitors' center, tours, and presentations. On New Hampshire Avenue is the George Meany Memorial Archives. The archives preserves the historical records of the American Federation of Labor and Congress of Industrial Organizations. The museum features exhibits documenting the worklife and the history of labor.

Bethesda, a Washington, D.C. suburb developed and was named for the Bethesda Presbyterian Church. At the church is a "Madonna of the Trail" Monument, honoring a pioneer mother and child. A memorial honoring General Richard Montgomery is also in Bethesda. On Deepwell Drive is the Frank Lloyd Wright House, built in 1957. It is an important example of Wright's design philosophy. Located in North Bethesda is the Strathmore Hall Arts Center. This beautiful mansion dates from the turn of the century, and houses the Art Center for Montgomery County. Concerts are held throughout the year, and Strathmore Tea is served Tuesdays and Wednesdays at 1 p.m., October to May.

Wheaton, home to the National Capital Trolley Museum, is located on Bonifant Road between New Hampshire Avenue and Layhill Road. Included here are two carhouses with American and European antique streetcars, and a two and a quarter mile trolley ride. Exhibits are free. Admission is charged for trolley rides.

The Chesapeake and Ohio Canal National Historical Park Visitors Center is at 11710 MacArthur Blvd., in Potomac, Maryland. The Park itself follows the Maryland shore of the Potomac River from Georgetown in Washington, D.C., to Cumberland, Md. Begun on July 4, 1828, the canal is one hundred eighty-four and one half miles long, sixty feet wide, and six feet deep with seventy-four locks, and was completed in 1850. Also along the way are eleven aqueducts and a number of historic lockhouses. The canal was operated from 1850 to 1924. Promoters of the canal believed it would provide vital transportation between the Ohio River and the eastern seaboard. Unfortunately for the canalers, supporters of the Baltimore & Ohio Railroad saw the same opportunities. On the same day the canal was begun, ceremonies were also held launching the rail service. Construction for the canal proved far more complex than imagined. Material and labor shortages, conflicts over rights-of-way, and financial problems slowed the project.

By the time the canal was completed in 1850 at a cost of over seven and one half million dollars, the railroad had been in operation for nearly eight years. The only advantage the canal had over the railroad was the hauling of heavy non-perishables, such as coal, flour, and lumber. But, at the same time, the railroad was faster, cheaper, and extended farther westward.

During the Civil War, heavy damage resulted to the canal, and service was disrupted. A severe flood in 1889 brought economic woes, and another flood came in 1924, putting the canal out of business. The National Park Service adopted the property in 1971. A museum details the story of the canal, and can be seen at the visitor center at the Great Falls Tavern, built in 1828, at Potomac. Two major points of interest are the aqueduct at Monocacy and the Paw Paw Tunnel, which is cut three thousand one hundred eighteen feet through solid rock and lined with nearly six million bricks.

Chesapeake and Ohio Canal Boat Trips are available from the visitor center at the Great Falls Tavern, providing a one and one-half hour ride down the canal. Admission is charged.

Also of interest is Great Falls, located about fifteen miles northwest of Washington, D.C. Here visitors can view the Great Falls of the Potomac as they make a thundering descent in a series of picturesque falls and rapids.

Great Falls

Although Montgomery County is heavily populated, agricultural is still an important industry, including dairying and livestock. Corn, wheat, barley , alfalfa, and other hay crops are raised. Industrial plants are another important industry with nearly two hundred plants located in the county. According to the first census of 1790, Montgomery County had a population of 18,003. By 1920 there were still only 34,921 people living there. Over the years it has experienced tremendous growth, growing to 340,926 in 1960, and to 574,106 by 1980. In 1990 the population was 757,027 and in 1994 grew to 802,721, an increase of 6.0% since 1990.

The State of Maryland owns very little land in the county compared to other counties. The largest section is Seneca State Park, a 6,200-acre park, located on a ninety-acre lake.   Other parks and gardens include: Black Hill Regional Park, and The Lodge at Little Seneca Creek, located in Boyds; Brighton Azalea Gardens; Brookside Gardens; Cabin John Regional Park, in Rockville; Little Bennett Regional Park, in Clarksburg; McCrillis Gardens in Bethesda; Meadowside Nature Center in Rockville; Rock Creek Regional Park, northeast of Rockville; Rockwood Manor Conference Center in Potomac; Wheaton Regional Park; Woodend Mansion in Chevy Chase; Woodlawn Manor in Sandy Spring and Cherry Hill Park, in College Park, which features a campground with full hook-ups, swimming pool, sauna and hot tub facilities.

Montgomery County is internationally recognized as the headquarters of many leaders in scientific research and medical technology. Some examples are the Shady Grove Life Sciences Center; the National Institutes of Health, which include the Visitor's Information Center, Disease Information, and National Library of Medicine; the National Institute of Standards and Technology; National Oceanic and Atmosphere Administration; and the Naval Medical Center.

Some of the attractions in Montgomery County are the Fantasy Flights, located in Gaithersburg which offers hot-air balloon flights, as well as aerial advertising and the Sugarloaf Mountain Works, Inc., which features the Sugarloaf Craft Festivals.

Montgomery County was the first in Maryland to obtain authorization to establish a charter form of government, and the first in Maryland to have an elected Board of Education. It is one of the wealthiest counties in the country, and the largest in population of Maryland's counties. In 1998, the population rose to 835,370, and by the year 2000, it is projected to be 855,000.

Being close to both Baltimore and Washington, Montgomery County continues to grow and thrive with each new year.

Form of Government: Charter (1948)

Clara Barton assisting a wounded soldier

Map of Montgomery County

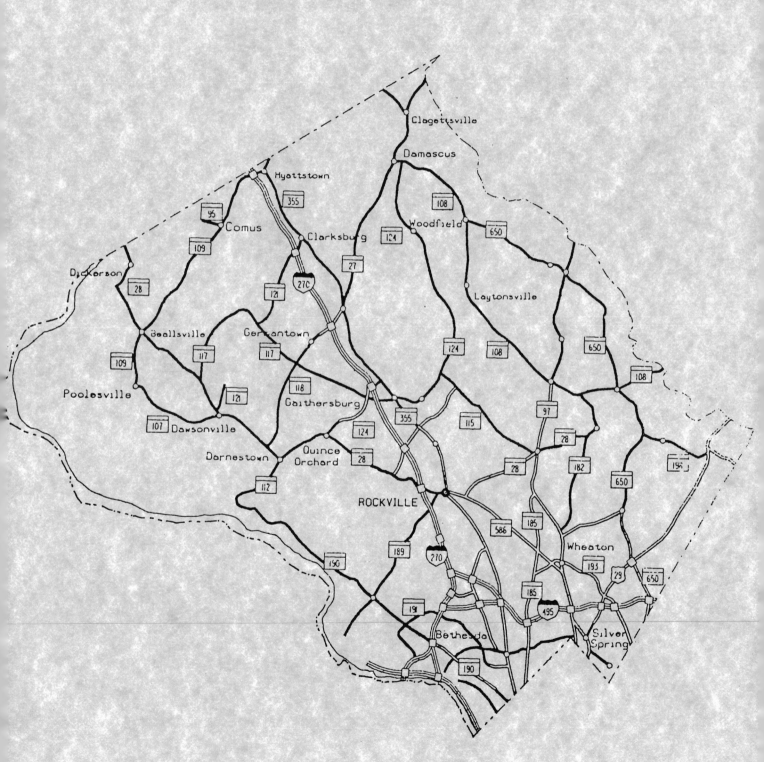

PRINCE GEORGE'S COUNTY

Prince George's County was created from Calvert and Charles counties in 1695 (Chapter 13, Acts of 1695, May session; to be established April, 1696). The County was named for Prince George of Denmark (1653-1708), the husband of Queen Anne.

Prince George's County and its seal are a history and heraldry dating back to the eleventh century. The red cross of St. George has been the symbol of Christian martyrdom since its first use during the great Crusades in the Holy Land. At the siege of Antioch in 1069, Crusaders believed they saw the ghost of St. George fighting at their side. Richard The Lionhearted adopted the red cross banner as a battle standard one hundred years later, using it as a special insignia on the white surcoats of English soldiers. The design continued as England's land and sea battle standard for many years.

The county seal in the flag's upper left quadrant did not officially become part of the flag until 1963 when a special committee suggested to the county government that it be added to "more definitely establish the colors as uniquely those of Prince George's County." The county seal was designed in 1696 by Charles Beckwith of Patuxent. Its crest is England's Imperial Crown, better known as St. Edward's Crown. The coat of arms in four quarters symbolizes Queen Anne, France and England in the first and fourth grand quarters, Scotland in the second grand quarter and Ireland in the third. Ribboned beneath is the county motto, "Semper Eadem," which means "Ever the Same." Originally, the seal depicted Prince George's without the apostrophe and using the old English style "u" in county. The seal was officially altered in 1971 to read "Prince George's County, Maryland" and made the lone official seal used on all documents and correspondence.

Prince George's County is located east of Washington, D.C., bordered by Howard County to the north, and Anne Arundel to the east. To the southeast lies Calvert, and Charles County is on the south. Washington, D.C. and Montgomery County border it to the west. Along the western boundary for a large area lie the Potomac River. Prince George's has an area of four hundred eighty-five square land miles and eleven square water miles.

Prince George's County has an elevation ranging from ten to four hundred twenty feet above sea level, averaging about two hundred fifty feet. The county was established by English people, and many of their descendants live there today. Having a population of 21,344 in 1790, it has risen to be the second largest county in Maryland, by population. By 1960 its population was 357,395; in 1980 657,707; and in 1990 728,553. By 1994 the population was 764,053, an increase of 4.9% since 1990. In 1998, the population again increased to 794,860, and by the year 2000, it is projected to be 812,100.

The County has twenty-eight incorporated cities, more than any other Maryland county. The largest incorporated city is Bowie with Hyattsville, second largest. The county seat is Upper Marlboro, founded in 1706, and named for the first Duke of Marlborough, John Churchill, an ancestor of Sir Winston Churchill. The Duke was the famous military leader of Queen Anne's reign. The chief agricultural crop in Prince George's county is tobacco, with some corn and grains also being raised. Livestock, poultry, and dairying are present, but less important than the field crops.

There are many interesting and historic places and homes in the county, both past and present. These include: Old Marlboro House which at one time was located on Main Street across from the courthouse. Built in 1732, it was once an inn, and according to tradition, when George Washington stopped here on his trip north, he always occupied room number seven on the second floor. Lafayette was also a guest, as well as Major General Robert Ross, commander of the British Army during the War of 1812. Some doubt that it was ever an inn, due to its distinguished Georgian Colonial design, believing it to be much too elaborate for a tavern during this period. Today this structure no longer stands.

Dower House: once known as Mount Airy was built in 1660 as a hunting lodge of the Calverts. In 1931 fire destroyed all but one two-and-a-half-story wing. Following the fire the house was restored. To the right of the house lies a terraced garden planned by Major Pierre Charles L'Enfant, who designed the city of Washington, D.C. Charles, fifth Lord Baltimore gave this estate to his natural son, Benedict Swingate Calvert. In 1748, Benedict married Elizabeth, daughter of Governor Leonard Calvert. Occasionally, George Washington would visit Dower House, according to his diary entries. In 1774, his stepson, John Parke Custis, married Calvert's daughter Eleanor, against the approval of Washington due to their young ages. The last of the Calverts to live at Dower House was Benedict's granddaughter Eleanor, who died in 1902 at the age of 95.

Poplar Hill: Built between 1784 and 1786 by Robert Darnall, who was the uncle of Mary Darnall, wife of Charles Carroll of Carrollton. They had two sons, Daniel and John. Robert and Mary lived at Darnall's Chance.

Darnall's Chance: Located at 14800 Governor Oden Bowie Drive in Upper Marlboro, Darnall's Chance is considered one of Prince George's County's and the State of Maryland's most significant historical landmarks. Built between 1694 and 1713, Darnall's Chance was owned for nearly four decades by the prominent Darnall and Carroll families. It is also the birthplace of Charles Carroll of Carrollton and his wife, Mary Darnall's two sons, Daniel and John. Daniel Carroll was a signer of the United States Constitution, and his brother John was the first bishop of the Roman Catholic Church in America. Darnall's Chance also features several design elements that are unique among the surviving colonial buildings of Maryland.

Montpelier in Laurel, was built by Thomas Snowden, between 1770 and 1785. Of interest is the interior woodwork, much of which is hand-carved. Especially notable is the detail of the stair railing between the north section and the library which has turned balusters (posts or supports) three to a step, each of different patterns. Montpelier is also significant for the many famous Americans who have visited it. These include George Washington, Martha Washington, Abigail Adams, and Franklin Roosevelt.

Throughout the eighteenth century, the Snowden family had considerable land holdings. In 1770, Major Thomas Snowden, a great-great grandson of the Welsh immigrant, Richard Snowden, inherited from his father, Thomas, the four hundred acres of land on which he would build Montpelier. Major Snowden married Anne Ridgely of Anne Arundel County in 1774. This marriage provided Major Snowden with the means with which to have the house constructed. He described this by saying, "having got a large fortune by his wife who was an heiress to a large estate." By the end of the eighteenth century, Major Snowden had landholdings totaling over nine thousand acres.

The Snowdens would also welcome a number of distinguished guests. Traveling to Philadelphia as a delegate to the Constitutional Convention in May, 1787, George Washington stopped by Montpelier where, "feeling very severely a violent headache and sick stomach (he) went to bed early." In September, on his return trip, he again stayed at Montpelier. In 1789, on their trip to attend his inauguration as the first president, George again stayed at Montpelier, along with his wife Martha. At the turn of the century,

Abigail Adams, on her way to join her husband in Washington, visited Montpelier. Adams stayed the night in the "large, handsome, elegant house, where I was received with my family, and with what we might term true English hospitality," she once wrote.

Major Snowden and his wife had five children. Following his father's death in 1803, a son, Nicholas, inherited Montpelier. In 1806, Nicholas married Elizabeth Warfield Thomas, and twelve children were born of the union. In 1824, Nicholas established a successful cotton mill that employed over 100 persons, known as Laurel Factory. Following the death of Nicholas in 1831, the estate was inherited by his daughter, Julianna, who married Dr. Theodore Jenkins in 1835. Julianna's daughters were the last Snowden descendants to own Montpelier. In 1961, Montpelier was acquired by The Maryland-National Capital Park and Planning Commission. In 1976, the Friends of Montpelier were formally chartered, and since that time, volunteer members have operated a giftshop, conducted tours and special events throughout the year. Today certain designated areas of the mansion are available on a rental basis for meetings, wedding receptions, etc.

Other historical sites are: Beltsville Agricultural Research Center, located in Beltsville. This is the home of the holiday turkey, the modern blueberry and strawberry, the lean hog, the "bug bomb," the human calorimeter, and the world's largest cloned orchard. Comprising 7,200 acres, it is the headquarters for the nationwide laboratories of the Agricultural Research Service, the science agency of the U.S. Department of Agriculture, and has been in operation for over eighty years. Guided tours are available by appointment.

In Greenbelt is the NASA/Goddard Space Flight Center/Visitor's Center & Museum: Established in 1959, the Goddard Space Flight Center was NASA's first major scientific laboratory devoted entirely to the exploration of space. Here scientists have some of the most advanced equipment available to design, build, test, and monitor a wide range of spacecraft. Tours are available.

The College Park Airport Museum, is the "World's Oldest Continually Operated Airport." It was established in 1909 when the Wright Brothers, Orville and Wilber, brought their newly accepted government airplane to this field to teach the first two army officers to fly. Between 1909 and 1934, many aviation firsts took place here. Some of the significant firsts in aviation occurring at College Park Airport include:

1909 - First woman passenger to fly in an airplane
       First military officer to fly a government airplane.
1911 - First testing of a bomb dropping from an airplane.
1912 - First testing of a machine gun from an airplane.
1918 - First U.S. Air Mail Service
1924 - First controlled helicopter flight.
1926 - First radio navigational aids developed and
       tested by the Bureau of Standards.

<u>Oxon Hill Farm</u>: At Oxon Hill Farm, horses still pull the plows, and a steam-powered thresher separates the wheat. This working farm, part modern and part turn-of-the century, is open to visitors, and was made a National Park in 1967. Also in Oxon Hill is the <u>Rosecroft Raceway</u>, one of the finest harness racing facilities on the East Coast.

In Upper Marlboro is the <u>Merkle Wildlife Sanctuary and Visitor Center</u>. In 1932 it began as a breeding and nesting ground for Canadian Geese. Interpretive programs and a new visitor center have made this one of the most unique and beautiful wildlife and environmental attractions in the State of Maryland. In Fort Washington is <u>Fort Washington National Park</u>. The fort was built between 1814 and 1824, constructed to replace the earlier Fort Warburton, named for the estate on which it was built in 1661, Warburton Manor. This was the home of the Diggs family, descendants of Edward Diggs, governor of Virginia. The fort was originally established to protect the capital in Washington. Following the War of 1812, Major L'Enfant, who designed the fort, labeled it one of the most interesting military structures in the United States. Featured at the fort are cannons, ramparts, earthworks, a drawbridge, and history tours.

Prince George's County is also the home of the University of Maryland, at College Park. The largest institution of higher learning in the State of Maryland, it also features sporting and cultural events year round. On the campus is Rossborough Inn, a historic inn dating from 1798, open for lunch during the calendar school year.

The <u>USAIR Arena</u>, located in Landover is the home of the Washington Bullets Professional Basketball Club and the Washington Capitals Professional Hockey Club. Also held at the arena are the Washington International Horse Show, and touring concerts featuring popular recording artists. A short distance from the USAIR Arena is <u>Adventure</u>

World at Largo. This family amusement/water theme park is the home of Maryland's tallest wooden roller coaster, and the "Wild Wave."

Belair: Built for Governor Samuel Ogle (1694-1752), who was 47 when he brought his 18 year old bride Anne Tasker here.

Marietta: Located in Glenn Dale, this was the plantation home of Gabriel Duvall. In 1811, he built this Federal style brick house, during which time he was also appointed an Associate Judge on the United States Supreme Court, a position he held for twenty-three years. Of the original six hundred fifty acre estate, only the Judge's law office and root cellar remain. In 1830, a second story was added when Duvall became guardian to his grandchildren.

Gabriel Duvall (1752-1844) spent over sixty years in public service. In addition to his position on the U.S. Supreme Court, he also was a member of the Maryland House of Delegates, the Maryland Supreme Court, and Comptroller of the United States Treasury. Marietta remained in the Duvall family until 1902. Today the mansion has been restored and is open to the public for tours.

Surratt House & Tavern: Located in Clinton, this middle-class farm house was built in 1852 for the family of John and Mary Surratt. This historic house also served as a tavern and hostelry, a post office, and a polling place prior to the Civil War. During the Civil War it became a safehouse in the Confederate underground system, which prospered in Southern Maryland.

In the fall of 1864, the Surratt family became involved in a plot by John Wilkes Booth to kidnap President Abraham Lincoln. This plan by Booth later turned to assassination on April 14, 1865. On his getaway, Booth stopped by the Surratt house to retrieve weapons and supplies which he had hidden there. As a result of this, Mary Surratt was tried in a military court and convicted of conspiracy to assassinate the President. On July 7, 1865, she became the first woman to be executed by the Federal Government. Today the museum features a variety of programs, focusing on the interesting events of the Lincoln assassination conspiracy.

Bladensburg, was founded in 1742 as Garrison's Landing on the Anacostia River. Some believe that it was named for Sir Thomas Bladen, governor of the province, but others believe the honor goes to his father, William Bladen. Once a busy port it shipped tobacco and flour in the early 1800s until the Anacostia River filled with silt, preventing large ships from entering the port. Bladensburg was also the site of a battle fought before the British capture of Washington in 1814. Bladensburg also has an area outside of the town which was used almost exclusively by fashionable gentlemen for dueling. On this site Commodore James Barron shot and killed Commodore Stephen Decatur and Colonel John McCarty killed his cousin Brigadier General Armistead Mason. Others involved in dueling include Henry Clay, John Randolph and Samuel P. Key, brother of Francis Scott Key. Another historical site in Bladensburg is the Market Masters House, built by Christopher Lowndes. During renovations in 1993, the original clocks were discovered.

Other places of interest in Bladensburg are: George Washington House, built in 1732, and located on Maryland Avenue, originally called the Indian Maid. The Bostwick House, was built in 1746 by Christopher Lowndes for his bride, Elizabeth Tasker. On the south chimney Lowndes placed his initials and date. The Magruder House; Built in 1743; The Ross House: Located near the Magruder House, was built in 1749 by Dr. David Ross, an officer in the French and Indian War. The Ross House was disassembled in the 1950s and was moved and reassembled in Baltimore County, and The Memorial Cross: erected in 1925 to the men from Prince George's County who died in the World Wars.

Another interesting place to visit in Prince George's County is the National Wildlife Visitor Center, located in Laurel. This center is the largest science and environmental education center in the Department of the Interior. Designed to accommodate one million visitors per year, this unique facility seeks to impart to young and old alike an increased knowledge of and appreciation for the earth's vital resources. It highlights the work of professional scientists who strive to improve the condition of wildlife and their habitats. Exhibits focus on global environmental issues, migratory bird studies, habitats, endangered species, creative life cycles and the research tools and techniques used by scientists.

The Visitor Center offers hiking trails, wildlife management demonstrations, and outdoor education sites for school classes. A gift shop, "Wildlife Images," operated by the Friends of Patuxent, Inc., offers a variety of books and educational materials.

Form of Government: Charter (1970)

Map and Seal of Prince George's County

QUEEN ANNE'S COUNTY

Queen Anne's County was created in 1706 (Chapter 3, Acts of 1706). The County was named for Queen Anne (1665-1714), who ruled Great Britain and Ireland, 1702-1714.

Queen Anne's County was the first English permanent settlement in the State of Maryland, under a 1631 patent from the king. In 1629, three years before the arrival of the Ark and the Dove at St. Mary's, Captain William Claiborne, an agent of the Virginia governor, established a trading post on an island he later named "Isle of Kent." Kent Fort Manor, built in 1640 and still standing is believed to be the oldest structure in Maryland.

On May 1, 1707, during the reign of Queen Anne, the second daughter of James II, and during the Royal Governorship of Colonel John Seymour, the county known as Queen Anne's was laid out by legislative enactment, and formed partially from Kent and Talbot Counties. From 1637 to 1692, the nine counties then in existence were permitted to use the lesser Seal of Lord Baltimore without official correspondence or legislative action proclaiming the fact. On October 13, 1692, following the Protestant uprising, the Council petitioned the Crown for permission to use the Arms of his Majesty William III as the seals of the various counties. Permission was granted and each county adopted the Kings Arms with the county name on the surrounding border. When Queen Anne's County was formed in 1707, no seal was requested or directed to be used. It is believed that various judges of the County Court used their own seals on official papers as no formal seal appears on official Queen Anne's County papers prior to the early seventeen hundreds.

Upon the death of Queen Anne in 1714, and the accession of George I to the throne, Calvert had his Colony restored to his family. Again for want of official records directing the type of seal to be used by Queen Anne's County, minor heraldic sleuthing proves that the original seal was produced after the Lords Baltimore regained control of the Colony. The Seal of Queen Anne's County is heraldicly described as follows: The Arms of Calvert, paly of six, Or and Sable, a bend counter changed. Above the Arms, the Royal Crown of England surmounted by the Ducal Coronet of Calvert and the two pennons, or and Sable, flying from staves of Gules. This indicated that Calvert is permitted to indulge the Royal prerogatives in the Colony of Maryland and the Banner above the Crest proclaims the governed area as Queen Anne's County. The Arms are supported by two lions rampant. Below the shield is the motto, "Crescite Et Multiplicamini" (Increase and Multiply).

In 1961, King William of England revoked the Calvert charter and Maryland reverted to the Crown. Upon his death in 1702, Anne, sister of his wife, for whom the county is named, became the Queen of England. At her death in 1714, she was succeeded to the throne by George I, who restored the Maryland Palatinate to the Baltimores.

When Queen Anne's County was first established in 1706, part of the territory included within its present bounds was taken from Kent County and part from Talbot County. At this time, the Calverts were out of power and because of this their western lands had been forfeited. The Arms of Lord Baltimore, which had been used as a basis for the official bearings of earlier sections, could no longer be used. Court records for the November term of 1728 contained the following directive: "A new County Seal is delivered to the Clerk of this Court, and it is ordered that all processes in matters of Record be henceforth sealed therewith, the said Seal being made pursuant to a late order of Council." Impressions made by this seal, on papers submitted to the Provincial Court at Annapolis for legal interpretation, are still on file at the Hall of Records in Annapolis. One of the clearest and most distinct of these appears on the case of Gilbert Barrow agt. Thomas Reed, 1743. Through contributions, Queen Anne's County was able to secure the services of Mr. Thomas E. Stokle, of Leonardtown, who is a competent heraldic artist of wide experience with the early bearings of Maryland. In conjunction with personnel from the Hall of Records, and utilizing their facilities for study of these impressions from which the original seal of the Queen Anne's County Court, reproduction was made, first in line drawings, then in color. This interesting work is at "Wright's Chance," the Historical Society's home in Centreville. Heraldically the seal is described as follows: Shield, a paly of six Or and Sable a bend counterchanged. Crest, out of a ducal coronet, two staves with pennons flying to the dexter side; the dexter Gold, the sinster Sable. Supporters, two lions guardant Or.

The unknown engraver who executed this original Court Seal, which was used to dignify and identify official pronouncements of the colonial court for Queen Anne's County, was faced with a problem in reducing its size. To accomplish this, the heading was shortened to Q Anne's County. The present seal of Queen Anne's County is made of the Shield, Crest, and Supporters, as described above. Below the shield is the motto, "Vincit Omnia Veritas." Its translation is "Truth Conquers All."

Queen Anne's lies between Kent County to the north, and Caroline and Talbot to the south. It stretches from the Chesapeake Bay to the State of Delaware, having a total of three hundred seventy-three square land miles and thirty-three square water miles. The land is generally flat, ranging from sea level to ninety feet above sea level.

Settled by the English, the county is mostly agricultural. Attracted by the flat terrain and good waterways, tobacco was the chief crop grown. Although each farmer was required by law to grow two acres of corn to insure a food supply, many were forced to grow more corn and wheat, because of the Revolutionary War, which curtailed the tobacco trade with England. Today the county remains the same. Corn, wheat, soybeans, small grains, and various varieties of vegetables are grown. Dairy, livestock, cattle and hog production are also important industries to the county.

The largest city is Centreville, the county seat, having a population of about two thousand. Other incorporated towns are Sudlersville, pop. 417; Queenstown, 387; Church Hill, 247; and Barclay, 187. Other towns include: Millington, 39 (total population is 474 of which 435 are in Kent County); Templeville, 83 (total population is 102, of which 19 are in Caroline County); Queen Anne, 141 (total population is 292, of which 151 are in Talbot County). In 1998, the total population of Queen Anne's County is 39,940, and by the year 2000, it is projected to be 41,600.

Centreville was founded in 1782 as the county's seat, originally named Chester Mill. In 1792, an act of the state legislature relocated the courthouse and center of government from Queenstown to land that was part of a four hundred acre tract, known as "Chesterfield," at the south side of the Chester River and north side of Corsica Creek. The town was officially incorporated on December 26, 1794. In 1797 the name was changed to Centreville because of its location and accessibility for all county residents. Centreville is a classic example of small town America. Its past is evident in the architecture of simple, austere federal period houses, as well as graceful Victorian era homes. Centreville has many interesting and historical places to visit. These include: The Courthouse and Statue, located at Lawyers Row is the oldest courthouse in the state in continuous use since 1791. The statue on the green commemorates Queen Anne, the county's namesake, who was the reigning monarch when the county was formed in 1706.

Also at Lawyers Row in "The Brass Pin" Site, a marker on the Centreville National Bank building denoting the survey reference point for all the original town lots since 1791. Located on South Commerce Street are three interesting places; Tucker House, c.1792, is the oldest house in the town with period furnishings and memorabilia. The house has six working fireplaces and the grounds contain a perennial herb garden. Wright's Chance, c.1744, is an early plantation house, moved to this location from its original 1681 site. Restored by the Queen Anne's Historical Society, the house has an impressive collection of Hepplewhite and Chippendale furniture. Housed here is also the Queen Anne's County seal, faithfully reproduced by Leonardtown heraldic artist Thomas E. Stokle. The Queen Anne's County Art Council, located at 206 S. Commerce Street, is a renovated church, serving as the headquarters of the art council. Fine arts are exhibited, and performances and workshops are held.

Also in Centreville is Chesterfield, c.1660, located on Chesterfield Avenue. All the land for the town of Centreville was carved from this plantation estate, originally owned by William Hemsley in 1660. This clapboard structure was once invaded by the Nanticoke Indians, and is today a private residence. The Wharf & Captain's House, c.1794, are located on Front & Corsica Streets. Once the center of commerce for the town's shipping trade, the wharf often hosted a floating theater and is now a public landing. The row of houses located here were built by Captain Osmond to accommodate the families of ships' crew members who transported goods and produce up and down the Bay. St. Paul's Church, c.1699, located at Liberty Street and Church Lane, still holds weekly services today. Built in 1692 under the authority of the parish vestry at the cost of fourteen thousand three hundred ninety-five pounds of tobacco, the site was first used in 1704.

Other towns and their origin are: Burrissville, founded in 1790 and named for the Burris family who first lived there; Church Hill, was founded in 1732 and grew up around St. Luke's Episcopal Church; Crumpton, was settled in the early 1700s, and was originally known as McAllister's Ferry. The present town was named in 1858 for William Crump, a prominent land owner; Grasonville, formally known as Winchester and Ford's Store, it was changed to Grasonville in honor of William Grason, governor of Maryland from 1839 to 1842; Ingleside, first known as Long Marsh then Beaver Dam after streams in the area. In 1812 the name was changed to Ingleside; Mattapex, named after an Algonquian Indian word meaning "junction of waters."

The City of Queen Anne, was settled in 1857. When the railroad arrived in 1878, the station was named Queen Anne. Because this station was the only place there, and the town was built around the station, the town was named Queen Anne. Queenstown, named for Anne, Queen of England, Scotland, and Ireland. Queenstown was established in 1707 as the first county seat. Although just a small village it had good shipping facilities and was used as an outlet for cargo received from England. During the War of 1812, the British considered the town important and launched a land and sea attack on the village. Located here is St. Peter's Catholic Church. Romanesque and Victorian architecture decorate the brick exterior, while the interior is refinished in colonial tradition with stained glass windows and mid-nineteenth century brass. Located on Rt. 18 and Del Rhodes Avenue is the Queenstown Colonial Courthouse. Built about 1708, this simple one-room wooden structure was the first courthouse in the county. Restored to its original state it contains authentic reproductions. Tours are available on request.

Also in the area is Gallows Field, the location where gallows, stocks and pillory were in operation, and the old colonial courthouse; Roe, was first known as Roes Cross Roads, named after James Roe, a storekeeper; Romancoke, was William Claiborne's Kent Island plantation, named after an Algonquian/Powhatan Indian word meaning, "where there is low lying ground"; Ruthsburg, named after Christopher Cross Ruth, a County Justice in 1765; Sudlersville, first known as Sudler's Cross Roads, was named after Joseph Sudler in the 1690s. Sudlersville Train Station, c.1885, is located at 101 Linden Street, and has been preserved as a museum devoted to the history of the railroad, the history of Sudlersville, and Baseball Hall of famer, Jimmy Foxx. Dudley's Chapel, c.1783, also in Sudlersville on Benton Corner Road, is the oldest Methodist church still standing in the county, and was a preaching station for Bishops Cooke and Ashbury.

The town of Stevensville, located near the William Preston Lane, Jr. Memorial Bridge, is the home of Christ Church. Built in 1880, and located at 117 East Main Street, this church was founded in 1631 and houses the oldest established congregation in the state. Sunday services are held and tours are available by appointment. The Stevensville Train Station, c.1902, is located on Cockey's Lane. This was the original station house when the stop became part of Queen Anne's Railroad System, and today has been restored to its original state.

Wye Mills, named after the Wye East River and the mills located there. The Talbot County line runs through the center of Wye Mills. Located on Route 662 in Wye Mills is

<u>Wye Mill</u>, the oldest grist mill on the Eastern Shore. Here visitors can observe how wheat and corn are stone ground by water power into flour and meal. Today's mill is much the same as it originally was, with a big water wheel, a pair of granite mill stones, and a maze of conveyors, shoots and sifting equipment designed to carry and process the grain as it becomes flour. A strong sense of the past is present at Wye Mill. Resting against the building are old worn mill stones, and the dust from many grindings has settled on the ancient wooden beams, adding to its charm.

Upon visiting Wye Mill, visitors get a real feeling of exactly what it was like years ago. When the mill is running, the floor-boards rumble, the sound of the machinery fills your ears, and the smell of grain permeates the air. Visiting the mill is a very interesting, historical, learning experience. Curators are on hand to explain the mill's history and operation, while volunteer millers demonstrate how water powers the stone grinding process. Also located in the picturesque village of Wye Mills is the site of the four hundred year old Wye Oak tree, and eighteenth century Wye Church.

There are many interesting places in Queen Anne's County, which have some of the finest examples of early architecture. These include: <u>The Chesapeake Bay Bridge:</u> Completed in 1952, the bridge cost $45 million and links the Western and Eastern Shores. At its greatest height the bridge roadway rises two hundred feet above the Bay, and is seven and one-tenth miles long, four and one-third miles of which are over water. In 1967, the bridge was renamed the <u>William Preston Lane, Jr. Memorial Bridge</u> in memory of a former governor of Maryland. A second span was opened in 1972, at a cost of $112 million; <u>Kent Island:</u> The largest island in the Chesapeake Bay, was the first permanent settlement in Maryland, founded and named by Captain William Claiborne in 1631, for his home country in England. Claiborne fought for many years with Lord Baltimore over the claim to the island, finally relinquishing it in 1658.

Some examples of early architecture include: <u>Queen Anne's County Courthouse:</u> Located in Centreville and built in 1790, it was remodeled in 1830 and again in the 1860s. Also in Centreville is the <u>St. Paul's Protestant Episcopal Church</u> built in 1885, and containing a chalice and flagon presented by Queen Anne, and <u>Walnut Grove</u>, the oldest dwelling in the county, built between 1681 and 1685 of logs and brick. In other areas are located: <u>Wye Plantation:</u> Built by Colonel Edward Tilghman in 1747, it was the home of William Paca (1740-1799), signer of the Declaration of Independence and governor of Maryland. Paca also had a residence in Annapolis. Among the noted guests who visited Wye Plantation are General Lafayette, the two Charles Carrolls, and Colonel Tench Tilghman. In the graveyard near the house is the tomb of William Paca. The Houghton Library at the plantation is notable. Wye Hall, designed by James Hoban, is located directly opposite Wye Plantation. This house was also built by William Paca. Destroyed in 1789 by fire, it was rebuilt only to be destroyed again by fire in 1920. The present house was rebuilt using the original foundation; Blakeford: Built in 1809 on the DeCourcy estate; Kennersley: Built in 1703; Bolingly: Targeted by British cannon fire during the War of 1812 contains a notable unusual double stairway.

Much of Queen Anne's County is still unspoiled by man. Areas such as Wye Island Natural Resource and Tuckahoe State Park, shared with Caroline County, are examples of this. Queen Anne's County remains a beautiful, pleasant place to live and one of the finest farming counties in the State.

Form of Government: County Commissioners

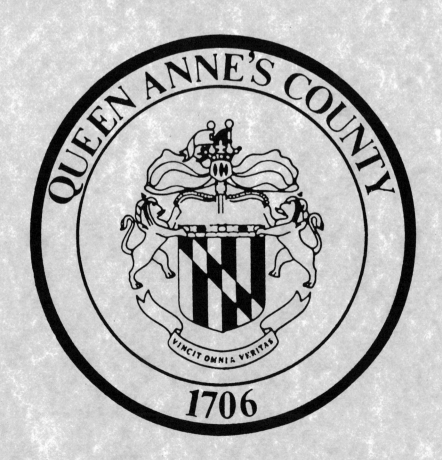

Map of Queen's Anne's County

ST. MARY'S COUNTY

It was here that the passengers on the Ark and the Dove landed in March, 1634. Except for a small trading post established on Kent Island by William Claiborne, St. Mary's City was the first Maryland colony, established in 1637. The county and city of St. Mary's are both named in honor of the Virgin Mary.

St. Mary's County Seal is described as having two lions on their hind feet, leaning on the State Coat of Arms. The motto across the bottom is the same as the Great Seal of Maryland, "Fatti Maschii Parole Femine," usually translated as "manly deeds, womanly words." The date on the seal, 1637, is assumed to be the date the seal was first used.

St. Mary's County is at the tip of the western shore of the Chesapeake Bay, and is bordered on the north by Charles County and the Patuxent River and on the south by the Potomac River. It has a land area of three hundred sixty-seven square miles and a water area of fifty-three square miles. By the time of the original census, the county had a population of 15,544 residents. By 1940, the number of residents had dropped to 14,626, but again picked up to over 38,000 in 1960. By 1990 the population rose to 75,975, and in 1994 was 80,323, an increase of 5.7% since 1990. In 1998, the population rose to 86,730, and by the year 2000, it is projected to be 90,700.

St. Mary's County is agricultural, producing tobacco, corn, wheat, oats, barley, rye and soybeans. Livestock products are also an important industry.

As Maryland's birthplace, St. Mary's County has many interesting and historical places. St. Mary's City is one such place. On March 25, 1634, Leonard, brother of Cecil Calvert, anchored his ships, the Ark and the Dove, by St. Clement's Island. On this day they came ashore to celebrate the Feast of the Annunciation. Today we celebrate March 25 as Maryland Day. While most of the crews lived on the ships, Leonard and others traveled up the Potomac River to meet with the Emperor of the Piscataway Indians, and arranged for a peaceful settlement for his people on the Indians' land. Two days later, on March 27, 1634, Leonard, with the Ark and the Dove sailed up the St. George's River (now St. Mary's) to an established village of the Yoacomico Indians. The Yoacomico Indians were in the process of evacuating their village for fear of attacks by the

Susquehannock Indians. Leonard and the new colonists took over the village and paid the Indians for it with hatchets, axes, farm tools and cloth. Soon the colonists built St. George's Fort, followed by a town laid out according to Leonard's plans. Year by year the colonists increased in number and in 1676 built a statehouse.

St. Mary's City was the first capital of the State of Maryland, and remained so until the capital was moved to Annapolis, a more convenient location, in 1694. Also originally the county seat, St. Mary's City lost this status, and declined rapidly, when the seat was moved to Leonardtown.

During the colonial days of St. Mary's, the money used to purchase items were the English pound, shilling and pence, the official currency of Maryland. But because of a shortage of these types of currency, other items of value were used. These included furs, tools, cloth, salt, corn, meat, livestock and tobacco. Because coins were so scarce, Cecil Calvert ordered shillings, sixpence, silver groats, and copper pennies to be made. To accomplish this the first mint was established in Maryland, in St. Mary's in 1660. The English king, learning of the minting of coins, disapproved and ordered the mint closed. Consequently, only several hundred coins were made. Some of these coins are still around today. One such collection, believed to be a complete set, may be viewed at Johns Hopkins University. These coins were the property of John W. Garrett, who willed them to the university in 1942, along with his estate "Evergreen," and his paintings and library of books.

As English money became more and more scarce to obtain, other forms of currency were used in Maryland by the 1700s. These include Spanish dollars, pistoles (gold), and doubloons (gold). French half-guineas and francs, Dutch guilders, and German pieces of gold. Because coins were hard to come by, some of the larger coins were cut into sections, sometimes halves and quarters. The quarter coin of the United States gets its name from this procedure. Also the Spanish used a money mark symbol which was inscribed as "$" which in modern times symbolizes a dollar sign. When the coins were cut into halves or quarters, this symbol "$" was placed on each coin meaning that it originally came from a dollar. Thus the "$" symbol became known or to mean "dollar."

Some of the original buildings built in St. Mary's City in colonial times are no longer there. Still, the city has many historic sites.

Historic St. Mary's, an eight hundred acre outdoor history museum includes <u>St. Mary's Old State House</u>; located on Middle Street. This old State House was built in 1934 to celebrate Maryland's tercentenary. Bricks from ruins of several old buildings were used to reconstruct the Old State House. The original building was built by Captain John Quigley in 1676, paid for with 300,000 pounds of tobacco and cask. Cannons which were buried for centuries and unearthed can be found at the entrance way and on the grounds.

St. Mary's Old State House (inside and outside views)

The Maryland Dove; located on the water behind the Old State House is a replica of one of the square-rigged ships that brought the settlers to Maryland.

The Maryland Dove

The <u>Leonard Calvert Monument</u> stands on the site where Calvert signed a treaty with the Yaocomico Indian Emperor, and the <u>Freedom of Conscience Monument</u>, erected in 1934, commemorates the Act Concerning Religion passed by the Maryland General Assembly in 1649. <u>Ruins of Smith's Town House</u> are located east of the Old State House. This building was erected in 1647 and was used for legislative meetings of the colony held in 1662. Only crumbled bricks and stone remain on the site. Formally Fort St. Mary's stood across the street from the town house.

Inside the museum at Historic St. Mary's City are many interesting exhibits. One such exhibit is a facial reconstruction. Nationally recognized forensic artist Sharon Long, from the University of Wyoming, created this (see photograph below) facial reconstruction of Anne Wolseley Calvert. Ms. Long first examined and measured the proportions of the recovered skull. Using molding and casting processes she reproduced a skull identical to the original. Ms. Long then referred to a tissue measurement index that lists an average thickness at key points on the skull which vary according to sex, race, age and weight. After locating and marking tissue depth on the plaster skull the areas were filled with clay. Features were then carefully sculpted and skin given color. Age markings, eyebrows, eyelashes, and hair were added to complete the likeness.

Trinity Protestant Episcopal Church was built in 1829 using bricks which were salvaged from the first State House. In the churchyard is located the Leonard Calvert Monument. The Copley Vault; located at the rear of the church, this vault holds the dust remains of Sir Leonard Copley and his wife. Copley was the first royal governor of Maryland. Also included in Historic St. Mary's is the Godiah Spray Tobacco Plantation, a fine example of a seventeenth century tobacco plantation. On the plantation are the main dwelling house, Freedman's Cottage, and a tobacco field, drying barns, kitchen garden and animal pens. Features also include archaeological excavations. Overlooking the Potomac River is the Margaret Brent Memorial Garden. The Visitor's Center at Historic St. Mary's includes an archaeology exhibit hall, guided walking tours, and a gift shop. Exhibits are open from Maryland Day (March 25) through the last weekend in November, Wednesday through Sunday. Several annual events are celebrated at this historic site, including Maryland Day and the Grand Militia Muster. St. Mary's College of Maryland; located nearby, is a State institution chartered in 1828.

St. Mary's County has many historic churches. These include the old St. Ignatius Catholic Church, located on Villa Road, and is on the National Register of Historic Places. The first St. Ignatius was originally an Indian hut in St. Mary's City. The first Catholic church in British North America was built here in 1636. In 1704, it closed for public worship by order of Colonel John Seymour, the royal governor. The church was demolished and the bricks moved to its present location. Here was built St. Ignatius Manor House, a private home where religious services could be legally held. In 1745 a small chapel was built behind the house, and when it became too crowded, a larger church was built in 1785, replacing the smaller one. This church, restored in 1950 is still standing, and contains stained glass windows and an altar that is exceptional. In its cemetery, the oldest on the Atlantic seaboard, are the graves of some of Maryland's well known families.

All Faiths Episcopal Church, was built in 1767. The church features a Rose window above the altar which symbolizes the gifts of God and His bountiful creation. The barrel-shaped ceiling, slave gallery, and the old hand-wrought hardware give evidence to the age of the church. All Saints Episcopal Church, is located in Avenue, on Route 470 and was built in 1846. The church actually began in 1642 when Dr. Thomas Gerard, a Catholic, built an Anglican Church for his wife, where she and her friends and servants could worship. Records indicate the existence of at least two church buildings on the Tomakoken Creek site prior to the erection of the present church.

Christ Episcopal Church, built in 1736, is located on Route 238 in Chaptico. The original church was founded in 1642 and established by Act of the Governor's King and Queen Parish. During the War of 1812, British troops occupied the church. On the grounds is a cemetery which includes the vault of the Francis Scott Key family.

On St. Andrew's Church Road (Route 4) in California is St. Andrew's Episcopal Parish Church, founded in 1767. Listed on the National Register of Historic Places, the interior of the church contains two balconies and the original box pews. A hand-lettered altar piece or reredos was painted in 1771, and displays the Lord's Prayer, the Ten Commandments, and Creed. The brick exterior of the church has an unusual inset portico and a large palladian window. The oldest Catholic Church in continuous use in English-speaking America is located in St. Mary's County. This is St. Francis Xavier Church, located on Route 243 in Compton. Listed on the National Register of Historic Places, St. Francis Xavier was built in 1731.

St. George's Episcopal ("Poplar Hill") Church, is located south of Leonardtown on Route 244 at Valley Lee. This William and Mary Parish began in 1638 and was established in 1692, the seventh Episcopal parish in Maryland. An interesting feature is four ancient gravestones of early rectors which have been incorporated in the church floor. The church is also listed on the National Register of Historic Places. At Charlotte Hall, on the grounds of the Veterans' Home is St. John's United Episcopal Church (Dent Chapel). Built in 1883, Dent Chapel was erected in memory of Reverend Hatch Dent, the first principal of Charlotte Hall Military Academy. Constructed of granite with a decorative brick belt, this church is perhaps the best example of Victorian Gothic architecture in Maryland.

Other Places of interest in the County are Cross Manor, built in 1642 and is believed to be the oldest house in the State. Sotterly Plantation was built in 1717, and is located in Hollywood on Route 245. This working plantation is graced with architectural beauty in a magnificent setting along the Patuxent River. The mansion contains period furnishings, Chinese Chippendale staircase, as well as other handcarved woodwork. Included in the tour are the formal gardens, north and south gate houses, slave cabin, farm museum and the gift shop. Also facing the Patuxent River is Cellar Hill, another example of an eighteenth century mansion. Looking out from Cellar Hill, four Maryland counties can be seen.

Of special historic interest, is a small piece of land, approximately sixty square acres in area. This land is at the mouth of the St. Clement's River, in the Potomac called <u>St. Clement's Island</u>. This "Birthplace of Maryland" is the most historic land in the State. It was here on March 25, 1634 that Governor Leonard Calvert and his colonists formally took possession of a part of the New World, eventually known as Maryland. In 1934, the Tercentenary Commission erected a forty-foot concrete cross commemorating the First Landing. This cross is located one-half mile off shore. Also located here is the <u>St. Clement's Island - Potomac River Museum</u>. This museum houses hundreds of artifacts from the local area. In the Potomac River Room visitors can learn the history of St. Clement's Island. Featured is a scale replica of the Island Lighthouse and Bell Tower which stood watch over the river for one hundred five years. Go back in time to the 1900s in the Country Store, and browse the gift shop. Also on the museum ground is the <u>Little Red Schoolhouse</u>, built in 1820. St. Clement's Island is accessible only by boat, and tours are available through the museum by prior arrangements.

Another area of historic interest in the county is Leonardtown, the county seat. Established in 1708, Leonardtown became the county seat in 1710, succeeding St. Mary's City. It replaced St. Mary's City because it was closer to the center of the county. Soon after the capital of Maryland was moved from St. Mary's City to Annapolis, it was made the county seat. Leonardtown was originally named Seymour Town after Governor Seymour of the province. Later it was renamed Leonardtown, in honor of Leonard Calvert, fourth Lord Baltimore.

In 1710 a log courthouse was built when Leonardtown became the county seat. St. Mary's Beacon, a Democratic weekly newspaper occupied a house built in 1704. Originally containing seven rooms, it was enlarged to twenty-one. It was here that the court sat until the log courthouse was built. Tudor Hall, located near the courthouse, was built in 1780 by Abraham Barnes. Tudor Hall has a deeply recessed entrance portico at ground level with four peculiar capped Doric columns, an unusual feature for a Maryland Georgian design. It was formerly owned by the family of Francis Scott Key. Also in Leonardtown is St. Mary's Academy, opened in 1885 by the Sisters of Charity, and the Old Jail Museum, containing county artifacts, memorabilia and houses many historic records. Displayed are a "lady's cell," along with Dr. Phillip Bean's Office, furnished as used during his practice, 1914-1980. The Old Jail Museum is also the headquarters of the St. Mary's County Historical Society.

At the southern tip of the County, where the Potomac River and Chesapeake Bay meet, is Point Lookout State Park. This five hundred eighty acre park is the site of Fort Lincoln, an earthen fort built by Confederate prisoners. Two monuments honor the three thousand three hundred sixty-four Confederate dead from the prison camp, with their names inscribed in the monument. The Visitor's Center contains a Civil War Museum. During the summer months, boat ramps, swimming, fishing, picnicking, and a playground are available in the park. In Piney Point on Route 249 is the Piney Point Lighthouse and Future Museum. Unique in its tower design, the lighthouse, constructed in 1836, was the first permanent lighthouse built on the Potomac River, and is the only remaining accessible lighthouse in its original location in Southern Maryland. Using a fixed beacon which was visible for over twelve miles, the lighthouse is one of only three in existence on the Potomac River today. The six acre park also houses a museum and gift shop.

St. Mary's County is also the home of the nation's only museum dedicated to testing and evaluation of naval aviation. This is the Naval Air Test Evaluation Museum located on Route 235 in Lexington Park. Featured are early photographs, vintage scale models, and full scale aircraft. Located outside the Naval Air Warfare Center is the home of the

U.S. Naval Test Pilots' School. It was here at the school that Astronauts Glenn, Shepard, Schirra and Carpenter received their test pilot training.

For an interesting trip back in time to Maryland's founding, St. Mary's County must not be missed.

Form of Government: County Commissioners

Map and Seal of St. Mary's County

SOMERSET COUNTY

Somerset County was created by an Order in Council in 1666 and was named after Lady Mary Somerset, sister-in-law of Cecil Calvert, Second Lord Baltimore. Originally it included the present areas of Wicomico and Worcester counties.

Located on the southern tip of the Eastern Shore, Somerset is bounded on three sides by water. It has an area of three hundred thirty-two square land miles and forty-six square water miles. The topography is generally flat, rising to only fifty feet above sea level in small areas. Smith Islands, South Marsh and Deal are all part of Somerset County. South Marsh and Smith Islands are separated from the mainland by Tangier Sound, and these areas provide some of the best fishing in the Chesapeake Bay.

The Great Seal of Somerset County was first used on documents in 1666 until 1707. After the year 1707, the seal was not used for two hundred fifty-one years. Through the efforts of the Board of Somerset County and members of the Olde Princess Anne Days Committee, the seal was again put into use in 1958. At this time it was only permissible to use the seal in black and white. Following this, the Board of County Commissioners requested the original colors of the seal, and through a legislative act, today the seal, including its original colors, is in use.

The Seal is described as an oval band with the words, "County Somerset." Within the oval a shield bearing a very slightly modified version of the Stuart royal arms. Above the shield the Royal "Semper Eadem," is written, which translated means, "always the same." Below this is written 1666, the year the County was founded. Several of the early County seals, including the present one, are based on the Stuart royal arms. The alterations in the Somerset County Seal are a reversal of the position of the fleur-de-lys (the royal arms has two above and one below), an absence of the flower design on the inside of the border around the rampant lion, and a simpler drawing of the harp. Also, the Garter encircling the royal arms has been reduced to a simple band.

A technical heraldry definition of terms and the establishment of colors used in the Somerset County Seal are:

England: In 1198 his arms (Richard I) were Gules, three lions passant guardant in pale or. This coat is referred to as England. France Modern: England was borne alone until 1340, when Edward III, adopting the new practice of quartering, took the arms of France, Azure, seme-de-lis, (Azure and or means, "Blue and Gold"), termed France Ancient, and bore <u>Quarterly France Ancient and England</u>. These arms expressed his claim to the French throne. These continued as the Royal Arms until about 1405. Subsequent to this, Henry IV, following the example of the French King, reduced the number of fleurs-de-lis to three, that is France Modern. The Royal Arms then became <u>Quarterly France Modern and England</u>. Scotland: The Royal Arms of Scotland are Or, a lion rampant within a double tressure flory counter-flory gules. Ireland: The arms of Ireland are Azure, a harp or, stringed argent. The Oval Band: The Garter has encircled the royal shield since the reign of Edward III. A colored illustration of the Order of the Garter and of the Royal Arms show the Garter to be blue, bordered with gold. It seemed logical, then, for the oval band on the Somerset County Seal to be colored in this way.

In 1910 the population was 26,455, the highest in its history. Since then it has decreased, being 19,623 in 1960. By 1990 the population rose to 23,440, and again to 23,727 in 1994, an increase of 1.2% since 1990. In 1998, the population is 24,710, and by the year 2000, it is projected to be 25,000.

Fishing, seafood processing and agriculture are the county's main industries. The seafood processed includes fish, oysters and crabs. Agricultural activities include corn, rye, barley, soybeans, and strawberries. Some poultry raising is also present.

Most of the early settlers who came in the 1660s were highly religious. Quakers, Catholics, Huguenots, Presbyterians and Methodists all arrived after being driven across Virginia's border by that colony's strict policy of religious intolerance. The new settlers knew little about seafood harvesting, but soon adapted to the life on the shore.

Following the Civil War, and with the beginning of the steam age, the county began to flourish. Railroads and steam ships opened a new way to distribute goods. Many once sleepy fishing villages now were transformed into busy towns. One especially affected was Crisfield, where ships competed for space in their now crowded harbor.

<u>Crisfield</u> is known as the Seafood Capital of the World. The first settler was Benjamin Somers, who staked his claim in 1666. Originally known as Annemessex, an Indian

name meaning "bountiful waters", it evolved into a fishing village known as Somers Cove in honor of Benjamin. At first the settlers did not realize the potential of the seafood found there. They would catch oysters, crabs, clams and fish for their own use. After the Civil War, the town began to boom thanks in part to John Woodland Crisfield a Princess Anne attorney, who convinced the Eastern Shore Railroad to extend its line to the water's edge. Now the once sleepy town of Somers Cove was accessible by land or sea, making the possibilities of commercial seafood unlimited.

In appreciation for the work done by John Crisfield, the town's name was changed to Crisfield. Crisfield became incorporated in 1872, and by 1900 there were over one hundred fifty seafood processing plants in the town. By 1910, the Crisfield Customs House boasted the largest registry of sailing vessels of any port in the nation. Today, Crisfield features Maryland's largest marina, designed for all types of boats. Although a paradise for fishers, Crisfield is still thought of as the Seafood Capital of the World, more for spirit then production. At one time oystering was the foundation of the local seafood industry. Today crabbing has replaced oystering. In addition to hard shell crabs, each summer over six million soft shell crabs are processed. Crisfield is also the county's largest city and is the home of J. Millard Tawes, former governor of Maryland. On June 16, 1962 The Maryland Port Authority dedicated the Somers Cove Marina. It has a basin ten feet deep, sixty feet wide and one-thousand feet long. The complex provides berths for five hundred boats to one hundred feet in length, and was built at a cost of $800,000. In the Visitor's Center at Somers Cove Marina is the Governor J.Millard Tawes Historical Museum. The Museum honors Governor Tawes (1894-1979) who had a long distinguished record of public service. The collection documents his career and highlights the history and culture of the Crisfield area. The Visitor's Center also has a swimming pool, bath house and a laundromat. Another area of interest in Crisfield is the Jane's Island State Park. This three thousand six hundred acre park is described as having unexcelled boating, fishing, and crabbing opportunities. The Hodson Area, located on the mainland, features campsites, cabins, a marina and boat rentals and pontoon boat service to Jane's Island during the summer months. The island itself is accessible only by boat, and is entirely undeveloped, with miles of isolated shoreline and sandy beaches.

Crisfield also has several fine examples of early colonial architecture. One example is called Makepeace, built in 1663. Another is the historic Crockett House, located on Main Street, a beautiful Victorian showpiece built in 1888.

Other interesting cities, towns and places in Somerset County are: <u>Princess Anne</u>, the county seat, which was laid out in 1773 when the General Assembly legislated its birth. Named for the daughter of King George II, it also is the home of Maryland State College. Famous buildings in Princess Anne include: <u>The Manokin Presbyterian Church</u> built in 1765; <u>Washington Hotel</u> (1774); <u>Teackle Mansion</u> (1801) was built by Littleton Dennis Teackle to duplicate the design of the Scottish castles he admired. This mansion provided the setting for Civil War author George Alfred Townsend's novel "The Entailed Hat," a fictional account of the notorious Patty Cannon. <u>East Glen</u> (1795); <u>E. Herrman Cohn House</u> (1800); <u>St. Andrew's Episcopal Church</u> (1700); and <u>Beckford</u> (1776) built by Henry Jackson and overlooking the Manokin River, its name combines two English words meaning "the wading place across the creek."

<u>Beverly of Somerset</u> (1796) located near King's creek, this house was built by Nehemiah King II. <u>Kingston Hall</u> (1750) was built by Robert King III and was the home of Thomas King Carroll, Governor of Maryland from 1830 to 1831.

Other towns and their origins are: <u>Champ</u>, originally named St. Peter's Peninsula, the name was changed by a local optometrist, I.Frank Beauchamp. Wanting the name "Beauchamp," but thinking that was too long, it was changed to Champ. <u>Chance</u>: when the community was in the process of hopefully getting a postal service, a local resident, Captain James Whitlock suggested the name Rock Creek, but the postal service rejected the name. Upon believing that there was no chance of ever getting a post office, he suggested the name Chance, which to his surprise was approved. <u>Costen</u> was named for one of its first settlers, Henry Costen in the 1660s and <u>Eden</u> was named after the last Proprietary Governor of Maryland, Sir Robert Eden.

<u>Kingston</u> was named for Maryland's famous King family. <u>Marion</u>: John C. Horsey had donated land for the railroad to extend through this area to Crisfield. To compensate him for his donation, he was permitted to pick the name, thus he chose Marion after his daughter. <u>Mt. Vernon</u>: although it predates George Washington's mansion, Mt. Vernon was named in honor of his birthplace. <u>Oriole</u>, originally was to be named St. Peter's, but the postal service turned the name down. Its name comes from the bird, the Oriole, which thrives in area trees. <u>Rehobeth</u> was founded in 1668. This community was named for the plantation on which it was built. William Stevens owned this land and donated many acres. On this land is also the Rehobeth Presbyterian Church, the first Presbyterian Church in America, built in 1706 by Francis Makemie. The name Rehobeth is derived from an Old

Testament word meaning "room for all." Somerset County was also the home to the first Methodist congregation in the United States.

Mentioned earlier were Deal and Smith Islands. Deal Island was originally named "Devil's Island" because it was regarded as only fit for the devil. One of the men who worked the island was Joshua Thomas. When Devil's was pronounced, it came out as "dee-uls," thus Thomas insisted that the spelling match the pronunciation, having it renamed Deal. Smith Island, founded in 1679, was named for its largest landowner, Captain Henry Smith. Today many of the small number of inhabitants are descendants of Captain Smith, and make their living by doing what he did, fishing for oysters and crabs.

The "Land of Pleasant Living" as Somerset is called is truly that. The time-honored simple lifestyles of days gone by are still carried out today. It is a beautiful and interesting place to visit.

Form of Government: County Commissioners

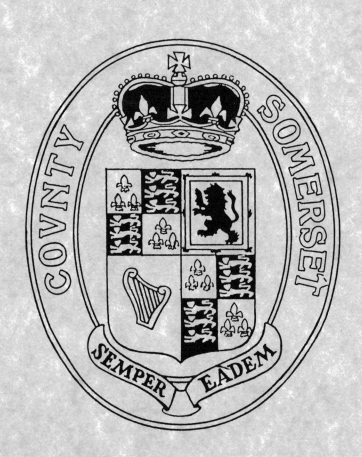

Map of Somerset County

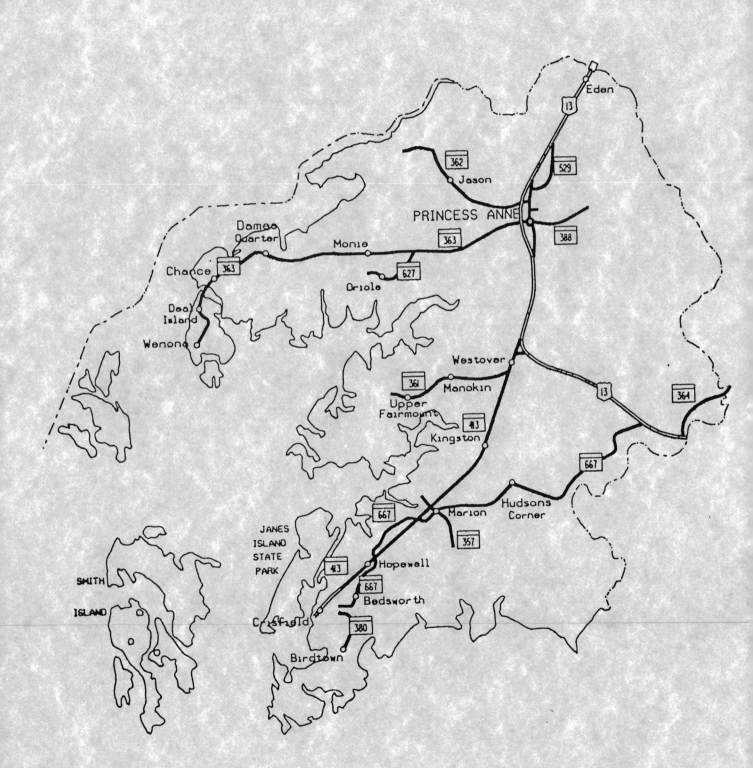

TALBOT COUNTY

Talbot County was created probably by virtue of an order of the Governor in Council. The County was in existence by February 18, 1661, when a writ was issued to the sheriff. The County was named for Lady Grace Talbot, sister of Cecil Calvert, Second Lord Baltimore, and the wife of Sir Robert Talbot, an Irish statesman.

Talbot County is bordered on the west by the Eastern Bay, Chesapeake Bay and the Choptank River, and on the east by Caroline County. To the north lies Queen Anne's County and to the south is Dorchester County. Talbot has an area of two hundred seventy-nine land and fifty-two water square miles. The county is part of the Coastal Plain and thus seldom has an elevation of over twenty feet above sea level. The highest point in the county is seventy-two feet above sea level, outside of Easton.

The Great Seal of Talbot County was officially adopted on July 26, 1966. As a result of Talbot County being named in honor of Grace Talbot, daughter of George Calvert, the first Lord Baltimore, and sister of Cecil Calvert, the second Lord Baltimore, the Talbot coat of arms was adopted as the design of both the seal and flag. This consists of a rampant lion in red, against a silver shield. The background color of the seal and flag is purple, which was the color assigned in 1694 to Talbot County by the royal governor of Maryland, Sir Francis Nicholson. The seal is circular in shape, with the words, "The Great Seal of Talbot County Maryland" along the edge. Below the rampant lion is written in Latin, "Tempus Praeteritum Et Futurum," which translates as, "Times, Past and Future."

Talbot's population was slow to rise, being 21,578 in 1960 and only 25,520 by 1980. By 1990 the population was 30,549, and rose again to 32,015 in 1994, an increase of 4.8% since 1990. In 1998 the population is 33,030, and by the year 2000, it is projected to be 33,500.

An agricultural county, Talbot's chief crop was tobacco. The first settler, Edward Lloyd as well as other English settlers, turned the acres and acres of land into tobacco plantations. These tobacco fields where established on the shores of the Choptank, Wye, Tred Avon and St. Michaels (now the Miles) Rivers, on the stretch of the Chesapeake Bay known as Bayside, as well as on the many creeks and coves. For over a century, life in

Talbot County centered around tidewater and tobacco, which served as money and traded for English manufactured goods, purchased directly from the English ships which would anchor off the plantation wharves. The first town in the county was Oxford, laid out in 1683. It served as a port of call for vessels from all over the world. The county's first shipbuilding center was St. Michaels, where the sailing craft, later known as "Baltimore Clippers" were built.

Many of the first settlers were Quakers, who were seeking a haven from persecution. In 1682, three acres of land were purchased from John Edmondson, and the erection of the Third Haven Meeting House was begun. Construction was slow and tedious, taking two years to complete, as the timbers had to be hewn with a broad-axe and finished with primitive tools of that day. One of the builders was William Southeby, regarded as the first American to write against slavery. In 1673, George Fox, the founder of the Religious Society of Friends (Quakers), visited the area of Easton. Upon returning to England, he sent a number of books to the Meeting (Society of Friends). These books were the beginning of the Meeting's library, believed to be the earliest public library in Talbot County, and most likely in the province. This was established long before the Bishop of London, England, through Commissary Bray, introduced parochial libraries in this province. The first held in this structure was in the fall of 1684. In 1693 Betty's Cove Meeting (1660-1693) was transferred to this Meeting House. Throughout the years, many notable Quakers have worshipped in this building. These include William Penn, John Woolman, John Fothergill, Samuel Bownas, and Rufus Jones. Continuous records have been kept on the various transactions of the Meeting House since 1676. Due to their extreme value, they are today held in the Hall of Records in Annapolis, Maryland. Concerning the Meeting House and the Quakers, Dr. Kenneth Carroll wrote in his book, Quakerism on the Eastern Shore, "A non-violent and peaceful approach to the solution of social problems has been the policy of the Society of Friends throughout its long history. Third Haven Friends are well aware of the past...at the same time however they are increasingly aware of the fact that Christianity as interpreted by Quakerism is a living religion based upon personal experience." The Third Friends Meeting House is located at 405 S. Washington Street. Visitors are welcome 9 a.m. to 5 p.m. daily, with Sunday service at 10 a.m.

Others who came to Talbot County were Puritans, driven from cavalier Virginia in the Cromwell era, and Irish and Scottish rebels transported to the colony as indentured servants. The county's first Negroes, came as slaves. One of their offspring, later turned into the nation's greatest nineteenth century leader towards Black freedom and justice. His name was Frederick Douglass.

Frederick Douglass was born Frederick Augustus Bailey in 1818 on a farm on Lewistown Road, now Trappers Corner, in Talbot County. Today the farm no longer exists. At an early age, Douglass was sold as a slave to the Lloyds at Wye House, located between the Miles and East Wye Rivers. Today the house is privately owned. At a later date he was again sold to Captain Auld who owned a store in St. Michaels, Maryland. Following several attempts, he finally escaped to the North, where he took the name Douglass. By the 1840s, Douglass had distinguished himself as the most effective abolitionist speaker. Considered less radical than other abolitionists of his time, his freedom was finally bought for $1,250. Douglass went on to become the U.S. Diplomat to Haiti under President Rutherford B. Hayes, a good friend to Abraham Lincoln, and served as a Marshall of Deeds in Washington, D.C., where he died in 1895. The only physical evidence of Frederick Douglass left in Talbot County is a birthplace marker on Matthewstown Road, located on the banks of the Tuckahoe River, just before the Tuckahoe River Bridge, in an area called the Chapel District.

During the American Revolution, several residents of the county played key roles. Matthew Tilghman was Maryland's acknowledged leader in the events leading to Independence, and his son-in-law, Tench Tilghman, was George Washington's aide. Tench was famous for his "ride" carrying the news of Cornwallis' surrender to the Continental Congress in Philadelphia. Another was Young Petty Bensen, a Revolutionary War hero, who later as Brigadier General, headed a citizen army which fought during a British attack on St. Michaels in 1813, during the War of 1812. Tobacco remained the chief crop until the Revolutionary War when the foreign market was disrupted, and was replaced by wheat to feed Washington's Continental Army. With the war disrupting foreign trade, and wheat needed to feed the army, farmers also turned to other crops, such as corn, and hay, and in later years added barley, rye, soybeans and various vegetables. With the outbreak of the Civil War, Talbot County was deeply divided, with hundreds of men fighting on both sides. In post Civil War times, Talbot gained national recognition as a site of summer homes for wealthy Northerners. Today Talbot ranks as one of the highest in sweet corn production, as well as tomatoes, fruit and dairy products, and is one of the main livestock feeding areas of the Shore.

The largest communities in the county are Easton, the county seat, St. Michaels, Tilghman Island, Oxford and Trappe.

Easton, the county seat was founded in 1788. The early name of the town was Court House, then Talbot Court House, and later Talbot Town. The town grew up around the Third Haven Meeting House, built between 1682 and 1684 and the county Court House, built in 1789. There are two stories as to the origin of the name Easton. The first is that it was named simply because of its location as the governmental center of Maryland "east" of Annapolis; the second being in memory of Easton on the lower Avon River in England, since the Tred Avon River flows nearby in the county. In 1788, the Maryland General assembly enacted legislation naming the town Easton, and further decreed that the courts and general business of the Eastern Shore be conducted here. As a result, this made Easton the "capital" of the Eastern Shore for a brief time. Easton is also known as a "Cathedral Town," being the location of the Episcopal Diocese, and for many "firsts" on the Eastern Shore. Easton had the first newspaper, the first bank, and the first gas plant. It also had the distinction of having the first steamer line and first airplane to Baltimore.

Historical sites in Easton include the Talbot County Courthouse, at Washington and Dover Streets, built in 1791. It was later Victorianized, with wings added in 1958. The original courthouse, built in 1711 stood nearby on land purchased from Philemon Armstrong, On the court grounds in May 1774, were adopted "The Talbot Resolves," which voiced the sentiments later appearing in the Declaration of Independence. In this present Court House on May 28, 1862, Circuit Court Judge Richard Bennett Carmichael was attacked while on the bench by hoodlums from Baltimore under a provost marshal, who disapproved of certain decisions. He was taken, bleeding to Baltimore and imprisoned. Having no formal charges he was later released and resumed a distinguished life.

The Talbot County Free Library, on Washington Street near Dover is one of the oldest public libraries on the Eastern Shore. The Bullitt or Chamberlain House, at 108 Dover Street was built in 1801 by Thomas James Bullitt, president of the Easton Bank from 1830 until his death in 1840. He was the ancestor of William C. Bullitt, who was U.S. ambassador to the Union of Soviet Socialist Republics in 1933 and also to France in 1936.

At Washington and Gay Streets is a house known as The Rest. This was the home of Franklin Buchanan, an admiral of the Confederate Navy. The Stewart Building, located across from the courthouse, was first known as the Easton Hotel, the Eastern Shore's first actual hotel. In later years it was known as the <u>Brick Hotel</u>, and continued to serve as the Eastern Shore's leading hotel through the nineteenth century. After the hotel closed, the building was remodeled, and became known as the Stewart Building. Today it is used for offices. The <u>Historical Society of Talbot County Headquarters</u> is located at 25 South Washington Street. The headquarters is a three-gallery museum with guided tours of two restored houses. These are the James Neall House, built in 1810, and the Joseph Neall House, built in 1795. Both James and Joseph were Quaker cabinetmakers, and their homes feature a Federal style garden and a woodshop, used for their woodworking. The gardens at the Historical Society have won national acclaim. Two churches of interest in Easton are the <u>Christ Church</u>, at 111 South Harrison Street, built between 1842 and 1845. This church was the first church in Easton to add a spire to its bell tower. On U.S. Route 50 is <u>No Corner for the Devil</u>. Built in 1881, it was originally used as a Methodist Church. This hexagonal structure was designed so that "the devil would have no corner in which to sit and hatch evil."

Easton's daily newspaper, <u>The Star-Democrat</u> is one of the oldest daily newspapers in the United States. It was established from <u>The Star</u> founded in 1799, and <u>The Democrat</u>, founded in 1855. Originally it was headquartered in Barlett's Mill, now One Mill Place. It since has recently relocated to 1 Airpark Drive, Easton. <u>The Star-Democrat</u> publishes <u>The Star-Democrat</u> and <u>The Delmarva Farmer</u> in Easton; <u>The Times-Record</u> in Denton; <u>The Record Observer</u> in Centreville; <u>The Dorchester</u> in Cambridge; and <u>The Bay Times</u> in Kent Island.

The <u>Site of the Slave Market</u>, in Easton, is located in a market house on Washington Street adjoining the Court House. It was here that slaves were purchased, as well as garden products, such as tobacco, the major crop. The Slave Market was used for many years prior to and after the Civil War.

Another very beautiful and interesting town is <u>St. Michaels</u>, laid out in 1778. Located on the Miles River it is about ten miles west of Easton. Founded in 1677, the town grew up around Christ Church of St. Michaels Episcopal Parish. St. Michaels both in colonial times and today, was a major shipping and watermen's town. Many famous Baltimore clipper ships were built in St. Michaels, and crabbers and oystermen still work at their trade. Years ago the Miles (then Myles) River and the town were both named St. Michaels. In 1675, William Hambleton of Martingham named the river "Myles" in his will. The spelling was later changed to Miles. The town's name remained St. Michaels because it grew up around the Episcopal Church, named after St. Michael the Archangel. During the War of 1812, St. Michaels escaped serious damage due do the ingenuity of the people who lived in the town. In 1813, the British bombarded the town, but prior to this, the townspeople put out all lights at the ground level. Instead, they placed many lanterns in the tree tops, so that when the British bombardment came, they took a false range and overshot the town.

Also located in St. Michaels is the Cannon Ball House on Mulberry Street, one of the oldest dwelling houses in the town, built in 1805. It got its name because a cannon ball shot through the roof and bounced down the stairs, past the owner's wife, without injuring the residents or doing great harm. Another of the oldest homes in St. Michaels is the Bruff House, built in 1791. The house stands on land purchased by John Bruff in 1791 for twenty pounds. The Amelia Welby House also on Mulberry Street was constructed during the 1700s and was the birthplace in 1819 of Amelia Ball Coppuck, the poet praised by Poe. Christ Protestant Episcopal Church, had a rector in 1672, and the present building was built in 1878. In the construction on the present church several muskets were discovered under the flooring, believed to have been left by the troops who were stationed at the church in 1810 during the battle of St. Michaels. The Perry Cabin, built before the Revolutionary War, was given its name by Samuel Hambleton, paymaster to Commodore Perry's flagship in the Battle of Lake Erie.

The Chesapeake Bay Maritime Museum, located on Mill Street consists of sixteen buildings devoted to the history and traditions of the Chesapeake Bay. Exhibited are skipjacks, other boats, guns and decoys, ship models, paintings and the 1879 Hooper Strait Lighthouse. Open most times of the year, daily 10-5. Admission is charged. The Patriot of St. Michaels is a historic one and one-half hour Miles River cruise, which departs from the Maritime Museum. Open seasonally, spring to fall. Admission is charged.

The Freedom's Friend Lodge is a prominent historic site for St. Michaels African-American Community. Chartered and built in 1867, it is the oldest Lodge still existing in Maryland. The original structure was replaced in 1883 by the present one, which was restored in 1991. The Old Inn, c.1816, is a red brick building constructed by Wrightson Jones. An unusual feature in St. Michaels is the cellar, which still houses a large Coal's fireplace. In 1877, the St. Michaels Comet advertised the Inn as having "Entertainment for Man or Beast." In Church Cove Park between Mulberry and Greene Streets are The Cannons. These cannons are replicas of the two given to the town of St. Michaels in 1813 by Jacob Gibson as a peace offering following a mischievous prank. The originals were confiscated by Federal Troops from the Arsenal in Easton at the beginning on the Civil War.

St. Mary's Square is located between Mulberry and Chestnut Streets. In 1770, an English factor, James Braddock, purchased land and laid it off in lots, later named Braddock's Ward. A central area, now called St. Mary's Square, was set aside for public use. Located here is the ship's carpenter bell cast in 1841 and the remains of an 1812 cannon used in defense of the town. The St. Mary's Square Museum, c.1800, was originally part of a steam grist mill. This structure was moved to its present site from land patented to John Hollingsworth in 1659. The "Teetotum" building serves as a general display area, and was thus named because of its resemblance to the toy top of the same name, c.1860.

St. Michaels is also known as the birthplace and home of major league baseball great Harold Baines. Harold was first drafted by another fellow-Eastern Shore resident Bill Veeck for the Chicago White Sox in 1977. Harold has played for Chicago, Texas, Oakland, and the Baltimore Orioles.

Stretching west and south from St. Michaels is a long, narrow peninsula that has been called "Bay Hundred" since the seventeenth century. At the end of this peninsula is Tilghman Island. Tilghman Island was admitted to Talbot County in May, 1707. Its name is derived from Matthew Tilghman who inherited the island in 1775. A beautiful area, Tilghman Island residents consist mainly of watermen, who make their livings from oystering, crabbing, party fishing, and gunning. A focal point of the island is the bridge connection to the mainland at Knapps Narrows. Through maps, it has been shown that some sort of bridge has been here since the late 1600s. The present bridge, a fascinating counter-balanced drawbridge, was built in 1932. Tilghman Island today offers a wide array of seafood, restaurants, lodging, bed and breakfasts, shops, sportfishing, hunting, crabbing services, marinas, and marine facilities.

The town of Oxford is on the southern tip of the peninsula between the Choptank and Tred Avon Rivers, and is one of the oldest towns in Maryland. Oxford was one of Lord Baltimore's planned port towns, founded in 1683. For over one hundred years Oxford was one of Maryland's leading shipbuilding and active port towns. Originally named Oxford, for the English university city, the name was changed to Williamstadt in 1695 in honor of the reigning king, William of Orange. In 1702, when Queen Anne took the throne, the name was changed back to Oxford.

The American Revolution marked the end of Oxford's glory days. With the British ships gone, as well as their variety of goods, and tobacco being replaced by wheat as a cash crop, businesses went bankrupt, cattle grazed in the streets, and the population dwindled. Following the Civil War, a new prosperity began with the completion of the railroad in 1871. The seafood industry, along with improved methods of canning and packing, opened up the national markets for oysters from the Chesapeake Bay. Businesses again boomed, population increased, and houses began going up everywhere. But this prosperity was not to last. In the early part of the twentieth century, as the oyster beds decreased, packing houses closed, businesses went bankrupt, and the railroad and steamships disappeared, Oxford became a sleepy little town. Its main inhabitants were the watermen who worked the waters of the Tred Avon. Today, Oxford is still a watermen's town, but is enjoying a new resurgence based on tourism and leisure activities.

Some of the points of interest in Oxford are the Academy House (Bratt Mansion), which was the residence for the Maryland Military Academy from 1848-1855. Today it is a private residence. Barnaby House, located at 212 N. Morris Street, was built in the 1770s by Captain Richard Barnaby. This private residence features pine woodwork, a corner fireplace, and a handmade staircase. The Tred Avon Ferry, at N. Morris Street, is believed to be the oldest privately operated ferry in the country that "runs free", that is, not attached to a cable. The line was started in 1760 by Elizabeth Skinner and connects Oxford and Bellevue. Skinner collected her fares in tobacco, the currency of the times. Today the ferry is modern and diesel operated, and serves many who take the ride for its scenic beauty. The Oxford Customs House, also on N. Morris Street, was built in 1976 and is an exact replica of the first Federal Custom House built by Jeremiah Banning, the first Federal Collector of customs and the Tench Tilghman Monument, located in Oxford Cemetery, at the grave of Tench Tilghman. Across the cove from the cemetery is Plimhimmon, former home of Tilghman's widow, Anna Marie Tilghman, who is also buried in the cemetery, as well as a number of their descendants. Originally, Tench Tilghman was buried in Baltimore. His body was moved to this location in 1973. On Old Villa Road near Easton is a carved stone marking Tench Tilghman's birthplace.

The town of Trappe is the birthplace of major league baseball great Frank "Home Run" Baker. The town's name origin is not known exactly, but three explanations are possible. The first is from a monastery built by French Trappist monks; the second is that is was named after a popular tavern called Partridge Trap, and the third from the numerous fur trapping activities in the area, inspiring the name Trap or Trappe.

Historical sites in Trappe include the Dickinson House, built between 1730 and 1740. Located at the corner of Main and Powell Streets, this was the home of John Dickinson. He was prominent in the American Revolution and was also a member of the Continental Congress. Dickinson College, in Carlisle, Pennsylvania was named in honor of John Dickinson. The Kemp House, located on the east side of Main Street, dates from 1810, and features a beautiful old sugar maple tree in the yard. Trappe Landing, located about two miles from Trappe, is a beautiful area beside deep water where the boats came in from Baltimore as well as other areas. This was at one time the principal point for shipments of grain from Talbot County.

On the Choptank River northeast from Trappe, is the quiet village of Windy Hill. At one time this was a thriving place for shipping peaches, vegetables, domestic animals, furniture, and other articles of trade. Windy Hill, as well as Kingston Landing, and Kirby's Wharf were once important Talbot County shipping points on the Choptank, where the old steamboats would line up as far as Denton.

One of the more interesting structures in Talbot County is the Wye House located near Easton. The house was built in 1780 by Colonel Edward Lloyd, ancestor of Maryland's Governor Edward Lloyd (1809-1811). On March 13, 1781, the house was raided by a British landing party, which took many possessions, including large pieces of silver plate. Years later these items came into the possession of the British royal family and, identified by their coat of arms, were returned to their owners in America. Colonel Lloyd who built the house was a delegate to the Continental Congress and a member of the Maryland Council of Safety. In the graveyard on the grounds lie the first American Edward Lloyd, and two-sons-in law of Governor Edward Lloyd, as well as Admiral Franklin Buchanan, and Commander Charles Lowndes.

The old Wye Church at Wye Mills, built on the foundation of an earlier church in 1721, is another interesting structure of colonial times. It is one of the oldest Episcopal Churches in America. In 1949 it was completely restored under the direction of William G.

Perry, who also was the supervising architect of Colonial Williamsburg. Features of the church include the high box pews, and the hanging pulpit on the north wall. The west gallery bears the Royal Arms of England, and the original church communion pieces are engraved, "William Hemsley, 1737."

Wye Mills is also the home of several other interesting sites. The Old Wye Mill was built on land patented in 1664 by James Scott. The Mill is considered to be the oldest institution historically continuous in Talbot and Queen Anne's Counties, as the Talbot and Queen Anne's County line runs directly through the Mill. Flour for Washington's troops at Valley Forge was produced here. Now restored, it operates on a limited basis. The Wye Vestry House and Parish House, is located at Wye Mills. The Vestry House has been reconstructed on the original foundation following the builder's plans of 1762. The Parish, built in 1957, follows early eighteenth century style.

In the churchyard between the Wye Church, Vestry House and Parish House is the Great White Oak Tree. The official State Tree of Maryland, and symbol of the Easter Shore, the Wye Oak is the largest white oak tree in Maryland and believed to be the largest in the United States. Its height is ninety-five feet, with a horizonal spread of one hundred sixty-five feet. The trunk is more than twenty-one feet in circumference, and its age is estimated at well over four hundred years. The Wye Oak is owned by the State of Maryland and is now a state park. Located nearby is an early-American school room displayed in a small building. The Wye Oak can be approached from Route 50 off of either Route 662 or Route 401.

Located a short distance from Wye Mills off Route 50 is Chapel District, the site of the first Court House in Talbot County. During the early days of the county, court was held in the homes of the justices. As the waterways were the principal means of travel, a court house site was selected on Skipton Creek, near Wye Landing. It was built on a farm owned by Philemon Freddeman Hemsley, known as "Hopton." Today the farm is privately owned by H.T. Slaughter known as "Winodee" which means "Win or Die." This Court House was built in 1679, and eventually a settlement grew up around it. Today the community and buildings are gone. At one time, besides the Court House there was also a jail, stocks and a whipping post. At times the Court House was also used as a hotel for those traveling far distances. In 1684 the Court House issued an order which read, "noe drink be sold in the Court House or drunke there dureing the setting of the court."

Each year in August at Chapel District near Cordova is held The Jousting Tournament, Maryland's official State Sport. It has been held here since 1868 for the benefit of St. Joseph's Catholic Church, the oldest Catholic Church on the Eastern Shore. Father Joseph Mosley, S.J., founded St. Joseph's Mission in 1765 through much toil and sacrifice. He lived in a shed of boards which he himself had hewed from trees. Having no stove, fireplace or chimney, he would build fires in the shed, and the smoke would find its way out through a hole in the roof. In 1874 the Mission became part of the Diocese of Wilmington.

Some of Talbot County's other towns and their origin are: Avalon founded in 1620 and named in honor of a Newfoundland settlement financed by George Calvert, first Lord Baltimore. Bellevue, was founded in 1683 and originally called Ferry Neck. The name was changed to Bellevue by Colonel Oswald Tilghman, in honor of his wife, Belle Harrison. Claiborne, named for the first permanent white settler in Maryland, Captain William Claiborne, was established in 1886. Copperville, named for Uncle John Copper, a slave at Wye House during the Civil War. Hambleton, was named after settler William Hambleton who served as the County Sheriff and later as a member of the United States Congress in the 1860s and Manadier founded in 1690 around the White Marsh Church, and named for the Reverend Daniel Maynadier, who was the church's rector in 1711. The cemetery is all that remains today where the graves of Rev. Maynadier and Robert Morris, Sr., another prominent Talbot County resident can be found.

The first settlers found a serene way of life in Talbot County, and this lifestyle is much the same today.

Form of Government: Charter (1973)

Map and Seal of Talbot County

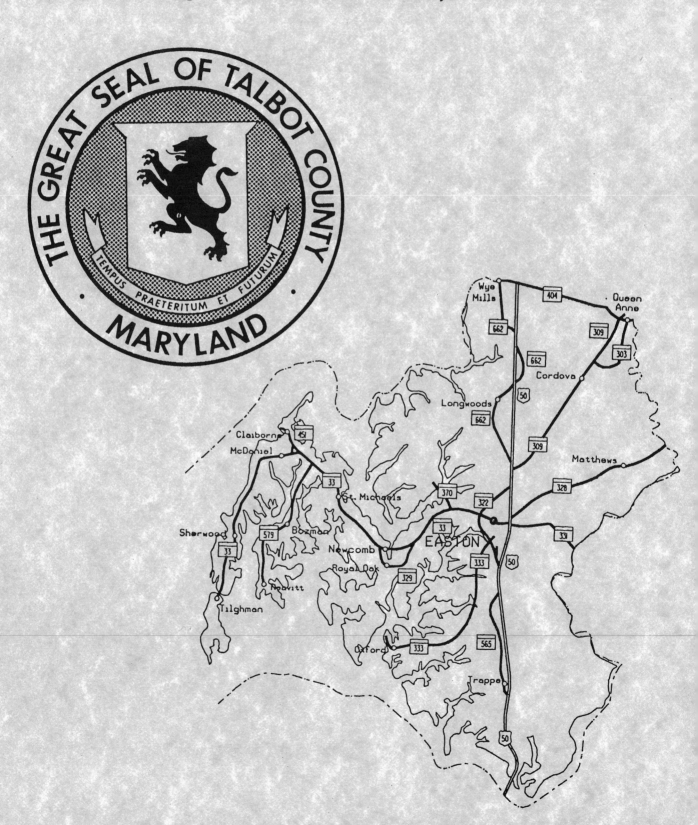

WASHINGTON COUNTY

Washington County was created from Frederick County by resolve of the Constitutional Convention of 1776. The County was named for George Washington. Washington County was the first county in the United States to use "Washington" as its name. Today there are approximately thirty others in the country.

There have been two Great Seals or logos of Washington County, although each has never been formally adopted. This original one, used between 1950 and 1988, though unofficially, is circular in shape, with the word "Washington" at the top center edge, and "County" directly centered below this on the bottom edge. Its design depicts farming through a barn and manufacturing through a factory, with the county map outline superimposed over these images. The present seal or logo has been in effect since 1988, although again, has not been officially adopted. It is oval in shape, with the words "Washington County" centered along the top edge, and "Maryland" centered along the bottom edge. It features a portrait of George Washington in the center. Above the portrait of Washington are nine stars. The larger star in the center represents Hagerstown, the County Seat. The remaining smaller eight stars represent the county's eight incorporated towns; Boonsboro, Clear Spring, Funkstown, Hancock, Keedysville, Sharpsburg, Smithsburg and Williamsport. To the right side of Washington's portrait is written the date, "1776" the year in which the county was founded.

Washington County is bordered on the north by Pennsylvania and on the south by the Potomac River, separating it from West Virginia. On the east lies Frederick County and on the west, Allegany County. It has an area of four hundred sixty-two land and nine water square miles. The terrain of Washington County is rugged, and includes the western slope of the Blue Ridge Mountains. The highest point in the county is Quirauk Mountain, part of the Blue Ridge. The lowland belt is known as Hagerstown Valley, which lies between the Blue Ridge and the Appalachian Ridge to the east which is also an extension of the Shenandoah Valley of Virginia.

The original settlers of the county were Swiss, English, Scotch and French, some of whom settled as early as 1735. Washington has the highest population of the four northwestern Maryland counties. In 1960 the population was 91,219, rising to 103,829 in

1970 and 112,764 in 1980. By 1990 it was 121,393, and in 1994 was 126,599, an increase of 4.3% since 1990. In 1998, it is 129,440, projected to be 131,100 by the year 2000.

Washington is known as Maryland's fruit growing county. Although the area is mountainous, it still ranks high in agricultural production. It ranks first in fruits and nuts sold. Also important are dairy products, and the raising of livestock. Corn, wheat, oats, barley, alfalfa, mixed timothy and clover hay are also grown.

The largest city in Washington County is Hagerstown, the county seat, having a population of about 36,000. In 1736, Jonathan Hager had arrived on the shores of the new colonies, debarking at the Port of Philadelphia. Within a short period of time, Hager decided to make his home in Maryland, because Charles Calvert, proprietor of the colony, offered land cheaply to those willing to settle in the western frontier. On June 5, 1739, Hager purchased two hundred acres of land from Daniel Duland for forty-four pounds. He named this tract of land, "Hager's Fancy." Having this land, he now needed to pick the location for his house. He carefully chose a section of land where there was cool spring water. Construction began over these two springs to insure a protected water supply. In 1740 Hager married a German neighbor, Elizabeth Kershner, and presented her with the new house. This new house was styled in German tradition, and built with uncut fieldstones carefully fitted by Hager. The walls in the house are twenty-two inches thick for added protection. The house features a large central chimney which provided added warmth, and rye straw and mud between the floors which served as insulation. During the summer months, the Hagers would retreat to the cellar area, where the spring water provided a cool environment, as well as protection against man and nature. The Hagers lived in this house for several years during which time, Jonathan grew very prosperous. He opened a trading post at his home while continuing to acquire additional land. On May 8, 1745 "Hager's Fancy" was sold to Jacob Rohner for two hundred pounds. The house remained in the Rohrer family until 1944, when it was acquired by the Washington County Historical Society, which restored it to its original colonial beauty. In 1954 it was presented to the City of Hagerstown, and in September, 1962, the Hager House was opened to the public on the bicentennial anniversary of Hagerstown.

As others began to settle here in 1762 the town was known as Elizabeth Town, after Hager's wife. In January 1814, the population had grown to 2,500 and the assembly passed an act to change the name of Elizabeth Town to Hagers Town and incorporated the same. Gradually the name became Hagerstown. During Jonathan Hager's time, the many townspeople named their tracts of land or farms. Some of the more interesting names were: Agreed to Have it Shared; All that's left; Discontent; I am Glad it is no Worse; Love in a Village; Near the Navel; Scared from Home; Search Well and You Will Find; The Third Time of Asking; Trouble Enough and The Widow's Last Shift.

During Jonathan Hager's lifetime, he became a leading citizen, and was involved in many activities. These include farming, cattle raising, and gunsmith. Hager was a volunteer Captain of Scouts during the French and Indian War. In 1762 he founded what would become Hagerstown and in 1771 and 1773 he was elected to the General Assembly in Annapolis. On November 6, 1775, Captain Hager was accidentally killed while supervising the building of the German Reformed Church (now Zion) on land which he had donated. Jonathan Hager has been called the "Father of Washington County" due to his having laid the groundwork for its separation from Frederick County in 1776, and the subsequent creation of Hagerstown as County Seat.

During the Civil War Hagerstown was not in a plantation district with many slaves. Because of this, in 1861 the majority of its citizens voted against secession. At the start of the war the town prospered, selling many items including foodstuff. This reputation of having supplies later had disadvantages. In 1863, General John McCausland appeared with one thousand five hundred Confederate troops and demanded twenty thousand dollars and twenty thousand sets of clothing. The townspeople raised the money and filled the clothing request in part.

By the close of the war, both the county and city of Hagerstown were left impoverished. Improvement was not felt until 1867 when Hagerstown was connected with the main line of the Baltimore & Ohio Railroad, at Weverton. This improved the hauling of goods to Baltimore, decreasing the traveling distance by sixty-three miles. In 1872 the first train finally reached Hagerstown, again cutting the distance by twenty miles. The first passenger train arrived on September 4, 1880, and the railroad established an office here. Between 1880 and 1900 the population finally increased, doing so more rapidly then it had in the previous century.

Hagerstown has many historical places of interest. These include: The Gruber Almanac Company Office: Originally established at 9 North Potomac Street, it was here that John Gruber published the Hagers-Town Town and Country Almanack. Gruber was born in Pennsylvania in 1768 and settled in Hagerstown (then spelled Hagers-Town), and in 1797 published the first issue of the "Almanack" in German. In 1798 through 1918 two issues were printed, one in German and one in English. Until Gruber's death in 1867, he did both the editing and typesetting. Over the years the Hagerstown Almanac has been proven to be very accurate. Former Governor of Maryland, William T. Hamilton used the Almanac as consultation before setting the date of any hanging, in an attempt to insure good weather for this popular event. Today the Hagerstown Almanac is still published and is widely used. The original location on North Potomac Street has since been torn down. The new headquarters is located nearby.

The Hager House and Museum located next to City Park at 19 Key Street, were built in 1739 by Jonathan Hager. The house is completely furnished in period style. The Hager Museum, adjacent to the founder's home contains hundreds of artifacts comprising the "finest archeological find in Maryland." The collection consists mainly of items uncovered under the stone porch of the Hager House during its restoration in 1953. These include eighteenth and nineteenth century coins, bone forks and combs, pottery, buttons, and ironwork, as well as other finds. Another item which can be seen in the Museum is "Little Heiskell," the symbol of Hagerstown. Little Heiskell is a weathervane in the shape of a Hessian soldier. It was commissioned by Jonathan Hager and designed by a German tinsmith of the same name. During the Civil War it was shot in the "heart" by a Confederate sharpshooter, while atop City Hall, where it remained until 1935. Also located on the grounds of the Hager House are the Elizabeth Kershner Hager Herbal Gardens. Located on all sides of the house, these herbal and flower gardens are plantings that are based on known colonial gardens. During the colonial period, herbs were used not only for flavoring and seasoning, but also for medicinal purposes.

The Miller House at 135 Washington Street is a Federal-style townhouse, built in 1818, and is the headquarters of the Washington County Historical Society. It contains exhibits such as Civil War artifacts, Doll and Clock collections, Bell pottery, and the first Hagerstown taxicab, a 1910 Regal. Admission is charged. The Washington County Museum of Fine Arts, in City Park displays paintings, sculptures, and Oriental art objects. Admission is free. On Potomac Street is the Maryland Theater, a restored 1915 vaudeville house designed by Charles Lamb, and home to the Maryland Symphony Orchestra. Four festivals are held each year in Hagerstown. These are the National Pike Festival in May, the Hagerstown Fair in August, the Alstatia Festival in November, and the Illuminary Festival in December. April through September the Hagerstown Suns, a Double AA Eastern League Division of the Baltimore Orioles Baseball Club play at Municipal Stadium.

Hagerstown's <u>City Park</u> where the Hager House and Museum, Washington County Museum of Fine Arts and the Mansion House Art Center are located is often called "America's second most beautiful city park." The centerpiece of the park is a fifty acre lake, home for over two hundred fifty waterfowl. The <u>Mansion House Art Center</u> located at the park is a Georgian style house built in 1846 by John Heyser. Today it houses a collection of local art. Other historical sites in Hagerstown include <u>City Hall</u>, opened in 1940. Inside is displayed a model of the original City Hall. <u>Hagerstown Roundhouse Museum</u> located at 300 S. Burhans Boulevard depicts the history of the Western Maryland Railroad, as well as six other railroads which made Hagerstown the Hub City.

Each year in July, the City of Hagerstown celebrates "The Ransom of Hagerstown," where the events of July, 1864 are re-enacted. In July, 1864, General Jubal Early moved from the Shenandoah Valley toward the Potomac River, threatening a third invasion of the North by Confederate forces. Fighting occurred at Harper's Ferry, Leetown, Darksville, and Martinsburg on July 3rd. Two days later, Early crossed the Potomac at Shepherdstown and there was skirmishing at Keedysville, Point-of-Rocks, Soloman's Gap and Hagerstown.

On Wednesday, July 6, Early sent one thousand five hundred cavalry commanded by John McCausland into Hagerstown to levy a ransom of twenty-thousand dollars, as well as clothing, in retribution for Federal destruction of farms, feed and cattle in the Shenandoah Valley. Through the cooperative effort by three banks and the Hagerstown City Council, the money was raised to save the town from being burned. At the same time the money was raised, the citizens and businesses surrendered pants, shirts, hats and shoes for the rebels. The banks that raised the needed funds were the Hagerstown Bank (later the Hagerstown Trust Co.); the Hagerstown branch of the Williamsport Bank (later the Washington County National Bank); and the Hagerstown Savings Bank (later the First National Bank).

About ten miles from Hagerstown is the site of one of the Civil War's most famous battles. <u>Antietam National Battlefield</u> is a nine hundred sixty acre site at Sharpsburg, Maryland. The Battle of Antietam, as it was called by the Union, or the Battle of Sharpsburg, as it was referred to by the Confederates, was fought on September 17, 1862. On this bloodiest day of the Civil War, the Union lost 12,440 men and the Confederates 10,941. On this battlefield General McClellan and his 87,000 troops met General Robert E. Lee's 41,000 men. One interesting structure at Antietam is the

Dunker Church, which many men, both Union and Confederate fought in and around, and died. My great great grandfather, William Benton Marck served in the 30th Regiment, Company C, Army of Northern Virginia, and was wounded this day as his regiment charged from behind the Dunker Church, only to be met by heavy Union artillery fire. Of the two hundred thirty-six men who fought this day from Company C, one hundred seventy-two died.

The battlefield today displays maps, tablets and monuments; vertical cannon barrels mark the area where three Union and three Confederate generals died. At various times, re-enactments are held here with costumed interpreters depicting camp life, military drills and other battle related demonstrations. The Visitors Center contains a museum and gift shop and book store and well as information on walking and car tours. Admission is charged. The <u>Antietam National Cemetery</u> was established in 1865 and contains the graves of four thousand seven hundred seventy-six Union soldiers and two hundred sixty-one graves of men who fought in subsequent wars. A notable landmark, "The Private Soldier" a monument dedicated to Civil War dead is located here.

Some larger towns in Washington County include <u>Boonsboro</u>, which was founded in 1774 by George and William Boone, who were related to the famous Daniel. Boonsboro was also very active during the Civil War. On September 11, 1862, "Stonewall" Jackson came close to being captured when he was seen walking his horse on the outskirts of town after a skirmish, but was able to return to his lines. Several days following the Battle of South Mountain, Fitzhugh Lee's cavalry was protecting the rear of Lee's army and had a skirmish with advancing Union troops on the streets of the town. Following the Battle of Antietam, the churches and many private homes of Boonsboro were used to care for the wounded. One of the churches used for the wounded was <u>Trinity Reformed Church</u>, on Church Street. In the church graveyard is a monument to William Boone, erected in 1935 to replace the former simple stone that had marked his grave for 137 years.

Daniel Boone

<u>Rose Hill</u> located on Main Street in Boonsboro was built in 1814. This home was the setting for David Belasco's play, "The Heart of Maryland," first produced in 1895. Several scenes of the film version were photographed here. On Main and St. Paul Streets is <u>Weldon</u>, a house built in 1741 by Moses Chapline. This old mansion was another of the settings used for "The Heart of Maryland." At Main and Church Streets was the United States Hotel, built in 1811, and used by many celebrities. Also on Main Street near Church Street is an old cannon that was cast in Boonsboro for use in the War of 1812. The <u>Boonsborough Museum of History</u> contains a unique collection of historical objects of local and national importance. These include Civil War relics, a firearms collection and American Indian artifacts.

Not far from the town of Hancock, in the historic Cumberland Valley near Big Pool, Maryland is <u>Fort Frederick</u>, one of the last fortifications built at the time of the French and Indian War (1754-1763). The stone Fort was named in honor of Maryland's Lord Proprietor, Frederick Calvert, Sixth Lord Baltimore, and erected by Governor Horatio Sharpe in 1756 to protect the English settlers against the French and their Indian allies. Most forts during this period were built of wood and earth and were small in size, but Fort Frederick is unique because of its size and its strong stone stockade walls. Though never attacked by the French, the Fort did serve as an important supply base for various English campaigns. In 1763, an Ottawa Indian Chief named Pontiac staged a massive Indian uprising. It was during this uprising that several hundred settlers and a militia force sought protection at the fort. During the American Revolution, Fort Frederick saw service again as a refuge for settlers and as a prison camp for Hessian and British soldiers. In 1791, the

State of Maryland sold the Fort, and for the next one hundred thirty-one years, the land was used for farming. During the Civil War, Union troops occupied the Fort and fought a brief skirmish with Confederate raiders on Christmas Day, 1861. This was the only military engagement Fort Frederick has seen.

In 1922, the State of Maryland repurchased the fort. Throughout the remainder of the 1920s the State began development of a State Park, Maryland's first. During this time and into the 1930s restoration of the fort began and continued in 1976 in honor of the nation's bicentennial. Today the fort has been restored to its original 1758 appearance. Historical displays are featured at the fort, the Museum and the Visitor's Center. Also available at Fort Frederick State Park are camping, picnicking, hiking, fishing and boating.

In the area of Fort Frederick, near Hancock was the former site of Fort Tonoloway, which was built in 1755 after Braddock's defeat. It was built on the Potomac River but was abandoned after Fort Frederick was opened. Today all that remains on this site is a picnic area.

At the town of Hancock is the St. Thomas Episcopal Church on Church and High Streets. It was built in 1835. In 1861 and 1862 this church was used to shelter the Union wounded. Union batteries were placed near the church to defend against the guns of Stonewall Jackson, located across the river. Also located here is the C & O Canal Museum, at 326 E. Main Street. Operated by the National Park Service, this museum features a slideshow presentation, artifacts, photos and books dedicated to canal life. On display also is a small canal boat replica. The C & O Canal National Park is a one hundred eighty-four mile park along the Potomac River, extending from Georgetown in Washington, D.C. to Cumberland, of which seventy-seven miles are in Washington County.

Williamsport is at the junction of the Potomac (meaning "among the black walnuts") and Conococheague Creek ("very long"). During the Revolution, Braddock's army used one of the many trails here on their way back to Frederick. The town Williams' Port was founded by General Otho Holland Williams for whom it was named. In April, 1786, by an Act of the Maryland General Assembly, the town of Williams' Port was assigned the name Williamsport, combining the two former names. When it was a busy shipping port, the townspeople petitioned the United States Congress to be selected as a Federal City, and the first U.S. Capital. The town was inspected by George Washington in 1790, but because Great Falls prevented large ships from entering the towns port, their request was denied. During the Civil War, Robert E. Lee along with his Army of Northern Virginia camped in the town, and held the town for a week following the Battle of Gettysburg, waiting for the swollen river waters to subside. During the prosperous C & O Canal days, Williamsport was a busy center of commerce. Today, visitors can see the unique rain spouts that hang out from the house tops over the streets of this quaint town. Williamsport is famous for its ghosts and legends as well as for the many historical haunts that attract visitors. An interesting feature of the town is that just about every resident has a nickname, such as "Duckfoot," "Moonbeam," "Apple," and "Zims."

Historic places of interest in Williamsport include the C & O Towpath and Aqueduct, where cargo boats once were pulled along the waterway by mules and tenders. The Bollman Steel Truss Bridge, located at the Potomac River is one of only two such bridges remaining in the United States. The other such bridge is located in Howard County. Also on the Potomac River is Lock House #44, along the canal. It was here that boats traveling on the canal were let to a different water level. At the end of Springfield Lane is the Springhouse, the oldest permanent building in Washington County. A visit to Williamsport captures a sense of times and events thought to be gone forever. The legend states, "take a drink of the clear spring water, and once you've visited, you'll always return."

Other attractions of interest in Washington County are the Albert M. Powell Fish Hatchery, located on Beaver Creek. The hatchery raises trout from eggs to adults for stocking various rivers and lakes throughout the state. As many as 200,000 fish in all stages of development are kept in outdoor pools. The Beaver Creek Schoolhouse, is an authentically refurbished turn-of-the-century one-room schoolhouse and museum.

Maryland's only commercial underground cave is in Washington County. Crystal Grottoes Cavern is located outside Keedysville, and is one of the largest solution caves in the world. Just across the Potomac River from Harper's Ferry (West Virginia) is John Brown's Farm. It was from this house that John Brown, in 1859, seized the Federal Armory at Harper's Ferry. Recently restored, this log house is on the National Registry.

Washington has many state and county parks. These include Gathland State Park/South Mountain State Park, of which a portion is located in Frederick County. Once the estate of Civil War correspondent George Alfred Townsend, Gathland is the only park in the world dedicated to the free press. The War Correspondent's Arch stands at the crest of South Mountain. <u>Greenbrier State Park</u>, is a one thousand two-hundred acre park which features a forty-two acre fresh water lake. The <u>Washington Monument State Park</u>, features the first monument completed in memory of George Washington, dedicated July 4, 1827. It is located atop South Mountain, the natural border between Frederick and Washington Counties.

The county parks include <u>Pen Mar County Park</u>, a redeveloped forty-four acre park featuring a panoramic view of the Cumberland Valley. Once an amusement park in the early 1900s, today it features concerts, and other entertainment in the summer months. <u>Piper Lane County Park</u>, is the county's smallest; <u>Camp Harding County Park</u>, was named after President Warren G. Harding. In the early 1920s, such notables as Harvey Firestone, Thomas Edison and Henry Ford camped here. <u>Devil's Backbone County Park</u>, is a scenic park located along Antietam Creek. It features a beautiful waterfall, picnic areas, picnic pavilion, swings, and an outdoor chapel.

Located on Millbrook Road off Route 67 is <u>Mt. Briar Wetland Preserve</u>. This environmental site is one of the most unique, non-tidal wetland areas in Maryland. Featured is a floating boardwalk which allows for walking through the park. The <u>Wilson Village/Wilson Bridge Picnic Area</u>, located off Route 40, contains a recently restored country store and schoolhouse, as well as other buildings along the old National Pike. The Wilson Bridge, the county's oldest and longest stone arch bridge has been restored and is today a walking bridge. Featured is a picnic area, a parking lot with canoe access and great fishing in the area.

Washington County not only enjoys great agricultural and industrial productivity, but remains as a beautiful mountainous county, rich in historical sites.

Form of Government: County Commissioners

Map of Washington County

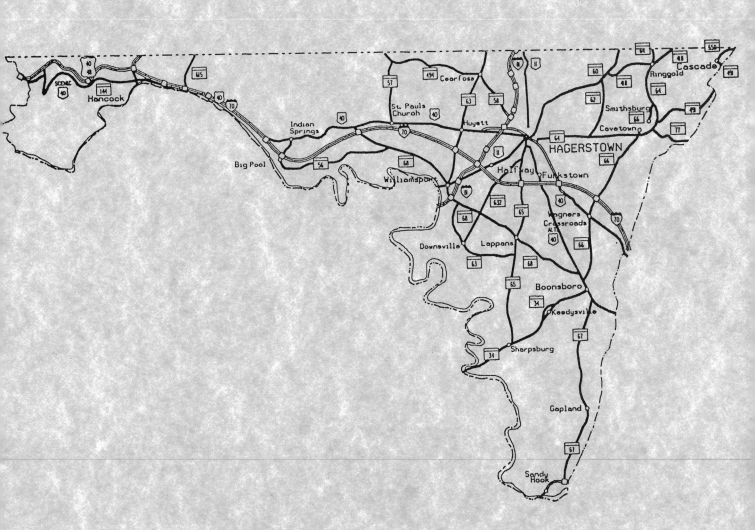

WICOMICO COUNTY

Wicomico County was created from Somerset and Worcester counties in 1867 (Const., Art. XIII, secs. 2-6). The County was named after the Wicomico River from the Indian words "wicko" and "mekee" meaning "a place where houses are built," referring to an Indian town on the river banks. Wicomico was the twenty-second of Maryland's twenty-three counties to be created.

The seal of Wicomico County has been in effect since August 24, 1965. It is described as circular in shape, bearing the words "Wicomico County" on the outer margin. In the center of the seal is a map of the outline of Wicomico County, with a profile of a Wicomico Indian superimposed over the map. Below the profile of said Indian is the date, 1867, the year Wicomico was founded.

Wicomico is bordered on the north by Dorchester County and the State of Delaware and the south by Worcester and Somerset. To the east lies Worcester and to the west Dorchester. It has an area of three hundred eighty square land and fifteen square water miles. Located in the Atlantic Coastal Plain its elevations range from sea level to forty feet above sea level generally. Its highest point is eighty-four feet above sea level.

The population of the county is mostly descendants of the early settlers who were English and Scotch. In 1950 there were 39,641 people in the county. By 1960 it increased to 49,050 and in 1980 it was 64,979. By 1990 it was 74,339, and in 1994 rose to 78,473, an increase of 5.6% since 1990. In 1998, the population is 81,620, and by the year 2000, it is projected to be 83,400.

Wicomico County is, and always has been agricultural. Corn was the mainstay in the lives of the Wicomico Indians, and it is now a main ingredient of the County's multimillion dollar poultry industry. Modern Wicomico boasts many other industries: seafood, clothing, lumber, canned and frozen food, bakery products, and several manufacturing plants. An estimated 32,000 people are employed today in the County's various industrial operations. Their products are distributed nationally and internationally, due to Wicomico's proximity to major markets.

Many prominent citizens of the colonial era settled in what was to become Wicomico County. Among these were Levin Winder, who was Governor of Maryland from 1812 to 1816, and the celebrated Revolutionary War General William H. Winder, who was married to Gertrude Polk, a relative of President James A. Polk. "Bounds Chance," situated on the south side of the Wicomico River, was the home of Matilda Lucas Bounds, a cousin of Samuel Chase. A signer of the Declaration of Independence, Chase often visited his cousin in this historic colonial home, which still stands. Annie Frances Rider, a great granddaughter of one of Wicomico's founders, was the wife of Elija E. Jackson, Governor of Maryland in the late 1800s. A short distance north of Upper Ferry on the Wicomico River resided Brigadier General Alexander Roxburgh of Revolutionary War fame, who received an award for his military services from President Thomas Jefferson. Other well-known natives of the county in the early 1900s were Congressmen William H. Jackson, David J. Ward and Senator William P. Jackson.

One of Wicomico County's best-loved links with history is St. Bartholomew's (Old Green Hill) Church on the banks of the river. Originally established around 1690, the present brick structure was erected in 1733 and is still used for services once a year in August. The Wicomico Historical Society, Inc. is located at Pemberton Historical Park in Salisbury. Included in the park is Pemberton Hall built in 1741, for Colonel Isaac and Ann (Dashiell) Handy. In 1683 Thomas Pemberton received the tract of land from William Stevens. The Pemberton family held on to the land for forty years before selling it to Isaac Handy, Salisbury's original settler. It was Handy who built the house and named it for the Pemberton family. The One-room Rockawalkin School is a typical example of a rural school house built about 1872. It was used as a school from that time until 1938. In 1973 the school building was moved to the site at Pemberton Elementary School and later restored. Today the building serves as a museum of early education in the county. The Nutters Election House, built in 1938, was used until 1976. It is the only election house still standing in Wicomico County, that was originally built as an election house. Balloting generally was done in private homes, churches or neighborhood stores. The building today houses the Society's collection of presidential and inauguration memorabilia and political campaign items. It is located at the water pumping station in Fruitland.

Poplar Hill Mansion in Salisbury, located on Poplar Hill Avenue was built in 1795 by Major Levin Handy. The house is a very good example of postcolonial style. Fortunately, it escaped the fires of 1860 and 1886. Long Hills is another example which dates from the eighteenth century.

Although Wicomico is a comparatively young County, Mardela Springs, located in the western section, was included in the Lord Baltimore grant and had beginnings as early as 1632. The City of Salisbury, which is the county seat, is situated so well geographically that it is the center of the commercial and cultural life of the entire Delmarva Peninsula.

In 1665, Colonel Isaac Handy established a small wharf at the Wicomico River and named it Handy's Landing. In 1732, this village was officially founded as Salisbury Town, named for either the Earl of Salisbury, a friend of the first Lord Baltimore or for Wiltshire, England's city of Salisbury. Many years later, in 1867, Salisbury was made the county's seat. During the Revolutionary War, Tories and riffraff pirates disguised as Tories ravaged the river settlements and farms. During the Civil War, Salisbury's citizens were badly divided. Most of the slave owners were Confederate sympathizers, and the rest favored the Union, whose volunteers from Maryland and Delaware were stationed here from 1861. They made various trips through Maryland, Delaware, and Virginia disarming secessionists, but were involved in no actual fighting. In 1860 and again in 1886 fires devastated the town, where hardly an old building escaped. One of the few buildings which did survive the fire of 1886 was the Wicomico County Court House. In rebuilding the city a second time, it was built in brick, as opposed to wood. The new construction, built between 1887 and 1935, reflects different architectural periods, from Victorian Gothic and Georgian to Queen Anne and Art Deco styles.

Downtown Historic Salisbury contains twenty-one structures consisting of stores, banks, historic buildings, and churches. All of these structures, with the exception of the Court House were destroyed in the fire and were rebuilt after 1887, and all use Downtown Plaza as their address, with their respective numbers. Several examples are the structure at 243 Downtown Plaza. This was originally the Merchant's Hotel and after its rebuilding became the West End Hotel. At number 237 is located the oldest building on the Plaza. This double storefront structure retains its original incised decorative cornice. The first owner operated both an ice cream shop and a grocery. The mansard slate roof structure located at number 300 was originally the Farmers & Merchants Bank. It is called the "Old Synagogue Building" because the Beth Israel Congregation met on the second floor for many years. The octagonal domed turret and Gothic windows with colored leaded glass have been maintained. At 220 Downtown Plaza were originally two structures, but were removed in 1935 when Montgomery Ward built the current structure. The front facade with its rare stone dormered windows at the top have remained the same as the original structure.

St. Peter's & West Church Street was established in 1768. The church was destroyed by fire in 1860 and again in 1886. The current edifice was copied from the architecture of the Church of the Annunciation in Philadelphia, and is of the Italian Renaissance style. At 110 West Church Street is a structure originally designed as a fire house. It includes a seventy-two foot tower where fire hoses were suspended to dry. It has formerly served as City Hall and the City Hall Museum, and now houses the city's police department.

In 1925 the State Normal School was founded in Salisbury. Over the years the name was changed twice. First to Salisbury State College and today is Salisbury State University. In addition to the usual undergraduate and graduate programs, the university offers workshops, seminars, and cultural activities for the benefit of the community.

In Salisbury's City Park is the Salisbury Zoo, considered one of the finest small zoos in the country. It is described as "a little jewel of a place that can be seen in an hour's time - but can be lingered over and savored for a great deal longer." The natural settings provide homes for a variety of birds and animals, including Sam the Macaw and rare Spectacled Bears. Additionally, Salisbury is known as the "poultry capital of the world" due to one of its famous residents, Frank Perdue.

The Peninsula General Hospital, completed in 1904, was built on high ground previously used for a tent hospital during the Civil War. Following a major rebuilding and expansion program, the Peninsula General Medical Center opened its doors in September 1977. The new Center contains three hundred seventy-five beds and has a staff of over one hundred fifty physicians and surgeons. This fine facility serves the entire Eastern Shore of Maryland, and portions of Delaware and Virginia, having an area population of about 300,000.

Maryland Lady provides one and one-half hour cruises on the Wicomico River, departing from the Salisbury marina. Tours are narrated and lunch and dinner cruises are also available. Admission is charged.

Ward Museum of Wildfowl Art is located on Beaglin Park Drive and Schumaker. Here the art of decoy carving of songbirds, ducks, geese and other waterfowl are preserved and displayed. Exhibits range from one thousand year old Indian decoys to the elaborate ones created today. Admission is charged.

Several other places of interest in the county are: <u>Tonytank Manor</u> built in 1800; <u>Cherry Hill</u> (1757); <u>Paul Jones House</u> (1773); <u>Anderson House</u> (1730); and <u>Nithsdale</u> (1732).

Other towns in the county and their origin are: <u>Allen</u>, established in 1672 by William Brereton and originally named Brereton, then Brewington. In 1882 the town finally received a post office, which took the name Upper Trappe. But because there were many other places named Trappe, the postmaster, Joseph S.C. Allen volunteered the use of his surname, and the town has been named Allen since. <u>Delmar</u>, located four miles north of Salisbury, straddles the state lines of Maryland and Delaware, thus its name Delmar. <u>Hebron</u>, gets its name from the religious-minded colonial founders, honoring the Old Testament village of Hebron, located in Israel. Hebron is notable because it is located exactly midway between the Atlantic Ocean and the Chesapeake Bay.

<u>Mardela Springs</u>, is named for a word created from Maryland and Delaware. Originally the town was named Barren Creek but was changed to Mardela Springs in 1906. <u>Nanticoke</u>, was named for the Nanticoke River on which it lies, and <u>Parsonsburg</u>, was named for Isaac H. Parsons who founded the town in 1854. <u>Pittsville</u>, was originally named Derrickson's Cross Roads. In 1868 the Wicomico and Pocomoke Railroad reached the town. The railroad president, Dr. Hilary R. Pitts could not fit the long former name on the train's sign, so he changed it to Pittsville, after himself, a shorter name.

<u>Wetipquin</u>, is derived from the Indian original name of Nassawango. The name was shortened to Wango because the citizens grew tired of multisyllabled Indian names, and <u>Whitehaven</u> was named by an English settler, Colonel George Gale for the English city from which he came. He was the stepfather of Augustine Washington who was George Washington's father.

In November 1943 the <u>Salisbury-Wicomico County Airport</u> opened, built four miles southeast of Salisbury. The Airport occupies nine hundred acres of land and is further protected by an additional five hundred twenty-nine acres held in easements for runway approach zones. Commuter services provide daily scheduled flights to Washington National, Baltimore-Washington International, and Philadelphia International Airports. The Airport is considered one of Wicomico County's principal assets and has the potential of becoming a major regional transportation facility and a center for air-oriented industrial development.

Wicomico has indeed made progress over the years and is an interesting place to visit.

Form of Government: Charter (1964)

Map and Seal of Wicomico County

WORCESTER COUNTY

Worcester County was created from Somerset County in 1742 (Chapter 19, Acts of 1742). The County was named after Earl of Worcester.

The official seal of Worcester County consists of a shield bearing the Calvert Arms above which is a coronet (symbolic of the Earl of Worcester) and a slightly oval band on which is inscribed the words "County Worcester," which surrounds the coronet and shield.

Worcester is located on the southeastern extremity of Maryland's Eastern Shore. It is bordered by the State of Delaware to the north and Virginia to the south. The northern section is bordered on the west by Wicomico County and the lower section by Somerset. To the east lies the Atlantic Ocean. Worcester County has an area of four hundred eighty-three land and one hundred six water square miles. There are four physiographic divisions in the county. These are the mainland, the coastal beach, the marshes and the freshwater swamps. Most of the county's elevation is sea level, rising to only thirty-five feet above sea level at its highest point.

The population of the county was 23,733 in 1960. In ten years it rose only to 24,442 and by 1980 was only 30,303. By 1990 it was 35,028; and in 1994 increased to 39,015. In 1998, it is 41,910, and by the year 2000, it is projected to be 43,300.

The economy of the county is chiefly agricultural. Corn, rye, soybeans, Irish potatoes, sweet potatoes, tomatoes, snap and lima beans, and strawberries are raised. Leading industries in the county are tomato canning, chicken processing, and tourism, thanks to the resort town of Ocean City.

The largest communities in the county are Snow Hill, the county seat, Ocean City, Pocomoke City and Berlin. Snow Hill was founded in 1642 and has served as the county seat since 1742. It was given its name by Colonel William Stevens who named it after the Snow Hill section of London, which had been his early home. As you walk through the Royal Port of Snow Hill, you can feel the sense of centuries ago. Along Federal, Church and Washington Streets the enormous sycamore trees and stately homes reflect the history of long ago. In 1742, when Worcester County was divided from Somerset County, Snow Hill became the county seat. A disastrous fire in 1893 destroyed Snow Hill's original downtown area, but many other historic homes and public buildings remain. These include several pre-Revolutionary War structures, carefully preserved and maintained by the present Snow Hill residents. As you continue walking on Washington Street, you pass the courthouse and library that brings you to the water. At the water are located Sturgis Park and Byrd Park. At these parks various recreational activities are held, including summer concerts, river tours, canoe rentals, and boat ramps.

At one time school in Snow Hill was held in a single room as recreated in the Mt. Zion One-Room School Museum. Today the Snow Hill Elementary, Middle and High School are within walking distances of most of the residents. As the county seat, Snow Hill is the center of many social services. The main library contains an extensive collective of local history material. Two very interesting attractions in Snow Hill are the Julia A. Purnell Museum on Market Street and Furnace Town. The Museum features a remarkable exhibit of area artifacts, memorabilia, costumes, tools and machinery, all dating from pre-historic ages through the early twentieth century. Furnace Town is a re-creation of the 1840s iron manufacturing village at the Nassawango Iron Furnace.

Ocean City was first developed in 1872 and given the name "The Ladies Resort to the Ocean." The town's promoters opened the first hotel, The Atlantic, in 1875. Later the name was changed to Ocean City and today is the most popular resort town in Maryland. The once small village is now a ten-mile long strip of many hotels, motels, condominiums, restaurants, amusement parks, and miniature golf courses. There is also a two-mile boardwalk, loaded with specialty and souvenir shops. Ocean City has the finest beach in the State. Activities include swimming, sun bathing, boating and fishing, and deep sea fishing where some of the finest white marlins have been caught. One museum of interest is the Ocean City Life-Saving Station Museum, on the Boardwalk at the Inlet. The Life-Saving Station Museum features Ocean City's colorful past at the Life-Saving Station, built in 1891. Included are an aquarium, a doll's house, shipwreck artifacts, programs, and numerous small exhibits.

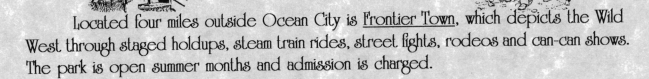

Located four miles outside Ocean City is <u>Frontier Town</u>, which depicts the Wild West through staged holdups, steam train rides, street fights, rodeos and can-can shows. The park is open summer months and admission is charged.

<u>Pocomoke City</u> was first established in 1670. Founded by Colonel William Stevens, it was first known as Stevens Landing. Other names that followed are Meeting House Landing, Warehouse Landing, Newtown and Pitts Creek. In 1878, Reverend I.O. Ayers of the Methodist Episcopal Church wanted a more distinguished name and chose Pocomoke City, which has lasted. The Pocomoke River, which has played an important role in the city's evolution also serves as a sanctuary for small animals and migratory birds. Visitors to the water may see up to twenty-seven species of mammals, twenty-nine reptiles, fourteen amphibians, and one hundred seventy-two species of birds. The Pocomoke River is also the northernmost habitat for the bald cypress trees.

Some interesting facts concerning Pocomoke City and the Pocomoke River are: The Pocomoke River gets its name from the Indian word "pocomoke," meaning "black Water"; many runaway slaves, bootleggers, and smugglers once found a safe haven from the law along the river in the Pocomoke Forest; the Pocomoke River is said to be the deepest river in the United States for its width; there were times in the past when the Pocomoke River was frozen so solid that people actually skated from Pocomoke City to Snow Hill; a fire in 1922 completely destroyed downtown Pocomoke City, leaving two hundred fifty people homeless; and the best location to enjoy the setting of the sun is at the Cedar Hall Wharf, at the end of Cedar Hall Road.

Some attractions in Pocomoke City include the <u>Costen House</u>, located on Market Street. This was the home of Dr. Isaac T. Costen, the first mayor of Pocomoke City. The house, designed after Victorian Italiante Architecture is on the National Register of Historical Sites. <u>Cypress Park</u>, in downtown Pocomoke City, features boat docks, a ball field, picnic areas, tennis courts and a playground. The <u>Pocomoke River State Park</u> is located on Route 113. In the park are the Shad Landing Area and the Milburn Landing Area. The Shad has water & electrical hook-ups, and features canoe and rowboat rentals. The Milburn is located off Route 113, on Route 364, and is in the Pocomoke Forest. Both areas provide for camping, and include nature trails, picnic areas, telephones, launching ramps, and parking for trailers.

Berlin was one of the first permanent settlements in the area, established in 1677 by Colonel William Stevens, on a tract of land known as "Burley." It was first named Burleigh Plantation, then Stephen's Cross Roads. Burleigh at the time was a local inn, and thus the present name is a combination of Burliegh and the inn, for Berlin.

Berlin was the birthplace of Stephen Decatur, the famous naval hero of the War of 1812. Although the Decaturs were from Philadelphia, Stephen's mother had been sent to the Eastern Shore for safety during the Revolutionary War. In the early 1900s Berlin became a pleasant and frequent rest stop for those on their way to the small coastal village of Ocean City. After World War II, as Ocean City began to develop, Berlin quietly took a back seat to the beach scene. But in recent years Berlin has resumed a prominent role at the crossroads between the beach resorts and the inland shore communities. A large section of Berlin has been designated as a National Historic District, and many of the homes, as well as the commercial district are included in the National Register of Historic Places.

Some of the historic sites in the Commercial and Residential Districts are the Stevenson-Chandler House, which was built in the 1790s. Although recently restored, the front portion of this Federal home is believed to be the oldest remaining structure in Berlin. The original part of the house, when viewed from the street, is represented by the two bays to the left of the front entrance. The distinctive gambrel roof is the only one of its type in the community. It is located at 125 North Main Street. Also on North Main Street at 300, is the Brueckmann House. This structure began as a Federal house, although it features Gothic Revival cross-gable, a steeply pitched roof, and a decoratively trimmed front porch.

South Main Street in Berlin contains many houses of historical interest. These include the Kenwood at 101, built about 1830; Burley Cottage, at 205, also built about 1830 and is notable for its four tall chimneys and front porch with a bull's eye window; Scott Cottage, at 204 which features a large Magnolia tree on the grounds, and the structure has a massive chimney with four flues located on the south side; Cantwell House, at 206, was built in the early twentieth century; Burley Manor, at 313, built in the 1860s; Telescopic House, at 413. This structure was built in 1840 and of interest is the placement of a smaller wing next to a larger one creating a "telescope effect."; and Waverly, located at 509, another of Berlin's Federal style houses.

Other historic places in the districts are the Taylor House Museum (1825); Thompson House (early nineteenth century); Keas House (1880); Barrett House (early nineteenth century); and Whaley House (Robin's Nest). The Whaley House, dating from 1800, is Berlin's earliest documented dwelling house. Located at 2 West Street, the main section with gable-front features a decorative cornice or band containing a Greek motif. The large section on the south side also dates from the early nineteenth century. Behind the main house are a number of buildings, including a granary, smokehouse, and outhouse.

Located on Germantown and Trappe Roads is the New Bethel United Methodist Church, the first black church in the Berlin area, and is the noteworthy seat of Methodism for the African-American community. New Bethel has also given the Methodist Church, and the world, the most prolific hymn writer of all time, Reverend Charles Tindley.

Other smaller towns in Worcester County include: Bishopville, founded in 1668 by the Bishop family. Littleton Bishop, later operated a saw and grist mill in 1830. Furnace, located several miles northwest of Snow Hill, was the home of the Maryland Iron Company founded in 1832. The company built an iron furnace but business was never much above marginal. The furnace was shut down in 1847, leaving Furnace a ghost town. The town is slowly being restored, and Furnace is part of the National Register of Historic Places. Girdletree located outside Snow Hill, was a shipping point for farm products and sea food. Originally known as Girdle Tree, its name comes from the word Girdle, in this case meaning to cut a ring of bark from a tree for the purpose of killing it. Prior to the Civil War, Charles Bishop acquired a large estate. Before he could build his house he had to remove a large beech tree. He girdled the tree, then named his farm Girdle Tree Hill. The village grew around his farm, and was later shortened to Girdletree.

Indiantown was the home of the Askiminikonsin Indians, in the 1660s. Once occupied by over five different tribes, it was the largest Indian settlement in Maryland. When the white settlers started cutting roads into this territory, the settlement was named Askiminikonsin, and later changed to Indiantown. Newark was originally founded as Queponco Station. During the Civil War a house in the town had an unusual shape. It was built in a boat-shaped design and called "The New Ark," thus the town took the name Newark after it.

Chincoteague Bay and Assateague Island National Seashore are two very well-known areas in the county. Chincoteague Bay is a long narrow channel separating Assateague

Island from the mainland. Chinocoteague is an Indian word meaning "large stream or inlet." It is known for its wild ponies that swim to Assateague and for the oysters found in its waters. Assateague Island is a long sandy strip extending from Ocean City. Assateague means "place across," from its location across the Chincoteague Bay. Assateague is a favorite place for tourists, campers, boaters and fishers. Visitors are also there to see the wild ponies who freely roam the island. Each year hundreds come to watch the wild ponies swim the Chincoteague Bay. The ponies were brought in the 1600s by mainland farmers and planters. Assateague Island National Seashore falls in both Maryland and Virginia. It is operated by the National Park Service, U.S. Department of the Interior. Chincoteague National Wildlife Refuge is located in Virginia, and is operated by the Fish and Wildlife Service, U.S. Department of the Interior.

Assawoman Bay is the inlet separating Ocean City from the mainland. Its name origin is Indian, but no meaning has been determined.

One famous church in the county is St. Martin's Episcopal Church, on the St. Martin's River. Built in 1759, it originally cost eighty thousand pounds of tobacco, which was about four thousand dollars. The church today is rarely used, although in remarkable condition. All Hallows Church in Snow Hill was built in 1756, and contains a Queen Anne bible, dated 1701.

Worcester County has a lot to offer, from boating, swimming, fishing and sunbathing at the famous Ocean City.

Form of Government: Code Home Rule (1976)

Map of Worcester County

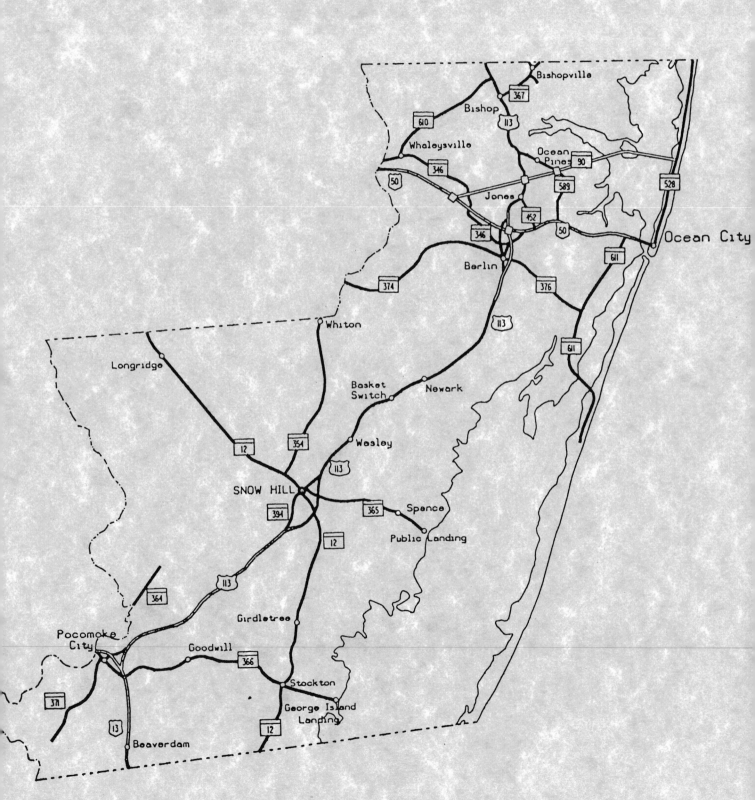

MARYLAND COUNTIES AND THEIR COUNTY SEAT

ALLEGANY COUNTY/ CUMBERLAND

ANNE ARUNDEL COUNTY/ ANNAPOLIS

BALTIMORE COUNTY/ TOWSON

CALVERT COUNTY/ PRINCE FREDERICK

CAROLINE COUNTY/ DENTON

CARROLL COUNTY/ WESTMINSTER

CECIL COUNTY/ ELKTON

CHARLES COUNTY/ LA PLATA

DORCHESTER COUNTY/ CAMBRIDGE

FREDERICK COUNTY/ FREDERICK

GARRETT COUNTY/ OAKLAND

HARFORD COUNTY/ BEL AIR

HOWARD COUNTY/ ELLICOTT CITY

KENT COUNTY/ CHESTERTOWN

MONTGOMERY COUNTY/ ROCKVILLE

PRINCE GEORGE'S COUNTY/ UPPER MARLBORO

QUEEN ANNE'S COUNTY/ CENTREVILLE

ST. MARY'S COUNTY/ LEONARDTOWN

SOMERSET COUNTY/ PRINCESS ANNE

TALBOT COUNTY/ EASTON

WASHINGTON COUNTY/ HAGERSTOWN

WICOMICO COUNTY/ SALISBURY

WORCESTER COUNTY/ SNOW HILL

MARYLAND COUNTIES AND THEIR ORDER OF ESTABLISHMENT

1.   ST. MARY'S (1637)
2.   KENT (1642)
3.   ANNE ARUNDEL (1650)
4.   CALVERT (1654)
5.   CHARLES (1658)
6.   BALTIMORE (1659)
7.   TALBOT (1661)
8.   SOMERSET (1666)
9.   DORCHESTER (1668)
10. CECIL (1674)
11. PRINCE GEORGE'S (1696)
12. QUEEN ANNE'S (1706)
13. WORCESTER (1742)
14. FREDERICK (1748)
15. CAROLINE (1773)
     HARFORD (1773)
17. WASHINGTON (1776)
     MONTGOMERY (1776)
19. ALLEGANY (1789)
20. CARROLL (1836)
21. HOWARD (1851)
22. WICOMICO (1867)
23. GARRETT (1872)

POPULATION

Maryland Counties and Baltimore City

	1998	2000*
Allegany	76,140	77,500
Anne Arundel	468,365	480,200
Baltimore	725,060	732,700
Baltimore City	663,110	643,300
Calvert	70,570	75,000
Caroline	29,920	30,600
Carroll	145,300	149,300
Cecil	81,420	83,700
Charles	118,340	123,200
Dorchester	30,210	30,350
Frederick	192,060	203,200
Garrett	30,170	30,650
Harford	219,600	226,600
Howard	239,310	253,500
Kent	19,120	19,350
Montgomery	835,370	855,000
Prince George's	794,860	812,100
Queen Anne's	39,940	41,600
St. Mary's	86,730	90,700
Somerset	24,710	25,000
Talbot	33,030	33,500
Washington	129,440	131,100
Wicomico	81,620	83,400
Worcester	41,910	43,300
State of Maryland Total	5,176,305	5,274,850

Source: State of Maryland, Office of Planning
*Year 2000: Projected

MARYLAND'S REGIONS:

THEIR COUNTIES & BALTIMORE CITY

WESTERN MARYLAND

Garrett, Allegany & Washington

CAPITAL REGION

Frederick, Montgomery & Prince George's

CENTRAL MARYLAND

*Carroll, Baltimore, Harford, Howard, Anne Arundel &
Baltimore City*

SOUTHERN MARYLAND

Calvert, Charles & St. Mary's

UPPER EASTERN SHORE

Cecil, Kent, Queen Anne's, Talbot & Caroline

LOWER EASTERN SHORE

Dorchester, Wicomico, Somerset, Worcester

MARYLAND STATE PARKS AND FORESTS

EASTERN REGION

Assateague State Park (Worcester County)
Choptank River Fishing Piers (Cambridge)
James Island State Park (Somerset County)
Martinak State Park (Caroline County)
Pocomoke River State Park (Worcester County)
Pocomoke River State Forest (Worcester County)
Shad Landing Area (Worcester County)
Tuckahoe State Park (Caroline & Queen Anne's Counties)
Wye Island (Queen Anne's County)
Wye Oak State Park (Talbot County)

CENTRAL REGION

Elk Neck State Park (Cecil County)
Gunpowder Falls State Park (Harford & Baltimore Counties)
Hart-Miller Island State Park (Baltimore County waters)
North Point State Park (Baltimore County)
Patuxent River State Park (Howard & Montgomery Counties)
Patapsco Valley State Park (Baltimore, Howard, Carroll, Anne Arundel Counties)
Rocks State Park (Harford County)
Seneca Creek State Park (Montgomery County)
Soldiers Delight (Baltimore County)
Susquehanna State Park (Harford County)

SOUTHERN REGION

Calvert Cliffs State Park (Calvert County)
Cedarville State Forest (Prince George's & Charles Counties)
Merkle Wildlife Sanctuary (Prince George's County)
Point Lookout State Park (St. Mary's County)
Sandy Point State Park (Anne Arundel County)
St. Clement's Island (St. Mary's County, in the Potomac River)
St. Mary's River State Park (St. Mary's County)
Smallwood State Park (Charles County)

WESTERN REGION

Big Run State Park (Garrett County)
Casselman River Bridge State Park (Garrett County)
Cunningham Falls State Park (Frederick County)
Dans Mountain State Park (Allegany County)
Deep Creek Lake State Park (Garrett County)
Fort Frederick State Park (Washington County)
Gambrill State Park (Frederick County)
Garrett State Forest (Garrett County)
Gathland State Park (Washington & Frederick Counties)
Greenbrier State Park (Washington County)
Green Ridge State Forest (Allegany County)
Herrington Manor State Park (Garrett County)
New Germany State Park (Garrett County)
Potomac State Forest (Garrett County)
Rocky Gap State Park (Allegany County)
Savage River State Forest (Garrett County)
South Mountain State Park (Washington & Frederick Counties)
Swallow Falls State Park (Garrett County)
Washington Monument State Park (Washington County)

CHRONOLOGY OF MARYLAND'S
BARONS OF BALTIMORE
LORDS OF PROPRIETARY
&
GOVERNORS
1625 to PRESENT

BARONS OF BALTIMORE AND LORDS PROPRIETARY

1625-1632 - George Calvert (1580-1632)

He received the title, Baron of Baltimore, from James I, King of England, and became 1st Lord Baltimore in February 1625.

1632-1675 - Cecilius Calvert (1605-1675)

2nd Lord Baltimore. Succeeded to title on death of George, April 13, 1632. Granted Charter of Maryland by Charles I, King of England, on June 20, 1632.

1675-1715 - Charles Calvert (1637-1715)

3rd Lord Baltimore. Succeeded to title on death on Cecilius, November 30, 1675.

1715-1715 - Benedict Leonard Calvert (1679-1715)

4th Lord Baltimore. Succeeded to title on death of Charles, February 21, 1715.

1715-1751 - Charles Calvert (1699-1751)

5th Lord Baltimore. Succeeded to title on death of Benedict Leonard, April 16, 1715.

1751-1771 - Frederick Calvert (1731-1771)

6th Lord Baltimore. Succeeded to title on death of Charles, April 24, 1751.

1771-1776 - Henry Harford (ca. 1759-1834)

Henry Harford did not succeed to title when Frederick died on September 4, 1771, because Harford was his illegitimate son, but was bequeathed the province of Maryland in Frederick's will. After the Revolution, Harford relinquished his claim to Maryland in return for a monetary settlement from British government.

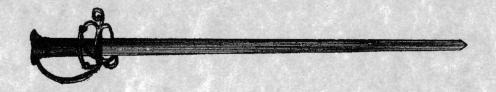

GOVERNORS
1634-1776

Governors under Proprietary and Parliamentary Government, 1634-1689

1634-1645 - Leonard Calvert

1645-1646 - Captain Richard Ingle
        Usurped the government and maintained control until about the middle of
        1646.

1646 -   Captain Edward Hill
        Elected governor by the council while Leonard Calvert was in Virginia. Hill
        claimed to have a commission from Calvert. His appointment was illegal, as
        he was not a member of the council when elected. It appears that he truly
        held office, for he later attempted to collect fees due him by virtue of his
        service.

1646-1647 - Leonard Calvert

1647-1649 - Thomas Greene

1649-1652 - William Stone
        During his absences, he left the following men to act in his place:
        Thomas Greene, 1649; Thomas Hatton, 1650.

1652-1658 - Parliamentary Commissioners: Richard Bennett and William Claiborne.

1652-1656 - William Stone
        Stone's commission as governor was contested by the Parliamentary
        Commissioners.

1654-1657 - Commissioners appointed by the Parliamentary Commissioners.
William Fuller/Richard Preston/William Durand/Edward Lloyd/John Smith/
John Lawson/Richard Wells/Leonard Strong/John Hatch/Richard Ewen.

Richard Bennett and William Claiborne, with authorization from the Puritan
government in England, issued an ordinance July 22, 1654, to ten Marylanders
as commissioners "for the well Ordering, directing and Governing the affaires
of Maryland" with powers that included the right to summon assemblies.
Later additions to the body of commissioners were: William Parker/Robert
Slye/Thomas Meeres/Thomas Marsh/Sampson Waring/Michael Brooke/John
Pott/Woodman Stockley/William Parrott/Philip Morgan/William Ewen/Thomas
Thomas/Philip Thomas/Samuel Withers and Richard Woolman.
The commissioners surrendered their powers to the restored proprietary
government March 24, 1657.

1657-1660 - Josias Fendall
During his absence, he appointed Luke Barber to serve in his place from
June 1657 to February 1658.

1660-1661 - Philip Calvert

1661-1676 - Charles Calvert

1676   Jesse Wharton

1676-1679 - Thomas Notley

1679-1684 - Charles Calvert, Lord Proprietary

1684-1688 - Council of Deputy Governors
George Talbot/Thomas Tailler/Colonel Vincent Lowe/Colonel William Stevens
Colonel William Burgess/Major Nicholas Sewall and John Darnall.

1688-1689 - William Joseph

Governors under Royal Government, 1689-1715

1689-1690 - John Coode
    Leader of the Protestant Associators who seized the government on
    August 1, 1689.

1691-1692 - Nehemiah Blakiston
    Appointed president of the committee for the Government of Maryland when
    Coode went to England.

1692-1693 - Sir Lionel Copley

1693   Sir Thomas Lawrence
    Served only two weeks until Sir Edmond Andros arrived in Maryland and
    assumed control of the government.

1693   Sir Edmond Andros
    Stayed in Maryland only ten days before returning to Virginia.

1693-1694 - Colonel Nicholas Greenberry
    Appointed president of the council by Andros.

1694   Sir Edmond Andros
    Stayed in Maryland one week.

1694   Sir Thomas Lawrence
    Appointed president of the council by Andros.

1694-1699 - Sir Francis Nicholson

1699-1702 - Colonel Nathaniel Blakiston

1702-1704 - Thomas Tench
>Appointed president of the council by Blakiston.

1704-1709 - Colonel John Seymour

1709-1714 - Major General Edward Lloyd
>Elected president of the council when Colonel Francis Jenkins, who was a senior member of the council, failed to assert his right in a timely manner.

1714-1715 - John Hart

Government under restored Proprietary Government, 1715-1776

1715-1720 - John Hart
>Continued to serve as governor after control of the province was returned to Charles, 5th Lord Baltimore.

1720 Thomas Brooke
>Became president by virtue of his seniority when Hart returned to England.

1721-1727 - Charles Calvert

1727-1731 - Benedict Leonard Calvert

1731-1732 - Samuel Ogle

1732-1733 - Charles Calvert, Lord Proprietary

1733-1742 - Samuel Ogle

1742-1747 - Thomas Bladen

1747-1752 - Samuel Ogle

1752-1753 - Benjamin Tasker
> Became president of the council on death of Governor Ogle.

1753-1769 - Horatio Sharpe

1769-1776 - Robert Eden
> During Eden's absence, Richard Lee governed the province. Lee also governed the province briefly in 1776 after Eden's departure and before the assumption of the government by the convention.

GOVERNORS 1777-Present

By the Maryland Constitution of 1776, the governor was chosen annually by a joint ballot of both houses of the General Assembly (Md. Const. 1776, section 25). The governor was required to be at least 25 years of age; a state resident for at least five years prior to the election; and was required to hold real and personal property in the state having a value of five thousand pounds or more, one thousand of which was to be freehold estate (Md. Const. 1776, section 30). The governor was limited to three successive one-year terms and in the four years thereafter could not serve again (Md. Const. 1776, section 31).

The first popular election for governor was held October 3, 1838, in accordance with a 1837 constitutional amendment (Acts of 1836, chapter 197). Per this amendment the state was divided into three gubernatorial election districts:

1st District (Eastern District)
Caroline, Cecil, Dorchester, Kent, Queen Anne's, Somerset, Talbot and Worcester counties.

2nd District (Northwestern District)
Allegany, Baltimore, Carroll, Frederick, Harford and Washington counties.

3rd District (Southern District)
Baltimore City, Anne Arundel, Calvert, Charles, Montgomery, Prince George's,
St.Mary's
counties.

The governor was to be elected every three years by the voters of one gubernatorial district, on a rotating basis. This process of voters from a single gubernatorial district selecting the governor continued through the election of 1864.

The Maryland Constitution of 1851 continued the system of gubernatorial election districts. It raised the minimum age of candidates to thirty. The governor was required to have been a U.S. citizen and state resident for five years, and a resident of the district from which he was elected for three years. The term of the governor was lengthened to four years (Md. Const. 1851, Article 2. secs. 1, 6).

Gubernatorial election districts were eliminated by the 1864 Constitution. Thereafter, beginning with the election of 1868, the governor was elected by vote of the entire state's electorate. The 1864 Constitution also ended district residency requirements for candidates (Md. Const. 1864, Article 2, sec. 5).

The Maryland Constitution of 1867 required the governor to have been a citizen of the state of Maryland for ten years, a Maryland resident for five years, and a qualified voter at the time of the election (Md. Const. 1867, Article 2, sec.5).

The governor was limited to two consecutive terms by constitutional amendment ratified in 1948 (Acts of 1947, ch.109).

In 1970, a constitutional amendment required that the governor be a resident and registered voter of the state for only five years preceding the election (Acts of 1970, ch. 532).

GOVERNORS, 1777-1839

Elected by Legislature for one-year term under Constitution of 1776

1777-1779 - Thomas Johnson - No Political Party
Born: November 4, 1732, Calvert County.
Died: October 26, 1819, Rose Hill, Frederick County
Buried: All Saints' Parish Cemetery, Frederick, Md.

1779-1782 - Thomas Sim Lee - No Political Party
Born: October 29, 1745, Prince George's County.
Died: October 9, 1819, Needwood, Frederick, County.
Buried: Mt. Carmel Cemetery, Upper Marlboro, Prince George's County.

1782-1785 - William Paca - No Political Party
Born: October 31, 1740, Abingdon, Harford County.
Died: October 13, 1799, Wye Hall, Queen Anne's County.
Buried: Wye Hall, Queen Anne's County.

1785-1788 - William Smallwood - No Political Party
Born: 1732, Charles County.
Died: February 14, 1792, Mattawomen, Charles County.
Buried: Smallwood's Retreat, Charles County.

1788-1791 - John Eager Howard - Federalist
Born: June 4, 1752, Baltimore, Md.
Died: October 12, 1827, Baltimore City.
Buried: Old St. Paul's Cemetery, Baltimore.

1791-1792 - George Plater - Federalist
Born: November 8, 1735, St. Mary's County
Died: February 10, 1792, Annapolis
Buried: Sotterley, St. Mary's County[1]

1792-1794 - Thomas Sim Lee - (see above 1779-1782).

1794-1797 - John Hoskins Stone - Federalist
Born: 1750, Charles County
Died: October 5, 1804, Annapolis, Md.
Buried: Annapolis, Md.

1797-1798 - John Henry - Federalist
Born: November 1750, Weston, Dorchester County
Died: December 16, 1798, Weston, Dorchester County
Buried: Christ Protestant Episcopal Church Cemetery, Cambridge, Md.

1798-1801 - Benjamin Ogle - Federalist
Born: January 27, 1749, Annapolis, Md.
Died: July 6, 1809, Annapolis, Md.
Buried: Annapolis, Md.

1801-1803 - John Francis Mercer - Democrat
Born: May 17, 1759, Marlborough, Stafford County, Virginia.
Died: August 30, 1821, Philadelphia, Pa.
Buried: Cedar Park, Anne Arundel County.

1803-1806 - Robert Bowie - Democrat
Born: March 1750, Mattaponi, Prince George's County.
Died: January 8, 1818, Mattaponi, Prince George's County.
Buried: Mattaponi, Prince George's County.

---

[1]James Brice (1746-1801) became acting governor on the death of Governor Plater on February 10, 1792. He served until April 2, 1792, when Thomas Sim Lee was elected for the balance of the unexpired term.

1806-1809 - Robert Wright - Democrat
Born: November 20, 1752, Queen Anne's County.
Died: September 7, 1826, Blakeford, Queen Anne's County.
Buried: Cheston-on-Wye, Queen Anne's County.[2]

1809-1811 - Edward Lloyd - Democrat
Born: July 22, 1779, Talbot County.
Died: June 2, 1834, Annapolis, Md.
Buried: Wye House, Talbot County.[3]

1811-1812 - Robert Bowie (see above 1803-1806).

1812-1816 - Levin Winder - Federalist
Born: September 4, 1757, Somerset County.
Died: July 1, 1819, Baltimore City.
Buried: Monie Creek, Somerset County.

1816-1819 - Charles Ridgely of Hampton[4] - Federalist
Born: December 6, 1760, Baltimore County.
Died: July 17, 1829, Hampton, Baltimore County.
Buried: Hampton, Baltimore County.

1819 - Charles Goldsborough - Federalist
Born: July 15, 1765, Hunting Creek, Dorchester County.
Died: December 13, 1834, Shoal Creek, Dorchester County.
Buried: Christ Protestant Episcopal Church Cemetery, Cambridge.

---

[2]Governor Wright resigned on May 6, 1809. James Butcher of Queen Anne's County became acting governor. He served until June 5, 1809, when Edward Lloyd qualified.

[3]By Acts of 1811, chapter 211, ratified in 1812, the date of the election of the governor was changed from the second Monday in November to the second Monday in December.

[4]Charles Ridgely of Hampton was named Charles Ridgely Carnan at birth. In 1790, he legally assumed the name Charles Ridgely in compliance with the terms of the will of his uncle, Captain Charles Ridgely.

1819-1822 - Samuel Sprigg - Democrat
Born: 1783, Prince George's County.
Died: April 21, 1855, Northampton, Prince George's County.
Buried: Oak Hill Cemetery, Georgetown, Washington, D.C.

1822-1826 - Samuel Stevens, Jr. - Democrat
Born: July 13, 1778, Talbot County.
Died: February 7, 1860, Compton, near Trappe, Talbot County.
Buried: Stevens family Cemetery, Talbot County.[5]

1826-1829 - Joseph Kent - Democrat
Born: January 14, 1779, Calvert County.
Died: November 24, 1837, Rosemount, Prince George's County.
Buried: Rosemount, Prince George's County.

1829-1830, - Daniel Martin - Anti-Jackson
Born: 1780, The Wilderness, Talbot County.
Died: July 11, 1831, Talbot County.
Buried: Spring Hill Cemetery, Easton, Talbot County.

1830-1831 - Thomas King Carroll - Jackson Democrat
Born: April 29, 1793, Kingston Hall, Somerset County.
Died: October 3, 1873, Dorchester County.
Buried: Old Trinity Church graveyard, Church Creek, Dorchester County.

1831 - Daniel Martin (see above 1829-1830).[6]

---

[5]By Acts of 1823, chapter 111, ratified in 1824, the date for holding the election for governor was changed to the first Monday in January.

[6]Governor Martin died in office on July 11, 1831. George Howard succeeded him. Governor Howard completed Governor Martin's term, which expired in January 1832 and was subsequently elected by the legislature for a one-year term.

1831-1833 - George Howard - Anti-Jackson
Born: November 21, 1789, Annapolis, Md.
Died: August 2, 1846, Waverly, Howard County.
Buried: Old St. Paul's Cemetery, Baltimore City.

1833-1836 - James Thomas - Anti-Jackson
Born: March 11, 1785, De La Brooke Manor, St. Mary's County.
Died: December 25, 1845, Deep Falls, St. Mary's County.
Buried: Deep Falls, St. Mary's County.

1836-1839 - Thomas W. Veazey - Whig
Born: January 31, 1774, Cecil County.
Died: July 1, 1842, Cecil County.
Buried: Family Cemetery, Cherry Grove, Cecil County.

GOVERNORS, 1839-1854

Elected by voters for three-year term under Constitution of 1776, amended 1837.[7]

1839-1842 - William Grason - Democrat
Born: March 11, 1788, Queen Anne's County.
Died: July 2, 1868, Queen Anne's County.
Buried: Queenstown, Queen Anne's County.

1842-1845 - Francis Thomas - Democrat
Born: February 3, 1799, Frederick County.
Died: January 22, 1876, Frankville, Garrett County.
Buried: St. Mark's Episcopal Church Cemetery, Petersville, Frederick County.

---

[7]By Acts of 1836, chapter 197, ratified in 1837, the term of the governor was extended to three years.

1845-1848 - Thomas G. Pratt - Whig
Born: February 18, 1804, Georgetown, Washington, D.C.
Died: November 9, 1869, Baltimore City.
Buried: St. Anne's Protestant Episcopal Church Cemetery, Annapolis, Md.

1848-1851 - Philip Francis Thomas - Democrat
Born: September 12, 1810, Easton, Talbot County.
Died: October 2, 1890, Baltimore City.
Buried: Spring Hill Cemetery, Easton, Talbot County.

1851-1854 - Enoch Louis Lowe - Democrat
Born: August 10, 1820, Frederick County.
Died: August 23, 1892, New York.
Buried: Catholic Cemetery, Frederick.

GOVERNORS, 1854-1866

Elected by voters for four-year term under Constitution of 1851[8]

1854-1858 - Thomas Watkins Ligon - Democrat
Born: May 10, 1810, Farmville, Prince Edward County, Virginia.
Died: January 12, 1881, Chatham, Howard County.
Buried: Family cemetery, Howard County.

1858-1862 - Thomas Holliday Hicks - Native American
Born: September 2, 1798, Dorchester County.
Died: February 13, 1865, Washington, D.C.
Buried: Cambridge Cemetery, Dorchester County.

---

[8]Under the Constitution of 1851, the term of the governor began on the second Wednesday in January following his election and was for four years.

1862-1866 - Augustus W. Bradford - Unionist
Born: January 9, 1806, Bel Air, Harford County.
Died: March 1, 1881, Baltimore City.
Buried: Green Mount Cemetery, Baltimore City.

GOVERNORS, 1866-1869
Elected by voters for four-year term under Constitution of 1864[9]

1866-1869 - Thomas Swann - Unionist
Born: 1806, Alexandria, Virginia.
Died: July 24, 1883, Leesburg, Virginia.
Buried: Green Mount Cemetery, Baltimore City.

GOVERNORS, 1869 to Present
Elected by voters for four-year term under Constitution of 1867

1869-1872 - Oden Bowie - Democrat
Born: November 10, 1826, Prince George's County
Died: December 4, 1894, Fairview, Prince George's County
Buried: Fairview, Prince George's County

1872-1874 - William Pinkney Whyte - Democrat
Born: August 9, 1824, Baltimore City
Died: March 17, 1908, Baltimore City
Buried: Green Mount Cemetery, Baltimore City

1874-1876 - James Black Groome - Democrat
Born: April 4, 1838, Cecil County
Died: October 4, 1893, Baltimore City
Buried: Presbyterian Cemetery, Elkton, Cecil County

---

[9]The only election held under this constitution was on the first Tuesday after the first Monday in November 1864.

1876-1880 - John Lee Carroll - Democrat
Born: September 30, 1830, Baltimore City
Died: February 27, 1911, Washington, D.C.
Buried: Bonnie Brae Cemetery, Howard County

1880-1884 - William T. Hamilton - Democrat
Born: September 8, 1820, Washington County
Died: October 26, 1888, Hagerstown, Md.
Buried: Rose Hill Cemetery, Hagerstown, Washington County

1884-1885 - Robert M. McLane - Democrat
Born: June 23, 1815, Wilmington, Delaware
Died: April 16, 1898, Paris, France
Buried: Green Mount Cemetery, Baltimore City[10]

1885-1888 - Henry Lloyd - Democrat
Born: February 21, 1852, Dorchester County
Died: December 30, 1920, Cambridge, Md.
Buried: Christ Protestant Episcopal Church Cemetery, Cambridge, Dorchester County

1888-1892 - Elihu E. Jackson - Democrat
Born: November 3, 1837, Somerset County
Died: December 27, 1907, Baltimore City
Buried: Parsons Cemetery, Salisbury, Md.

1892-1896 - Frank Brown - Democrat
Born: August 8, 1846, Carroll County
Died: February 3, 1920, Baltimore City
Buried: Green Mount Cemetery, Baltimore City

---

[10]Governor McLane resigned on March 27, 1885. Henry Lloyd, who was president of the Senate, succeeded him as acting governor until January 21, 1886, when the legislature elected him to complete the remainder of McLane's term

1896-1900 - Lloyd Lowndes - Republican
Born: February 21, 1845, Clarksburg, West Virginia
Died: January 8, 1905, Cumberland, Md.
Buried: Rose Hill Cemetery, Cumberland, Allegany County

1900-1904 - John Walter Smith - Democrat
Born: February 5, 1845, Worcester County
Died: April 19, 1925, Baltimore City
Buried: Presbyterian Cemetery, Snow Hill, Worcester County

1904-1908 - Edwin Warfield - Democrat
Born: May 7, 1848, Howard County
Died: March 31, 1920, Baltimore City
Buried: Family burial ground, Cherry Grove, Howard County

1908-1912 - Austin L. Crothers - Democrat
Born: May 17, 1860, Cecil County
Died: May 25, 1912, Elkton, Md.
Buried: West Nottingham Presbyterian Cemetery, Cecil County

1912-1916 - Phillips Lee Goldsborough - Republican
Born: August 6, 1865, Cambridge, Dorchester County
Died: October 22, 1946, Baltimore City
Buried: Christ Protestant Episcopal Church Cemetery, Cambridge, Dorchester County

1916-1920 - Emerson C. Harrington - Democrat
Born: March 26, 1864, Dorchester County
Died: December 15, 1945, Cambridge, Md.
Buried: Christ Protestant Episcopal Church Cemetery, Cambridge, Dorchester County

1920-1935 - Albert C. Ritchie - Democrat
Born: August 29, 1876, Richmond, Virginia
Died: February 24, 1936, Baltimore City
Buried: Green Mount Cemetery, Baltimore City[11]

1935-1939 - Harry W. Nice - Republican
Born: December 5, 1877, Washington, D.C.
Died: February 24, 1941, Richmond, Virginia
Buried: Green Mount Cemetery, Baltimore City

1939-1947 - Herbert R. O'Conor - Democrat
Born: November 17, 1896, Baltimore City
Died: March 4, 1960, Baltimore City
Buried: New Cathedral Cemetery, Baltimore City[12]

1947-1951 - William Preston Lane, Jr. - Democrat
Born: May 12, 1892, Washington County
Died: February 7, 1967, Hagerstown, Md.
Buried: Rose Hill Cemetery, Hagerstown, Md.[13]

1951-1959 - Theodore R. McKeldin - Republican
Born: November 20, 1900, Baltimore City
Died: August 10, 1974, Baltimore City
Buried: Green Mount Cemetery, Baltimore City

---

[11]Acts of 1922, chapter 227, provided for quadrennial elections. The governor elected in November 1923 held office for three years. Beginning with the election held on the first Tuesday after the first Monday in November 1926, elections were held in the even-numbered years which were not presidential election years.

[12]Governor O'Conor resigned on January 3, 1947 to accept a seat in the United States Senate. William Preston Lane, Jr.,was elected by the legislature on January 3 of that year to complete the unexpired term. Governor Lane was inaugurated on January 3 for the remainder of Governor O'Conor's term and on January 8, 1947, for the full four-year term.

[13]Acts of 1947, chapter 109, established a two-term limit for each governor.

1959-1967 - J. Millard Tawes - Democrat
Born: April 8, 1894, Somerset County
Died: June 25, 1979, Crisfield, Md.
Buried: Sunny Ridge Memorial Park, Crisfield, Somerset County[14]

1967-1969 - Spiro T. Agnew - Republican
Born: November 9, 1918, Baltimore City
Resigned: January 7, 1969[15]

1969-1979 - Marvin Mandel - Democrat
Born: April 19, 1920, Baltimore City[16]
Lieutenant Governors[17]
Lieutenant Governor: 1971-1979 Blair Lee III - Born: Silver Spring, Md., May 16, 1916; Died: October 25, 1985

1979-1987 - Harry R. Hughes - Democrat
Born: November 13, 1926, Easton, Talbot County
Lieutenant Governor: 1979-1982; Samuel W. Bogley - Born: Washington, D.C., November 16, 1941
Lieutenant Governor: 1983-1987; J.Joseph Curran, Jr. - Born: West Palm Beach, Florida, July 7, 1931

1987-1994 - William Donald Schaefer - Democrat
Born: November 2, 1921, Baltimore City
Lieutenant Governor: 1987-1994; Melvin A. Steinberg - Born: Baltimore City, October 4, 1933

1994-Present - Parris N. Glendening - Democrat
Born: June 11, 1942, Bronx, New York
Lieutenant Governor: 1994-Present; Kathleen Kennedy Townsend[18] - Born: July 4, 1951.

---

[14] Acts of 1964, chapter 161, changed the date of the beginning of the governor's term to the fourth Wednesday in January following his election.

[15] Governor Agnew resigned on January 7, 1969, having been elected vice-president of the United States. Marvin Mandel was elected by the General Assembly on the same day to fill the balance of Governor Agnew's term, which expired in January 1971. Governor Mandel was subsequently elected by the voters to a full four-year term on November 3, 1970.

[16] Acts of 1970, chapter 576, changed the date of the beginning of the governor's term to the third Wednesday in January following his election. By a letter dated June 4, 1977, Governor Mandel notified Lieutenant Governor Blair Lee III that Lee would serve as acting governor until further notice according to the terms of Article 2, Section 6b, of the Maryland Constitution of 1867. Lee continued to act in the capacity of acting governor until January 15, 1979, when Mandel rescinded his letter of June 4, 1977, two days before the expiration of his second full elective term. Governor Mandel also designated Lee acting governor for a brief period on January 16, to, permit Lee to preside at the installation of Rita C. Davidson to the Court of Appeals.

[17] The office of lieutenant governor was created by the Constitution of 1864. The lieutenant governor served as president of the Senate, and acted as governor in case of the death, resignation, removal from the state, or other disqualification. The only incumbent of that office under the Constitution of 1864 was Christopher C. Cox, who was elected on November 8, 1864, took the oath of office on January 11, 1865, and served until January 8, 1868. The Constitution of 1867 did not provide for a lieutenant governor. The office was reestablished by a constitutional amendment ratified on November 3, 1970.

[18] Kathleen Kennedy Townsend is the daughter of Robert F. Kennedy, and is Maryland's first woman lieutenant governor.

MARYLAND'S

OFFICIAL STATE

SYMBOLS

THE GREAT SEAL OF MARYLAND

The Great Seal of Maryland is used by the Governor and the Secretary of State to authenticate Acts of the General Assembly and for other official purposes. The first Great Seal was sent from England shortly after settlement of the colony. With the exception of the period during crown rule (1692-1715), when different seals were used, the first Great Seal remained in use, although slightly altered, until the Revolution. The State of Maryland then adopted a new seal similar in form and spirit to those of other states. One hundred years later, the State of Maryland readopted its old seal (Joint Resolution no. 5, Acts of 1876). The reverse of this seal is the only part which has ever been cut. The obverse is still considered part of the seal and is often used to adorn public buildings.

The reverse consists of an escutcheon, or shield, bearing the Calvert and Crossland arms quartered. Above is an earl's coronet and a full-faced helmet. The escutcheon is supported on one side by a farmer and the other a fisherman. It symbolizes Lord Baltimore's two estates: Maryland, and Avalon in Newfoundland. The Calvert motto on the scroll is "Fatti maschii parole femine," which is usually translated "manly deeds, womanly words." The Latin legend on the border (the last verse of Psalms 5 from the Vulgate) is translated "with favor wilt thou compass us as with a shield." The date, 1632, refers to the year the Maryland charter was granted by Charles I, King of England, to Cecilius Calvert, second Lord Baltimore. The obverse of the Seal shows Lord Baltimore as a knight in full armor mounted on a charger. The inscription translated is "Cecilius, Absolute Lord of Maryland and Avalon, Baron of Baltimore."

FORMER

GREAT SEALS

OF

MARYLAND

GREAT SEAL OF ca. 1634

All that remains of the first Great Seal of Maryland is a fragment on a St. Mary's County land patent, dated July 10, 1640. The seal probably was similar to the 1648 seal. The great Seal of ca. 1634 was lost when it was "Treacherously and Violently taken away" by Richard Ingle and his accomplices in the antiproprietary rebellion of 1644.

GREAT SEAL OF 1648
(Reverse)

Fashioned of silver, the Great Seal of 1648 was sent to Maryland by Lord Baltimore to replace the seal lost in Ingle's Rebellion. The reverse shows Lord Baltimore's hereditary coat of arms, incorporating heraldic elements of the Calvert (paternal) and Crossland (maternal) families. The plowman and fisherman supporting the shield probably signify the bounties of Maryland's land and water resources.

GREAT SEAL DEPUTED OF WILLIAM & MARY, 1692

During the royal period, 1692-1715, the Great Seal of the Calvert family was replaced by royal seals, called deputed seals, for use on all official acts of government. The first of these deputed seals, the William & Mary Great Seal, is known by a single example on a proclamation of Governor John Seymour. The border design cannot be determined, but the center bears the WMR royal cipher. The Maryland great seals deputed were unique among colonial royal seals in incorporating the royal cipher.

GREAT SEAL DEPUTED OF QUEEN ANNE, 1706

No impression of the first Queen Anne Seal (1706-1712), or of the second Queen Anne Seal (1712-1715), which was dispatched to Maryland after the unification of England and Scotland, has been found on a Maryland document. A proof impression of the first Queen Anne Seal for Maryland was deposited in the British Royal Mint, however, and wax copies produced from the proof show its form.

GREAT SEAL OF 1648
(Obverse)

When Benedict, fourth Lord Baltimore, embraced the Anglican faith, full control of Maryland was returned in 1715 to the formerly Catholic Calvert family. Use of the Great Seal of 1648 was resumed on all official acts of government. The obverse, showing Lord Baltimore in an equestrian pose, originally bore on its border the name of Cecilius, second Lord Baltimore. Sometime after Charles, third Lord Baltimore, became proprietor in 1675, the seal was recut substituting the Latin "Carolus" for the former Cecilius.

GREAT SEAL OF 1794
(Reverse)

The first Constitution of Maryland provided that the Governor's Council determine what the great seal of the state should be. At first the Council simply ordered that the Great Seal of 1648 be continued. But in 1794 the Council ordered a new seal that eliminated all reference to the Calvert family. The new seal was designed by the noted American artist, Charles Willson Peale. The seal shows a tobacco hogshead and tobacco leaves, sheaves of wheat, a cornucopia, and a ship in the background, all symbols of Maryland's agriculture and trade.

GREAT SEAL OF 1817

Impressions of all earlier Maryland seals had been made in softened wax. The wax seal was then suspended, pendant-like, from the document by a paper or cloth ribbon. The Great Seal of 1817 was designed to emboss the image into the paper itself, a more efficient means of sealing. The engraved seal was made of steel. Its main decorative device is the American eagle surrounded by a border ornamented with thirteen points, symbolizing the original thirteen states.

THE GREAT SEAL OF MARYLAND

1632 1854

CRESCITE ET MULTIPLICAMINI

OF
MARYLAND

GREAT SEAL OF 1854

In 1854 the General Assembly ordered a new seal. Agreeing with Governor E. Louis Lowe that Maryland's seal should "consist of the arms of the state, and not of a device which has no significant relation to its local history," the legislature ordered a return to the Calvert design. Unfortunately, a crude woodcut was used as the model. Several inaccuracies resulted, most notably the use of only five bars, or pales, in the Calvert quadrant of the shield, and the use of the "increase and multiply" motto on the scroll.

GREAT SEAL OF 1876

The Great Seal of 1876 was ordered to correct the inaccuracies of the 1854 seal. The only important deviations from the original Calvert design were the addition of the date, 1632, to mark the years that the Charter of Maryland was granted, and reversing the direction of the pennons atop the two staffs. The seal was cut in brass in Paris, France, and placed in use in early 1879. Although new die have been cut, the 1876 seal remains the Great Seal of Maryland.

STATE FLAG

The father of George Calvert, first baronet of Baltimore, was Leonard Calvert, a country gentlemen of Yorkshire. He married Alicia Crossland, daughter and heiress of John Crossland, another Yorkshire gentlemen. Both families were of the class entitled to have arms. But, it was not until George Calvert was made baronet in 1617, that there was a petition to have the arms of the Calverts certified.

The first exemplification was made by the English heralds in 1622. It showed the black and gold pales with bend that makes the first and fourth quarters of the Maryland State Flag today. The Calvert and Crossland arms are first shown quartered together in the Seal of Maryland. The original Seal probably had the quartering, but unfortunately, it was lost, and there is no exact description of its design. It was replaced in 1648 by Cecil Calvert, the second Lord Proprietary. He remarked that the replacement was very much like the first. The quartering of the two coats of arms together, therefore, is of old usage of the Seal. However, it does not appear in the Flag until much later.

From 1634 until the Revolution, there are from time to time mentions of the Maryland Flag, and always these refer to the "yellow and black" of Lord Baltimore's colors, never to the red and white of the Crosslands. After the Revolution, there was no definite state flag in existence, either in custom or in law. There were a number of variations of the design, used pretty much ad libitum, for decorations and military emblems.

In 1885, Clayton C. Hall, a scholar from Baltimore, delivered an address on the Maryland Seal to the Maryland Historical Society, subsequently having the speech reprinted in pamphlet form. He gave a copy of the pamphlet to a Mr. Sisco, a flagmaker of Baltimore, the following year. Mr. Sisco manufactured a number of flags in the pattern of the one used today, apparently basing his design on information about the Seal gathered from the work of Mr. Hall.

In 1888, on the twenty-fifth anniversary of the Battle of Gettysburg, Maryland dedicated five monuments to Maryland regiments of the Army of the Potomac, that had taken part in the battle. A photograph of the ceremonies shows a flag in the pattern of the present one. The report of the monument commission, moreover, refers to this flag as the "State Flag." In 1889, on the seventy-fifth anniversary of the Battle of North Point (or Battle of Baltimore), flags were lavishly used in decorating buildings in Baltimore. The Baltimore Sun, describing these banners, makes it clear that they used both the Calvert and Crossland arms, but, from the wording of the story, one is in doubt as to whether the arms of the two families were combined in one flag or were shown in two different flags. In 1904, the present flag was adopted by law. The statute refers to it as the historic and traditional emblem of Maryland from the earliest times. It would appear, however, that in colonial days, the flag was simply the black and gold of the Calverts, and that during the first century of national existence, there was no official flag at all, and little agreement on any unofficial one.

The design of the Maryland Flag consists of the arms of the Calvert family quartered with the arms of the Crossland family. The Calvert family was that of the Lords Baltimore, the first Lord, George Calvert, being the founder of the colony of Maryland in 1634. The Crossland family was that of the first Lord's mother. As she had no brother and so was the heiress of her family estate, she was permitted under heraldic law to quarter her arms with those of her husband. Reading horizontally from the top of the staff, the first and second quarters are the Calvert and Crossland arms, respectively. Below are the same arms in reverse order.

The Calvert arms are six pales (perpendicular stripes) alternately or (gold) and sable (black), transverses from dexter chief (upper right corner) to sinister base (lower left corner) by a bend (band probably representing an ancient shoulder belt for carrying a sword) counterchanged (black where it crosses a gold stripe, gold where it crosses a black one). In the upper quarter, the first gold pale must be next to the flagstaff, and the extreme upper corner of the bend will be black. This is important, because if the flag is displayed upside down, a black pale will be next to the flagstaff, which is incorrect. The Crossland arms are quarterly, argent (silver) and gules (red), and a cross bottony counterchanged. In flags the color silver is represented by white. The cross bottony is a cross with extremities resembling a tre-foil plant. Article 60A, Chapter 862, Acts of 1945, Annotated Code of Maryland, is the authority for ornamenting the staff of the Maryland Flag with a gold cross bottony. This Act reads, "If any ornament is affixed to the top of a flagstaff carrying the Flag of Maryland, it shall be a gold cross bottony." The adjective is usually spelled either "botone" or "botony," but as the form in the law is "bottony," that spelling becomes correct and legal in Maryland.

STATE SONG

"Maryland, My Maryland," a nine-stanza poem, was written by James Ryder Randall in 1861. Randall wrote the poem in the early days of the Civil War because he was outraged when Union troops marched through Baltimore. This poem articulated his Confederate sympathies. "Maryland, My Maryland" was adopted as the State song in 1939.

My Maryland.

STATE TREE

The State tree is the White Oak or the Wye Oak. While King Henry VIII ruled England (1509-1547) a white oak acorn sprouted in the earth of the atlantic seaboard on the newly discovered continent of North America. The little seedling took root on a peninsula called "Chesopieoc" by the Indians. By the time Lord Baltimore's English settlers came and proclaimed the colony Maryland (1634) our oak was a magnificent, mature tree. Plantations sprang up along the Wye River site in the 1660's and a mill was established at the site. By the time the United States had successfully survived the Revolution and Maryland had ratified the U.S. Constitution (1788) the Wye Oak still lived and continued to live and survive the second war with England and leaf out every spring through the Civil War. Today the venerable oak is a part of the Wye Oak State Park, located in Talbot County. State foresters and the Maryland Arborists' Association care for the Wye Oak which is still in a state of remarkably good health. Its height is ninety-five feet, with a horizonal spread of one hundred sixty-five feet. The trunk is more than twenty-one feet in circumference, and its age is estimated at well over four hundred years. Because of its inspiring tenacity and impressive size the State of Maryland designated the Wye Oak the official tree of Maryland in 1941.

STATE SPORT

The equestrian sport of jousting was made Maryland's official sport in 1962. Jousting in its original form has generally been credited to a French man named Geoffori de Pruelli. The "sport" which at the time was more of an occupation, spread from France to Germany, to England, and into Europe during the tenth and twelfth centuries. Jousting tournaments were held as military exercises between the various nobles. These tournaments, which started peacefully, often turned into bloody battles between jealous champions. Winning these tournaments was one way for a low-born knight to make a quick name for himself and win riches beyond ordinary means. Over time, these petty local wars became more sport oriented and sophisticated and less a matter of life or death. Knights were considered gentlemen and were required to abide by the ideas of chivalry and fair play, then in vogue. Much of the credit for this fair-play code has always gone to King Arthur and the tales of the Round Table, a thirteenth century publicity stunt dreamed up by monks to raise money for rebuilding their abbey.

The first accounts of "Running at the Rings" dates to the days of James I of England, whereby knights demonstrated their skill, since the rings were obviously much smaller to lance than a man. The death of several nobles and at least one king, King Henry II of France in 1559, brought about the demise of the man-to-man type jousting. Also during this time gunpowder was introduced into Europe from the Orient. Thus guns made warfare by horse-mounted lancers obsolete overnight. Although the precise evolution of ring jousting is not known, history does provide us with many well-documented great tournaments throughout the next several centuries. Cecil Calvert, Lord Baltimore, was the first to introduce jousting in Maryland. In present times, jousting in Europe has declined, whereas Americans have built interest steadily. Each autumn in Washington, D.C., a national title is contested, with riders from many states competing.

So what exactly is jousting? In keeping with traditions the modern knight is mounted on horseback, but instead of being dressed in a cumbersome suit of armour and charging at an opposing rider with a long pointed lance in an effort to unseat him, the knight of the twentieth century wears a conventional riding habit, and charges his mount down a dirt track laid out beneath three overhanging arches. He carries a traditional lance, and with it he endeavors to spear a ring suspended from each arch as his horse gallops down the track. In accordance with the rules of the sport, each rider is given three rides or charges at the so-called large rings, which are one inch in diameter. It is possible to have a total score of nine rings on three rides, since the knight has a chance to spear three rings on each charge.

After all the knights have completed their three turns, the rings are reduced in size to three-quarters of an inch in diameter, and all the riders with a perfect score on the larger rings are allowed to have one ride on rings of this size. Subsequently the remaining riders with a perfect score again ride on rings of one-half inch in diameter, and this is where the victor usually emerges, as these very small rings are a severe test for even the best of the knights. In the case of a tie on one-half inch rings, the smallest is then used being one-quarter inch in diameter.

To the inexperienced spectator, it may appear simple, but it isn't as easy as it looks. The knights spend many hours practicing, and depend heavily on their horses, as a well-trained mount is indispensable to a tournament rider. For this reason, jousters spend weeks teaching their horses to respond to words rather than to the reins. Each rider's undivided attention must be on the rings, and without a horse that is well-trained it would be impossible. Often it takes two to three years before a horse is ready for riding in tournaments.

Unlike their ancestors, the modern knights do not devote their lives to jousting. They come from all walks of life; farmers, businessmen, professionals, as well as many others. Many represent the third, fourth and fifth generations of their family to participate in the sport. There are men, women, fathers and sons, brother combinations, and sister and brother combinations, all of whom ride for the love of the sport as there are no profits for the participants. Although prize money is awarded, this generally only covers the cost of the trip to the tournament, as many travel hundreds of miles with a car, horse and trailer. Each knight in keeping with the tradition has a title such as "Knight of Cedar

Lane" or "Knight of Little Woods" or in the case of a lady, it might be "Maid of Bartram Manor." These titles are chosen by the knights themselves and are usually names of estates, hometowns, streets, and occasionally one or two of them will take on a humorous aspect, such as "Knight of Will If I Can."

Jousting equipment has never been standardized, and is impossible to purchase from any store. For example, all the jousting lances are handmade. They average anywhere between five feet and seven feet in length and weigh anywhere between one and fifteen pounds, depending on the material used. The point of the lance is, on the average, two feet long and made of metal, aluminum, or stainless steel. The stock is usually made of wood, and its length depends largely on how long and how heavy the point is. The main concern in making a lance should be the balancing point, because when the lance is used it is held at the balance point. Additionally, very few jousting fields are alike, due to inadequate space available. An example of a field would be: Forty yards of starting room before the first arch. Thirty yards between the first and second, and second and third arches, then sixty yards after the last arch for stopping the horse, for a total of one hundred sixty yards. If this in not possible, yardage may be subtracted from the beginning and the end, however the thirty yards between each arch must stay the same, for the purpose of timing. A timing mark or pole is placed twenty yards before the first arch. Timing starts at this point and ends at the third arch, a total of eighty yards. Standard time to complete the course is nine seconds in regular jousts and eight seconds in championship jousts.

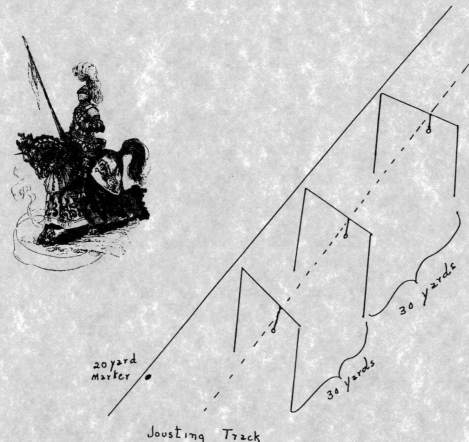

20 yard Marker

30 yards

30 yards

Jousting Track

By tradition, immediately following a joust, the crowning ceremony is held. The winning knight steps forward to claim his prize and to place upon the head of the lady of his choice the traditional wreath of flowers. In performing this ritual he crowns her "Queen of Love and Beauty." At this time the knights who placed second, third, and fourth also crown the ladies of their choice with wreaths of flowers, and these ladies become the first, second, and third maids of the Queen's Court.

The National Jousting Association as well as the Jousting Hall of Fame are located in Natural Chimneys Regional Park, in Mt. Solon, Virginia. Each year since 1821 the "Hall of Fame Joust" has been held here. The Hall of Fame depicts an honor roll of Jousting Champions, as well as a history of the sport and jousting memorabilia.

There are five jousting clubs or associations in Maryland. These are: The Maryland Jousting Tournament Association; The Amateur Jousting Club of Maryland, Inc.; The Central Maryland Jousting Club, Inc.; Eastern Shore of Maryland Jousting Association and the Western Maryland Jousting Club. Each year there are approximately fifty jousting tournaments, exhibitions, and championships held at various locations throughout the State of Maryland.

STATE FLOWER

The Black-Eyed Susan has been the official State flower since 1918. A yellow daisy, it blooms in late summer.

STATE BIRD

The Baltimore Oriole has been the official State bird since 1947. In 1882 special provisions were made for its protection. (Chapter 154, 1882). The oriole's colors are black and yellow, the same colors as in the Calvert shield.

STATE DOG

The Chesapeake Bay Retriever was declared the official state dog in 1964.

STATE BOAT

The skipjack was designated the State Boat in 1985. Skipjacks, named after a leaping fish, are the last working boats under sail in the United States.

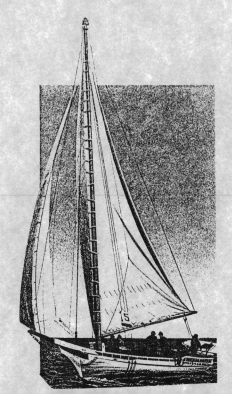

STATE FISH

The striped bass or rockfish was designated as the official State Fish in 1965.

STATE CRUSTACEAN

In 1989, the Maryland Blue Crab was designated as the official State Crustacean.

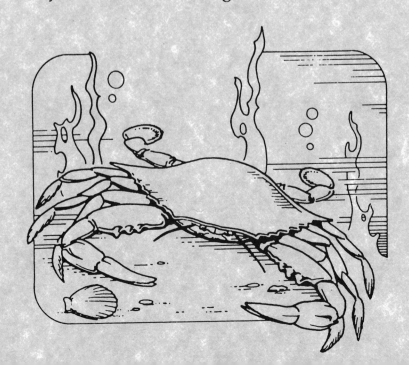

STATE FOSSIL SHELL

The Ecphora quadricostata, an extinct snail was designated as the official State Fossil Shell in 1984. The Ecphora inhabited the Chesapeake Bay 5 to 12 million years ago. One of the shells was found in St. Mary's County in 1685, believed to be the first North American fossil illustrated in scientific works.

STATE INSECT

The Baltimore Checkerspot Butterfly is the official arthropodic emblem of the State, designated in 1973.

Maryland

People, Places, Things and Events

as Commemorated

on

United States Postage Stamps

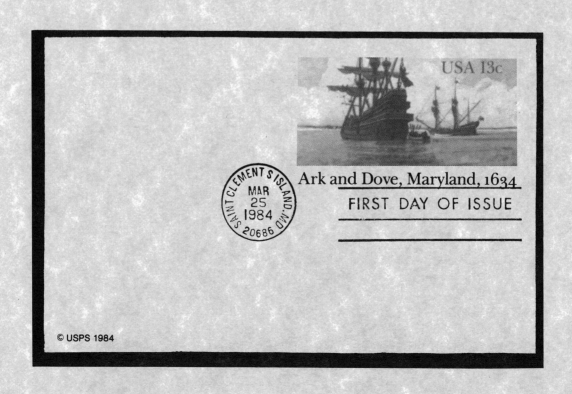

Ark and Dove, Maryland, 1634

FIRST DAY OF ISSUE

USA 13c

SAINT CLEMENTS ISLAND, MD
MAR 25 1984 20686

Maryland Tercentenary Commemorative, The Ark and the Dove
Issued at St. Mary's City, Maryland, March 23, 1934

Annapolis Tercentenary Commemorative, Issued at Annapolis, Maryland
May 23, 1949

Seal of the United States Naval Academy and Naval Cadets Issue
Issued at Annapolis, Maryland, May 26, 1937

American Bicentennial Issue, The Spirit of '76
Issued at Washington, D.C., February 15, 1988

15-Star Fort McHenry Flag Issue, Issued at Baltimore, Maryland
June 30, 1978

Historic Flag Issue, Fort McHenry Flag
Issued at Pittsburgh, Pennsylvania, July 4, 1968

Francis Scott Key, Issued at Frederick, Maryland, August 9, 1948

American Credo Issue, Francis Scott Key Quotation
Issued at Baltimore, Maryland, September 14, 1960

Black Heritage USA Series, recognizing the contributions of Black Americans
to the growth and development of the United States
Harriet Tubman and Cart Carrying Slaves, Issued at Washington, D.C., February 1, 1978
Benjamin Banneker and Benjamin as Surveyor, Issued at Annapolis, Maryland, February 15, 1979

Clara Barton Commemorative, Issued September 7, 1948 at Oxford, Massachusetts

State Birds and Flowers Issue
The Baltimore Oriole, Maryland's State Bird and the Black-eyed Susan, Maryland's State Flower
Issued at Washington, D.C., August 14, 1982

Butterflies Issue
Issued in a block of four different butterflies, one of which is the Checkerspot Butterfly,
Maryland's State Butterfly, Issued at Indianapolis, Indiana, June 6, 1977

American Trees Issue
Issued in a block of four different trees, one of which is the White Oak,
Maryland's State Tree, Issued at Hot Springs, Arkansas, October 9, 1978

Constitution Bicentennial Issue, Statehood, Issued at Washington, D.C.,
February 15, 1988

Maryland

Obsolete Bank Notes

&

Stock Certificates

Obsolete Bank Notes

What are obsolete bank notes? In the broadest sense of the term, U.S. obsolete paper money includes numerous types of no-longer-current paper money issued in the United States. It begins with the paper money of Britain's colonies in New England prior to the Revolutionary War. It also includes a myriad of merchants' issues of the seventeenth and eighteenth centuries, as well as issues of municipal, county and state governments, and the treasury notes of the Confederacy of 1861-1865.

One commonly hears the term "broken bank notes" applied to U.S. obsolete paper money. This term goes back to the days when bank failures were common. These failed banks were "broken" and their paper was "broken bank" notes. Nevertheless, many state banks either honorably wound up their business or converted over to national banks. Many of those early national banks or their successors exist today and some still redeem the old issues of their predecessors. So the term "obsolete paper money" is much preferred over "broken bank notes" because many of the banks did not fail and also because many issuers were merchants and other non-banks.

With the National Currency legislation of 1863-1865, the right of issuing their own notes was essentially removed from the banks by the Federal Government. For practical purposes, the state banks were obliged to close, carry on without issuing notes or convert to national banks and issue the new National Currency. Most close the latter option. Thus, the state bank note period ended in 1866.

During the period that these now obsolete notes were issued, thirty-four states did so. They are: Alabama, Arkansas, Connecticut, Delaware, Florida, Georgia, Illinois, Indiana, Iowa, Kansas, Kentucky, Louisiana, Maine, MARYLAND, Massachusetts, Michigan, Minnesota, Mississippi, Missouri, Nebraska, New Hampshire, New Jersey, New York, North Carolina, Ohio, Pennsylvania, Rhode Island, South Carolina, Tennessee, Texas, Utah, Vermont, Virginia and Wisconsin. Additionally, notes were also issued by the District of Columbia, as well as many merchants and non-banks such as The Baltimore and Susquehanna

Railroad Company, The Chesapeake & Ohio Canal Company, and many others.

During this period the banks in Maryland that issued notes were: Allegany County Bank, American Bank, Baltimore Bank, Bank of Baltimore, City Bank of Baltimore, Bank of Caroline, Cecil Bank, Central Bank, Central Bank of Frederick, Centreville Bank, Chesapeake Bank, Chesapeake Bank of Baltimore, Bank of Chestertown, Citizens Bank, Citizens' Bank of Baltimore, Clinton Bank, Bank of Columbia, Bank of Commerce, Commercial & Farmers Bank of Baltimore, Commercial & Farmers Bank, Commercial Bank, Commercial Bank of Baltimore, Commercial Bank of Millington, Conococheaque Bank, Consolidated Bank of Maryland, Cumberland Bank of Allegany, Cumberland City Bank, Bank of Dorchester, Easton Bank of Maryland, Elkton Bank of Maryland, Exchange Bank, Farmers & Mechanics Bank, Farmers & Mechanics Bank of Carroll County, Farmers & Mechanics Bank of Frederick, Farmers & Mechanics Bank of Frederick County, Farmers & Mechanics Bank of Kent County, Farmers & Merchants Bank, Farmers & Merchants Bank of Baltimore, Farmers & Merchants Bank of Cecil County, Farmers & Merchants Bank of Greensborough, Farmers & Millers Bank of Hagerstown, Farmers & Planters Bank, Farmers & Planters Bank of Baltimore, Farmers Bank of Maryland, Farmers Bank of Somerset & Worcester, Farmers' & Merchants Bank, Farmers' Bank of Leonardtown, Fells Point Bank of Baltimore, Fisherman's Bank of Charlestown, Franklin Bank of Baltimore, Frederick County Bank and Frostburg Bank.

Others were: Hagerstown Bank, Hamilton Bank, Havre de Grace Bank, High Bridge Bank, Howard Bank, Bank of Howard County, Marine Bank of Baltimore, Bank of Maryland, Mechanics Bank, Mechanics Bank of Baltimore, Merchants Bank, Merchants Bank of Baltimore, Mineral Bank, Mineral Bank of Maryland, North & South Bank of Potomac, Patapsco Bank of Maryland, Peoples' Bank, Peoples' Bank of Baltimore, Planters Bank of Prince George's County, Real Estate Bank of Baltimore, Real Estate Bank of Frederick County, Bank of Salisbury, Bank of Somerset, Susquehanna Bank, Susquehanna Bridge and Bank Company, Union Bank, Union Bank of Maryland, Valley Bank of Maryland, Washington County Bank, Western Bank, Western Bank of Baltimore, and Bank of Westminster.

On the following pages are examples of several of these obsolete bank notes from various Maryland banks and companies. Today these notes are a much sought after item for collectors. They range in price from about twenty-five to thousands of dollars each, depending on type, quality, and rarity. Although shown here in black and white, many of these notes are quite colorful, and the engravings are of magnificent quality.

The first two notes featured below are very old and quite rare.

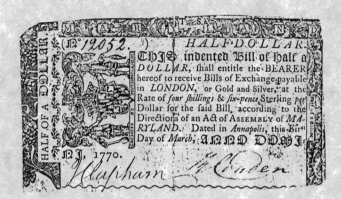
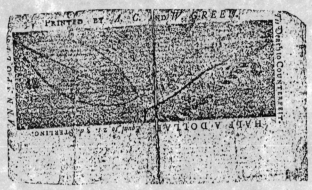

Half-Dollar Note, #12052 issued by the Directors of an Act of Assembly of Maryland
Dated in Annapolis, March 1, 1770
(Note: reverse side is written, "'Tis Death to Counterfeit")

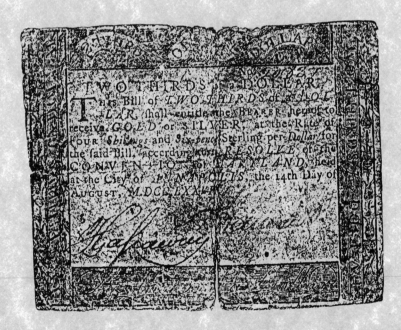

Two-Thirds of a Dollar note, issued by Resolve of the Convention of Maryland,
held at the city of Annapolis, August 14, 1776

One Hundred Dollar Note, #357, issued by The Baltimore and Susquehanna
Railroad Company, December 19, 1837

Five Dollar Note, #502, issued by The Susquehanna Bridge & Bank Company,
July 20, 1831

Ten Dollar Note, #3590, issued by The Chesapeake & Ohio Canal Company,
September 9, 1840

Twenty Dollar Note, #220, issued by The Chesapeake & Ohio Canal Company,
October 9, 1840

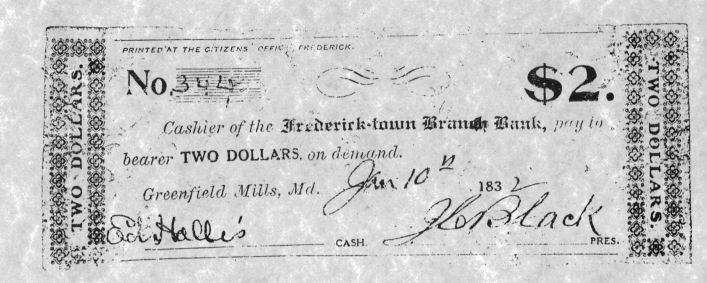

Two Dollar Note, #344, issued by the Frederick-town Branch Bank,
Greenfield Mills, Maryland, January 10, 1832

One Dollar proof note, issued at Baltimore, Maryland, 1860

Twenty Dollar proof note, issued by The Bank of Commerce, Baltimore, Maryland, 1850

Five Dollar note, #6665, issued by The Valley Bank, Hagerstown, Maryland,
April, 1856

Three-Dollar note, #322, issued by the Farmer and Merchants Bank of Greensborough, Maryland,
August 15, 1862

One-Dollar note, #2713, issued by The Allegany County Bank, at Cumberland, Maryland,
June 1, 1861

Five-Dollar note, #234, issued by The Commercial Bank of Millington,
October 20, 1839

Fifty-Dollar proof note, issued by The Hagerstown Bank, Hagerstown, Maryland,
1830 to 1850

Five-Dollar proof note, #4284, issued by The Hagerstown Bank, Hagerstown, Maryland,
1850s - 1860s

Ten-Dollar proof note, #5864, issued by the Hagerstown Bank, Hagerstown, Maryland,
1850s - 1860s

The following three notes were issued by the Somerset and Worcester Bank at Salisbury, Maryland, November 1, 1862

One-Dollar note, #1976, issued by the Havre de Grace Bank,
Havre de Grace, Maryland, Nov. 18, 1846

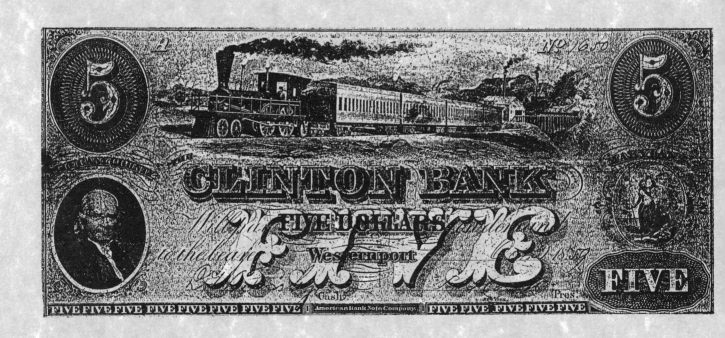

Five Dollar note, #1650, issued by the Clinton Bank, Westernport, Maryland
October 31, 1859

Stock Certificates

On this and the following pages are examples of Stock Certificates, issued by
The Baltimore and Ohio Railroad Company, Incorporated by the State of Maryland,
February 28, 1827.

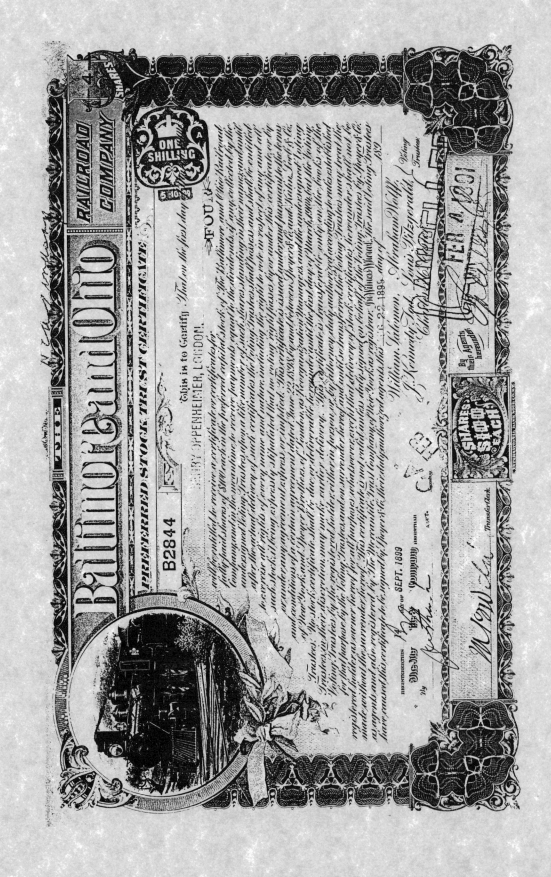

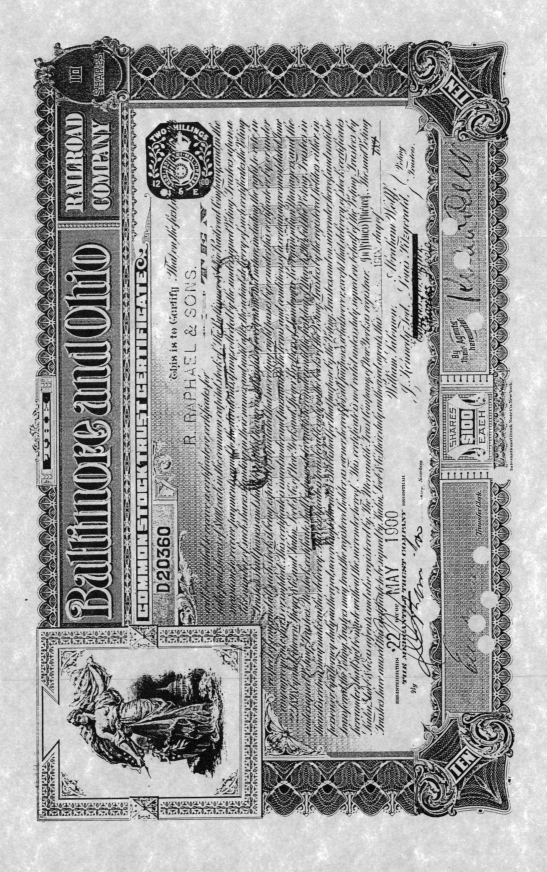

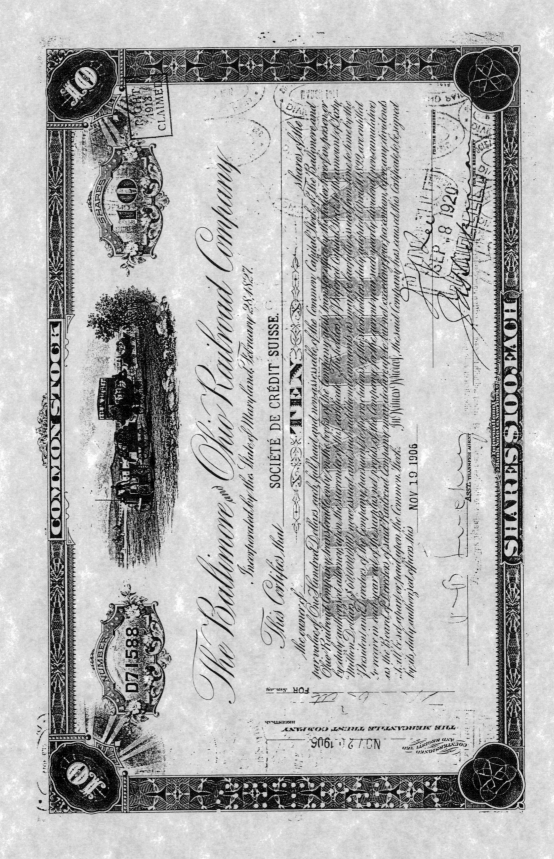

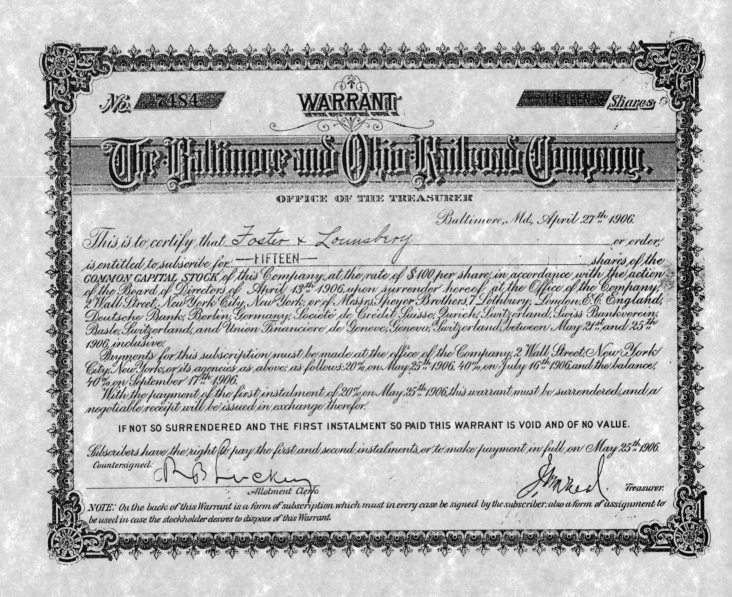

No. 7484   **WARRANT**   FIFTEEN Shares

The Baltimore and Ohio Railroad Company.

OFFICE OF THE TREASURER

Baltimore, Md., April 27th 1906.

This is to certify that *Foster & Lounsbery* or order,
is entitled to subscribe for ——FIFTEEN—— shares of the
COMMON CAPITAL STOCK of this Company, at the rate of $100 per share, in accordance with the action
of the Board of Directors of April 13th 1906, upon surrender hereof at the Office of the Company,
2 Wall Street, New York City, New York, or of Messrs. Speyer Brothers, 7 Lothbury, London, E.C. England,
Deutsche Bank, Berlin, Germany, Société de Crédit Suisse, Zurich, Switzerland, Swiss Bankverein,
Basle, Switzerland, and Union Financière de Genève, Geneva, Switzerland, between May 21st and 25th
1906, inclusive.

   Payments for this subscription must be made at the office of the Company, 2 Wall Street, New York
City, New York, or its agencies, as above, as follows: 20% on May 25th 1906, 40% on July 16th 1906, and the balance,
40% on September 17th 1906.

   With the payment of the first instalment of 20% on May 25th 1906, this warrant must be surrendered, and a
negotiable receipt will be issued in exchange therefor.

IF NOT SO SURRENDERED AND THE FIRST INSTALMENT SO PAID THIS WARRANT IS VOID AND OF NO VALUE.

Subscribers have the right to pay the first and second instalments, or to make payment in full, on May 25th 1906.
   Countersigned:

_____ *Allotment Clerk.*   _____ *Treasurer.*

NOTE: On the back of this Warrant is a form of subscription which must in every case be signed by the subscriber; also a form of assignment to
be used in case the stockholder desires to dispose of this Warrant.

Miscellaneous Documents

of Interest

from

Maryland's Past

MARYLAND PENSION—EIGHTY DOLLARS PER ANNUM, Payable Quarterly, in Equal Installments.

$20

Baltimore, July 25ᵗʰ 1867

The Treasurer of the State of Maryland,

Pay to the Order of *Nicholas Brewer* the sum of TWENTY DOLLARS, for one quarter's Pension due me under the act of the General Assembly of Maryland of 1867.

John Reed

Witness: *Mich. Diffenderffer*
R P Pinckee

75ᵗʰ Regt Col Colvin
Capt Colvin

YOUNG, PRINT.

Twenty-Dollar check issued by The Treasurer of the State of Maryland,
Maryland Pension Fund, July 25, 1867

$700.⁰⁰

Hagerstown Bank

Hagerstown Oct. 7 1876

Pay to the order of R. Miehle & Co

Seven Hundred Dollars 7/100

To Citi Natt Bank
Baltimore Md

J. S. Keusler Cashier

No. 11025

AMERICAN BANK NOTE COMPANY, PHILA.

Check for seven-hundred dollars, drawn on the Hagerstown Bank, October 7, 1876

Below is the front and reverse side of a certificate, advertising the Lottery in Maryland, issued by the Office of Egerton & Bro., Addrefs Egerton & Bro., Baltimore, Maryland.

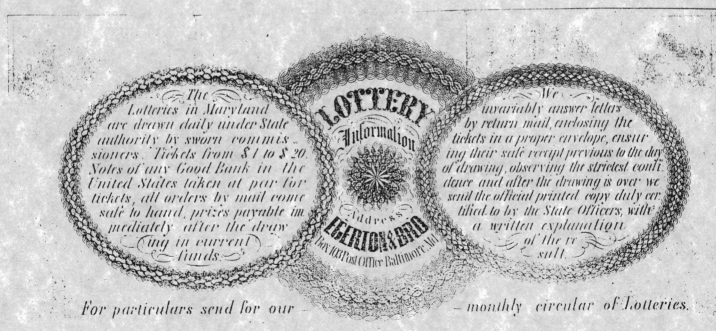

Below is a copy, showing the front and reverse side of an advertisement for Rose Jelly, Patented June 23, 1885, by The Rose Jelly Manufacturing Company, New Midway, Frederick County, Maryland. A most interesting and humorous advertisement.

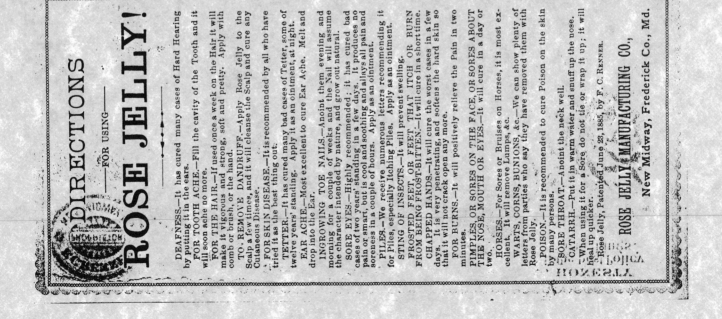

Below, and on the pages that follow, are several examples of different types of receipts, all issued from various departments from the City of Baltimore, as well as other Baltimore City companies.

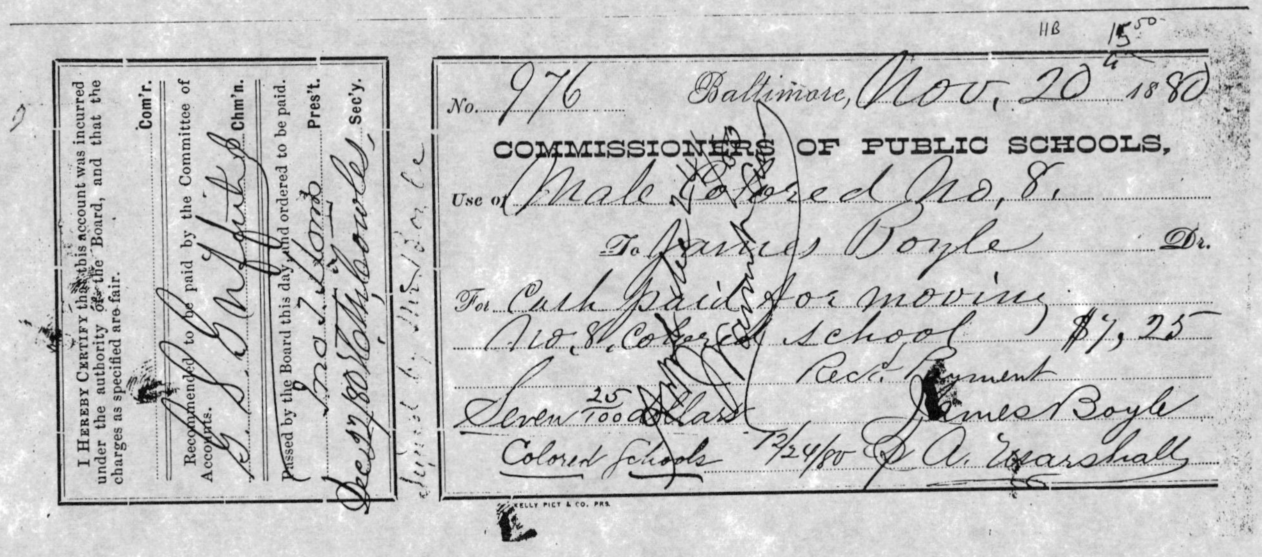

No. *976* Baltimore, *Nov, 20th 1880*

COMMISSIONERS OF PUBLIC SCHOOLS,

Use of *Male Colored No. 8.*

To *James Boyle* Dr.

For *Cash paid for moving*
No. 8 Colored School $7, 25

Rec'd Payment

Seven 100 Dollars *James Boyle*

Colored Schools *7/24/80* *S. A. Marshall*

I HEREBY CERTIFY that this account was incurred under the authority of the Board, and that the charges as specified are fair.

Com'r.

Recommended to be paid by the Committee of Accounts.

G. S. Griffith Chm'n.

Passed by the Board this day and ordered to be paid.

Pres't.

Jno. T. Morris Sec'y.

Baltimore, *February 11 1882*

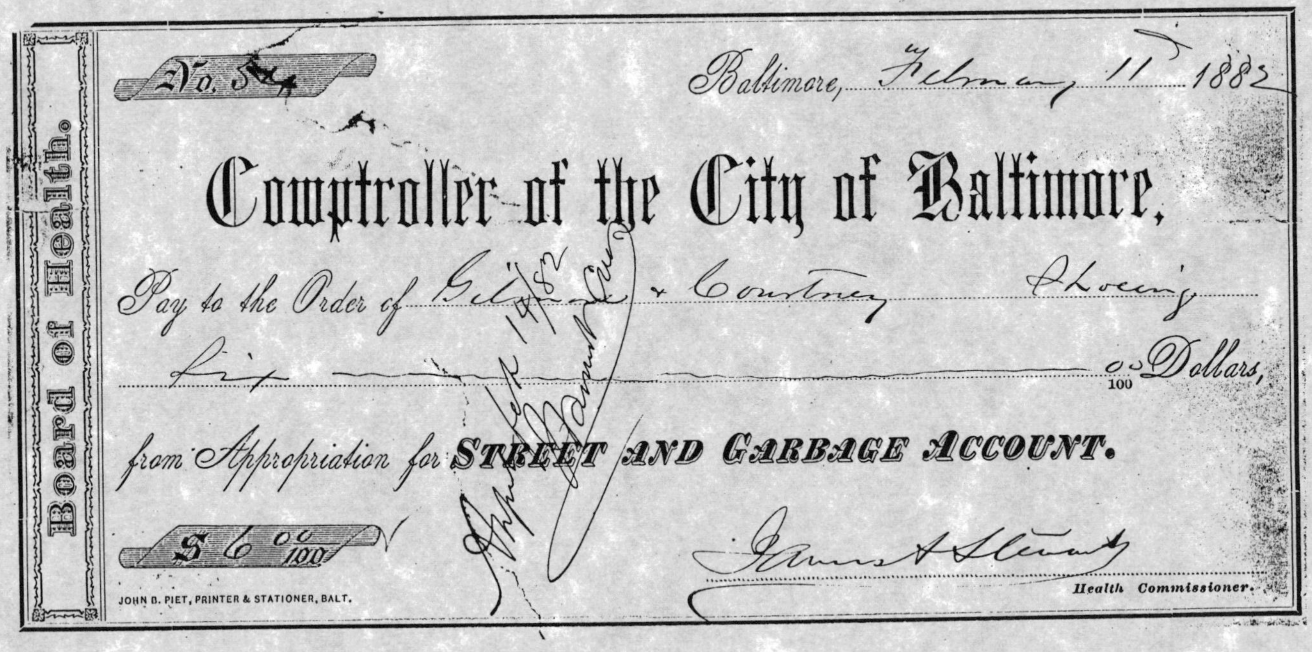

Comptroller of the City of Baltimore,

Pay to the Order of *Gile's & Courtney* *Loving*

Six 00/100 Dollars,

from Appropriation for **STREET AND GARBAGE ACCOUNT.**

James A. Stewart

Health Commissioner.

No. 5

$ 6 00/100

JOHN B. PIET, PRINTER & STATIONER, BALT.

Board of Health.

Baltimore, Nov 26 1878

HB 15.00

Received of The Mayor and City Council of Baltimore,

Fifteen Hundred ————————————— x Dollars,
100

on for a/c of appropriation for House of Reformation and Instruction for Colored Children
for the Year 1878.

1500 Dolls. X Cts.

Wm E. Woodyear
Treasurer

Horses Shod according to the Natural Formation of the Foot.   All Diseases of the Foot successfully treated.

HB 17.50

Baltimore, Feebuary 31st 1882

M. Board of Helth

Gilmore & Courtney, Dr.

PRACTICAL

HORSE SHOERS,

SAPP BROS. Printers, Balto. & Holliday Sts.   No. 59 SOUTH CENTRAL AVENUE.

do to shoeing $ 6 00

Rec Pay

Gilmore & Courtney

Correct

118 15 50

OFFICE OF THE COMMISSION OF PUBLIC PARKS,
CITY HALL.

No. 457

Baltimore, *November 29th* 1881

City Comptroller, Pay to *Henry C. Brown* or Order,

One 60/100 Dollars,

out of the appropriation for

D. H. Park

as per bill annexed

Dominick Raphece Sec'y and Treas.

$1 60/100

MARYLAND SAW MANUFACTORY.

CIRCULAR, MILL, MULAY, CROSS CUT, PIT.
HAND AND WOOD SAWS.
Saws re-toothed, Gummed, Hammered and Straightened,
Saws of every Description Repaired.
Sheet Steel Cut and Straightened. An assortment of
Saws of Superior Quality always on hand
Orders Executed with Punctuality and Despatch.

Baltimore, *November 1st* 1881.

Mess Park Commissioners

To HENRY C. BROWN, Dr.

Manufacturer of Every Description of
CAST STEEL SAWS,
ON THE MOST APPROVED PRINCIPLE,
UHLER'S ALLEY, in the Rear of 58 S. Charles St.

Oct	6	To setting & sharping 2 x cut saws	1.10	
"	17	" " " sharping " saw	.50	
				1.60

Received payment

Henry C Brown
for L. Scott

Eno W Caskell
Correct. A. Faul

GENERAL INFORMATION

Maryland's Nickname is "Old Line State." General George Washington gave Maryland this nickname as a result of the courageous Maryland Line Troops who served in the Revolutionary War.

Government: Maryland has three branches of Government;

1.) Executive:
Consisting of the Governor and his cabinet members.

2.) Legislative:
The Maryland General Assembly which consists of the Senate and House of Delegates.

3.) Judicial:
Consisting of four court divisions, the Court of Appeals, the Court of Special Appeals, the Circuit Courts, and District Courts.

Maryland is divided into three physiographical areas:

1.) The Coastal Plain:
Runs from the Delaware boundary line (referred to as Fall Line) to Washington, D.C.

2.) The Piedmont Area:
Runs from the Fall Line to the base of the Catoctin Mountains.

3.) The Appalachian Area:
Runs from the base of Catoctin Mountains to the western boundary of the state.

Maryland's Land:
Maryland is 12,407 sq. miles in area; 9,775 sq. m., land; 2,633 sq. m. water.

Maryland's length is 250 miles, and its width is 90 miles. Maryland's highest point is Backbone Mountain (3,360 ft.) and lowest point is sea level (Atlantic Ocean)

Maryland's Population:
5,176,305 (1998)
5,274,850 (projected, Year 2000).

Maryland's rank in size among the fifty states: 42nd

Maryland's National Wildlife Refuges:

Blackwater, Route 1, Box 121, Cambridge, Md. 21613

Eastern Neck, Route 2, Box 255, Rock Hall, Md. 21661

Maryland's Wild Acres Trail:
Open dawn to dusk, except Wednesday. Wild Acres Trail is located at: 3740 Gwynnbrook Avenue, Owings Mills, Md. 410-974-3195

Useful Addresses and Telephone Numbers in Maryland:

Office of the Governor, State House, 100 State Circle, Annapolis, Md. 21401-1925 (410-974-3901)

Maryland Office on Aging, 310 W. Preston Street, 10th Floor, Baltimore, Md. 21201 (800-243-3425)

Better Business Bureau, 2100 Huntingdon Avenue, Baltimore, Md. 21211-3215 (410-347-3990)

Office of Attorney General and Consumer Protection Division 200 St. Paul Place, Baltimore, Md. 21202-2021 (800-969-5766)

Maryland Network Against Domestic Violence (410-268-4393)

Federal Information Center, Baltimore, (800-347-1997)

Maryland Motor Vehicle Administration 6601 Ritchie Highway, N.E. Glen Burnie, Md. 21062 (410-768-7420)

Maryland's Television Networks :

WBAL-TV 11 (NBC) 11 TV Hill, Baltimore, Md. (410)467-3000

WBFF-45 (FOX) 2000 W. 41st Street, Baltimore, Md. (410)467-4545

WHSW-TV Channel 24, 4820 Seton Avenue, Baltimore, Md. (410)358-2400

WJZ-TV Channel 13 (CBS) Television Hill, Baltimore, Md. (401)466-0013

WMAR-TV Channel 2 (ABC) 6400 York Road, Baltimore, Md. (410)377-2222

WMPB Channel 67 Public Television, 11767 Owings Mills Blvd., Owings Mills, Md. (410)356-5600

WNUV-TV Channel 54 3001 Druid Park Drive, Baltimore, Md. (410)462-5400

The Discovery Channel 8201 Corporate Drive, Landover, Md. 20785

WFTY, Channel 50, Rockville, Md.

Maryland's Daily Newspapers

The Sun, Baltimore; Established 1837; Circulation 340,000

The Capital, Annapolis; Established 1884; Circulation 47,000

Prince George's Journal, Lanham; Established 1975; Circulation 40,000

Montgomery Journal, Rockville; Established 1973; Circulation 38,376

Cumberland Times-News, Cumberland; Established 1870; Circulation 32,548

The Daily News, Salisbury; Established 1923; Circulation 30,000

Frederick News-Post (Morning Edition), Frederick; Established 1910; Circulation 29,284

Carroll County Times, Westminster; Established 1911; Circulation 21,260

The Diamondback, College Park; Established 1908; Circulation 21,000

The Daily-Mail, Hagerstown; Established 1828; Circulation 17,469

Cecil Whig, Elkton; Established 1841; Circulation 17,000

Star-Democrat & Sunday Star, Easton; Established 1799; Circulation 16,000

Frederick News-Post, Frederick; Established 1883; Circulation 13,902

The Daily Banner, Cambridge; Established 1897; Circulation 7,212

The Daily Record, Baltimore; Established 1888; Circulation 5,350

Maryland State Police

Headquarters, 1201 Reisterstown Rd., Pikesville, Md. (410) 486-3101
Airport Division, BWI Airport, Linthicum, Md. (410) 859-7040

Barrack "A", Jessup, Md. (410) 489-4600

Barrack "B", Frederick, Md. (301) 663-3101

Barrack "C", Cumberland, Md. (301) 729-2101

Barrack "D", Bel Air, Md. (410) 838-4101

Barrack "E", Salisbury, Md. (410) 749-3101

Barrack "F", North East, Md. (410) 398-8101

Barrack "G", Westminster, Md. (410) 848-3111

Barrack "H", Waldorf, Md. (301) 645-1500

Barrack "I", Easton, Md. (410) 822-3101

Barrack "J", Annapolis, Md. (410) 974-3301

Barrack "L", Forestville, Md. (301) 568-8101

Barrack "M", Perryville, Md. (410) 575-6540

Barrack "N", Rockville, Md. (301) 424-2101

Barrack "O", Hagerstown, Md. (301) 739-2101

Barrack "P", Glen Burnie, Md. (410) 761-5130

Barrack "R", Essex, Md. (410) 686-3101

Barrack "S", Centreville, Md. (410) 758-1101

Barrack "T", Leonardtown, Md. (301) 475-8955

Barrack "U", Prince Frederick, Md. (410) 535-1400

Barrack "V", Berlin, Md. (410) 651-3101

Barrack "W", McHenry, Md. (301) 387-5511

Barrack "X", Princess Anne, Md. (410) 651-3101

Cambridge Detachment, Cambridge, Md. (410) 228-3101

Chestertown Detachment, Chestertown, Md. (410) 778-4511

Denton Detachment, Denton, Md. (410) 479-3101

By Another Name:

The town of New Market, in Frederick County, is called, "Maryland's Antique Capital."

Elkton, in Cecil County, is called, "The Marriage Capital of the East."

Garrett County is called, "America's Switzerland," "Maryland's Last Frontier," "Maryland's Best Kept Secret."

Pocomoke City, in Worcester County calls itself, "The Friendliest Town on the Eastern Shore."

New Cathedral Cemetery in Baltimore is called, "Bonnie Brae."

Dorchester County, because of its heart shape is known as "The Heart of the Chesapeake Bay."

In Eastern Shore dialect, if a woman is "gone to Canaan," it means that she is pregnant.

Emmitsburg, in Frederick County is known as "Poplar Fields."

Maryland's reference to being "America in Miniature," was first used by a writer for *National Geographic*.

The "Squire of Oakington," refers to former Maryland Senator Millard Tydings.

Crisfield, in Somerset County is known as the "Seafood Capital of the World."

The slogan, "Born in Baltimore but raised everywhere," refers to the umbrella, which was first manufactured in Baltimore.

H.L. Mencken, the famous writer and editor, who lived at 1524 Hollins Street most of his life, was known as the "Sage of Baltimore."

Some of Maryland's Famous authors :

Leon Uris, the author of *Exodus*, was born in Baltimore.

Thorne Smith, the author of *Topper*, was born in Annapolis.

Upton Sinclair, the author of *The Jungle*, and others was born in Maryland.

The Greatest Story Ever Told, was written by Maryland-born author Fulton Oursler.

Walter Lord, who wrote *A Night To Remember*, the story of the famous ship *Titanic*, was born in Baltimore.

James M. Cain, from Hyattsville, wrote *Double Indemnity*, and *The Postman Always Rings Twice*.

Lucille Fletcher from Oxford, in Talbot County wrote *Sorry Wrong Number*.

Dashiell Hammett, the author of the *Maltese Falcon*, was born in St. Mary's County.

Tom Clancy, who is Maryland-born has written many books including *The Hunt For Red October*, *Red Storm Rising*, *Patroit Games*, (Filmed in part in Annapolis and features the Naval Academy), and *Clear and Present Danger*.

The first novel written by a black woman in America was by Maryland-born Frances Ellen Watkins Harper, titled, *Shadows Uplifted*, in 1892.

Lane Kauffman, who won an Edgar award in 1954 for the mystery novel *The Perfectionist*, died in Glen Arm in 1988.

Films in or about Maryland and actors , actresses, musicians & other famous people from Maryland:

Goldie Hawn, who spent most of her youth in Takoma Park.

Clara's Heart, starring Whoopi Goldberg, was filmed in Baltimore.

And Justice For All, starring Al Pacino and *Bedroom Window*, a 1986 thriller were filmed in Baltimore.

John Astin, who is well-known for his role as Gomez Adams on the *Adams Family*, was born in Baltimore in 1930.

Baltimore-born Francis X. Bushman starred in the 1926 silent version of *Ben Hur*.

Barry Levinson, from Maryland, has directed many movies in Maryland, including *Avalon*, and most recently the television series *Homicide: Life On the Streets*, which is based on the novel by Baltimore's David Simon. The street scenes for *Avalon* were filmed on Appleton Street in Baltimore.

Frank Zappa, from Baltimore formed the famous rock group, Mothers of Invention.

Mildred Dunnock, from Baltimore won an Oscar for her role in *Death of a Salesman* in 1952.

Her Alibi starring Tom Selleck and Paulina Porizkova was filmed in Baltimore.

Diner, from 1982 and *Tin Men* from 1986 were filmed in Baltimore. The wedding scene in *Diner*, starring Steve Guttenberg was filmed in the Engineers Society, a 150+ year-old building at Mount Vernon Place.

Two films, *Hairspray* and *Polyester*, were both filmed in Maryland by John Waters, a Maryland resident.

David Hasselhoff, famous for his roles in *Knightrider* and *Baywatch* and others, and Jameson Parker, who played A.J. Simon on *Simon and Simon* were born in Baltimore.

The Seduction of Joe Tynan was filmed in part in Annapolis.

Noel Paul Stookey, a member of the famous Peter, Paul and Mary trio was born in Baltimore.

Eubie Blake, who was born in Baltimore in 1883, wrote such hit songs as *Shuffle Along* and *I'm Just Wild About Harry*.

Men Don't Leave, a film starring Jessica Lange was filmed in part in Baltimore.

Mount Rainier, a small town in Prince George's County, was the site of an exorcism in 1949, which was the basis for the film *The Exorcist*.

Charles Dutton, famous for many roles in television and movies including, *The Piano Lesson*, for which he won a Tony nomination; *The Best Little Whorehouse in Texas, Roc, Homicide: Life On the Streets*, and others, was born in Baltimore.

Billie Holiday, the famous jazz and blues singer, was born in Baltimore.

Aubrey Bodine, Maryland's famous photographer was born in Maryland and died in 1970. He is buried at Green Mount Cemetery.

Edwin Booth, a famous Shakespearean actor in the 1800s and brother of John Wilkes Booth, performed his first theatrical performance on the site of the original Harford County Courthouse in Bel Air. Edwin was also born in Bel Air.

Actress Lynda Carter, known for her role in televisions *Wonder Woman*, and her husband Robert Altman live in Potomac, Maryland, as does singer Roy Clark, and boxing champions Mike Tyson, and Sugar Ray Leonard.

The famous dog with a black ring around his eye from the *Our Gang Series* is buried in Aspen Hill Pet Cemetery in Wheaton, Maryland.

Maryland's Walk of Fame, which commemorates movies filmed in Baltimore is located at the Senator Theatre on York Road.

Garry Moore, noted for his bow-tie and crew-cut and famous for his television variety and game shows, was born in Baltimore.

The movie *Violets are Blue*, which starred Kevin Kline and Sissy Spacek was filmed in Baltimore and Ocean City.

The film *The Accidental Tourist*, starring Geena Davis, was based in Baltimore.

From 1925 to 1928, General Douglas MacArthur lived in Owings Mills, and United States Vice-President Hubert Humphrey once lived at 3216 Coquelin Terrace, Chevy Chase, Maryland.

Bowie Kuhn, former baseball commissioner from 1969 to 1984, was born in Takoma Park.

Sam Lacy, from Maryland, was the first black member of the Baseball Writers Association of America, while working as a sports editor for the Baltimore *Afro-American* Newspaper.

Francis Beirne, from Baltimore wrote *The Amiable Baltimoreans*.

Edna Ferber, who wrote *Show Boat*, based her novel on a Maryland floating theater.

The actress, Tallulah Bankhead, is buried at St. Paul's Churchyard in Chestertown, Kent County.

Miscellaneous Facts:

Each year during the Christmas season, the small town of Bethlehem in Caroline County postmarks nearly 100,000 Christmas Cards.

The first woman elected to the Maryland House of Delegates and Senate was Mary E.W. Risteau. She was elected to the House in 1921, and the Senate in 1934.

Maryland's first Jewish governor was Marvin Mandel.

In 1952, at the Republican National Convention, Maryland Governor Theodore McKeldin nominated Dwight D. Eisenhower for president.

During the Civil War, approximately 62,000 Marylanders fought for the Union, and 22,000 for the Confederacy.

The youngest man elected governor of Maryland was Herbert R. O'Connor, age 42.

Maryland's General Assembly has 188 members; 47 senators and 141 delegates. One senator and three delegates are elected from each of the 47 legislative election districts.

During World War II, four Marylanders received the Congressional Medal of Honor.

In 1608, explorer Captain John Smith referred to Maryland as the "Delightsome Land."

The coldest temperature ever recorded in Maryland was -40 degrees F. in Oakland, Garrett County, on January 13, 1912.

MARYLAND CRAB CAKES

1 pound crab meat

1 teaspoon salt

1 teaspoon Old Bay Seasoning

1 tablespoon chopped parsley

1 tablespoon baking powder

1 egg beaten

1 tablespoon worcestershire sauce

2 tablespoons mayonnaise

2 slices bread with crust removed. Break in small pieces and
   moisten with milk.
   Oil

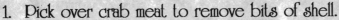

1. Pick over crab meat to remove bits of shell.
2. Add salt, Old Bay, parsley, baking powder and bread pieces.
3. Combine egg, worcestershire sauce and mayonnaise, then gently mix
    with crab meat.
4. Shape into cakes and fry 2 to 4 minutes on each side.
    Drain on paper towel.
    Makes 8 crab cakes.

Variations:

Deep Fried Crab Cakes - Fry cakes in deep fat at 375 degrees for
2 to 3 minutes.

Broiled Crab Cakes - Place crab cakes on greased broiler pan,
4 inches from heat. Broil 4 to 5 minutes
on each side.

The

Lords Baltimore

George and Cecilius Calvert
First and Second Lord Baltimore

Calvert Family Coat of Arms

George Calvert was a member of a family that dates back to 1366 in Yorkshire, England. George was born in 1580, in England, at Kipling, in the chapelry of Bolton. His father was Leonard Calvert, a country gentleman, and his mother, Grace Crossland. These two families' coat-of-arms, the Calverts and Crosslands, are used in the design of the Maryland State flag.

At the young age of fourteen, in 1594, George entered Trinity College, Oxford. It was here that he became proficient in Latin, and earned a bachelor's degree in 1597, and an honorary degree of Master of Arts in 1604. In this year on November 22, he married Anne Mynne in St. Peter's, Cornhill, London. Anne was the daughter of George Mynne and Elizabeth Wroth, of Hertingfordbury, Hertfordshire, England. Together George and Anne had eleven children.

They were:

1.) Cecil Calvert, second Lord Baltimore, born August 8, 1605 and died November 30, 1675.
2.) Ann Calvert, born 1607, married William Peasley in 1627, and died in 1672.
3.) Dorothy Calvert, born 1608, and died January 13, 1624.
4.) Elizabeth Calvert, born 1609. Death date unknown.
5.) Leonard Calvert, Maryland first governor, born 1610, and died June 9, 1647.
6.) Henry Calvert, born 1611, and died in November 1635.
7.) Francis Calvert, born 1612, and died c.1630.
8.) George Calvert, born 1613, and died in 1634 at sea.
9.) Grace Calvert, born 1615, married Robert Talbot in 1630 at Keldare County, Ireland, and died on August 15, 1672.
10.) John Calvert, born 1618, and died February 1618.
11.) Helen Calvert, born 1619, married James Talbot, sq. Death date unknown.
George and Anne divorced about 1622.

In the summer of 1597, upon earning his degree, he traveled throughout the continent, and in doing so, learned the French, Spanish and Italian languages. In 1606, Calvert became the primary secretary to Sir Robert Cecil. Cecil, was the secretary of state and controller of the policy of King James I, (Ruled 1603-1625) and served in this capacity until his death in 1612. Through Sir Robert's influence, Calvert advanced quickly and soon earned the confidence of the king.

Over the years Calvert held many important positions. In 1606, he was made the clerk of the crown of assize and peace in County Clare, Ireland. In 1609, he was made a member of Parliament for Bossiney, in Cornwall; was sent on a special mission for the king to France in 1610; and assisted the king in a theological dispute with Vorstius, a Dutch theologian.

In 1613, Calvert was appointed a clerk of the Privy Council where he also served on a commission to look into religious grievances in Ireland. In 1617, George Calvert was knighted, and two years later, the king, in direct opposition to the desires of the Duke of Buckingham, appointed him the principal secretary of state. In this position, he would serve as a companion to Sir Robert Naunton. By virtue of this position, he was automatically made a member of the Privy Council. In his position as principal secretary of state, he steadfastly discharged vital diplomatic functions. He was a zealous defender in Parliament of the unpopular policies of King James I, especially the negotiations for an alliance with Catholic Spain. In 1624, when these negotiations failed, Calvert lost his seat in Parliament; a position he had held for Yorkshire since 1621. Upon losing his Parliament seat, he was then returned to Parliament without delay as one of the members for the University of Oxford. Upon his return to Parliament, one of the issues facing him was a measure for the persecution of Catholics. Being a Catholic, and having announced his conversion to that faith, he resigned his secretaryship. In February 1625, King James I retained him as a member of the Privy Council and created him Baron of Baltimore, First Lord Baltimore, in the Kingdom of Ireland.

Calvert always had an interest in the colonization of America. This became apparent by his membership in the Virginia Company from 1606 to 1620 and through his admission as one of the council of the New England Company in 1622. In 1620, King James I granted Calvert an increased duty on silk that enabled him to purchase part of the peninsula of Avalon, in the southeastern section of Newfoundland. Two years later he received a grant from the King for the entire country of Newfoundland. In March 1623, a re-grant was issued, restricting his territory to the original peninsula of Avalon. On April 7, 1623, by virtue of a royal charter, was erected into the province of Avalon, the powers of whose lord were regal in kind and inferior only in degree to those of a king. Meanwhile, a small colony had been established there in Ferryland in 1620.

Although some buildings were erected, and some planting was done, the colony did not flourish.

In the summer of 1627, Calvert made a short visit to the colony. He returned in 1628 with his second wife, Joanne, whom he married sometime after 1622, and some of his children from his first wife, except his son Cecilius. During the summer of 1628, the colony was attacked by three French ships, whereby several engagements ensued. Because of this, Lord Baltimore appealed to the King for protection.

On March 20, 1628, George and his second wife, Joanne, had one son, Philip. He would go on to marry Anne Wolseley (see page 264). Together, Philip and Anne arrived in Maryland in 1657. They were sent by Cecil Calvert, Second Lord Baltimore to oversee the re-establishment of Lord Baltimore's government which the radical Protestants, with the support of Virginia, had taken over in 1654.

George Calvert disliked the cold, harsh winters. During the period from October to about May, his house was used as a hospital. For these reasons, Calvert appealed to the King for a grant of land in Virginia, where the weather was warmer. Although the King denied this request, Calvert had left for Jamestown where his wife, Lady Baltimore had gone in the fall of 1628, before the King's reply had reached him. The Virginians, who objected to Catholics, treated him badly. To hasten his departure for England, they tendered him the oaths of supremacy and allegiance. In 1632, King Charles I granted the Lord Baltimore the territory extending southward from the James River to the Roanoke River and west to the mountains,

as the province of Carolina. However, members of the Virginia Company, resentful of this, opposed such a grant. The King, responding to this opposition, substituted the land. This new territory was between the fortieth degree of north latitude and the Potomac River extending west from the Atlantic Ocean to the longitude of the first source of the river, as the province of Maryland. King Charles I, who ruled from 1625 to 1649, was married to Queen Henrietta Marie, for whom Maryland was named.

On April 13, 1632, George Calvert, first Lord Baltimore died, before the charter had passed the great seal, or was issued. This charter, which was copied from that of Avalon, had the date of June 20, 1632, and thus was issued to George's son, Cecilius.

George Calvert, was very diligent and a most trustworthy public servant, who maintained an earnest intent for the welfare of England. With the charter of Maryland, he laid the foundation for one of the most successful governments in the American colonies. George Calvert was buried April 15, 1632, at St. Dunstan's Church, England.

Cecil or Cecilius Calvert, succeeded to the title of second Lord Baltimore upon his father, George's death. Cecil Calvert married the Catholic Anne Arundell, the daughter of Thomas Arundell in 1629. Anne Arundel County, Maryland is so named after Lady Anne Arundell. Cecil and Anne had two children, one son, and one daughter.

Cecil Calvert was raised a Catholic and attended Trinity College, Oxford, England. Upon his father's death, Cecil inherited the title, the Irish estates, and about twelve million acres of land, in what would become Maryland. He served as the first designer and Lord Proprietor of the Maryland colony from 1632 to 1675.

Although he never visited America, he proficiently preserved his charter rights from adversaries over the course of several decades. He established Maryland on a sturdy and wealthy footing, to the depletion of his personal fortune. Additionally, he consistently promoted religious toleration for all Christians living in his colony.

Cecil Calvert died on November 30, 1675. His only son, Charles, served as governor of Maryland from 1661 to 1676, and the third Lord Baltimore from 1675 to 1715.

Charles, Benedict Leonard and Charles Calvert
Third, Fourth, and Fifth Lord Baltimore

Charles Calvert was born August 27, 1637, and was the only son of Cecilius Calvert, second Lord Baltimore, and his wife, Anne Arundell, daughter of Lord Arundell of Wardour. Charles had only one sibling, a sister.

Charles was commissioned governor of Maryland on September 14, 1661, and served as such until the death of his father, November 30, 1675. Upon his father's death he succeeded to the proprietorship of the province, and the third Lord Baltimore.

Being a Catholic, his position as governor and as proprietor came with many problems, as Protestants in the colony outnumbered the Catholics ten to one. Additionally, the ranks of the dissatisfied were increased with recruits from those who had come to the colony as convicts or as indentured servants. His problems continued with the Susquehanna Indians, who were hostile.

Because of a boundary dispute with William Penn, Calvert was required to travel to England where his troubles continued in the Protestant Revolution of 1688, as well as the antagonistic attitude of King William III toward proprietary charters. King William III ascended to the throne jointly with his wife, Queen Mary II in 1688, upon the death of King James II. Although executive power was given to William, they served together from 1689 to 1694. Upon Mary's death in 1694, William III ruled alone until his death in 1702. William III was succeeded by Queen Anne, who ruled from 1702 to 1714.

Although Charles was industrious in coping with these many difficulties, he did so with a bad temper, especially toward any opposition. In 1670, following a heated experience with the Assembly in 1669, votes in the Assembly were restricted to those freemen who had at least fifty acres of land, or who had an estate worth at least forty pounds sterling. Meanwhile, the practice began of summoning to the Assembly only one-half of the delegates who had been elected. Calvert was accused of abusing his privilege of appointing sheriffs to control elections. In 1672, Charles caused the election of Thomas Notley, a strong supporter of Calvert, as speaker. When delegates to the Assembly did not see issues Calvert's way, he would summon them to his chamber, where he prevailed upon them to yield. Calvert had a habit of vetoing acts in the Assembly years after they had been passed.

Charles Calvert was married four times. His second wife, Jane, was the daughter of Vincent Lowe and the widow of Henry Sewall. Charles and Jane had several children, one of which was Benedict Leonard Calvert, the fourth Lord Baltimore. Charles' children were intent on making government a family affair. This attitude was successful for a short time, but passed to incompetent guardians soon after Charles's

departure from England in 1684, when Charles went to defend his charter and territory from attacks by William Penn. Calvert's charter and territory were overthrown in 1689 by a Protestant association led by the irreverent John Coode. In 1692 a royal government was established.

Charles Calvert died on February 21, 1715. Although Charles lacked vision and personal magnetism essential to success, he continued to fight against encroachment of his territorial rights until his death. He is buried at St. Panoras, Panoras, England, located outside London. Charles and Jane Calvert's son, Benedict Leonard Calvert succeeded to the title of fourth Lord Baltimore upon his father's death. In January 1698, Benedict married Charlotte Lee, the daughter of Edward Henry Lee. Benedict Leonard and Charlotte had seven children:

1.) Charles Calvert, fifth Lord Baltimore, born September 29, 1699, and died April 24, 1751.
2.) Benedict Leonard Calvert, born September 20, 1700, and died June 1, 1732, at sea.
3.) Edward Henry Calvert, born August 31, 1701. Death date unknown.
4.) Cecilius Calvert, born November 1702. Death date unknown.
5.) Charlotte Calvert, born November 1702, and married Thomas Brenrwood, Esq., in 1723. She died in 1744.
6.) Jane Calvert, born November 1703, and married John Hyde, Esq., in 1720. Her death date unknown.
7.) Barbara Calvert, born October 3, 1704 and died in 1704.

Benedict Leonard Calvert died on April 16, 1715. Having claimed the title of Lord Baltimore on February 21, 1715, and having died on April 16, 1715, he served less than two months in this position. Upon his death, his son, Charles Calvert succeeded to the title of fifth Lord Baltimore.

Charles Calvert, the fifth Lord Baltimore married Mary Janson on July 20, 1730, the daughter of Theodore Janson and Williamza Henley. Charles and Mary had three children:

1.) Frederick Calvert, born February 6, 1731 and died September 14, 1771. Frederick, upon the death of his father Charles, succeeded to the title of sixth and last Lord Baltimore. On March 9, 1753, Frederick married Liana Egerton. Frederick died on September 14, 1771.
2.) Benedict Swingate Calvert, his birth and death dates unknown. In 1748, he married Elizabeth, the daughter of Governor Leonard Calvert.
3.) Louisa Calvert, her birth and death date unknown, married John Browning, Esq.
4.) Caroline Calvert, her birth and death date unknown, married Robert Eden.

Frederick Calvert, Sixth Lord Baltimore
and
Henry Harford

Frederick Calvert was born February 6, 1731 in Epsom, Surrey, England. He was the son of Charles and Mary Jansen Calvert, and was Maryland's sixth and last Lord Baltimore. Frederick's father, Charles Calvert, fifth Lord Baltimore, died on April 24, 1751. Frederick had two sisters, Louisa and Caroline.

Upon his father's death, Frederick inherited the proprietorship of Maryland, making him the sixth Lord Baltimore, and immense wealth and considerable political connections. His wealth included an income of about ten thousand pounds sterling a month, derived from collected rents and taxes, large shares of stock of the Bank of England, and his resident estate at Woodcote Park, in Surrey. It was through this wealth that enabled Frederick to live a life of high style and leisure.

Through this life of leisure, Frederick traveled extensively, but never visited Maryland. His travels took him throughout Europe, especially Italy where he would stay for long periods and Constantinople, where he lived for a while. Interestingly, Frederick's extravagant lifestyle actually interfered with his duties as the Proprietor of Maryland; however, at the same time he is credited with building Anglo-American relations in Maryland. The building of these relations, although believed to be accidental on Frederick's part, did come at a good time during the imperial crisis of the 1760s and 1770s. Although raised as a Catholic, he professed the Anglican faith to which his grandfather converted, to aid in regaining his proprietary colony after the crown held it.

Frederick had very good political ties, not only in London and throughout Europe, but also in Maryland. Three of Maryland's governors were related to him. Thomas Bladen, who served as governor from 1742 to 1752 married his aunt; Horatio Sharpe, governor from 1753-1769 was the brother of his guardian; and, Robert Eden, governor from 1769-1776, married his sister. Even though Lord Baltimore picked Robert Eden and Horatio Sharpe because of his relationship with them, they were good choices for the colonists of Maryland. Their relationship with the Lord Baltimore enabled them to easily solve problems between the proprietor and the colonists, at least to a point. However, because Frederick never visited Maryland, his attitudes and policies were responsible in shaping Maryland's reaction to the imperial crisis that led to the Revolution.

Although both Sharpe and Eden were very capable and well-liked governors, and maintained a good relationship with Frederick, they did become frustrated with Frederick. Frederick did abuse his trust the colonists had in him, which eventually distanced his colonial subjects. He did not allow Maryland to have an agent in London, which was the norm in many other colonies. He believed that taxation was a violation of his liberty, and thus refused his property or income to be taxed to support the war with France. He also refused to have the income he obtained from licensing redirected from his private holdings to help support the military costs.

Naturally, the colonists took exception to these policies believing them unfair, and the crown saw Frederick's actions as a hindrance to the war effort. It began apparent that Frederick's only goal was money, and not the interests of the colony.

One of Frederick's appointments, Bennett Allen, who was an Anglican clergyman, and good friend to Frederick, engaged in pluralism, by serving as pastor to several parishes at the same time, violating Maryland law and customs. Those that opposed Bennett would be threatened, that if they did not cooperate, Bennett would report their actions to Frederick, by virtue of his personal connections with him. Through repeated events such as this, the colonists respect for Frederick diminished, and tension arose among his governors.

Throughout these strained times, Frederick made himself difficult to contact. To avoid any confrontation, he traveled frequently, making it difficult for even his provincial secretary to locate him to conduct business.

Frederick's personal relationships were a disaster as well. In 1753 he married Lady Diana Egerton, the daughter of the Duke of Bridgewater. As he did not get along with his wife, he usually lived apart from her. Upon her death, he then lived with Hester Whalen of Ireland, with whom he had an illegitimate son and daughter. Additionally, by the year 1770, Frederick had twins by a different woman, and a daughter by another.

In Constantinople, because of his illegitimate children, scandals broke causing him to leave, as well as charges of him having his own private harem. These charges followed him to London as well. Frederick did support his illegitimate children, sending money to the stepfather of his heir Henry, by Hester Whalen.

In 1768, another scandal befell Frederick at home in London. This time he was accused of abduction and rape by Sarah Woodcock. During the trial, Frederick was tried as much by the press as he was in the courtroom. The jury, believing that Sarah did not make adequate attempts to escape or to report the crime properly, acquitted Frederick. To avoid any further disgrace, Frederick retreated to the continent.

On September 4, 1771, Frederick died in Naples, but unfortunately the many problems he created still existed for his colony. Before his death, Frederick made his illegitimate son Henry Harford, his heir. Using elaborate steps, Frederick instructed Governor Eden to declare the province of Maryland for Henry upon his death. The province of Maryland did recognize Henry as the heir, but his cousins, the Brownings, did not. Frederick's sister, Louisa Calvert, had married John Browning earlier. The Brownings, therefore contested the will, but were later bought off.

With the coming of the Revolution in 1774, Governor Eden left Maryland to pursue his own interests by initiating action on his wife's behalf in court, regarding her claim to her brother Frederick's estate. By leaving, he abandoned his colony to the revolutionaries. In his absence, the Loyalist cause and stabilizing force that Eden had thus far exerted on the Revolution was lost. Although Eden made a claim of Frederick's estate on his wife's behalf, this legal battle ended quickly when Sir Robert Eden decided to honor Frederick's instructions to him in his will, to recognize Henry as the true proprietor. All claims toward Frederick's estate against Henry made in 1774 and again in 1778, were finally settled in Henry's favor by Parliament through the Estate Act of 1780. As such, Henry received the bulk of his father's estate, totaling about 96,000 pounds.

Frederick Calvert can be credited with much of the unrest in Maryland that contributed to the anti-imperial attitudes that lead to American Independence. The colonists, once they displaced the proprietary authority, were reluctant to join the remaining colonies against the King of England.

Henry Harford, Frederick's illegitimate son by Hester was born April 5, 1758. Henry was raised, as was his sister, by Peter Prevost, Esq., their stepfather through marriage to their mother Hester. In caring for his son and daughter, Frederick paid large sums of money to Peter, who in turn raised them with all the advantages afforded the wealthy. Henry also was the heir to his father's fortune.

Henry attended Richmond School, in Surrey, then Eton, and Exeter College, Oxford University, where he obtained a degree in 1779. Following college, Henry ran for Parliament in 1781. Although he tied his opponent in the popular vote, he lost when the House of Commons decided the election. His opponent was favored due to him being a prominent land owner.

Although Henry inherited Maryland from his father in 1771, he paid little if any attention to his province, being only thirteen years old. Consequently, his uncle, Cecilius Calvert, Maryland's provincial secretary, managed his affairs. By the time Henry reached the age of majority, his province of Maryland had declared their independence and was at war with Great Britain. Because of his loyalty to the crown, Henry lost all his extensive property holdings in Maryland during the American Revolutionary War. However, having great wealth in England, he still was able to maintain the lavish life of a country gentleman.

In 1783, Henry and Sir Robert Eden returned to Maryland, where Henry tried to reclaim his land lost during the Revolutionary War. Believing it to be a simple task as the English courts settled in his favor, he soon learned that this claim would not come easily. Henry was however, accepted into the social circles upon his arrival in Annapolis. While there, he and Eden were the house guests of Dr. Upton Scott, at his elegant home. Dr. Scott was the uncle of Francis Scott Key, where Francis stayed while attending school in Annapolis in 1789. Having been accepted into the social graces of Annapolis, Henry was invited and attended the ceremony at Maryland's State House when George Washington resigned his commission as commander-in-chief on December 23, 1783.

In his attempt to regain his lost land, Henry petitioned the Maryland General Assembly in 1785. In this claim he also asked for lost rents on his land from 1771 until independence was declared. Henry's total claim was 327,441 pounds.

The assembly members reacted to Henry's claims with mixed emotions. One problem was that in 1780, the state had issued bills of exchange guaranteed by Henry Harford's confiscated property. So, if they returned the land to Henry, what then would happen if the bills of exchange were redeemed? This possibility made the assembly members nervous. Additionally, the Treaty of Paris, which ended the Revolutionary War, did not make clear the disposition of loyalists and their property claims.

In his request to the assembly, Henry wrote a letter by which he recognized the "free state" and appealed to "the dictates of equity and the feelings of humanity," citing that he needed this property for the "relief of his financial situation to avoid further embarrassments." This was a somewhat disputable statement in lieu of his considerable wealth.

Samuel Chase, a member of the Maryland Delegation, and one of four Marylanders who signed the Declaration of Independence, supported Henry's petition. It was felt that he did so to enhance his own chances as Maryland's agent to regain stock held in the Bank of England. Charles Carroll of Carrollton, another delegation member, and Maryland signer of the Declaration of Independence, also supported Henry's petition, which was consistent with his opposition to confiscation during the war. The petition received favorable votes in the House, but was unanimously rejected by the Senate in 1786. In their reasoning for this rejection, the Senate sited Henry's absence during the war, and his father, Frederick's alienation of his subjects, as major factors.

Having lost his petition in Maryland, Henry returned to England and attempted to gain compensation there. Following the Revolutionary War, Parliament established a system for reimbursing those loyalists who suffered losses during the war. In this claim, Harford and the Penn family, who also filed a claim, were recognized in Class VIII of the loyalists' losses that included proprietors. This classification was considered those of low risk, subject to a lower rate of compensation.

Henry Harford requested losses in the amount of 400,000 pounds, and the Penn family at 500,000 pounds. Over the next thirty years through litigation, Henry received more than 100,000 pounds, which turned out to be the second highest award given.

In 1792, Henry married Louisa Pigou, and through his inheritance, they lived a very comfortable life. Henry and Louisa had five children. Their first born son, Henry, died in infancy. Following Henry were Frederick Paul, Louisa Ann, Frances, and Fredericka Louisa Elizabeth.

In 1802, Henry's wife Louisa died. Four year's later, in 1806, Henry married Esther Ryecroft. They had two sons, George and Charles, and three daughters, Charlotte Penelope, Esther, and Emily.

At the time of the Revolution, Henry was too young to have taken an active role. Although the Revolution cost him his province, he still was able in later years to provide popular leadership that helped in shaping events. We remember Henry as Maryland's last proprietor, and the last trace of the Lords Baltimore's many failed attempts to bring supremacy to America.

Henry Harford is characteristic of the cost of loyalty to the crown, all the while having the position that permitted him to live a lavish lifestyle, in spite of his many losses.

Leonard Calvert
Maryland's First Governor

Leonard Calvert was born in 1610, the second son of George Calvert, first Lord Baltimore, and his wife, Anne Mynne. His eldest brother was Cecilius Calvert, second Lord Baltimore, and the first proprietor of the province of Maryland.

Although Leonard's brother Cecilius was the first proprietor of Maryland, he never visited there. As his presence was needed in England to defend his charter from repeated attacks, Cecilius entrusted the exercise of his authority to Leonard.

Much of Leonard's early life is little-known. It is recorded that in 1628, at the age of twenty-two, Leonard traveled with his father to Newfoundland, then returned to England where he petitioned the king for letters of marque. A letter of marque is a document issued by a nation that allows a private citizen to seize citizens or goods of another nation or to equip a ship with arms to attack enemy ships.

On behalf of Cecilius, Leonard sailed from Cowes, England with two ships, the *Ark* and the *Dove* on November 22, 1633. With him on this voyage was his brother, George, and about three hundred colonists. After a long voyage, they arrived at St. Clements Island, in Maryland, and went ashore on March 25, 1634. Today, March 25th is celebrated as Maryland Day. It was here that Leonard took "solemn possession of the Country for our Saviour and for our Sovereign Lord the King of England."

About one month later, after many days of exploring and establishing friendly relations with the Indians, Leonard established the seat of government at St. Mary's City in St. Mary's County, Maryland. On instructions he had received from Cecilius on November 15, 1633, before his journey on the *Ark* and the *Dove*, Leonard addressed himself as governor, and further had the authority to appoint two commissioners to assist him. He was further instructed to give no offense to the Protestant members of the colony, and to develop friendly relations with Virginia.

As governor, Leonard was granted many powers. On April 15, 1637, Leonard received his first commission as governor, by which he was made commander-in-chief of all armed forces by land and sea; was made chief magistrate with a large power of appointment; was authorized to call, prorogue, and dissolve the legislative assembly; was made the chancellor and chief justice with full authority to hear and determine all criminal and civil cases not involving life, member, or freehold, and grant pardons. Further, he was authorized to grant patents for lands and designate places for ports of entry, and markets.

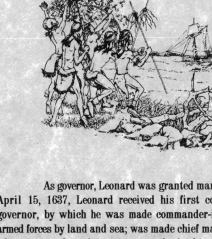

Governor Calvert gave special attention to the encouragement and regulation of trade with the Indians. In the summer of 1634, he sent the *Dove* to Boston with a cargo of corn to trade for fish and other products. He called the first Assembly of freemen to meet at St. Mary's in 1635, and those laws that they passed were sent to Cecilius the proprietor, for his approval. Cecilius rejected them and sent others in their place for approval by the second assembly. In January, 1637, all the members of the Assembly, except Governor Leonard and his secretary of the province, voted against them. A suggestion was made that some laws be agreed upon until the proprietor again responded. Leonard's reply to this was that the Assembly had no such power to take this action. Finally, he gave in to a proposal that stated that he govern during this period according to the laws of England, and if necessary, by martial law. Because of this, forty-two bills were passed. Governor Leonard signed the bills, and wrote to Cecilius saying, *"I am persuaded they will appear unto you to provide both for your honor and profit as much as those you sent us did."* Cecilius, as proprietor gave in and the right of initiative in the legislation passed to the Assembly. This became the first important step in the conversion to popular government in Maryland.

In February 1638, Governor Calvert leading a small force, caused the compliance of a trading post on Kent Island that William Claiborne had established there in 1631.

In 1642, Leonard Calvert married Anne Brent, the daughter of Richard Brent and Elizabeth Reed. Together they had two children: William Calvert, who was born in 1643, and died May, 1682 in Baltimore County, Maryland; and, Anne Calvert, born in 1645.

In 1643, Leonard sailed to England to confer with his brother. Upon his return in September 1644, William Claiborne and Richard Ingle incited a rebellion of Protestants against the Catholics. In this, St. Mary's City was confiscated, causing Governor Leonard to take refuge in Virginia. In 1646, Leonard returned with a force of Virginians and Marylanders, and regained possession of St. Mary's City, and restored order.

Leonard Calvert died on June 9, 1647. He left two children, William and Anne, by his wife, Anne Brent, who had died years before. In the days that preceded his death, Leonard made his sister-in-law, Margaret Brent his executrix. In this position she possessed the powers to look after his estate, and pay the soldiers Leonard had hired to recover St. Mary's City.

Leonard Calvert was a hard working man, and very faithful to his brother's interests. He did lack in diplomacy and governed mostly by force rather than leadership.

Margaret Brent
Francis Scott Key
Frederick Douglass
James Edward Lewis
Harriet Tubman

Margaret Brent
America's First Feminist

Margaret Brent was born in 1601 in Gloucester, England. She was one of thirteen children born to Richard Brent, lord of Admington and Stoke, and his wife, Elizabeth Reed, the daughter of Edward Reed, lord of Tusburie and Witten, all of Gloucester.

The history of the Brent family of Stoke, can be traced to Ode Brent, a knight in the year 1066. Margaret's mother's family claims a descent to William the Conqueror.

Being excited at the resources of the new world, Margaret, along with her sister Mary and two brothers Giles and Fulke, set sail on the ship *Charity* from Plymouth England in early October 1638. They decided to travel to Maryland, arriving at dawn on November 22, 1638. As they entered the Potomac River, they traveled upriver, settling in St. Mary's City. Once in Maryland, their family political affiliations afforded them favors giving them the ability to obtain large land grants and high offices. Margaret's brother Giles had been to Jamestown, Virginia previously, and soon became one of Governor Leonard Calvert's trusted assistants.

Margaret, being a very strong-willed independent person went directly to Governor Leonard Calvert equipped with letters from Lord Baltimore which claimed large land portions and privileges for the Brent sisters. These land portions were as large as those granted to the first arrivals at St. Mary's City. Because the Brents brought with them five men and four maid servants, they were entitled to eight hundred acres of land, under the rule of colonization inducements offered to women. However, because of the letters from Lord Baltimore, they were granted parcels much larger than the entitled eight hundred acres.

On October 4, 1639, Margaret obtained from the Assembly a patent for seventy and one-half acres in St. Mary's City, which she called, "Sister's Freehold." This was the <u>first</u> grant recorded at St. Mary's City and Margaret was the <u>first</u> woman of Maryland to hold land in her own right. In later years she acquired a tract of 1,000 acres of land, and in time, because of her help in transporting men and women, she accumulated even more.

Margaret Brent was a very forceful and fearless woman. When Governor Calvert returned to Maryland from Virginia in 1646, she helped him in suppressing the rebellion by William Claiborne, by gathering an armed group of volunteers to join in with Calvert.

Governor Calvert had much confidence and faith in Margaret's abilities, and proved this further by his appointing her his executrix in 1647. Additionally, the Provincial court appointed her Lord Baltimore's attorney, a position under which they empowered her to collect rents and handle both his estates. In this position as an attorney, Margaret entered more law suits than any other in the colony, and successfully prosecuted a claim involving seven thousand pounds of tobacco against the Calverts. In 1647, upon the death of Governor Leonard Calvert, Thomas Greene succeeded Calvert as governor, and served in this capacity until 1649. When Governor Greene left office in 1649, William Stone succeeded Greene, however, at times in 1649, upon Stone''s absence, Stone appointed Greene as acting governor.

Because of her many responsibilities, Margaret appealed to the Assembly on January 21, 1648 for a voice in their counsels, and for two votes in their Assembly proceedings. One vote was for herself as a landowner, and the second as attorney for Lord Baltimore. This request was more than two hundred fifty years before women were given the right to vote in the United States. Governor Thomas Greene considered her request, but refused her the right to vote. His decision was written as follows:

"Came Mistress Brent and requested to have vote in the House for herself and voice also; for that at the last Court 3rd January, it was ordered that the said Mrs. Brent was to be looked upon and received as his Lordship's attorney. The Governor denied that the said Mistress Brent should have any vote in the House. And the Mistress Brent protested against all the proceedings in this present Assembly, unless she may be present and have vote as aforesaid."

Cecil Calvert, second Lord Baltimore, upon learning that Margaret Brent had requested the right to vote as well as a seat in the Maryland legislature, was displeased at best. As England was so far away, by the time news reached there from Maryland, and other parts of the New World, it was, at times, erroneous. From the information conveyed to him, Cecil Calvert construed her actions to be those that opposed him, and turned against her. On August 15, 1648, Cecil Calvert wrote a letter to Margaret Brent, which included accusations, that although untrue, Margaret could not forgive. This letter included, in part, the following:

"We, most painfully learn of your scandalous, even avaricious conduct there in your presumptuous management of our own affairs by no other direction than that of a sick and suffering man. Our late lamented good brother on his deathbed was so tormented by pain and suffering that, in a delirium, he bestowed honors upon you which your modesty does not reject and your greed grasps tenaciously. The mortification brought upon our Province and our family by your ambitious brother's degrading union in matrimony with one of the savages there... (referring to her brother Giles's marriage to an Indian girl). We are now aware that for six years past you have appeared for the recovery of presumed debts due you and those persons represented by you...that as a result, we are now informed, you have mostly taken up land in lieu of the regular currency, so that there is grave danger that the family of Brent will or may have now the title to more of Maryland than the rightful Proprietary. Further, we are inflicted by your indelicacy in demanding a voice and vote in our Assembly there on our behalf. This mortification might well be brought upon us by the spouse of a fishmonger; that one of your high birth should so publicly forget her position gives us embarrassment and great vexation of spirit. We are persuaded the retirement of all the Brents from our Province would be conducive to domestic peace therein. We forward this day a commission to our well-affected friend, William Stone, Esq., empowering him to act as our Lieutenant General and attorney in Maryland."

Cecil Calvert continued in his letter to say further that this friend, William Stone, had convinced "five hundred souls of British and Irish decent" to settle in Maryland, but not for land for himself, but in essence for the good of Maryland. This further inferred that all actions taken by Margaret were for personal gain, and not for the benefit of Maryland. As it turned out, these five hundred souls that Stone brought to Maryland were all Puritans from Virginia. Eventually, they brought about a state of civil war, in which Governor Stone was captured, jailed, and threatened with execution.

In Margaret's defense upon receiving her letter from Lord Baltimore, the General Assembly with Governor Stone wrote a reply to Lord Baltimore, dated April 21, 1649. It included the following on her behalf:

"As for your bitter invective against Mistress Brent for her undertaking and meddling with your Lordship's estate, here we do verily believe and in conscience report, that it was better for the colony's safety at that time, in her hands, than in any man's else in the whole Province after your brother's death. For the soldier's would never have treated any other with that civility and respect. They were even ready at several times to run into mutiny yet still she pacified them, till at last, things were brought to that strait that she must be admitted and declared your Lordship's attorney by an Order of Court, or else all must go to ruin again. The Mistress Brent with our full concurrence did deputize Mr. Thomas Copely, who is well respected here, to receive rents, else no one might receive them and they remain a loss to you. Mistress Brent to well-affected soldiers has given a few of your cattle in lieu of wages, not above eleven or twelve cows. Your Lordship may well remember these soldiers had ventured their lives and fortunes in the defense, recovery and preservation of your Lordship's Province..."

Resentful of the decision not to permit her to vote, and in conjunction with the accusations from Calvert, Margaret left Maryland in 1650, and established a new home in Westmoreland County, Virginia that she called, "Peace." Earlier her brother, Giles had moved to Virginia, and one of her sisters, Anne, had married Governor Leonard Calvert. Anne died several years before Governor Calvert. Margaret, now owning vast estates in Maryland and Virginia, became very powerful. She was known as "lady of the manor," and held large feasts for her people.

Margaret Brent died in 1671. Although the exact month and day are unknown, she did make a will on December 26, 1663, which was admitted to probate on May 19, 1671.

Margaret Brent was considered a lady of queenly dignity, with extreme intelligence, and understanding sympathy and charm, who possessed progressive visions considerably beyond her day.

Francis Scott Key

When Key entered St. John's College at the age of ten, he did so at the grammar school section. Upon completion, he progressed to the intermediate section, then called the "French School." He graduated with a Bachelor of Arts degree in 1796, and later earned a second degree, Master of Arts, on November 12, 1800.

Key had an interest and desire to study law, in part through encouragement from his father, also a lawyer. Additionally, his father was a Justice of the Peace, and Associate Justice of his Judicial District, which comprised Allegany, Washington, and Frederick Counties. Philip Barton Key, Francis's uncle, was also an attorney, and arranged for Francis to study law under his friend, Judge Jeremiah Townley Chase in 1800. While studying under Judge Chase, Francis met Roger Brooke Taney, and the two became close friends. In later years, Taney, became a chief justice and is remembered for his famous "Dred Scott Decision."

A year later, in 1801, Francis opened his own law practice in Frederick. On January 19, 1802, Francis married Mary Tayloe Lloyd, the daughter of Colonel Edward Lloyd, at the "Chase House" owned by Colonel Lloyd in Annapolis. Together, Francis and Mary had eleven children; six sons and five daughters.

Following their marriage, Francis and Mary moved from Frederick to Georgetown, where Key went into practice with his uncle Philip. During the War of 1812, as the British were retreating from Washington in September 1814, a well-known physician, Dr. William Beanes was seized and taken to a British ship and confined. The British claimed that Beanes attacked one of their soldiers. Francis Scott Key, was asked to negotiate his release, and agreed to do so. On September 5, Key, along with Colonel J. S. Skinner, the government agent for the exchange of prisoners, sailed down the Chesapeake Bay from Baltimore en route to Beanes location. Upon their arrival, they met with British Rear Admiral George Cockburn, and secured Beane's release. They boarded an American ship, but stayed in the bay, due to the pending attack by the British. During the attack on September 13-14, 1814, Key stayed on deck in suspense, wondering what the outcome of the battle would be. At daybreak on the 14th, Key was overjoyed to find the American flag still flying over Fort McHenry. In his excitement he wrote his famous poem, originally titled, "The Defense of Fort McHenry." This poem later became known as "Star-Spangled Banner," and was adopted the official National Anthem of the United States on March 3, 1931.

Following the War of 1812, Francis, being a very religious person, considered entering the clergy. From 1814 to 1826, he was a delegate to the general conventions of the Episcopal Church, and was the lay reader at St. John's Church in Georgetown.

Francis Scott Key was born August 1, 1779 on the family estate, "Terra Rubra," a 1,865 acre plantation located then, in Frederick County, but today in Carroll County, Maryland. Francis was the son of John Ross Key and Ann Phoebe Penn Dagworthy Charlton. His great-grandfather was Philip Key, an Englishman, who came to Maryland in 1726. Francis had one sister, Anne Phoebe Carlton Key, who later married Roger Brooke Taney.

In 1789, at the age of ten, Francis was sent to Annapolis to obtain an education. He entered St. John's College, and due to little dormitory space, he lived with his blind grandmother, Ann Ross Key, and his great-aunt and uncle, Dr. and Mrs. Upton Scott. Key's middle name was given to him as a tribute to his great-uncle, Dr. Scott. The Georgian house owned by the Scotts, is on Shipwright Street, and is in pretty much the same condition today as it was in the 1700s. It is said that this is the home of Richard Carvel's grandfather in Winston Churchill's famous Annapolis romance. Dr. Scott originally came to Maryland as the personal physician to Royal Governor Sharpe. Scott fled Maryland for Ireland as a Tory refugee during the American Revolutionary War. Tories were outlawed in Maryland, and many were hanged. Tories were those persons that during the Revolution favored the side of the English.

Key was an effective speaker, with a quick logical mind. As an attorney he had extensive practice in the federal courts. Consequently, he was a United States attorney for the District of Columbia from 1833 to 1841. In this position, President Andrew Jackson, in October 1833, sent him to Alabama where he negotiated a settlement between the state and federal governments over the Creek Indian Lands.

In the middle 1830s, Key moved from Georgetown to Washington, D.C. On January 11, 1843, Francis Scott Key died of pleurisy at the home of his daughter, Mrs. Charles Howard, at Mt. Vernon Place, Baltimore. His body was first placed in the Howard family vault at St. Paul's Cemetery, Baltimore, then transferred to Mt. Olivet Cemetery, Frederick, in 1866.

Francis Scott Key was a slender man with dark blue eyes, who loved riding horses, and was generous in nature. In his lifetime he wrote many poems, all of which he considered more of a hobby, than serious writing. In 1857, a collection of his poems was published posthumously titled, "*Poems of the Late Francis Scott Key, Esq.*"

Today there are monuments dedicated to his memory at Mt. Olivet Cemetery, Fort McHenry, Eutaw Place in Baltimore and in Golden Gate Park, San Francisco, California.

Frederick Douglass

Frederick Douglass was born Frederick Augustus Washington Bailey in February 1818. He was born on a farm on Lewiston Road, Tuckahoe, near Easton, in Talbot County, Maryland. Frederick was the son of an unknown white father, and Harriet Bailey, a slave who was a part African and Native American. Frederick was born a slave on the great plantation owned by the Lloyd family. At times, they referred to him as Frederick Lloyd. When he was eight years old, he was separated from his mother and never saw her again.

As a child, Frederick was legally classified as real estate or property rather than as a human being. He experienced much neglect and cruel treatment, and hard work brought on by the tyranny toward slaves. Resistance by slaves usually resulted in even more cruel treatment. However, in Frederick's case it paid off. By fighting back toward his cruel master, Colonel Lloyd, and following a failed escape attempt, he was sent to Baltimore as a house servant at the age of eight. In Baltimore he learned to read and write with the assistance of his mistress, although was mostly self-taught. Having now learned to read and write he soon began to conceive of his freedom. Frederick was fortunate in that the Lloyd family often would severely whip slaves who were hard to manage or who tried to escape, then sent them to Baltimore, only to be sold to a slave trader, as a warning to all other slaves.

Upon the death of his master, Frederick was returned to the country as a field hand. Here, he conspired with six other fellow slaves to escape. Their plan a failure, and betrayed by another, he was placed in jail. His new master, being a tolerant sort, arranged for his release from jail and returned him to Baltimore. Again, in Baltimore, Frederick learned the trade of a ship carpenter, and in time, was permitted to hire his own men.

On September 3, 1838, Frederick made another escape attempt, and this time was successful. He traveled to New York, changed his last name to Douglass, and married a free black woman named Anne Murray, whom he had met in Baltimore earlier. Together they moved to New Bedford, Massachusetts, where Frederick worked as a laborer.

In search of a new career, Frederick read Garrison's *Liberator*, and in 1841 attended a convention of the Massachusetts Anti-Slavery Society in Nantucket. One of the attending abolitionists overheard Douglass speaking with some of his black friends. Impressed, this man asked Douglass to speak at the convention. Although reluctant, he did so, and although he stammered, his speech had a remarkable effect. As a result, and to his surprise, they immediately employed him as an agent to the Massachusetts Anti-Slavery Society, and a new career was born.

In his new position, he participated in the Rhode Island campaign against the new constitution that proposed the disfranchisement of blacks, which denied them the right of citizenship and the vote. He was the main figure in the famous "One-Hundred Conventions," of the New England Anti-Slavery Society. Here he was mobbed and beaten and forced to ride in "Jim Crow"[1] cars and denied overnight accommodations. Yet through this all, he remained and saw the planned program to the end.

Douglass possessed a strong physique, being more than six feet tall, with a strong constitution and an excellent speaking voice. Because of this, those who heard him speak, began to doubt his story of having ever been a slave, and that he was basically self-taught. Because of these doubts, Frederick wrote his *Narrative of the Life of Frederick Douglass*. However, a friend, Wendell Phillips, advised Douglass to burn the book because he recounted his life as a slave, and Phillips believed releasing it would re-enslave Douglass. Douglass refused and published the book in 1845. However, to avoid any possible consequences, he traveled to Great Britain and Ireland. He remained there for about two years where he had the opportunity to meet and get to know the English Liberals. In this environment, they treated him as a man and an equal for the first time in this life. This resulted in improving his character and self-esteem. From this experience, he truly started to believe that freedom, not only physical, but social equality and economic and spiritual opportunities were possible.

In 1847, he returned to the United States, and having enough money, he bought his freedom and established a newspaper dedicated to his race. Many of his white abolitionist friends disagreed with his views in this newspaper, and others

---

[1] "Jim Crow" refers to the "legal" repression of slavery or segregation.

believed that the ability to purchase his freedom was in fact condoning slavery. However, Douglass, upon learning these criticisms, handled them in a practical manner.

On June 22, 1894, Douglass gave an address at the Sixth Annual Commencement of a Colored High School in Baltimore, Maryland. In his address, Douglass said: *"The colored people of this country have, I think, made a great mistake, of late, in saying so much of race and color as a basis of their claims to justice, and as the chief motive of their efforts and action. I have always attached more importance to manhood than to mere identity with any variety of the human family..." "We should never forget that the ablest and most eloquent voices ever raised in behalf of the black man's cause were the voices of white men. Not for race, not for color, but for men and for manhood they labored, fought, and died. Away, then, with the nonsense that a man must be black to be true to the rights of black men."*

Frederick Douglass died on February 20, 1895. Active to the end, on the day he died, he attended a woman-suffrage convention.

Douglass went on to establish his newspaper, the *North Star*, and published it for seventeen years. Furthermore, he lectured, was a supporter of woman suffrage, took an active part in politics, and helped Harriet Beecher Stowe establish an industrial school for black youth. He also met with John Brown, and counseled him. Upon Brown's arrest, the Governor of Virginia attempted to arrest Douglass as a conspirator. To avoid arrest, Douglass fled to Canada, then England and Scotland, where he again lectured.

With the outbreak of the Civil War, additional opportunities came his way, by which he passionately fought against slavery as its major cause. He assisted in convincing black men to join the Union army, and he helped in recruiting for the 54th Massachusetts colored regiment, offering his own sons as the first recruits. Twice during the war, President Lincoln invited him to the White House to discuss important matters concerning the black soldiers in the Union Army.

Following the Civil War in 1877, Douglass was appointed as United States Marshall for the District of Columbia by President Hayes, and in 1881, President Garfield appointed him Recorder of Deeds for the District of Columbia.

In 1884, Douglass married again. His second wife was Helen Pitts, a white woman, which brought about much criticism. Concerning this, he maintained his sense of humor by saying, "my first wife was the color of my mother, and my second wife, the color of my father." In 1891, President Harrison appointed Douglass as Minister-Resident and Consul-General to the Republic of Haiti, and as Charge d'affaires for Santo Domingo.

James Edward Lewis
Sculptor

James Edward Lewis was born in Charlotte County, Virginia, in the town of Phoenix, and was the only child of Pearlean E. and James T. Lewis.

Both Pearlean and James T. were born to sharecropping families, and in their quest to leave the poverty of the South, moved to Kentucky after their marriage. Within a short time, they moved back to Virginia, where they planned a move to Baltimore. James T. came to Baltimore first, where he settled in a small house on Durham Street, before sending for his wife and the newborn James Edward in 1924. In Baltimore James T. worked for the United States Post Office, while his son attended segregated city schools.

In 1942 James graduated from Paul Laurence Dunbar High School. Having a reputation as a serious and determined young man, James also possessed a talent in art. This determination drove him to his desire to become a professional artist. Following his graduation from high school, James wanted very much to attend the Maryland Institute of Art, however, the school did not offer any separate facilities for black students. Consequently, he left Baltimore to study in Philadelphia, attending the Philadelphia College of Art. While in Philadelphia, he met Jacqueline Lucille Adams, who would later become his wife.

During this time, the United States was involved with the war with Japan and Germany. Committed to duty, James enlisted in the Marine Corps, serving in the 51st Defense Battalion, which temporarily interrupted his studies. He attained the rank of corporal, and was fortunate that his artistic ability was of use to the antiaircraft battalion. Today, many of his drawings are a part of the permanent records of the 51st Defense Battalion.

In 1946, James received an honorable discharge. In this year he and Jackie were married, and James continued his education at the Philadelphia College of Art. In 1949 he graduated with a Bachelors of Fine Arts Education degree, and a year later received a Master of Fine Arts degree from Temple University. Upon receiving his Master's degree in 1950, Morgan's President, Martin D. Jenkins, recruited him to build an art department at Morgan State College. James accepted this position and for the following thirty-six years he cultivated the Art Department at Morgan. This effort created what would become the James Edward Lewis Museum of Art at Morgan State University. In 1990, to honor him, the Regents of Morgan State University dedicated the Morgan Art Gallery in his name. Additionally, throughout his carer at Morgan, James also devoted time in continuing his own education as well as educating others in art and art history, through Ford Faculty Fellowships at Syracuse and Yale Universities, and frequent research and lecture tours in Africa.

In addition to his educational pursuits, James also was an accomplished sculptor and painter for more than forty years. When one would visit his home, the smell of oil-based clay would permeate the house. Throughout his life, he continued the habit of staying up until the early hours of the morning to complete various commissions.

His many commissions include:

1952: A bronze portrait of Dwight O.W. Holmes, late President of Morgan State University;

1953: An eight-foot bronze statue of Frederick Douglass, on the campus of Morgan State University.

1954: A heroic size sculpture of the Theodore R. McKeldin, the late Maryland Governor and Mayor of Baltimore City.

1956: A portrait bust of Frederick Douglass for the National Association of Colored Women's Club's, Inc.

1959: A portrait painting of Charles Key, the late Dean of Men at Morgan State University.

1960: A portrait painting bronze bust of Frederick Douglass for Douglass High School in Baltimore.

1968: A nine-and-one-half foot bronze sculpture depicting the historical role of the Negro soldier in wars involving the United States, titled, "The Salute to the Black Soldier." It is on the North end of the Battle Monument Plaza, Calvert and Lexington Streets, Baltimore. Attending during the dedication was General Chappie James, USAF, America's first Black Four-star general.

In 1986, James retired and devoted his attention to studying and expanding his personal collection of African traditional and modern art, modern American art as well as many other art objects.

On August 8, 1997, James Edward Lewis died at the age of seventy-four. He dedicated his life to collecting and creating art that represents the spirit, heart and meaning of the African in America and in Africa. Mr. Lewis was a wonderful, talented, caring man. Family, friends and colleagues who loved him will always remember, and admire not only the man, but his lifetime commitment to art.

Harriet Tubman
The Moses of her People

Harriet Tubman was born in 1820 in a cold, dark, windowless slave shanty on the Bucktown plantation owned by Edward Brodess in Dorchester County on Maryland's Eastern Shore. She was the daughter of black slaves, Benjamin Ross and Harriet Green, and was originally named Araminta by her master. As she defied slavery and its customs, she later changed her name to Harriet, after her mother.

During her childhood Harriet sustained a serious head injury when an angry overseer tossed a two-pound weight at her, striking her in her forehead. This injury nearly killed her and that caused her to have sudden, periodic sleeping seizures her entire life. The injury left an ugly scar, which throughout her life, reminded her of the horrors suffered as a slave. Being raised as a slave, she had to perform extremely hard work, and as such she acquired unusual strength. Because she was forced to work as a slave, Harriet did not have the opportunity to attend school. She did however, possess an innate intelligence with remarkable foresight and judgment. As time passed, and when fully recovered from her injury, her master, Brodess, hired her out to work on neighboring farms. This allowed her some independence, and the opportunity to earn small amounts of money. Some of the work Harriet would do was cut and split wood, drive oxen, and haul logs. By this work, Harriet grew quite strong in physical strength.

When a master hired out a slave, the slave would pay the master part of their earnings. For male slaves, the cost was one-hundred dollars a year, and for female, sixty dollars. In time, Harriet earned enough money not only to repay her master the sixty dollars, but also enough to buy her own pair of oxen.

Normally, female slaves at a young age were forced to marry a mate chosen by their masters. Because of her injury, Harriet was spared this tradition. However, Harriet, now in her twenties was getting too old to remain unmarried. Having worked and earned her own money, she attracted a free black man named John Tubman, who also worked odd jobs at various plantations. Although marrying a free man was quite unusual for a slave, they permitted Harriet and John to marry. Although forced to do so by her mother, Harriet in 1844, at the age of twenty-four, married John Tubman.

Having married a free man, Harriet thought of nothing but to one day be free herself. Interestingly, they should never have enslaved Harriet. One day, determined to trace her roots, she hired a lawyer at the cost of five dollars to trace the will of her mother's first master. In doing so, a will was found that gave her mother, Harriet Green, to an heir named Mary Patterson. The will provided that Ms. Green was to serve Mary Patterson until Patterson was forty-five years old. However, Patterson died before reaching this age, and was unmarried. Because there was no provision in the will concerning Harriet Green upon Patterson's death, she was therefore free. Unfortunately, no one told Ms. Green of this right, consequently she and her children remained enslaved. Harriet Tubman, now armed with this information was now more than ever determined to be free.

Having spent her first twenty-nine years as a slave plantation hand, in 1849, upon the death of her master, she learned that she was to be sold to the Deep South. Determined not to be sold, Harriet, along with her two brothers, escaped. Guided by the North Star on her journey to freedom, she was also aided by the Underground Railroad, which was a secret network of safe-houses created to help escaping slaves. Two of the principle "conductors" of the Underground Railroad who aided Harriet were Ezekiel Hunn and Thomas Garrett, both of Delaware.

Along the journey, her two brothers returned to Maryland, but Harriet continued and arrived in Philadelphia, she changed her name to Harriet, and worked for about a year to earn money. She then left Philadelphia and returned to Maryland. Once in Maryland she disguised herself as a man in an attempt to find her husband to bring him back north with her. Upon finding her husband, she found that he had married another. Devastated by this news, she set her mind and determination devoting her life to freeing slaves.

With her newfound freedom obtained in Philadelphia, where slavery was outlawed, Harriet found little solace in her freedom, while the masses of her race remained enslaved. Consequently, she spent the next ten years serving as a "conductor" on the Underground Railroad. She made more than twenty trips into the South and rescued about three hundred Negroes from slavery. In her rescue efforts, Harriet would move these persons from the South to a secret station near

Wilmington, Delaware, to freedom in Philadelphia. On her journeys, she usually started Saturday night, because this would give her more than a day's start before the owners discovered that their slaves were missing the following Monday morning. At times along the way to freedom, some of those she rescued would become frightened and want to turn back. Harriet would not hear of this. Often she would admonish those wanting to turn back at gunpoint, saying, "Live North, or die here." She also carried opium with her on her journeys to quiet crying babies.

Upon arriving at her destination, she frequently worked as a cook, dressmaker, or a laundress to earn money to help sustain the fugitive slaves. Both black and white abolitionists praised her as the *"Moses of her people."* She became widely respected, and was honored by such noteworthy persons as Frederick Douglass, Susan B. Anthony and Ralph Waldo Emerson. Similarly, slave holders and other pro-slavery advocates also hated her in the South, and as well in the North by antiabolitionists.

Once in April 1860, in Troy, New York, the police had captured a runaway slave by the name of Charles Nalle. It was Harriet who led a group that freed Nalle, and in doing so, they attacked Harriet and severely beat her. Still, possessing courage and confidence, she avoided capture.

Despite the Fugitive Slave Act of 1850, which provided for harsh treatment, nor the forty-thousand dollar bounty on her for her arrest, dead or alive, could stop Harriet. In 1857, she performed an inconceivable mission of freeing both her aged parents. Now free, she took her parents to a home in Auburn, New York; land that Harriet purchased earlier from William H. Seward.

In 1858, Harriet traveled to Canada, where she had the opportunity to meet John Brown. A friendship developed, by which Brown referred to her as *"General Tubman,"* and said, *"Harriet is one of the bravest persons on this continent."* Harriet approved of and provided support for Brown's plan to seize the government arsenal at Harper's Ferry, West Virginia. However, due to circumstances beyond Harriet's control, she was unable to recruit others to join Brown, nor was she able herself to join. Upon Brown's defeat and hanging, Harriet was deeply saddened. She regarded Brown as the "Savior of her people."

When the Civil War began, she, without delay asserted her right to participate. Armed with a letter from John Andrew, the governor of Massachusetts, she traveled to Hilton Head, South Carolina, where she reported to General David Hunter. Here she worked in the Union Army as a scout, spy, nurse, and cook. She continued this activity throughout the war, and in 1865 near the war's end, she briefly worked at a freedman's hospital in Fortress Monroe, Virginia.

Upon the end of the Civil War, she continued her mission and concern for the Negro masses. In North Carolina she worked hard and tirelessly to establish schools for the hundreds of freedmen.

In 1869 Harriet married Nelson Davis, a black Civil War veteran. Additionally, she had a book of her own, titled, *Scenes in the life of Harriet Tubman* (1869), which she dictated to Sarah Hopkins Bradford who wrote it for her. They printed and sold this book with help from Gerrit Smith, Wendell Phillips, and some of her Auburn friends and neighbors. With the royalties from her book, she was able to pay off the mortgage on her house in Auburn.

During this time she applied for a pension for her wartime service, however the government showed her much less gratitude than she deserved. Finally, after thirty years of trying to collect her pension, Congress, with the support of former Secretary of State William H. Seward, awarded her the trifle amount of twenty dollars a month. Private citizens helped and contributed money for the support of the Harriet Tubman Home for Indigent and Aged Negroes in Auburn.

In her later years, Harriet continued to work for the women's right's movement, as well as her continued work with aged and indigent Negroes. On March 10, 1913, Harriet Tubman died of pneumonia. A full military service was provided for her. They buried Harriet with full military honors in Fort Hill, Auburn.

In 1914, the Cayuga County Historical Society Association built a tablet in her memory and in recognition of her service, in a ceremony delivered by Booker T. Washington. Additionally, in further recognition of her tireless service the United States Postal Service issued a stamp in her memory. They issued this thirteen-cent stamp depicting her image in Washington, D.C. on February 1, 1978, as the first stamp in a "Black Heritage Series."

Harriet Tubman was a woman of greatness who represented nearly a century of struggle and difficulties fighting slavery toward her goal of social justice.

In 1886, Sarah Hopkins Bradford, who had written Harriet's book for her in 1869, issued an expanded version titled, *Harriet Tubman, The Moses of her People.* They reprinted this book in 1961.

Today, the Brodess plantation no longer exists, but there is a historic marker noting the former site of Harriet's birthplace. The Harriet Tubman Coalition, Inc., hosts guided tours, by appointment only to major sites of interest in and around Bucktown and Cambridge. These include the historic marker, the Bazzel Methodist Episcopal Church, the Stanley Institute, Waugh United Methodist Church, the Harriet Tubman Park, and the Scenic Long Wharf. This wharf is the site where Harriet arrived when she rescued her sister whom they were auctioning outside the courthouse, a few blocks away on Historic High Street.

aryland's

FIRSTS

Maryland's Firsts

Maryland, being rich in history has the distinction of having many "firsts." Listed here are just some of the events, discovery's, and inventions that occurred first in Maryland, and in some cases America. Many of these happenings you have probably heard before, but perhaps did not realize that they happened first in our great State.

Maryland's first jury composed entirely of women was used in the trial of Judith Catchpole, accused in the murder of her child. This jury of seven married and four single women was ordered by the Generall Provinciall Court at Patuxent on September 22, 1656. The jury acquitted her.
Maryland Archives

In 1657, Rev. Francis Doughty, the first Presbyterian minister came, to Maryland.
Maryland Historical Society

Instructed by Lord Baltimore to record the proceedings held in the Provinciall Court, St. Johns, on November 15, 1681, this is the earliest shorthand record, made by John Llywellin, a Clerk of the Council.
Maryland Archives

The first Presbyterian Church in America was established in Snow Hill in 1684, by Francis Makemie, the father of American Presbyterianism.
From *History of the Presbyterian Church in the United States*, by E.H. Gillett,1964

The engraved bookplate of Charles Carroll the immigrant, who came to Maryland in 1688, was the first used in the Province.
from *Early Maryland Bookplates*, by Edith R. Bevan, 1944

William Nuthead was the first printer in Maryland. He established his press in St. Mary's City in August 1685.Upon his death, his wife, Diana inherited his Maryland printing business and became the first woman licensed as a printer in America.
From *The St. Mary's City Press: A New Chronology of American Printing*, by Lawrence C. Wroth

Maryland's first hospital was established in what is now Charlotte Hall in St. Mary's County.
From *History of Baltimore's Medical Profession*, by Ralph J. Robinson, 1954

Maryland's first brewery was established in Annapolis in 1703 by Benjamin Fordham. It remained in operation until his death in 1716.
From *Brewing in Maryland, Colonial Times to the Present*, by William Kelley, 1965

The first Maryland portrait painter was Justus Engelhardt Kuhn, of German descent from the Rhine Valley. He applied to the General Assembly for naturalization on December 3, 1708, and continued his painting until his death in November 1717.
From *The Earliest Painter in America*, by Charles Henry Hart, 1898

Maryland's first newspaper was *The Maryland Gazette*, printed on September 12, 1727 in Annapolis by William Parks.
From *A History of Printing in Colonial Maryland*, by Lawrence C. Wroth, 1922

English-style racing of pedigreed horses, the first in America was introduced in Maryland by Governor Ogle in 1745. A short time alter the Maryland Jockey Club was formed.
From *History of Maryland*, by J. Thomas Scharf, 1879.

The first drug store in Maryland and Baltimore was located at the corner of Market (now Baltimore) Street and Calvert Street and was established by Dr. William Lyon in 1746.
From *Medical Annals of Baltimore*, by John R. Quinan, 1884

Baltimore's earliest volunteer fire company was organized September 22, 1763. It was later known as the Mechanical Company.
From *Maryland Business Corporations*, by Joseph G. Blandi, 1934

The first school in Maryland and Colonial America was established by the Rev. Dr. Thomas Bacon, Rector of the Parish of St. Peter in Talbot County in 1750.
From *The History of Talbot County*, by Oswald Tilghman, 1915

Baltimore's first bakery was founded by William Speer in 1764 on a small island in the basin off Gay Street.
From *1729 Baltimore Town and City 1929*, by G.W. Worsham, Jr., 1929

The first book printed and published in Baltimore in 1765 was:
The Detection Of The Conduct and Proceedings of Messrs. Annan and Henderson,.....Baltimore-Town, By John Redick-Le-Man, printed by N.Hasselbach.
From *A History of Printing in Colonial Maryland 1686-1776*, by Lawrence C. Wroth, 1922

The first smallpox hospital in Baltimore was established in 1769 by Dr. Henry Stevenson, an Oxford graduate. It was located several feet north of Eager Street on the west side of Greenmount Avenue.
From *History of Baltimore's Medical Profession*, by Ralph J. Robinson, 1954

The earliest granting of a business charter by the Maryland Legislature was to the Susquehanna Canal Company on December 26, 1783.
From *Maryland Business Corporations*, by Joseph G. Blandi, 1934

The first balloon ascension in the United States was made in Baltimore on June 24, 1784. Built by Peter Carnes, a Bladensburg attorney, the balloon was 35 feet in diameter and 30 feet high. Although Carnes wanted to make the flight, he believed his was too heavy, so a volunteer was sought. A thirteen- year- old Baltimore boy, named Edward Warren made the first ascension.
From *The First Century of Flight in America*, by Jeremiah T. Milbank, Jr., 1943

The first water company to be chartered in the United States was the Baltimore Water Company, founded in 1792.
From *The State of Maryland Economy 1776-1807. By* Mary Jane Dowd.

The first African-American immigrant who came to Maryland on the *Ark* and the *Dove* in 1634 was Mathias Sousa. A plaque dedicated in his honor is located today near the waters edge near the *Maryland Dove*, in St. Mary's City.

Dr. Jacob Lumbrozo was the first Jew to immigrate to Maryland, arriving on January 24, 1656. He was also the first Jewish physician to come to America.
From *The Making of An American Jewish Community*, by Isaac M. Fein, 1971.

In 1650, Reverend Robert Brooke and his family arrived in Maryland from England. He brought with him some English fox hounds. Today, the American fox hounds are those descended from those he had brought with him.
From *The Maryland Dents*, by Harry Wright Newman, 1963.

The "Maryland Act of Religious Toleration," was the first colonial religious liberty act enacted by an established legislature.
Maryland Historical Society

The earliest court jury of twelve to meet occurred on January 31, 1637, at Mettapient in St. Mary's County. They were investigating the death of John Briant, and determined that his death was caused by a tree having fallen on him.
Maryland Archives

Augustine Herman became the first naturalized citizen in Maryland on January 14, 1660.
Maryland Historical Society

The first printing of the laws of Maryland occurred in 1700. They were printed by Thomas Reading. The only known copy is owned by the Library of Congress, Washington, D.C.
From *A History of Printing in Colonial Maryland, 1686-1776*, by Lawrence C.Wroth, 1922

The first open market in Maryland was established in Baltimore in 1763, and was located at the corner of Baltimore and Gay Streets.
From *1729 Baltimore Town and City 1929*, by G.W. Worsham, 1929

John Archer of Harford County was the first American to receive a Bachelor of Medicine degree on June 21, 1768, from the College of Medicine in Philadelphia. A Bachelor's degree was the only one given at the time.
Historical Society of Harford County & The Medical and Chirurgical Faculty of Maryland

The first Native-American Methodist minister in Maryland was Richard Owings, who began his preaching in 1772. He was born in 1738 and died in Westminster in 1786.
From *Those Incredible Methodists*, by Gordon P. Baker, 1972.

In 1774, William Goddard of Baltimore was responsible for the establishment of the first "Constitutional Postal System," which in later years formed the United States Post Office. Baltimore's first official postmaster was William Goddard's sister, Mary. She was appointed to this position in 1775 and served until February 16, 1790. On December 31, 1793, George Washington reappointed her as postmaster where she held his position until 1800.
From *A Brief History of the Baltimore Post Office from 1753-1930*, by Ernest Green, 1930

The first paper mill in Maryland was founded by William Hoffman in 1776. Known as the Hoffman Paper Mill, it was located in Baltimore County on the Gunpowder Falls. When paper currency was first adopted by the Continental Congress, it was Hoffman's Mill who made the paper for it.
From *Maryland's First Papermaker*, by Dieter Kunz, 1945

The first printing of the Declaration of Independence that contained the signers was done in Baltimore. It was printed by Mary Katherine Goddard in 1777. This first printing contained all the signatures except one, that of Thomas McKean of Delaware, who was in the army and did not get the opportunity to sign it until 1781.
From *A History of Printing in Colonial Maryland, 1686-1776*, by Lawrence C. Wroth, 1922

The first college in America named for George Washington was Washington College, in Chestertown, founded in 1782. This was also the only college so named with the consent of Washington.
From *A Double Anniversary at Chestertown*, by Anthony Higgins, 1932.

The first Methodist College in America was Cokesbury College, located in Abingdon, Maryland. It was founded in 1785 and named in honor of Bishops Thomas Coke and Francis Asbury. It opened on December 6, 1787, and was destroyed by fire in 1795.
From *An Authentic History of Cokesbury College*, by George W. Archer, 1894.

Maryland's first glass maker was John Frederick Amelung, a German immigrant. His business was located in Frederick in 1787.
From *The Maryland Press 1777-1790*, by Joseph T. Wheeler, 1938.
Maryland Historical Society

John Carroll became the first Bishop of Baltimore and the first Bishop of the Catholic Church in the United States on November 6, 1789.
From *The Story of American Catholicism*, by Thomas Maynard, 1942
Maryland Historical Society

Benjamin Banneker, who was born in Ellicott's Mills (now Ellicott City) was America's first African-American scientist. He was born in 1731 and died in 1806.
From *The Life of Benjamin Banneker*, by Silvio A. Bedini
Maryland Historical Society

The first magazine published south of the Mason-Dixon Line was done in Maryland in 1793. It was titled, "The Free Universal Magazine," Volume I, # III, and was printed by Philip Edwards, in Baltimore. Volumes I and II were published in New York City.
From *A History of Printing in Maryland 1791-1800,* by A. Rachel Minick, 1949

The first fire insurance company in Maryland was the Baltimore Equitable Society. It issued its first policy on April 10, 1794, to Humphrey Price. The policy covered a three-story building located on Baltimore Street.
From *A Mark of Tradition,* by John C. Schmidt, 1966 Baltimore Equitable Society

Maryland was the home of the first Sunday newspaper published in America. It was *The Sunday Monitor,* from Baltimore, and was issued December 18, 1796.
From *A History of Printing in Maryland 1791-1800,* by A. Rachel Minick, 1949.
Maryland Historical Society

Fort McHenry, in Baltimore's harbor, was the first fort built by the United States government. Surveying began in 1798, and construction started in 1799. It was named in honor of James McHenry of Baltimore, who served as the first Secretary of War under George Washington.
From *History of Baltimore City and County,* by J. Thomas Scharf, 1881

In 1803, Thomas Moore of Brookville invented the first refrigerator.
Maryland Historical Society

Established in 1805, the Farmers Bank of Annapolis was the first financial institution in America to pay interest on deposits. It paid four percent on deposits held longer than six months, and three percent on demand deposits.
From *Sesqui-Centennial The Farmers National Bank* of Annapolis 1805-1955, 1955 Maryland Historical Society

The first highway in America that was funded by the United States Treasury was the Cumberland Road. It ran from Cumberland, Maryland to Vandalia, Illinois, and was constructed between 1806 and 1840.
From *The Old Pike, A History of the National Road,* 1894

The first money loaned to the United States government was by William Wilson. He loaned the government $50,000 to help with the war with England in 1814. Upon its repayment, Wilson refused to accept any interest.

The first time the "Star-Spangled Banner" appeared in any newspaper in America, was in the *Baltimore Patriot.* It appeared on September 20, 1814, and was titled, "Defense of Fort McHenry."
Maryland Historical Society

The first war memorial built in the United States was the Battle Monument . It is located at Calvert and Fayette Streets in Baltimore, and it's cornerstone was laid on September 12, 1815, on the first anniversary of the Battle of Baltimore. It was not complete until ten years later.
Historical Society of Carroll County, Maryland

The first railroad to be chartered in the United States was the Baltimore & Ohio Railroad. It received its charter on February 28, 1827.
Maryland Historical Society

The first patent in the United States for a steam locomotive was issued to William Howard of Baltimore on December 10, 1828. His design was for the Baltimore & Ohio Railroad, but was never built.
Maryland Historical Society

The first magazine in America dedicated to sports was issued in Baltimore in September 1829. It was called the *American Turf Register and Sporting Magazine.* It ran until December 1844.
From *A History of American Magazines 1741-1850,* by Frank A. Mott, 1930
Maryland Historical Society

The first train in America to run at a speed of thirty miles per hour was owned by the Baltimore & Ohio Railroad on April 30, 1831. The Baltimore & Ohio was also the first in America to have a double-track line. It ran from Baltimore to Ellicott 's Mills (now Ellicott City) and was first used in February 1831.
Maryland Historical Society

The first ordained rabbi in America was Abraham Rice, who came to Baltimore from Bavaria in 1840.
From *The Early German Jews of Baltimore,* by Moses Aberbach, 1972

The first dining cars on a train in America were put in use by the Baltimore & Ohio Railroad in 1843.
Maryland Historical Society

The first YMCA building built in the United States was in Baltimore at Pierce and Schroeder Streets. It was built in 1859.
From *Of Time and A Triangle,* by Thomson King, 1953

The first synthetic sweetening agent, Saccharine, was discovered by Constantine Fahlberg on February 27, 1879. Fahlberg worked at Johns Hopkins University.
From *On the Liquid Toluenesulphochloride,* by Constantine Fahlberg, 1879.

The first commercial electric street car in America and the world, was put into operation in Baltimore on August 10, 1885. It ran from Oak Street to Roland Avenue and 40th Street. It was powered by an exposed rail, and thus was hazardous, and lasted in operation less than one year.
From *A Contraption Run by Lightning,* by John G. Baker, 1951

The first Linotype machine in America was invented by Ottmar Mergenthaler in Baltimore in 1884.
Maryland Historical Society

The first steam tanker, the *Maverick,* was built in America by the firm of W.T. Malster of Baltimore in 1890.
Maryland Historical Society

The Ouija board was invented in Baltimore by brothers, William and Isaac Fuld. In 1892, William received a patent.
From *Strange Aftermaths Not Foreseen by the Ouija's Inventors. The Baltimore American,* 1940

The first and only major league baseball player to hit seven for seven in a game was accomplished by Wilbert Robinson, a catcher for the Baltimore Orioles. It occurred on June 10, 1892 in a game against St. Louis. Robinson hit six singles and a double and the Orioles won the game 25-4.
From *A Full Century of Baseball in Baltimore,* by James H. Bready, 1959.

The first use of rubber gloves in surgery in America was introduced by Dr. William S. Halsted, a Chief Surgeon at Johns Hopkins Hospital in 1894.
From *Ligature and Suture Material, Journal of the American Medical Association,* by William S. Halsted, 1913. Maryland Historical Society

Maryland was the first state in America to adopt the "Shield Law," which protected reporters and newspapers from revealing their sources of information.
The Washington Post, 1973 Maryland Historical Society

The first Rural Free Delivery service of the United States Post Office in America was in Carroll County, Maryland. It began on December 20, 1899.
Historical Society of Carroll County, Maryland.

The first bookmobile in the United States was put into operation from an idea of Miss Mary Titcomb, a librarian at the Washington County Free Library. It went into operation in April 1907.
From *Story of Washington County Free Library,* by Mary L. Titcomb, 1931 Washington County Free Library & Maryland Historical Society

The first orchestra in the United States to have municipal support was the Baltimore Symphony Orchestra. Their first concert was held on February 11, 1916, and was conducted by Gustav Strube.
From *The Story of Music in America, Baltimore,* by George Kent Bellows, 1948 Maryland Historical Society

The first newspaper in America to use an airplane for news gathering was the *Evening Sun* in Baltimore. It began its operation on September 1, 1920. Piloted by Lt. William D. Tipton, it became a useful tool, sighting a train wreck on its first outing, and two days later sighted a submarine in trouble off the Delaware Capes.
From Gerald W. Johnson, Frank R. Kent, H.L. Mencken and Hamilton Owens, *The Baltimore Sun,* 1937 Maryland Historical Society

James Hubert (Eubie) Blake, who was born in Baltimore, composed the first black musical in 1921, titled, "Shuffle Along."
Maryland Historical Society

In 1922, Dr. Elmer V. McCollum discovered Vitamin D at the Johns Hopkins School of Hygiene and Public Health.
Maryland Historical Society

In April 1930, the Baltimore & Ohio Railroad was the first in America to introduce and use an air-conditioned car. In May 1931, the B & O was also the first in America to have a completely air-conditioned train.
Maryland Historical Society

In 1964, the Holiday Inn in Baltimore was the first commercial building in the United States to have a revolving restaurant.
From *The Use of Turntables in Buildings,* by D. Bruce Johnston, 1965
Maryland Historical Society

The first African-American to be appointed to the United States Supreme Court was Thurgood Marshall of Baltimore. He was appointed to the Supreme Court in 1967.

The first gas lighting of a building was demonstrated by Benjamin Henfrey of Baltimore in 1802.
Maryland Historical Society

The first automatic elevator was invented in Baltimore by James Bates in 1856.

Monuments in Maryland's Counties

Revolutionary War Monuments

Anne Arundel County:
Daughters of the American
Revolution Plaque
City Hall, Duke of Glouster Street,
Annapolis

John Paul Jones Plaque
St. Anne's Church, Annapolis
John Paul Jones Crypt
Erected in 1924
U.S. Naval Academy, Annapolis

De Kalb Monument
Erected in 1886
State House, Annapolis

French Soldiers & Sailors
Erected in 1911
St. John's College, Annapolis

Carroll County
War Memorial
Main Street &Pennsylvania Avenue
Westminster

Cecil County
Michael Rudolph
East Main Street at courthouse
Elkton

Charles County
Monument to General Smallwood
Smallwood State Park
Rison

Frederick County
SAR Plaque
Old National Pike at Jug Bridge
Frederick

Harford County
State of Lafayette
Erected in 1976
Union Avenue at Warren Street
Havre de Grace

Chestertown
Patriots of Kent County
Memorial Park, High Street

Montgomery County
Daughters of the American
Revolution Plaque
Courthouse
Rockville

John C. Brown Memorial Bridge
Plaque
Erected in 1950
Rockville Pike &
Edmondson Drive
Rockville

Washington County
Washington Monument
Erected in 1827
Washington Monument State Park
Boonsboro

Civil War Monuments

Allegany County
Capture of Generals
Kelly and Cook
Erected in 1910
Baltimore & George Streets
Cumberland

Confederate Stone Shaft
Erected in 1912
Union Soldier Monument
Erected in 1895
Rose Hill Cemetery
Cumberland

U.S. Colored Troops Monument
Erected in 1991
Sumner Cemetery
Cumberland

Anne Arundel County
Civil War Centennial Plaque
Erected in 1964
Interior, State House
Annapolis

Caroline County
GAR Soldier Statue
Erected c. 1903-1910
Hillcrest Cemetery
Federalsburg

Carroll County
Woman Relief Corps Monument
Erected c. 1888-1910
Ebenezer Methodist
Church Cemetery
Winfield

Cecil County
Bronze Plaque
Courthouse, Elkton

Civil War Tablets
Erected in 1965
Methodist Cemetery
Cherry Hill

Memorial Gates
Erected in 1928
North East Cemetery

Dorchester County
Governor Thomas Holliday Monument
Cambridge Cemetery
Cambridge

Frederick County
General Meade Marker
Erected in 1930
Grounds of Prospect Hall Seminary
Frederick

Monocacy National Battlefield
Frederick

Confederate Monument

Maryland Soldiers of the Union &
Confederacy Monument

Mount Olivet Cemetery
Frederick

Confederate Unknown Soldier Statue
Erected in 1881

Frederick County Confederates Tablet
Erected in 1933

Garrett County
Scofield Monument
Crest of Meadow Mountain
Grantsville

Harford County
Civil War Veterans Monument
Erected in 1900
Cemetery, 600 Ohio Street
Havre de Grace

Howard County
Confederate Monument
Erected in 1948
Courthouse grounds
Ellicott City

Kent County
Soldiers of Kent in the Federal &
Confederate Armies Monument
Erected in 1917
Memorial Park, High Street
Chestertown

Montgomery County
Confederate Dead Obelisk
Erected in 1896
Grace Episcopal Church
Silver Spring

Confederate Soldier Monument
Erected in 1913
Courthouse, East side
Rockville

Davis Plaque
Cabin John Bridge
Cabin John

Ridgeley Brown Plaque
Erected in 1924
St. John's Church
Olney

Montgomery County
Monocacy Cemetery
Beallsville
Confederate States of America
Monument
Erected in 1911 & 1975

Monocacy Chapel
Erected in 1915

St. Mary's County
Point Lookout National Cemetery
Confederate Monument
Erected in 1876

Confederate POWs Monument
(Federal)
Erected in 1911

Talbot County
Confederate Monument
Erected in 1916
Courthouse
Washington Street
Easton

Washington County
Antietam National Battlefield
Sharpsburg

1st Maryland Battery, C.S.A.
Erected in 1900

1st Maryland Light Artillery Battery
A, USA
Erected in 1900

1st Maryland Light Artillery Battery
B, USA
Erected in 1900

2nd Maryland Infantry, USA
Erected in 1900

3rd Maryland Infantry, USA
Erected in 1900

5th Maryland Infantry
Companies A & I
Erected in 1890

5th Maryland Infantry
Erected in 1900

Baltimore Battery, C.S.A.
Erected in 1900

Maryland State Monument
Erected in 1900

Purnell Legion Infantry, USA
Erected in 1900

United States Soldiers Monument
Erected in 1900

Washington County
Doubleday Hill Monument
Erected in 1897
Williamsport

Garland Monument
Erected in 1993
Reno Monument
Erected in 1889
Reno Monument Road
off Rt. 67, Fox's Gap

Lee Headquarters Marker
Boonsboro-Shepherdstown Road,
Rt. 34, Sharpsburg

War Correspondents Arch
Erected in 1896
Gapland State Park
Crampton's Gap

Washington Confederate Cemetery
Potomac Street
Hagerstown

World War I
World War II
Korea & Vietnam Monuments

Allegany County
World War I Doughboy Monument
East Main Street
Lonaconing

Anne Arundel County
AMVETS Carillon
Erected in 1984
Maryland State Veterans Cemetery
Crownsville

World War I Memorial
St. John's College
Erected in 1920
Annapolis

Baltimore County
World War I Memorial
Wayside Cross
York Road, south of Joppa Road
Towson

Calvert County
World War I Monument
Erected in 1920
County Courthouse at
Route 765
Prince Frederick

Cecil County
World War I Monument
Town Hall, Bohemia Street
Chesapeake City

World War I Doughboy Monument
101 Railroad Avenue
Maryland National Guard Armory
Elkton

Carroll County
Memorial Gateway
City Park at Center Street
Westminster

War Memorial
High Street
New Windsor

War Memorial
Main Street and
Pennsylvania Avenue
Westminster

Western Maryland Railroad Honor
Roll
Erected in 1920
Main Street
Union Bridge

World War I Memorial
Town Hall
Manchester

Charles County
World War I & II Monument
SE of U.S. 301 & Rt. 225
LaPlata

Dorchester County
World War I Memorial Fountain
Long Wharf
Cambridge

World War I Monument
Erected in 1930
Cemetery, Rt. 331
Hurlock

Frederick County
Spirit of the American Doughboy
Erected in 1923
West end of Main Street
Emmitsburg

World War I
Erected in 1926
Memorial Park
Bentz and 2nd Street
Frederick

Harford County
World War I Monument
Erected in 1923
Maryland National Guard Armory
Main Street
Bel Air

World War I Honor Roll
Erected in 1919
Commerce and
Washington Streets
Havre de Grace

Kent County
Sunrise Peoples Monument to
World War I, World War II
Korea and Vietnam
Erected in 1989
Memorial Park, High Street
Chestertown

Montgomery County
World War I, World War II
Korea and Vietnam
Cheltenham, Woodmont & Norfolk
Streets
Bethesda

Prince George's County
World War I Monument
Courthouse Garden
Upper Marlboro

Somerset County
Spirit of the American Doughboy
Monument
Erected in 1923
Veterans' Cemetery
Crisfield

World War I, World War II
Korea and Vietnam Memorial
Ewell

St. Mary's County
World War I Monument
City Square
Rt. 5 and Washington Street
Leonardtown

Washington County
World War I Monument
Erected in 1919
Main Street
Boonsboro

World War I Doughboy Monument
Erected in 1921
Baltimore Road at
Alternate Rt. 40
Funkstown

World War I Monument
Main Street
Keedysville

World War I and II Monument
Church Street, Rt. 65
Sharpsburg

World War I Doughboy Monument
Erected in 1926
Williamsport

Wicomico County
World War I
(captured German
artillery piece)
City Park
South Park Drive
Salisbury

Worcester County
World War I, World War II
Korea and Vietnam
Snow Hill

Maryland Veterans Vietnam Memorial
Dedicated May 28, 1989
Located in Baltimore at Middle
Branch Park, overlooking the
Patapsco River.

The Maryland Veterans Vietnam Memorial is a ring of stone with a granite wall upon which is inscribed the one thousand forty-six names of those Maryland men who lost their lives in Vietnam. The names of those thirty-five men who remain missing are also inscribed in the stone. Although formal records reflect that of the women who were killed in Vietnam, none were from the State of Maryland. The Memorial features two forty-five foot flag poles flying both the flag of the United States and the Maryland State flag. Below the Maryland flag flies a POW-MIA flag. Immediately outside the Memorial ring are sixteen spires which represent the Vietnam years from 1959 to 1975. The three and one-half acre Memorial is also enhanced further by groves of trees and greenery. In addition to the financial contributions of corporations, and citizens, the Maryland General Assembly provided funds equaling $2,250,000 for the construction of the Memorial, thus making the Memorial a contribution from all citizens of Maryland as a tribute to all Marylanders who served in Vietnam. This Memorial stands as a humble and simple tribute to all who served their country, their State and their fellow citizens with honor.

Maryland Korean War Memorial
Dedicated May 27, 1990
Located at Canton Waterfront Park,
Baltimore City.

The Maryland Korean War Memorial contains the names of those five hundred twenty-five Marylanders known to have been killed in the Korean War or who are still listed as missing in action. Using the land's slope to the water, the designers of the Memorial developed a spatial hierarchy including a most private zone of a curved wall topped with yew, the symbol of eternal life. This sanctuary with the carved names would represent the incomplete, the unbroken circle of a war that never ended and would create a contemplative experience and an area of the living and the dead facing inward for a memorial function.

The pavement area with a map of Korea embedded in the pavement floor separates the two paths of the circle. The lower part of the circle contains information relative to the conduct of the war, participants and casualty information. From the Memorial facing toward the water is a wedge-shaped lawn, formed by trees, symbolic of the Chinese offensive wedge down the peninsula.

Funding of $750,000 was obtained through the enacting of a bond bill by the Maryland General Assembly. Construction of the Memorial was started on November 20, 1989, and completed May 22, 1990, with its dedication five days later.

TRIVIA & INTERESTING FACTS. SEE HOW YOU DO!

(answers on following page)

1. One area in Maryland is only one mile wide, the arrowest of any State. Can you guess where?

2. Where does Maryland rank in size among thefifty states?

3. What was the name and year of Maryland's first colony?

4. Where is Maryland's capital located?

5. The Mason-Dixon line divides Maryland fromwhat other state?

6. Which county name means "beautiful stream" in Indian language?

7. Which county is the smallest in area?

8. How long is the Mason-Dixon line bordering Maryland?

9. Four states border Maryland. Can you namethem?

10. Which county was the last to be established?

11. Francis Scott Key is buried in what town?

12. Which county is Maryland's geographic center?

13. What river forms Maryland's southern and southwestern boundary?

14. What county is largest in area?

15. What is the oldest public building in Maryland?

16. When is Maryland Day?

17. When and Where did George Washington resign his commission as commander-in-chief?

18. Maryland was named for an English Queen. Can you name her?

19. Name the two ships that brought Maryland's original settlers?

20. Which ship of the two was the larger?

21. Who were the first people in Maryland, andwho gave them their name?

22. How many people founded the first Maryland colony?

23. What Indian tribe owned the land which is now St. Mary's?

24. Name the woman who was the first to attempt to vote and be denied?

25. What was the main effect the French and Indian War had on Maryland?

26. In 1811, what political group urged war with England?

27. The Battle of Baltimore is also known by another name. Can you name it?

28. What poem was written by Francis Scott Key during the War of 1812?

29. Name the Treaty that ended the War of 1812?

30. Name the four colors contained within the Maryland flag?

31. Who was the First Lord Baltimore and what was his wife's name?

32. Which Calvert arrived at St. Clements Island on March 25, 1634, and what title did he hold?

33. Name the abolitionist who established and published the newspaper, *North Star.*

34. Name the sculptor who created the statue of Frederick Douglas displayed at Morgan State University?

35. What was the "Underground Railroad, and who was known as the "Moses of her People?"

36. Whose Coat of Arms are used in the Maryland Flag?

37. Name the four signers of the Declaration of Independence from Maryland?

38. In what Baltimore hotel did Francis Scott Key finish his famous poem?

39. For whom is Caroline County named?

40. Name the second largest vertical drop water falls in Maryland?

41. What famous actress grew up in Kent County?

42. Name the six Lord's Baltimore.

43. What is the oldest warship in the United States?

44. What is Maryland's nickname?

45. When and where were the Articles of Confederation ratified?

46. Who made the flag that flew over Fort McHenry during the Battle of Baltimore?

47. What were the first and last counties in Maryland to be established?

48. What county in Maryland is named after a President?

49. What ornament must be affixed atop theflagstaff bearing the Maryland flag?

50. What is the name of the first black Marylander who came to Maryland on the *Ark*?

ANSWERS TO QUESTIONS

1.) Hancock, Maryland
2.) 42nd
3.) St. Mary's in 1634
4.) Annapolis
5.) Pennsylvania
6.) Allegany
7.) Calvert
8.) 230 Miles
9.) Pennsylvania, Delaware, Virginia, West Virginia
10.) Garrett in 1872
11.) Frederick
12.) Prince George's (4½ miles NW of Davidsonville)
13.) Potomac
14.) Frederick
15.) Old Treasury Building, Annapolis
16.) March 25th
17.) December 23, 1783 at the Maryland State House, Old Senate Chamber
18.) Henrietta Marie
19.) The Ark and the Dove
20.) The Ark
21.) Indians, Christopher Columbus
22.) 220
23.) Yaocamicoe Indians
24.) Margaret Brent
25.) It slowed growth of Western Maryland and increased growth in Frederick, Annapolis and Baltimore.
26.) War Hawks
27.) The Battle of North Point.
28.) Star Spangled Banner
29.) Treaty of Ghent
30.) Black, Gold, Red, White
31.) George Calvert and Grace Crossland
32.) Leonard Calvert, First governor of Maryland
33.) Frederick Douglass
34.) James Edward Lewis
35.) A secret network of safe-houses created to help escaping slaves. Harriet Tubman.
36.) Calvert and Crossland families
37.) Charles Carroll of Carrollton, Samuel Chase, William Paca, and Thomas Stone.
38.) Indian Queen Inn
39.) Caroline Eden, the daughter of Charles Calvert, Fifth Lord Baltimore
40.) Falling Branch or Kilgore Falls
41.) Katharine Hepburn
42.) George, Cecilius, Charles, Benedict Leonard, Charles, and Frederick Calvert
43.) U.S. Frigate *Constellation*
44.) Old Line State
45.) March 1, 1781, at Annapolis, Maryland
46.) Mary Young Pickersgill
47.) St. Mary's and Garrett
48.) Washington
49.) Gold Cross Bottony
50.) Mathias de Sousa

ACKNOWLEDGEMENTS

1.)   Maritime: Ark and the Dove, Painting by Moll, courtesy of The Maryland Historical Society. Reprinted by permission.

2.)   Map: The Route of the Ark and the Dove, courtesy of The Maryland Historical Society. Reprinted by permission.

3.)   Photograph, Mason-Dixon Stone Markers, The Maryland Historical Society. Reprinted by permission.

4.)   Map of Maryland, page 6, General Drafting Company, Inc.

5.)   Maryland State Official Symbols, except State Flower, State Sport, and State Bird courtesy of The Maryland State Archives, Maryland Manual, 1994-1995 Edition. Reprinted by permission.

6.)   Maryland County Maps, courtesy of The Maryland Department of Transportation, State Highway Administration.

7.)   Maryland Chronology, in part, Maryland Manual, 1996-1997 Edition, courtesy of The Maryland State Archives. Reprinted by permission.

8.)   Maryland County Seals, courtesy of the respective Maryland County, except where otherwise noted. Reprinted by permission.

9.)   Allegany County Seal, courtesy of Cathy E. Blank, secretary to the County Commissioners. Reprinted by permission.

10.)   Baltimore City Seal, courtesy of the Honorable Kurt Schmoke, Mayor. Reprinted by permission.

11.)   Baltimore County Seal, courtesy of Nicholas C. Spinnato, Sr., Executive Assistant. Reprinted by permission.

12.)   Calvert County Seal, courtesy of Colletta Fox, secretary to Administrator. Reprinted by permission.

13.)   Carroll County Seal, courtesy of Jay A Graybeal, Director, Historical Society of Carroll County, Maryland, Inc. Reprinted by permission.

14.)   Dorchester County Seal, courtesy of the County Commissioners and Doris Goslin, Administrative Assistant. Reprinted by permission.

15.)   Harford County Seal, courtesy of the Honorable Eileen M. Rehrmann, County Executive. Reprinted by permission.

16.)   Howard County Seal, courtesy of Gail H. Bates, Assistant to the County Executive. Reprinted by permission.

17.)   Kent County Seal, courtesy of the County Commissioners and Janice F. Fletcher, Administrative Assistant. Reprinted by permission.

18.)   Montgomery County Seal, courtesy of the Honorable Neal Potter, County Executive and Judith F. Scioli, Director, Office of Public Information. Reprinted by permission.

19.)   Queen Anne's County Seal, courtesy of the County Commissioners. Reprinted by permission.

20.)   Somerset County Seal, courtesy of the County Commissioners, and Rita R. Merklein, secretary. Reprinted by permission.

21.)   Talbot County Seal, courtesy of Blenda W. Armistead, County Manager. Reprinted by permission.

22.)   Washington County Seals, courtesy of Paulette Sprinkle, Program Coordinator, Hagerstown-Washington County Convention & Visitors Bureau.

23.)   Wicomico County Seal, courtesy of Henry S. Parker, President, County Council. Reprinted by permission.

24.)   Worcester County Seal, courtesy of John A. Yankus, Chief Administrative Officer. Reprinted by permission.

25.)   Prince George's County Seal, courtesy of the Honorable Parris N. Glendening, County Executive. Reprinted by permission.

26.)   Photographs: Antietam National Battlefield Park; Bloody Lane; Burnside Bridge; Cannon; old State House at St. Mary's City; Great Falls; Barbara Fritchie House; old Senate Chamber, State House, Annapolis, Md.; State House, Annapolis; Margaret Brent plaque; Middleham Chapel; Likeness of Anne Wolseley Calvert; Maryland Dove; Falling Branch Falls; Tudor Hall; Havre de Grace Lighthouse; Great Falls; Black-eyed Susans, The Mudd House, 1993, 1994, 1995, by John T. Marck. Obsolete bank notes, currency, stock certificates, and miscellaneous documents 1995, from the author's collection.

27.)   Back cover Maryland State seal, courtesy of Maryland State Archives. Reprinted by permission.

28.)   Drawings of Charles Carroll, Samuel Chase, William Paca, and Thomas Stone, courtesy of The Maryland Historical Society. Reprinted by permission.

29.)   Carroll County First Rural Delivery Service plaque, courtesy of The United States Postal Service. Reprinted by permission.

30.)   Indian Queen Inn Logo, courtesy of The Baltimore Journal, 1929, Baltimore TwoHundredth Anniversary, 1729-1929.

31.)   Photograph of the Kenmore Inn and F. Bond Boarman, courtesy of the Bel Air Centennial Committee, Inc., 1874-1974.

32.)   Advertisement and photograph of the Kenmore Inn, from the author's collection.

33.) <u>Westminster During the Civil War</u>, by Jay A. Graybeal, Director, Historical Society of Carroll County, Maryland, Inc. Reprinted by permission.

34.) Photographs of United States Postage Stamps, by James L. Marck, MarWest Publications, Mesa, Arizona, from the collections of James L. Marck and John T. Marck. United States Postal Card, Ark and Dove, from the author's collection.

35.) The author wishes to thank Miss Katharine Hepburn for her kind letter.

36.) Post cards used throughout this book, of Star-Spangled Banner Flag House and Museum; Original copy of Star-Spangled Banner penned by Francis Scott Key; Francis Scott Key Monument; Clara Barton Monument; Government House; Fort McHenry National Monument; U.S. Frigate Constellation; Mount Clare Mansion; Barbara Fritchie and Barbara Fritchie House; Washington Monument; Battle Monument; Roger Brooke Taney House and Museum; War Correspondents Arch; and St. Clement's Island cross are from the collection of John T. Marck.

37.) Drawing of the Star-Spangled Banner Flag House and Museum, courtesy of the Star-Spangled Banner Flag House and Museum and Cindy Nauta, Director. Reprinted by permission.

38.) Baltimore City Chronology, 1668-1929, reprinted in part, Courtesy of <u>The Baltimore Journal, 1929, Baltimore Two Hundredth Anniversary, 1729-1929.</u>

39.) The author wishes to thank the following county agencies, departments, and historical societies for their informational help and assistance: Allegany County Visitor's Bureau; Baltimore Area Convention and Visitors Association; Annapolis and Anne Arundel County Conference & Visitors Bureau; Calvert County Office of Economic Development; Carroll County Tourist and Information Center and the Historical Society of Carroll County, Md. Inc.; Commissioners of Caroline County; Cecil County Office of Economic Development; Charles County Government, Department of Community Services; Dorchester County Tourism Office; Tourism Council of Frederick County, Inc.; Board of Garrett County Commissioners; Harford County Tourism; Howard County Tourism Council, Inc.; Kent County Chamber of Commerce, Inc.; Conference & Visitors Bureau of Montgomery County, Md. Inc. and the Montgomery County Government, Office of Information; Prince George's County, Maryland, Conference & Visitors Bureau, Inc.; Queen Anne's County Visitors Service; St. Mary's County Government, Department of Economic and Community Development; Somerset County Tourism; Talbot County Chamber of Commerce; Washington County Convention and Visitors Bureau; Wicomico County Convention & Visitors Bureau; and the Department of Economic Development, Worcester County.

40.) Excerpts from <u>The Charles County Seal</u>, by Frederick Tilp. Used with permission of the County Commissioners of Charles County.

41.) Various line art drawings used throughout this publication by DeskGallery, Zedcor, Inc.; Whelan Design Studios, under license to Zedcor, Inc.; Berol Corporation, under license to Zedcor, Inc.; Visual Delights, under license to Zedcor, Inc.; DoverPublications, under license to Zedcor, Inc. DeskGallery is a registeredtrademark of Zedcor, Inc. Placement concept by the author; used and reprinted by permission.

42.) The author wishes to thank Mrs. Peggy Hoffman for her kind informational assistance regarding Maryland jousting. Jousting photograph of Mr. Bruce Hoffman, courtesy of Mrs. Peggy Hoffman. Reprinted by permission.

43.) Drawing of Maryland jousting knight by Rick Rector, reprinted by permission.

44.) Information on the Maryland State Flag, in part, supplied by the Annapolis and Anne Arundel County Conference & Visitors Bureau. Reprinted by permission.

45.) Drawing of State Bird, Baltimore Oriole, from the author's collection.

46.) The author conveys a special thank you to his father, William John (Jack) Marck, Jr., for his valuable assistance with this project.

47.) The author wishes to thank Mr. Rocky J. Rockefeller, Archivist, Maryland State Archives, for his informational assistance on Frederick Calvert and Henry Harford.

48. My thanks to Mr. Frederick I. Douglass, historian and photo archivist of Morgan State University and a decendant of Frederick Douglass for his informational assistance on James Edward Lewis.

49.) Photo of the Frederick Douglass statue and Jmaes Edward Lewis, courtesy of Frederick I. Douglass. Reprinted by permission.

50.) Calvert Coat of Arms appearing in Maryland Chronolgy from John Ogilby, *Nova Terrae-Maria tabuka, 1671*. Courtesy of the Maryland Archives.

51.) Baltimore Orioles logo courtesy of the Baltimore Orioles Professional Baseball Club, and Major League Baseball.

52.) The author wishes to thank Ms. Jill J. Seipe, Manager, The Baltimore Zoo, for providing the information and photograph of The Baltimore Zoo Mansion House. Reprinted by permission.

53.) "The History of the Baltimore Zoo, 1801-1997," by Marlene England, reprinted in part by permission of The Baltimore Zoo.

54.) Photograph of The Baltimore Zoo Mansion House by Jeff Bill, reprinted by permission of The Baltimore Zoo.

55.) The Baltimore Colts "horseshoe" is a registered trademark of the Baltimore and Indianapolis Colts, and the National Football League. The Baltimore Colts Fight Song, "Let's Go Colts," words and music by Jo Lombardi & Benjamin Klasmer.

56.) The Baltimore Ravens logo is a registered trademark of the Baltimore Ravens and the National Football League.

57.) Photograph of the *"Pride of Baltimore II,"* courtesy of Mr. Mark Belton, Director, Pride of Baltimore II. Reprinted by permission.

Index

A

B

Y

Z

NOTE: The year written in parenthesis, and the page # that directly follows, refers to the location of said item in the Baltimore City Chronology.

The End

Jostens Commercial Printing
David O'Brien
Sales Representative
Bel Air, Maryland
410-515-0202

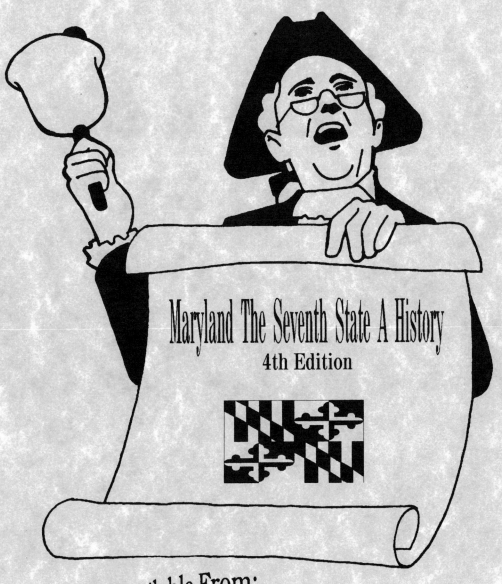

Maryland The Seventh State A History
4th Edition

Additional Copies Available From:

Creative Impressions, Ltd.
P.O. Box 188
Glen Arm, Maryland 21057

Phone:410-592-7068
Fax: 410-592-7067

Visa, MasterCard & American Express Accepted

A Page in American History

Historic Surratt House Museum

*Where 19th-century culture mingles with the ghosts
of the Lincoln assassination story.*

9118 Brandywine Road
P. O. Box 427
Clinton, Maryland 20735

Phone and TTY: 301-868-1121
Fax: 301-868-8177

The Maryland-National Capital
Park and Planning Commission